11.01.05

Global Forces and Local Life-Worlds

Social Transformations

Edited by Ulrike Schuerkens

SAGE Studies in International Sociology 51
Sponsored by the International Sociological Association/ISA

SAGE STUDIES IN
INTERNATIONAL SOCIOLOGY

Editor
Julia Evetts, University of Nottingham, UK

© Ulrike Schuerkens 2004

First published 2004

 SAGE Publications Ltd
1 Oliver's Yard
55 City Road
London EC1Y 1SP

SAGE Publications Ltd
2455 Teller Road
Thousand Oaks, California 91320

SAGE Publications India Pvt Ltd
B-42, Panchsheel Enclave
Post Box 4109
New Delhi 100 017

British Library Cataloguing in Publication Data

A catalogue record for this book is available from the British
Library

ISBN 1 4129 0004 2

Library of Congress Control Number: 2003108065

Typeset by Type Study, Scarborough, North Yorkshire
Printed in Great Britain by The Cromwell Press Ltd,
Trowbridge, Wiltshire

Contents

About the Authors

Nina Bandelj is both assistant professor of sociology and faculty associate at the Center for the Study of Democracy at University of California, Irvine. Her research interests are in comparative economic sociology, political economy, sociology of culture and change in Central and Eastern Europe. Her recent articles were published in *Social Forces*, *Current Sociology* and *Sociological Forum*. *Address*: Department of Sociology, University of California, Irvine, 3151 Social Science Plaza, Irvine, CA 92697, USA. [email: nbandelj@uci.edu]

Helmuth Berking is professor of sociology at the Technical University Darmstadt, Germany. His research interests are in the fields of cultural globalization, political sociology and urban sociology. His recent publications include *Sociology of Giving* (Sage, 1999) and *Städte im Globalisierungsdiskurs* (Königshausen and Neumann, 2002). *Address*: Technische Universität Darmstadt, Institut für Soziologie, Fachbereich 2, Residenzschloss, 64283 Darmstadt, Germany. [email: hbe295@t-online.de]

Lauren Langman is professor of sociology at Loyola University, Chicago. His interests include alienation studies, Marxist sociology and cultural sociology. Recent publications include: 'Suppose They Gave a Culture War and No-one Came: Zippergate and the Carnivalization of Political Culture', *American Behavioral Scientist* (December 2002); 'The Body and the Mediation of Hegemony: From Subject to Citizen to Audience', in Richard Brown (ed.) *Body, Self and Identity* (University of Minnesota Press, 2002); 'From the Poetics of Pleasure to the Poetics of Protest', in Paul Kennedy (ed.) *Identity in the Global Age* (Macmillan and Palmore, 2001); with Douglas Morris and Jackie Zalewski, 'Globalization, Domination and Cyberactivism', in Wilma A. Dunaway (ed.) *The 21st Century World-System: Systemic Crises and Antisystemic Resistance* (Greenwood Press, 2002). *Address*: Department of Sociology and Anthropology, Loyola University of Chicago, Chicago, IL 60614, USA. [email: llangma@luc.edu]

George Morgan teaches sociology and cultural studies in the School of Humanities at the University of Western Sydney. His book on black/white reconciliation in Australia will be published in 2003. *Address*: Humanities/Centre for Cultural Research, University of Western Sydney, Locked Bag 1797, Penrith South DC, NSW 1797, Australia. [email: george.morgan@uws.edu.au]

Christine Müller studied sociology, social anthropology and the history of arts at the University of Basle (Switzerland). She received her PhD from the Sociology of Development Research Centre, University of Bielefeld, and is currently a research assistant in the project 'Globalization of Knowledge – Development Experts in World Society' at the Institute of Global Society Studies associated with the University of Bielefeld. Her main research interests are methodology, knowledge, gender, development politics and epistemic cultures. Recent articles are published in Markus Kaiser (ed.) *Weltwissen, Entwicklungsexperten in der Weltgesellschaft* (Verlag, 2002). *Address*: Graf-von-Stauffenbergstr. 7a, 33615 Bielefeld, Germany. [email: christine.mueller@uni-bielefeld.de]

Eric Popkin is assistant professor of sociology in the Department of Sociology at Colorado College. He has published a number of articles on various facets of Central American immigration in Los Angeles and transnational migration. *Address*: Department of Sociology, Colorado College, 14 E. Cache La Poudre St, Colorado Springs, CO 80903, USA. [email: epopkin@ColoradoCollege.edu]

Shalini Randeria is professor of sociology and anthropology at the Central European University, Budapest and a member of the working group on 'Civil Society' at WZB, Berlin. Professor Randeria's interests include globalization, law and public policy, development studies and postcolonial theory. Recent publications include chapters in Yehuda Elkana et al. (eds) *Unraveling Ties: From Social Cohesion to Cartographies of Connectedness* (St Martin's Press, 2002) and in Sebastian Conrad (ed.) *Jenseits des Eurozentrismus: postkoloniale Perspektiv in den Geschichts- und Kulturwissenschaften* (Campus Verlag, 2002). *Address*: Department of Sociology and Anthropology, Central European University, Nador Utc. 9, 1051 Budapest, Hungary. [email: 100703.1663@compuserve.com]

Ulrich Schiefer is a sociologist and professor at the Instituto Superior de Ciências do Trabalho e da Empresa (ISCTE), Lisbon and researcher at the Centro de Estudos Africanos, Lisbon and the Institute Sociology, University of Münster (Germany). He has conducted field research in Guinea-Bissau, Mozambique and Portugal. His published books include *Guinea-Bissau zwischen Weltwirtschaft und Subsistenz. Transatlantische Strukturen an der oberen Guinea Küste* (ISSA, 1986) and *Von allen guten Geistern verlassen? Dissipative Ökonomie: Entwicklungszusammenarbeit und der Zusammenbruch afrikanischer Gesellschaften. Eine Fall–Studie zu Guinea-Bissau* (IAK, 2002). *Address*: ISCTE, Avenida das Forças Armadas 100, P 1649 026 Lisbon, Portugal. [email: schiefer@iscte.pt]

Johanna Schmidt is a PhD candidate in the Department of Sociology, University of Auckland, New Zealand. Her thesis, which will be completed mid-2003, is an investigation of the impact of westernization and migration on Samoan *fa'afafine*. Her teaching interests include globalization and popular culture. *Address*: PO Box 1869, Shortland St, Auckland, New Zealand. [email: schmidtjo@hotmail.com]

Ulrike Schuerkens has doctorates in sociology and in social anthropology and ethnology from the École des Hautes Études en Sciences Sociales in Paris. She received the diploma 'Habilitation à diriger des recherches' from the University Paris V – René Descartes. Currently, she teaches at the École des Hautes Études en Sciences Sociales in Paris. She was a lecturer at Humboldt University Berlin (Germany). She has published extensively on development, social change, migration, multiculturalism, and colonialism. Her latest books are *Changement social sous régime colonial: Du Togo allemand aux Togo et Ghana indépendants* (L'Harmattan, 2001); *Transformationsprozesse in der Elfenbeinküste und in Ghana* (Lit, 2001). *Address*: 10, Jonquoy, F-75014 Paris, France. [email: ulrike.schuerkens@caramail.com]

Willfried Spohn is adjunct professor at the Free University of Berlin, has been visiting professor at several American universities and is currently research director of an EU-funded Western/Eastern European comparative project on European and national identities (EURONAT) at the European University Viadrina, Frankfurt-Oder, Germany. He has published widely in the area of historical and comparative sociology. His major publications include: Can Europe Work? Germany and the Reconstruction of Post-communist Societies (ed. with S. Hanson, 1995); Europeanization, National Identities and Migration: Changes in Boundary Constructions between Western and Eastern Europe (ed. with A. Triandafyllidou, 2002); Modernization, Religion and Collective Identities: Germany between Western and Eastern Europe (forthcoming). *Address*: Konradin Str. 5, 12105 Berlin, Germany. [email: Willfried.Spohn@IUE.it]

Marina Padrão Temudo is an agronomist at the ISA, Lisbon and senior researcher at the Instituto de Investigação Científica Tropical (IICT)/Centro de Estudos de Produção e Tecnologia Agrícolas (CEPTA), Lisbon. Her ethno-agronomie field research has been conducted mainly in Guinea-Bissau, Mozambique, Cape Verde, São Tomé and Principe. Her article 'A escolha do sabor, o saber da escolha: selecção varietal e segurança alimentar na Guiné-Bissau' was published in *Revista de Ciências Agrárias* (Lisbon) 4: 69–95 (1996). *Address*: CEPTA, IICT, Tapada da Ajuda, Edifício das Agro-industrias e Agronomia Tropical, Ap[do] 3014, P 1300–901 Lisbon, Portugal. [email: Marina_Temudo@hotmail.com]

Preface

Global Forces and Local Life-Worlds assembles the most interesting contributions to the Research Committee 09, 'Social Practice and Social Transformation', of the International Sociological Association over the four years between the 14th World Congress of Sociology in Montreal, Canada (1998) and the 15th World Congress of Sociology in Brisbane, Australia (2002). These contributions thematize from different theoretical approaches and sociological perspectives current socioeconomic, political and cultural processes of 'glocalization' – the manifold entanglements of globalization, modernization and traditional life-worlds in various western as well as non-western regions, societies and localities. The focus here is less on macro-theories of globalization, though they are always implicitly or explicitly addressed, rather than on micro-sociological analyses of global macro-processes in specific social life-worlds. With this focus, we hope to transcend not only the methodological nationalism of most national sociological traditions, but also the Euro- or western-centrism of many world-system and globalization theories. In this methodological and analytical direction, the assembled contributions attempt to join the growing multi-perspective endeavours for an international, transnational and global sociology.

This publication presents a summary of recent activities of RC 09 and simultaneously a prelude to a thorough reorientation and restructuring of its future research activities and organizational format. This is indicated by the planned name change of RC 09 from 'Social Practice and Social Transformation' to 'Social Transformation and Sociology of Development'. At its creation in 1974, the RC 09 was named 'Innovative Processes in Social Change' and shortly thereafter (1980) renamed as 'Social Practice and Social Transformation'. Originating from the impulses of the cultural revolution and its constitutive social movements in the 1960s, both names intended to bring together critical and participatory social research in the first, the second and the third worlds. The concept 'social transformation' was directed at the then predominating modernization paradigm and its focus on western-centred, teleological, macro-theories of social change and intended to open the sociological eye to contingent, open and actor-centred processes of social transformation. The concept 'social practice' referred to the then predominating notion of social engineering in the direction of western modernization. Its intention was to support – 'emancipatory social movements' by critical and participatory sociological research.

In the meantime, however, both labels, 'social practice' and 'social transformation', have lost their critical self-evidence. The classical modernization theories and related macro-theories of social change, not at least as a response to their critics, have undergone a thorough self-critique and reconceptualization from neo-modernist to multiple modernity approaches with an analytical focus on social structure, culture and social agency or macro–micro links in social reality. As a result, the distinction between social change and social transformation has lost its critical implications. As well, the concept of social practice aiming at participation in emancipatory social movements, at least after the breakdown of Communist and socialist regimes all over the world, has often turned out as a naive romanticization of social movements – better to be replaced by a value pluralism of committed and disengaged sociological research. Furthermore, the emerging new world order in the context of intensifying globalization processes has dissolved the clear-cut distinctions between the first, second and third worlds, and has been replaced by a multilayered, multipolar, hierarchical, asymmetric and unequal global order of manifold social changes, developments and transformations.

Under these new world conditions and their implications for and challenges to a transnational and global sociology, the envisaged title 'Social Transformation and Sociology of Development' of RC 09 wishes to invite particularly the growing number of sociologists who concentrate their work on the comparative sociological analysis of transnational and transhistorical macro- and micro-processes of social development and social transformation in the non-western world and its embedded linkages to the western world. This invitation is particularly directed to: (1) traditionally western or western-located sociological scholars who work in the fields of 'developmental sociology', 'Entwicklungssoziologie', 'sociologie du développement' or 'sociología de desarrollo' and related international or area studies; (2) scholars in the increasingly developing national sociologies in the non-western world in Africa, Asia, Australia/Oceania, Latin-America and Eastern Europe; (3) scholars in the western and non-western world who concentrate their work on the transnational and global interconnections and interactions in the emerging global society in non-western and western world regions; and (4) sociological scholars who focus on related theoretical approaches of multiple modernities, globalization, world-system and postcolonialism in a civilizational, international, transnational and global comparative perspective.

Global Forces and Local Life-Worlds assembles contributions in different theoretical, analytical and methodological orientations as interesting examples of such a reorientation of RC 09 'Sociology of Social Transformation and Social Development'. My special thanks for the materialization of this publication go particularly to Ulrike Schuerkens, the designated new president of RC 09 for the coming four-year period, who prepared the book with unremitting energy, and Julia Evetts, the editor of the Monograph Issues of the Sage Studies in International

Sociology, without whose sympathetic support this idea would never have been realized.

Willfried Spohn
President of RC 09 1999–2002

1

Social Transformations Between Global Forces and Local Life-Worlds: Introduction

Ulrike Schuerkens

During the last decade, the activities of our Research Committee 09, 'Sociology of Social Transformation and Social Practice',[1] have concentrated on micro-sociological analyses of socioeconomic, political and cultural transformations of local life-worlds through the continuing and intensifying processes of globalization. Our regional focus has been particularly on the non-western world, but it has also included a western comparative perspective. In the emerging contemporary world, two processes of social transformation increasingly and inextricably intertwine. On the one hand, there are universalizing processes of modernization and globalization, mostly of western origins, that are spreading all over the world. On the other hand, there are tendencies to maintain traditional life-worlds, attempting at keeping up the authenticity of their cultures. The interaction of these processes results in varying forms of implantation of and adaptation to western modernity and culture, crystallizing in differing mixtures and hybrid modes of western modernity and non-western traditions, various forms of reaction and resistance to the imposition of the western model, or various forms of dissolution and destruction of traditional life-worlds through the impact of the western civilization.

In order to present the recent activities of our Research Committee to a wider sociological and anthropological public, we bring together in this monograph issue of *Current Sociology* and in the book in the SSIS series theoretically informed case studies and empirically based theoretical reflections within this research framework. These research activities are of interest to a relatively specialized public of sociologists and anthropologists, students and professional researchers. We think moreover that the topic will interest a wider public in the countries of the South, such as university institutes, NGOs and offices of governments.

It seems actually that there are no comparable books in English in spite of the fact that this topic has interested several researchers during the last years. In German, there are two interesting books on similar topics: Dieter Neubert et al. (1999) *Gemeinschaften in einer entgrenzten Welt* and Helmut Buchholt et al. (1996) *Modernität zwischen Differenzierung und*

Globalisierung. Kulturelle, wirtschaftliche und politische Transformation-sprozesse in der sich globalisierenden Moderne. Focusing on the countries of the South, another book exists, edited by Hans-Peter Müller (1996), *Weltsystem und kulturelles Erbe. Gliederung und Dynamik der Entwick-lungsländer aus ethnologischer und soziologischer Sicht.* On a more theoretical level, a book from Jonathan Friedman (1994) is also related to our topic: *Cultural Identity and Global Process.* The book *Global Culture, Island Identity: Continuity and Change in the Afro-Caribbean Community of Nevis,* by K.F. Olwig (1993), represents a case study. In French, a small introduction to the topic by an ethnologist exists: Jean-Pierre Warnier's (1999) *La Mondialisation de la culture.* Moreover, Centre Tricontinental published a book in 2000 with the title *Cultures et mondialisation. Résis-tances et alternatives,* where some interesting case studies on cultural glocalization can be found written by scholars and practitioners from different parts of the world. Though some theoretical and a growing number of empirical studies exist, there is no comprehensive collection of theoreti-cally informed case studies either in English, or in German or French.

Our publication is divided into three parts: (1) an introduction and a historical overview on the topic, empirical methods and theoretical approaches; (2) a systematic part focusing on comparisons across empirical case studies; and (3) an empirical part containing studies of the topic in different world regions. The composition of this collection of articles is based on the participants' contributions to the activities of our Research Committee 09. The common theme is the link between global forces and local life-worlds. In this introductory article, we briefly present the current glocalization debate and research agendas and introduce, within this frame-work, the core topic and the individual contributions of this publication.

The core topic or *leitmotif* is the issue of glocalization. Some of the social and cultural phenomena we are confronted with at the beginning of the third millennium are rather new in the history of humankind. There are three basic reasons for this fact: first, an increasing part of human beings all over the world are interconnected with each other; second, the cumulative effects of human actions and interactions are leading to, for instance, global ecological problems; and, third, the resulting increasing complexity of the world. All this means that our disciplines have to investigate globalizing interactions between nation-states, economies, societies and cultures. However, globalization is not simply dissolving local life-worlds in their traditional local structures and settings, but is interacting with them in a sort of localization, or 'glocalization' as some scholars name this hybrid mix. As sociology and cultural anthropology analyse the conditions of humankind in a global age, local changes resulting from the impact of global forces mean a new form of interdependence of cultures. Thus, nationally con-stricted approaches such as modernization and dependence theories have lost their explanatory power. Instead, new theoretical and analytical approaches are needed to study social tranformation in various world regions under conditions of globalization.

The different articles of this publication are linked systematically to the general framework. They are presented in a few words. In the second introductory article written by Ulrike Schuerkens, the historical-intellectual origins and the theoretical aspects of the glocalization debate are systematically developed in order to outline in a global era, a new sociological and anthropological approach to social transformation in non-western world regions and the geographic South. An alternative theoretical framework to approaches such as the westernization of the South, the theory of endogenous development and the world-system theory is developed in the form of contemporary characteristics of modernity between global and local forces.

On this basis, the first article systematically presents the current sociological and anthropological debate on globalization and localization, summarizes the research agendas and findings, and outlines a number of topics for further research. In particular, it is argued that the mapping of global cultural flows is still at an impressionistic stage and should be complemented by a systematic methodology of empirical enquiry outlined in our collection of articles. This can lead to a more differentiated assessment of the often assumed processes of global cultural homogenization. It allows for empirically based solutions to several theoretical problems such as cultural convergence, non-western globalization and alternative modernities. A cross-culturally valid notion may thus help to conceptualize and analyse cultural exchanges that circumvent 'the West'. Finally, the core question of whether humanity is gaining or losing in the globalization process calls for further empirical investigations.

Langman's article about the link between culture and transformation shows that globalization processes create forces that both homogenize and differentiate identities. He demonstrates how global consumerism fosters ludic identities that sustain the hegemony of the global system. His thesis is exemplified by American football games, which provide males with a sense of empowerment and implicitly reinforce their gender privileges and their feelings of superiority. Langman recalls that the Superbowl's mass spectacle in the USA began in the era that gave rise to modern feminism and globalization. The game has become intertwined with global consumerism insofar as, for several years now, football games appeal to men all over the world. Even if the games in different regions of the world are a little different from the Superbowl of the US, the fundamental idea – domination through violence – seems to be the same: the football player acts out the erotic/aggressive fantasy desires of many male spectators. In these celebrations of male performances, aggressive male identities are confirmed and constantly renewed. The otherwise disciplined behaviour in the marketplace or in bureaucracies can be preserved by the participation in ludic activities which permit one to maintain the rational order of the global economic model.

Even if Langman only analyses American Superbowl, football has been considered, like Christianity, as something which was good for the countries of the South (see Brown, 1998: 27). The mission of European countries was to develop the game in the farthest regions of the globe. Today, we see that this mission has been realized with the Football World Cup being held in South Korea in 2002 and the participation of Latin American and African countries in the games. In the countries of the South, the game has been adopted as the people's game and as one of the most potent symbols for the assertion of national identity. Football has become a political and cultural transnational practice with effects not only on ludic culture, but on conceptions of masculinity, too. In this sense, football can be seen as a powerful factor spreading patriarchal conceptions all over the world. The support which these games find with political elites, who do not hesitate to be linked to them and who officially sanction successes and failures of their national teams, witnesses the social and cultural importance of the ideology which football conveys.

Another example from Langman tackles body modifications which consist in permanent transformations of the body of young people who reject the repression and conformity intrinsic to postmodernity. In order to allow the current consumerism of large parts of the world to flourish, the ludic spaces which Langman describes allow the repressed to return. The author furthermore describes how the globalized spectacle of the local Carnival of Rio de Janeiro attracts tourists and emphasizes an inversion of the social order and a realization of individual desires. He shows that the local touristic spectacle is influenced by tourists who introduce western habits, western meanings and customs. The countries of origin of these tourists are most often the western industrialized regions, which contributes to the fact that the local attraction becomes more and more linked to global factors: tourists and the global system of international tourism influence the transformation of local socioeconomic structures. As Langman demonstrates, tourism can be seen as an important element of the intertwining of human beings and their 'cultures'. The link between the global and the local via tourism thus represents a powerful inflow of external cultural elements.

In this sense, cultural elements contribute to stabilize the dominant order of our globalized world. The different cultural elements he describes are characterized by global and local elements: the Rio Carnival attracts global tourists, Superbowl is a game which has parallel meanings all over the globe, body modifications can be found in rather different world regions, even if their sense as a means of rejection or acceptance of the dominant society is dependent on further cultural factors, such as religious worldviews.

Helmuth Berking underlines in his article the increasing importance of the ethnicization of cultural identities in a world characterized by globalization. He argues that the globalization of production, commodity markets and financial markets is increasingly breaking territorial links and is seeking autonomy from national rules. Moreover, services and rights guaranteed by states are no longer dues only to citizens but to all people – a fact which feeds the hate and the xenophobia of autochthonous groups. Berking underlines that neither global flows of cultures nor transnational migrants stop at the borders of nation-states. He is surely right to suggest the growing influence of ethnic groups who begin to become an important factor of social inequality in western countries, and also between the North and the South, a factor which causes struggles for recognition and fights for territorial presence in numerous non-western and western regions of the globe. The importance of the ethnic dimension in international relations is obvious, too, if we consider the hierarchization of states, as it is established by UN organizations: a colour structure can be found with overall white nations at the top of the ladder, coloured nations occupying the middle levels and black nations at the bottom of the ladder. This ethnic inequality, which was first evoked by Wallerstein and Balibar some years ago, currently influences life-chances, social relations, the direction of international migrations, and political relations between states. Since September 11, these ethnic and/or cultural factors of international relations have arrived at the foreground of the political agenda. Conflictual situations in the geographic North are now often linked to ethnic belongings which may have their origins in the geographic South. In the geographic South and East, war or warlike situations have become more and more frequent. A new form of racism has emerged, which has become widespread in some European countries with the growing political importance of extreme right-wing parties. However, for the time being, the nation and its culture are not replaced by transnational cultures. Instead diasporic, transnational ethnic cultures are emerging which may contribute to the enlargement of political associations between different nation-states, as the example of the European Union suggests.

The article by Willfried Spohn analyses a phemonenon which has become important since the events of September 11. The author suggests that in the last two decades, an enormous revitalization of nationalism and religion can be found, often combined in the form of religious nationalism. This development is characteristic for almost all continents: the revolution in Iran and the rise of religious fundamentalism and religious nationalism in the Islamic countries, the radicalization of Hinduism in Southern Asia, the revival of nationalisms and Christian – Catholic and Orthodox – religion with the fall of Communism in Eastern Europe, the development of sectarian Protestantism in Latin America as well as the rise of Protestant fundamentalism in North America. Following these movements, the predominant classical sociological modernization paradigm *cum* secularization thesis has been increasingly replaced by globalization theory with its perspective on the revitalization of nationalism and religion as structural consequences of globalization. Within this theoretical controversy, the author develops a historical-sociological comparative approach (on the basis of Shmuel Eisenstadt and David Martin) that argues for multiple modernities combining specific religious types and secularization patterns, which are characteristic not only for the 'modern age', but also the 'global age'. This core thesis is theoretically developed and exemplified by a variety of empirical case studies on religion and nationalism from different world civilizations and regions.

The article by Ulrike Schuerkens shows the structural change of societies of the South due to their often colonial past. She argues that the interaction of societies of the South and the North meant a globalization and westernization of important elements of the social, economic, cultural and political systems of these societies. The study of colonial and neocolonial development policies and of the resulting interactions between autochthonous societies and European colonial societies lets appear a gradual integration in a world system, not only of economies, but of politics, social systems and cultural systems, too. The author underlines the universality of several structures beneath the diversity and multiplicity of possible developments. Ulrike Schuerkens suggests that local particularities are accepted, yet that the actual tendency is one of an existing universality, which is difficult to demonstrate because of large local differences.

Events such as the death of Diana Princess of Wales, the Olympic games and acts of terrorism show that a global present exists, that communication flows permit local events to spread in a globalized world where people have the possibility to know more and more about each other, even if opportunities to move physically are still limited to a restrained number of people, which has nevertheless grown extensively in the last 20 years.

Ulrike Schuerkens argues that the acceptance of fundamental elements of western models allows increasing groups of people to communicate and understand each other. A way of life has been introduced in former colonial societies of South America, Asia and Africa which allows movement beyond local boundaries in a globalized world. Ulrike Schuerkens uses the example of the labour system to demonstrate these processes of appropriation of new forms of behaviour, new ideas, new meanings of local life-worlds introduced by global elements. Sure, these possibilities are not accessible to the entire population of a country. Due to diversities of different orders, such as life-chances, gender, or geographic origin, the access to globalized life-worlds is limited. Yet it is obvious that mass media, tourists and migrants contribute to the fact that local people have begun to accept more and more elements of globalized life-worlds. Often, these elements are looked for, a fact which rejoins strategies of transnational enterprises and international organizations (see Sklair, 2001). Consumerism as part of the neoliberal economic model is spread all over the world and leads people to accept material consumer goods, even if the meaning of these goods is still influenced by local cultures and may be different according to geographic regions (see Miller, 1994). Common economic and political models are implanted in various regions of the world. Market and democracy are institutions which the dominant order tries to establish all over the world. The challenge of the 21st century may thus be no longer the globalization of a hegemonic structural model, but the unequal distribution of participation chances in our globalized world. The anti-globalization movements assemble parts of these groups who put up with the more or less negative aspects of the globalized world. Even if these movements are not able to stop processes which have been initiated by powerful institutions and structural models, they will emphasize problems inherent in the globalization project. Forgotten groups, such as peasants of the agrarian societies in the South who are still forced to adapt to challenges by focusing on 'traditional' mechanisms, poor city dwellers in overcrowded urban areas, populations exposed to natural disasters, all these people risk not being included in the globalization project. Members of these groups may be accessible to forces which the world knows since September 11. In this sense, we have to observe critically the globalization project. It is surely not a garden of Eden for every human being, but it is a powerful project which may permit humanity to resolve common problems. Global conferences and transnational events let a new era appear, which explores new challenges.

The article by Shalini Randeria addresses the issue of law by examining the interplay between the World Bank, NGOs and the state at federal and regional level in India. Her article shows the intertwining of traditional norms, national law, World Bank standards and international human rights. The author discusses current conflicts around natural resources and the right to livelihood in western India. She displays in several case studies some of the contradictory effects of World Bank policies and projects. The monopoly of the state with regard to law is challenged by a diversity of state, supra-state and non-state actors at the local, national and supranational level, as Shalini Randeria shows. However, law remains an important but ambivalent issue, whose regulation is questioned by NGOs and social movements who constitute important interfaces between state, international institutions and local groups. The article demonstrates strategies of the state in the face of attempts by civil society actors and international organizations. The connections between local actors and global discourses reveal that globalization is locally experienced, that transnational social movements link local actors to global discourses, that World Bank loans have an impact on local risks of impoverishment and displacement. In this sense, Shalini Randeria's article contributes to the growing debate in social and cultural anthropology, which challenges its former tradition as a localized discipline. Instead, she shows the international and transnational links of local groups in the face of conflictual issues.

The article by Christine Müller shows the organization of women at local, regional, national and transnational levels. She argues that the interesting point today is the interconnection between women. Since the UN women's world conferences, the knowledge of the local life-world is transformed on a global level into common strategies and programmes. A worldwide permanent collaboration and global networking structure in a North–South as well as in a South–South relationship has been established. Müller underlines that local interactions are still based on face-to-face communications, but this knowledge flows across distances, common meetings and mutual visits; it circulates from the urban to the rural parts of countries, but also from the rural to the urban context. Global discourses are brought down to the local level by acts of translation embedded in local issues. Moreover, local and global institutions react by changing their structures and their policies.

The case studies from different regions of the world illustrate the very differentiated outlook we discuss in the theoretical chapter written by Ulrike Schuerkens. The article of Eric Popkin discusses the topic of transnationalism, which occupies an important place in glocalization studies, insofar as transnational migrants maintain strong links to their home country and their country of residence. These relations have social, political, religious, economic and organizational forms. The process of transmigration means an increasing inflow of cultural elements in the regions of origin, but in the regions of arrival, too. Migrants bring their lifestyles, their knowledge, their values, their goods, also their culture or parts of their culture to other geographical regions. Furthermore, due to mutual visits, return migration, contacts by phone, post or email, an intense flow of goods, consumption patterns, values, representations and information takes place. Countries of origin thus acknowledge a large inflow of external cultural elements. Long (1996: 49) writes: 'migration networks also function as important conduits of information and opinions about the "world outside" and disseminate the latest fashions in dress, music and films'. In the country of residence, cultural elements penetrate such as different eating habits, religious beliefs, healing methods and different fashions, which all contribute to an enrichment of the often western cultures. Moreover, parts of the elites of countries of origin and residence, working in embassies, in universities, in transnational companies contribute to a transnational professional culture which is often influenced by western values of social contacts, fashion and cuisine. These transnational cultures are created by deterritorialized activities and connections of their members. The transnational culture is a hybrid and syncretic culture influenced by different communities. As Hannerz (1993: 43) argues, 'cultures travel . . . when people travel'. Travelling across frontiers signifies a growing cross-cultural (in)flow of cultural elements. In a second step, migrants integrate their new social and cultural surroundings in their local life-worlds and let multicultural situations emerge, which I described for African migrants in France (Schuerkens, 2000, 2001). Processes of transnational migrations thus contribute to a growing deterritorialization of cultures.

In her article, Nina Bandelj analyses the foreign direct investment flows in Slovenia and puts the question how such an amount of global capital impacts on economic practices in local settings. She displays that foreign direct investment as a key indicator of economic globalization is embedded in a process of continuous negotiation between global pressures and local interests. Even if initially after the independence of the country Slovenian policy favoured domestic owners over foreign investors, since 1997 provisions have been put in place which have given domestic and foreign investors equal rights to enter and exit business. Since 1999, free transfers of profits and the repatriation of capital have been permitted. The idea that foreign direct investment can contribute to the economy's restructuring and development has entered the official political discourse. Since its independence in 1991, Slovenia joined more and more international organizations which strongly advocated the opening of borders to foreign direct investment. Insofar as these organizations propagate worldwide models of economic action, they exert formal and informal pressures on new member states to align their legislation with neoliberal institutions, which promote worldwide convergence processes in economic policies. However, the adoption of formal arrangements has not meant that network ties, political alliances and cultural affinities between investors and domestic hosts have disappeared. Actually, Nina Bandelj shows that prior business contacts and similar cultural practices provide an impetus for the majority of Slovenian enterprises to invest. Nevertheless, the rather short period of international economic contact does not permit a final answer. Even if global processes encourage today convergence *and* divergence, institutional globalization may be decisive for further processes of economic globalization initiated by transnational enterprises.

Marina P. Temudo and Ulrich Schiefer's article presents the case of an agrarian society confronted by a war situation. The authors show that the agrarian society of Guinea-Bissau did not lose its potential for reconstruction because of the fact that its production did not depend on the secondary economy of development aid. They demonstrate the capacity for reconstitution of this agrarian society by analysing its exchange of work, its produce and its system of loans. The authors demonstrate the complex web of social rules of solidarity and reciprocity which allowed relatives and urban refugees to do harvest work in the fields. Change in the work organization and in resource management permitted the majority of the urban population to survive war inside the agrarian societies of Guinea-Bissau. During this period, relief aid was rather limited and the construction of refugee camps was not necessary. After the war and with the return of refugees to urban areas, the relationship between city dwellers and rural groups underwent important changes. The return of the displaced urban population means that the newly created networks may give young rural people a better chance to migrate to cities. The outcome of these processes can currently only be presumed.

A larger integration of these agrarian populations in an international division of labour, as is the case in other African rural areas involved in production for the world primary goods market, may become a political target (see McMichael, 1996: 66ff.). Temudo and Schiefer show that, for the time being, the agrarian societies of Guinea-Bissau are still capable of activating their own resources, even under extreme pressures. Their conclusion on the widening gap between urban and rural areas in this country shows the fragility of agrarian societies in Africa, which still strive to restore their traditional mechanisms in a continent where agrarian societies are often involved in the global labour division. The authors argue that rural development policy seems to be interested in these social processes which permit urban dwellers to find acceptable solutions in difficult situations.

Jo Schmidt shows in her article that the Samoan gender framework as a whole has reacted to Samoa's increasing westernization. The work that the *fa'afafine*[2] do is gendered, but the product of labour – the money they earn – is rendered gender neutral. The increasing influence of the western culture has led to an emphasis on appearance and bodily expression as a marker of gender. Other clothing habits have been introduced and a move towards concepts of individual expression can be found. This means for the fa'afafine that to be feminine is now centred on who one has (or would have) sex with and no longer on the labour one performs. Samoan understandings of gender have intertwined with western discourses of sexuality which consider gender to be fundamental for self-identity. Sex between a man and a fa'afafine did not threaten the man's heterosexuality insofar as creating families was seen by Samoans as a central social imperative. Jo Schmidt distinguishes the existence of the fa'afafine 50 years ago from the present generation where marriage is seen to be a contradiction to the sense that fa'afafine have of themselves as feminine. She argues however that, in Samoa, a marked disapproval of homosexuality exists until today. The fa'afafine begin nevertheless to identify themselves as gay and fa'afafine at the same time. In this way, they are adapting to the globalized western discourse on gender and sexuality without abandoning their tradition.

The article by George Morgan explores the attraction of autochthonous traditions both for Aboriginal people in Australia and for the broader public. He shows that the autochthonous identity of most Aboriginal people living in cities is not something which is invented or contrived. Aboriginal culture is forced to adapt to the pressures which are placed on it. The everyday significance of inherited forms of ancient rituals, spirituality and connections to land recedes. The author argues that these phenomena continue to be forms that serve to constitute Aboriginal solidarity, but Aborigines currently produce emergent cultures from the material available through global cultural flows. For instance, young people appropriate the symbolism of black American protest and youth cultures. Already 30 years ago, Aborigines had adopted afro hairstyles. Today, they embrace the styles of hip-hop and rap, and young men have been inspired by the politics of Malcolm X and Louis Farrakahn. Thus, Aboriginal people adopt motifs which receive local significance, but acquire a subcultural meaning different from the original setting.

George Morgan underlines that ancient symbols continue to provide people in urban dwellings with a point of anchorage against the pressures to assimilate to an Australian global modernity. Living around European population centres in often difficult social situations, they support a political culture based on recovering aspects of the past. His article shows furthermore that there is a growing contemporary interest in autochthonous traditions by middle-class citizens and counter-cultural movements. Their romanticism reflects, as George Morgan demonstrates, a popular disillusion with western rationality and modernity and reveals a yearning for fulfilment through a connection which what is considered as natural. This movement witnesses the links of the local Aborginal culture to cultural expressions in other parts of the globe, often situated in western countries.

What can we conclude from these different contributions on the problematics of glocalization between globalization and local life-worlds? The different case studies show multiple facets of the interaction of the local and the global, which I outline conceptually in the theoretical introduction. One of the research findings of this publication is certainly the image of a global world linked to local life-worlds all over the world. Today, we can no longer accept the existence of distinct cultural units which are circumscribed by a geographic territory. Instead, we are currently confronted with cultures which are influenced by migration, tourism, international communication flows, transnational enterprises and international organizations. The image of an isolated culture which was the main interest of social and cultural anthropology and ethnology some years ago, can no longer be the main focus of this discipline. Our selection of articles shows that most of their authors are working as social and cultural anthropologists, and as sociologists. In fact, the combination of these disciplines allows one to analyse current problematics of non-western countries situated between global processes and local life-worlds. Certainly, social anthropology still permits a better understanding of some of the aspects of cultures studied here. Yet a sociological approach to these cultures is essential to understand some of their global aspects. The notion of 'global cultures' suggested by Featherstone (1995: 10) helps in understanding these processes of differentiation between local cultures all over the globe influenced by global factors. It seems that research on cultures of the southern hemisphere can only continue to play a societal role if we accept that we must tackle influences originating from the global system on these societies. Some years ago, ethnologists still manifested a silent denial of studies which tackled global systems. Currently, these ethnologists are becoming a minority, with younger students and scholars who will not accept any longer being restrained to research topics which they consider as belonging to the past. Concepts as 'endogenous' and 'exogenous', which described research endeavours of the disciplines some years ago, are more and more replaced by notions such as global and local, which are more adapted to current situations.

Different articles underline the fact that the link between global forces and local life-worlds cannot only be explained by structural transformation but also by agency. This means that, for instance, political commitment may emphasize either the long-term perspective of globalization, or the diversity of national or regional life-worlds. The topic which we tackle touches important social values and policy issues, even in the scientific community where research on this issue is done. But there is a general avoidance to recognize the problem of incongruence between processes of globalization and localization. The principle of 'unity in diversity', which we can find in the discourse of ethnologists, does not specify if it concerns particular elements of a system or if it is understood as the integration of some cultural systems into a larger one. It seems that the declaration of values, such as 'we must preserve diversity . . . acts as a substitute for the analysis of the actual changes' (Mlinar, 1992: 168). As Mlinar underlines with a similar example, the right to be different tends to be directed towards global forces, while the right to underline unity tends to be directed towards local life-worlds. Globalization is achieved by the domination of a given system element at the expense of others, or by a common acceptance of global standards. Distinctive localization is achieved by the preservation as an item of folklorization, by a widely shared (globalized) element, or by the (re)construction of a particular surrounding. Our case studies show that we cannot dissociate global forces from local life-worlds as they are linked by mutually dependent processes. Thus it is not coherent to promote globalization without differentiation of 'local' communities. Globalization may not provide long-term protective mechanisms for localized identities without more or less changes in the context of global economic, political, social and cultural flows. In the long term, global forces may induce far-reaching transformations in local life-worlds as some of our case studies underline; in the short term, protective mechanisms may contribute to the survival of several aspects of local life-worlds. Thus it seems important to acknowledge the necessity of a notion such as glocalization which tries to include aspects of both sides: global forces and local life-worlds which can no longer be considered as separate entities.

Today, people are confronted by transnationals, global images, markets. They try to get to grips with these external elements. We can no longer speak of the globalized world in terms of 'centre–periphery', which implied asymmetries in economies, politics and culture. Instead the current globalization implies a form of homogenization and diversity: globalization is linked to localization. As our case studies show, we have to analyse the ways in which local systems, values, social relations are reworked in interaction with global conditions. For several decades, we have found the creations of new local social forms as an answer to the process of globalization. In order to be meaningful to social actors, these new social meanings must build on existing cultural schemes. It becomes obvious that this sort of reinvention of tradition and creation of new meanings is different from persisting local traditions. Thus glocalization permits the opening up of a new theoretical understanding of social transformation and change.

The implication of this conception is that large aspects of current economic, social and cultural relations need to be explored by insisting on global and local processes. This opens up numerous questions in various fields of research which go further than what has been possible in this publication. It is now even possible to suggest another research agenda. We need more studies on the treatment of global dimensions in various local life-worlds, enterprises, politics and counter-movements. Further theory-oriented, comparative and micro-sociological empirical research on social transformation and development has to take account of the understanding of glocalization which we try to pursue in the present publication.

Notes

1 The name of RC 09 will probably soon be changed to 'Social Transformation and Sociology of Development'.
2 The Samoan *fa'afafine* are biological males who express feminine gender identities.

Bibliography

Brown, Adam, ed. (1998) *Fanatics, Power, Identity, and Fandom in Football*. London and New York: Routledge.

Buchholt, Helmut, Heidt, Erhard U. and Stauth, Georg, eds (1996) *Modernität zwischen Differenzierung und Globalisierung. Kulturelle, wirtschaftliche und politische Transformationsprozesse in der sich globalisierenden Moderne*. Hamburg: Lit.

Centre Tricontinental (2000) *Cultures et mondialisation. Résistances et alternatives*. Paris and Montreal: L'Harmattan.

Featherstone, Mike (1995) 'Global Culture: An Introduction', in Mike Featherstone (ed.) *Global Culture: Nationalism, Globalization and Modernity*, pp. 1–14. London: Sage.

Friedman, Jonathan (1994) *Cultural Identity and Global Process*. London: Sage.

Hannerz, Ulf (1993) 'Mediations in the Global Ecumene', in Gísli Pálsson (ed.) *Beyond Boundaries*, pp. 41–57. Oxford: Berg.

Harmsen, Andrea (1999) *Globalisierung und lokale Kultur. Eine ethnologische Betrachtung*. Hamburg: Lit.

Long, Norman (1996) 'Globalization and Localization: New Challenges to Rural Research', in Henrietta L. Moore (ed.) *The Future of Anthropological Knowledge*, pp. 37–59. London and New York: Routledge.

Long, Norman (2001) *Development Sociology: Actor Perspectives*. London and New York: Routledge.

McMichael, Philip (1996) *Development and Social Change: A Global Perspective*. Thousand Oaks, CA, London and New Delhi: Pine Forge Press.

Miller, Daniel (1992) 'The Young and the Restless: A Case of the Local and the Global in Mass Consumption', in Roger Silverstone and Erich Hirsch (eds) *Consuming Technologies*, pp. 163–82. London and New York: Routledge.

Miller, Daniel (1994) *Modernity an Ethnographic Approach: Dualism and Mass Consumption in Trinidad*. Oxford: Berg.

Mlinar, Zdravko, ed. (1992) *Globalization and Territorial Identities*. Aldershot: Avebury.

Müller, Hans-Peter, ed. (1996) *Weltsystem und kulturelles Erbe. Gliederung und Dynamik der Entwicklungsländer aus ethnologischer und soziologischer Sicht*. Berlin: Reimer Verlag.

Neubert, Dieter, Koessler, Reinhart and von Oppen, Achim, eds (1999) *Gemeinschaften in einer entgrenzten Welt*. Berlin: Arabische Buch.

Olwig, Karen Fog (1993) *Global Culture, Island Identity: Continuity and Change in the Afro-Caribbean Community of Nevis*. Chur: Harwood Academic Publisher.

Schuerkens, Ulrike (2000) 'L'Intégration sociale des migrants africains en France: une problématique interculturelle', *Revue Internationale de Sociologie* 10(3): 365–84.

Schuerkens, Ulrike (2001) 'African Women and Migration in France', in *African Development Perspectives Yearbook* 8, pp. 765–82. Hamburg: Lit.

Sklair, Leslie (2001) *The Transnational Capitalist Class*. Oxford and Malden, MA: Blackwell.

Warnier, Jean-Pierre (1999) *La Mondialisation de la culture*. Paris: Éditions de la Découverte.

2

The Sociological and Anthropological Study of Globalization and Localization

Ulrike Schuerkens

Introduction

This article sketches the development of the topic of globalization and localization within sociology over the last two or three decades and summarizes the research findings of this period. Subsequently, a number of topics for further enquiry are outlined. It is argued that the mapping of global cultural flows is still at an impressionistic stage and should be supplemented by systematic procedures. This leads to a more differentiated assessment of global cultural homogenization. We tackle the problems of cultural convergence, non-western globalization and alternative modernities. Cultural exchanges that circumvent 'the west' have not yet received sufficient attention. A cross-culturally valid notion of modernity may help in conceptualization. Finally, the question whether humanity is gaining or losing in the globalization process calls for further investigation.

Social Transformations between Processes of Globalization and Differentiation

The expectation that modernization would promote a world of increasing homogeneity has been contested in proposals for countries of the South to 'delink' from the capitalist world economy (Amin), and the resurgence of alternative cultural agendas such as those of Islamic fundamentalism. Wallerstein's historical research about the position of Europe at the core of development of capitalism illustrates that processes of globalization have very intimate connections with processes of westernization. The simple statement of modernization theory that social progress is equal to the spread of western institutions and norms is now defunct, but Hettne's (1995) identification of 'Eurocentric bias' in thinking about development leads us to rethink fundamental categories of this understanding of the world. In the West, the expanded contact with other cultures brought about by globalization has had the effect of undermining certainties on which ideas of western superiority were based, making it increasingly difficult to specify what it means to be western. It seems to be a fact that processes of globalization and westernization are closely interconnected. But an account of globalization as westernization runs into the difficulty of the progressive blurring of the West's geographical boundaries as people and ideas cross those boundaries. One of the most important effects of globalization is that social relationships are less and less bound by spatial location. According to this, it has been acknowledged that the interconnectedness of local and global social relationships makes problematic the idea of societies as discrete, bounded entities. While the movement in one direction might be understood as westernization, as the export of western values and ways of life, globalization also involves processes which import to western societies the encounter of the postcolonial reality.

Globalization might be regarded as synonymous with westernization in the sense that it has its historical origins in the West, but it is not a process which promotes global homogeneity through the imposed reproduction of western patterns elsewhere in the world. It is the case that the countries of the South have not imitated the North in any mechanical fashion, while there has also been extensive appropriation of ideas and practices by the West from the rest of the world. There are theorists for whom it is import- ant to highlight capitalism as the driving force within globalization. Sklair (2001) has argued that the role of transnational capitalism has been import- ant in the spread of transnational corporations and the globalization of mass media, both of which have promoted consumerism as a central piece of modern global culture. This allows the distinction between 'capitalist development' and alternative definitions of development framed in terms of economic growth, criteria of the distribution of the social product, demo- cratic politics and the elimination of class, gender and ethnic inequalities. In the analysis of third world societies, there is extensive resort to concepts such as postcolonialism and post-development (Escobar). This idea is echoed in the notion of postmodernization and the claim that a transition from modernity is underway. Postmodernists like the first raise fundamental doubts not only about the direction of social change, but also about the very idea of attempting to predict the future.

One of the most important aspects of globalization is that it is essentially 'action at distance'. The post-traditional society is the first global society. Until relatively recently, much of the world remained in a quasi-segmental state, in which many large enclaves of traditionalism persisted. The local community continued to be strong. A global world is one where pre-existing traditions cannot avoid contacts not only with others but also with many alternative ways of life. By the same token, it is one where the 'other' cannot any longer be treated as inert. The point is not only that the other 'answers back', but that mutual interrogation is possible. In a post-traditional order, we see the formation of a cosmopolitan conversation of humankind. If there is no dialogue, tradition becomes fundamentalism. Fundamentalism may be understood as an assertion of a formula truth without regard to consequences. This counter-current has arisen in opposition to the inter- mingling of western and traditional attitudes and behaviour. It is likely to be prominent in nations which find themselves structurally at the lower end of the international stratification ladder, which is dominated by the western and western-orientated nations. On the other side, the current assertion that cultural pluralism is the final shape of world reality and its enthusiastic advocacy as an absolute doctrine, or goal to work towards, is surely naive and unrealistic. The western world provides today standards of living, life-styles and behaviour to which, as a matter of sociological fact, people of other nations seek to aspire. It is likely that the compelling force of this structure of power will, in the long run, prove irresistible.

Currently, the destruction of the local community in developed societies, as Giddens (1984) showed, has reached its apogee. Traditions which survived or were actively created, have increasingly succumbed to forces of cultural evacuation. The world of the 'traditional society' is one of *traditional societies*, in which cultural pluralism takes the form of multiple mores and customs, existing in separated spaces. The post-traditional society is quite different. It is globalizing in an intense manner. In the post-traditional order cultural pluralism can no longer take the form of separated forms of power. With the intensifying of globalizing processes, these traditions become undermined. Traditions are called to justify themselves. Giddens suggests that 'traditions only persist in so far as they are made available to discursive justification and are prepared to enter into open dialogue not only with other traditions but with alternative modes of doing things' (Giddens, 1984). The post-traditional society is characterized by global aspects, by new forms of interdependence. In this sense, the modernity which is discussed in sociologies' theoretical debates is global, universal insofar as all over the world traditional societal aspects are questioned. Individuals are linked in local societies to changes at the global level. Actions are done without personal contacts via the global net of mass media, phone, fax and computers. The structures of local communities are thus constructed no longer at the local place, but are constructed by organizations far away. Social groups are linked less and less by a common local history, common relations and a common worldview. Abstract systems, values and symbols define the daily social reality. Local groups have to distinguish between face-to-face relations and links via impersonal symbols. New social systems emerge which have been influenced by global and local aspects during transformation processes, linked to colonialism and neo-colonialism.

More empirical research about these processes seems to be needed to demonstrate the links between local social mechanisms and global patterns which influence everyday actions. In this publication, we try to fill this gap in scholarly work. Links between global and local patterns are shown as the emergence of new cultural forms in different countries of the South. Anthropology and sociology, which tackle as social sciences developments in the countries of the South, have to treat local answers to global patterns in a changing international world. The traditions which we can find in these societies are thus no longer static ones, but have to be adapted by each new generation. The social sciences can thus no longer tackle a stable social world, but must tackle a world which is influenced by knowledge aspects coming from the whole world. Some decades ago, anthropologists still spoke about their objects as if they were static ones. Today, societies of the South investigated by sociologists and anthropologists are confronted with processes of continual change. They answer back and anthropological studies tackle processes which touch changing life-patterns of social groups. It seems today that processes at lower integrative levels (nation-state, region, community, kinship) are becoming increasingly governed by orders of the higher level.

It seems to me that we have to take account in our empirical research in countries of the South of local aspects and global influences, without exaggerating the tendency of one side or neglecting the other side. If we accept the definition of Giddens, his image of humankind helps us to consider people of the South not as victims of global processes, but to show the varieties of their experiences and actions. The interdependencies between groups within nations and between nations across the globe have to be investigated much more. The different articles of this publication contribute to a critical examination of these processes in the post-developing world.

The Sociological and Anthropological Study of Globalization and Localization

One of the most significant tendencies of the 21st century is the interdependency of the world caused by many transnational relations, processes and flows. Hannerz (1996: 17) writes: 'In the most general sense, globalization is a matter of increasing long-distance interconnectedness, at least across national boundaries, preferably between continents as well.' These processes of linkages across borders include a restructuration of spaces. A growing process of deterritorialization, the disappearance of fixed links of human beings to towns, villages and national frontiers can be found. Today, life-spaces, activities and social links of individuals and societies are larger than national frontiers. Spatial distances include the world as a space. According to time periods, the most intensive globalization processes took place in the last 20–30 years, which can be considered as an 'accelerated phase of globalization' (Waters, 1995: 36). During this period, a global network of flows, processes and links across frontiers was formed. European colonialization and the worldwide expansion of capitalism during the 19th and 20th centuries had already signified an intensification of worldwide networks. However, we focus on the processes of the last 20–30 years.[1]

In this article, we show how transnational networks contribute to the establishment and intensification of global processes and how these global processes are linked to multiple flows of cultural elements which are crossing frontiers. From the perspective of local (national or subnational) units, this means a growing integration in global and transnational contexts and growing contacts with 'external' cultural elements. External cultural elements are elements which cross national and 'cultural' frontiers to enter a local context. These external elements may become local elements when they try to get a foothold in their new cultural context. Featherstone (1995: 8) writes: 'One consequence of these changes is that more and more people are now involved with more than one culture.'

Even if these local implications can be found in former cross-frontier relations and activities, at the current state of globalization, they are much more important. Because of the increase in and the intensification of cross-frontier processes during the last decades, the importance of these processes at the local level has become larger compared to the past. To speak in the words of Hannerz, we can say that the intensification and the extent of global links had increasing consequences on the life and the culture of men. Hannerz (1987: 555) writes: 'From First World metropolis to Third World village, through education and popular culture, by way of missionaries, consultants, critical intellectuals and small-town storytellers, a conversation between cultures goes on'.

With regard to a local perspective, these links and contacts across frontiers imply that the 'habitat of meaning' (Hannerz, 1996: 22–3) of a group and an individual includes on an increasing scale external meanings and cultural forms. Here the interesting questions are to see what the cultural consequences and implications on a local level are of these increasing flows of external cultural elements. In the following paragraphs, I will analyse how the local react in front of global external cultural elements. In particular, I put the questions of whether a global cultural homogenization is in the making and what the local processes opposed to this development are.

Globalization and the Perspective of a Global Cultural Homogenization

Different authors from various social and cultural sciences consider processes of globalization and flows of cultural elements across frontiers as a global cultural homogenization, as a 'westernization' or an 'Americanization'. For instance, Nederveen Pieterse (1993: 1) writes: 'The most common interpretations of globalization are the idea that the world is becoming more uniform and standardized, through a technological, commercial and cultural synchronization emanating from the West.'

This perspective is based on the fact that the flow of cultural elements across frontiers is dominated by western industrial nations, such as the United States. According to these scholars, the global flow of cultural forms and meanings takes place along a one-way street from the core countries to the peripheral countries. Hannerz (1992: 219) writes: 'When the center speaks, the periphery listens, and mostly does not talk back.' Mass media, products from mass media and (material) consumption goods are considered to contribute to a global cultural homogenization. The spread of these goods from core countries implies an increasing development of consumption societies close to the western model.[2] Mlinar (1992b: 21) speaks of 'cocacolization', Appadurai (1995: 295) of 'commoditization' and Hannerz (1996: 24) of a global 'takeover by giant cultural commodity merchants'.

These predictions cannot only be founded on western dominance in the global flow of cultural elements. These ideas assume that western cultural elements are uncritically absorbed in the countries of the South. Moreover, cultural inflows are considered suppressing of existent local meanings and forms. Due to processes of saturation and continuing inflows of western cultural elements, the thesis is that 'the center cumulatively colonizes the minds of the periphery, with a corresponding institutionalization of its forms, getting the periphery so committed to the imports that soon enough there is no real opportunity for choice' (Hannerz, 1992: 236).

Most often, this sort of scenario is based on superficial and anecdotal examples which can rarely be proven with scientific methods. An exact analysis of local reactions and interpretations to inflowing cultural elements and a detailed examination of interactions between local cultures and global cultural flows can only rarely be found (see, for example Hannerz, 1989a: 207; Tomlinson, 1991: 38–44). Often, these writings reflect fears of authors or critical perceptions of their own cultures. These scholars oversee the long-term implications of contacts established for several centuries in some coastal regions. Hannerz (1992: 242) points out for instance: 'There has been time to absorb the foreign influences, to modify the modifications in turn, and to fit shifting cultural forms to developing social structures, to situations and emerging audiences. This is not a scene where the peripheral culture is utterly defenseless, but rather one where locally evolving alternatives to imports are available, and where there are people at hand to perform innovative acts of cultural brokerage.'

Often, these authors ignore the existence of local cultural alternatives and the active role of local populations in face of inflowing elements. They do not take account of the fact that inflowing cultural forms and meanings do not meet a cultural *tabula rasa*, but existing local meanings and cultural forms. The penetrating cultural elements enter a dialogue with these local forms and meanings, these perspectives and experiences of local populations. Local groups in the countries of the South are not only passive consumers and uncritical recipients of the western culture. Often, groups play an active and creative role in the transformation of their own culture while handling inflowing cultural elements. The local handling of these elements is neither an imitation, nor an uncritical takeover. Hannerz (1989a: 212) argues: 'The cultural flow from center to periphery . . . does not enter a void, nor does it wash out everything that comes in its way.'

On the other hand, it cannot be denied that increasing flows of cultural elements across borders meant in different fields a global and worldwide cultural approach. This is true for some consumption patterns and wishes, for some values and perceptions. Following this insight, many authors emphasize today that, on the one hand, a combination of increasing global cultural approaches exists, and, on the other, a continuing global cultural heterogeneity and differentiation. Appadurai (1995: 295) states for instance: 'The central problem of today's global interactions is the tension between cultural homogenization and cultural heterogenization.' Some authors stress, moreover, that a globalization of material forms can be found beside a global differentiation of cultural meanings and contents.

Globalization and the Problem of Global Cultural Diversity

Currently, processes of local absorption of global cultural flows and the mixture between global and local cultural elements are increasingly studied. It became evident that the global cannot exist without the local. The local is the space 'in which a variety of influences come together, acted out perhaps in a unique combination, under those special conditions' (Hannerz, 1996: 27).

The essential elements of the local can be found in local daily life, which Hannerz calls the 'form-of-life frame'. This frame includes daily activities in household, workplace and neighbourhood, daily emotional face-to-face relations to other close people, daily uses of symbolic forms; in short, all these elements 'which we largely take for granted as parts of local life' (Hannerz, 1996: 28). These events and experiences of the local daily life are considered as direct and real. Often, these elements have a great influence on the life of human beings. This local daily life is considered to be a central area for the organization, production and spread of culture. Here, we can find a constant circulation of meanings, which includes every individual who participates in local life, every consumer and every producer. Hannerz (1996: 73) writes: 'It is by way of people's attentions to one another in situations within the form-of-life frame . . . that meanings are most continuously and precisely constructed.'

This central role of the 'form-of-life frames' for the organization of culture implies that external cultural inflows have to be negotiated with daily local actions and interactions. A cultural inflow is filtered by local human experiences which allow the acceptance, refusal, interpretation and transformation of actions and forms. Long (1996: 50) explains: 'In fact globalization itself can only be meaningful to actors if the new experiences it simultaneously engenders are made meaningful by reference to existing experiences and cultural understandings.'

If one takes account of this cultural power of the local daily life – its central role in the construction of meanings and in the reception of external cultural elements – possibilities of cultural influences from the global culture are severely restricted. But this local 'form-of-life frame' is subsumed to change; it is temporal and cannot assure an unchanged cultural continuity. The local is changed by the influence of external cultural elements. Inflowing cultural elements, such as television series, western consumer articles and values introduced by migrants, can become elements of the local daily life, often in changed forms and adapted to local contexts. Hannerz (1996: 27) considers thus the local as an area 'where the global, or what has been local somewhere else, also has some chance of making itself at home'. Even in the field of the family, which is one of the most import- ant places of cultural reproduction and transmission of traditions, external influences appear due to processes of globalization: a transgenerational con- tinuity of attitudes, representations and desires is thus more and more undermined.

The local culture and the local daily life can no longer be considered as a 'tacit realm of reproducible practices and dispositions' (Appadurai, 1990: 18). The life and the cultural identity of a human being are less and less con- structed according to a traditional framework. This signifies that 'standard cultural production ... is now an endangered activity' (Appadurai, 1991: 199). Due to mass media and other processes of globalization, numerous possible lifestyles and models of identification are currently presented to individual actors in local settings. They represent ideas which permit the construction of fantasies and perspectives which are not the same as tra- ditional local representations and lifestyles. Imagination and tentative adaptation begin to play an ever more important role in the creation of an individual life. Appadurai (1991: 205) points out: 'Lives today are as much acts of projection and imagination as they are enactments of known scripts or predictable outcomes'. Individual lifestyles, values and behaviours of people are more and more different from local cultural traditions.

The mutual influence of the local and the global has been described thus by Long (1996: 47): ' "local" situations are transformed by becoming part of wider "global" arenas and processes, while "global" dimensions are made meaningful in relation to specific "local" conditions and through the under- standings and strategies of "local" actors'. There exists consequently a situ- ation of continuous interaction of local cultural elements and global cultural influences. Both participate in the local cultural construction of local meanings and cultural forms.

Globalization and the Emphasis on the Local

We have already evoked global links and the extension of people's frame of reference: 'the possibility of being exposed ... to the whole infinity of places, persons, things, ideas' (Strassoldo, 1992: 46). Parallel to global integration and the increasing importance of transnational levels, we can find an intensification of local cultural traditions. MacLeod (1991: 11) underlines: 'Turning in the direction of traditional symbols, customs, images and behavior forms an important countertrend in a modernizing world.' We can thus find an intensification of local particularism and differentiation.

Buell (1994: 9) argues: 'Tighter integration has thus paradoxically meant, and continues to mean, proliferation of asserted differences.'

These processes can be found in numerous societal fields: in the economy, politics, environmental movements, cultural values, etc. They can be an expression of fortification, revitalization or reinvention of local cultural identities and traditions based on ethnic, social, or religious elements they have in common. Different factors explain the appearance of these trends: local groups may interpret global links and their influences on local elements as an attack which leads to indistinct fears in the face of their own culture. The rapidity and the extent of global changes, the complexity of global systems may furthermore contribute to fortify a desire for stability and continuity. As Strassoldo (1992: 46) argued: 'The New Localism is the search for a refuge from the unsettling confusion of the larger world.' References to local communities and local values, a revitalization of traditional cultures and an emphasis on local cultural identity may permit a feeling of stability and confidence in the face of processes of globalization. Beyer (1994: 62) argues: 'To the extent that relativizing forces make themselves felt, individuals seek to orient themselves in our impersonal, global society through identification with a particular group and its specific culture.'

From this perspective, the emphasis on an own culture is not orientated against another real culture – even if groups who are concerned often underline this factor – but against feared effects of processes of globalization. At the same time, emphasis on local cultures can mean an opposition to globalization processes originating in western countries. Bright and Geyer (1987: 69–70) write: 'the assertion of local and particular claims over global and general ones . . . is rather an effort to establish the terms for self-determining and self-controlled participation in the processes of global integration and the struggle for planetary order'.

There is another tendency which needs to be considered here: the world-wide development of a new cultural self-confidence. This cultural self-confidence is growing because of the global spread of ideas and values, and the global recognition of culture and cultural elements as a universal value. A global recognition of the right to an own culture and cultural self-determination accompanies these processes. As the ideo-scapes studied by Appadurai show, a global spread of ideas and values is part of current processes of globalization. The fact that more and more groups consider their culture and lifestyle as a political right lets them put an emphasis on their own culture. Today, due to mass media and global migration flows, global cultural differences are thus more easily established and found out.

Conclusion

In conclusion, we can state that many of the inflowing cultural elements are transformed during processes of integration and embedding in new local environments. They are interpreted in relation to local cultures and particular experiences of local populations. They are appropriated by local requirements and are filled with corresponding contents and functions. Hannerz (1992: 238) indicates: 'the periphery . . . takes its time in reshaping that metropolitan culture which reaches there to its own specifications'. But processes of local appropriation and transformation of cultural elements allow the emergence – due to the mixture of local and imported cultural elements – of something new and unique. The local clash of different cultural elements signifies a creation of new cultural forms, new lifestyles, new representations. In a global perspective, this means a global cultural diversity: but a diversity resulting from the present global cultural links, from the cultural appropriation of external elements by local populations and from the creative mixture of 'global' elements with local meanings and cultural forms. Hannerz describes these processes in the following way:

> The world system, rather than creating massive cultural homogeneity on a global scale, is replacing one diversity with another; and the new diversity is based relatively more on interrelations and less on autonomy. Yet meanings and modes of expressing them can be born in the interrelations. We must be aware that openness to foreign cultural influences need not involve only an impoverishment of local and national culture. It may give people access to technological and symbolic resources for dealing with their own ideas, managing their own culture, in new ways. (Hannerz, 1987: 555)

The global flow of culture is certainly not a one-way street, but may be interpreted rightly as 'a global intercultural interplay' as Nederveen Pieterse (1993: 9) describes it. Countries of the South export, for instance, their music, their literature, their spirituality, or healing methods to countries of the northern hemisphere. These trends are not new, but due to processes of globalization, their importance increases: migrants and media, tourists and scientists are looking permanently for innovations in other cultures and are interested in 'exotic' and 'authentic' cultures.

Notes

I would like to thank Willfried Spohn for his longstanding support of this publication.

1 The influence of colonialism on social transformations in the countries of the South has been tackled in my book (Schuerkens, 2001) on colonial change in the former German Togo.
2 See in this sense the chapter 'Global Vision and the Culture-Ideology of Consumerism' in Sklair (2001: Ch. 8).

Bibliography

Appadurai, Arjun (1990) 'Disjuncture and Difference in the Global Cultural Economy', *Public Culture* 2(2): 1–24.
Appadurai, Arjun (1991) 'Global Ethnoscapes: Notes and Queries for a Transnational Anthropology', in Richard G. Fox (ed.) *Recapturing Anthropology*, pp. 191–210. Santa Fe, NM: School of American Research Press.
Appadurai, Arjun (1993) 'Patriotism and its Futures', *Public Culture* 42(5): 411–29.
Appadurai, Arjun (1995) 'Disjuncture and Difference in the Global Cultural Economy', in

Mike Featherstone (ed.) *Global Culture: Nationalism, Globalization, and Modernity*, 6th edn, pp. 295–310. London: Sage.

Appadurai, Arjun (1996) *Modernity at Large: Cultural Dimensions of Globalization*. Minneapolis: University of Minnesota Press.

Axford, Barrie (1995) *The Global System: Economics, Politics and Culture*. Oxford: Polity Press.

Beyer, Peter (1994) *Religion and Globalization*. London: Sage.

Bright, Charles and Geyer, Michael (1987) 'For a Unified History of the World in the Twentieth Century', *Radical History Review* 39: 69–91.

Brumann, Christoph (1998) 'The Anthropological Study of Globalization: Towards an Agenda for the Second Phase', *Anthropos* 93(4–6): 495–506.

Buchholt, Helmut, Heidt, Erhard U. and Stauth, Georg, eds (1996) *Modernität zwischen Differenzierung und Globalisierung. Kulturelle, wirtschaftliche und politische Transformationsprozesse in der sich globalisierenden Moderne*. Hamburg: Lit.

Buell, Frederick (1994) *National Culture and the New Global System*. Baltimore, MD and London: Johns Hopkins University Press.

Dahmani, Mohamed (1983) *L'Occidentalisation des pays du Tiers Monde. Mythes et réalités*. Algiers: Economia.

D'Iribarne, Philippe (1998) *Cultures et mondialisation. Gérer par-delà les frontières*. Paris: Seuil.

Ekholm-Friedman, Kajsa and Friedman, Jonathan (1995) 'Global Complexity and the Simplicity of Everyday Life', in Daniel Miller (ed.) *Worlds Apart: Modernity through the Prism of the Local*, pp. 134–89. London and New York: Routledge.

Featherstone, Mike, ed. (1995) *Global Culture: Nationalism, Globalization and Modernity*, 6th edn. London: Sage.

Friedman, Jonathan (1994) *Cultural Identity and Global Process*. London: Sage.

Friedman, Jonathan (1995) 'Being in the World: Globalisation and Localisation', in Mike Featherstone (ed.) *Global Culture: Nationalism, Globalization and Modernity*, 6th edn, pp. 311–28. London: Sage.

Geertz, Clifford (1986) *Savoir local, savoir global*. Paris: PUF. (First American edn 1983, *Local Knowledge: Further Essays in Interpretive Anthropology*.)

Giddens, Anthony (1984) *The Constitution of Society: Outline of the Theory of Structuration*. Cambridge: Polity.

'Globalization' (1999) *International Social Science Journal* 51, 160(4): 135–261.

Godelier, Maurice (1995) 'L'Anthropologie sociale est-elle indissolublement liée à l'Occident, sa terre natale?', *International Social Science Journal* 47, 143(1): 165–83.

Hannerz, Ulf (1983) 'Tools of Identity and Imagination', in Anita Jacobson-Widding (ed.) *Identity: Personal and Socio-Cultural*, pp. 347–60. Uppsala: Academia Upsaliensis/Atlantic Highlands, NJ: Humanities Press.

Hannerz, Ulf (1987) 'The World in Creolization', *Africa* 57(4): 546–59.

Hannerz, Ulf (1989a) 'Culture between Center and Periphery: Toward a Macroanthropology', *Ethnos* 54(3–4): 200–16.

Hannerz, Ulf (1989b) 'Notes on the Global Ecumene', *Public Culture* 1(2): 66–75.

Hannerz, Ulf (1991) 'The Global Ecumene as a Network of Networks', in Adam Kuper (ed.) *Conceptualizing Societies*, pp. 34–56. London and New York: Routledge.

Hannerz, Ulf (1992) *Cultural Complexity: Studies in the Social Organization of Meaning*. New York: Columbia University Press.

Hannerz, Ulf (1993) 'Mediations in the Global Ecumene', in Gísli Pálsson (ed.) *Beyond Boundaries*, pp. 41–57. Oxford: Berg.

Hannerz, Ulf (1995a) 'Cosmopolitans and Locals in World Culture', in Mike Featherstone (ed.) *Global Culture: Nationalism, Globalization and Modernity*, 6th edn, pp. 237–51. London: Sage.

Hannerz, Ulf (1995b) ' "Kultur" in einer vernetzten Welt. Zur Revision eines ethnologischen Begriffes', in Wolfgang Kaschuba (ed.) *Kulturen – Identitäten – Diskurse. Perspektiven Europäischer Ethnologie*, pp. 64–84. Berlin: Akademie-Verlag.

Hannerz, Ulf (1996) *Transnational Connections: Cultures, People, Places*. London: Routledge.

Harmsen, Andrea (1999) *Globalisierung und lokale Kultur. Eine ethnologische Betrachtung.* Hamburg: Lit.

Hettne, Björn (1995) *Development Theory and the Three Worlds*, 2nd edn. Harlow: Longman.

Kearney, Michael (1995) 'The Local and the Global: The Anthropology of Globalization and Transnationalism', *Annual Review of Anthropology* 24: 547–65.

Long, Norman (1996) 'Globalization and Localization: New Challenges to Rural Research', in Henrietta L. Moore (ed.) *The Future of Anthropological Knowledge*, pp. 37–59. London and New York: Routledge.

MacLeod, Arlene Elowe (1991) *Accommodating Protest: Working Women, the New Veiling, and Change in Cairo.* New York: Columbia University Press.

McMichael, Philip (1996) *Development and Social Change: A Global Perspective.* Thousand Oaks, CA, London and New Delhi: Pine Forge Press.

Mattelart, Armand (1983) *Transnationals and the Third World: The Struggle for Culture.* South Hadley, MA: Bergin and Garvey.

Mense-Petermann, Ursula (2002) 'Kontinuität und Wandel. Zum Erklärungspotenzial institutionalistischer Ansätze in der Transformationsforschung', *Berliner Journal für Soziologie* 2: 227–42.

Miller, Daniel (1990) 'Fashion and Ontology in Trinidad', *Culture and History* 7: 49–77.

Miller, Daniel (1992) 'The Young and the Restless: A Case of the Local and the Global in Mass Consumption', in Roger Silverstone and Erich Hirsch (eds) *Consuming Technologies*, pp. 163–82. London and New York: Routledge.

Miller, Daniel (1994) *Modernity an Ethnographic Approach: Dualism and Mass Consumption in Trinidad.* Oxford: Berg.

Miller, Daniel, ed. (1995a) *Worlds Apart: Modernity through the Prism of the Local.* London and New York: Routledge.

Miller, Daniel (1995b) 'Introduction: Anthropology, Modernity and Consumption', in Daniel Miller (ed.) *Worlds Apart: Modernity through the Prism of the Local*, pp. 1–22. London and New York: Routledge.

Miller, Daniel (1997) *Capitalism: An Ethnographic Approach.* Oxford: Berg.

Mlinar, Zdravko (1992a) 'Introduction', in Zdravko Mlinar (ed.) *Globalisation and Territorial Identities*, pp. 1–14. Aldershot: Avebury.

Mlinar, Zdravko (1992b) 'Individuation and Globalization: The Transformation of Territorial Social Organization', in Zdravko Mlinar (ed.) *Globalisation and Territorial Identities*, pp. 15–34. Aldershot: Avebury.

Mlinar, Zdravko (1992c) 'Epilogue', in Zdravko Mlinar (ed.) *Globalisation and Territorial Identities*, pp. 165–9. Aldershot: Avebury.

Müller, Hans-Peter, ed. (1996) *Weltsystem und kulturelles Erbe. Gliederung und Dynamik der Entwicklungsländer aus ethnologischer und soziologischer Sicht.* Berlin: D. Reimer Verlag.

Müller, Hans-Peter, Kock, Claudia and von Ditfurth, Anna (1991) *Kulturelles Erbe und Entwicklung: Indikatoren zur Bewertung des sozio-kulturellen Entwicklungsstandes.* Munich: Weltforum Verlag.

Nederveen Pieterse, Jan (1993) *Globalization as Hybridization*, Working Paper 152. The Hague: Institute of Social Studies.

Nederveen Pieterse, Jan (1996) 'The Development of Development Theory: Towards Critical Globalism', *Review of International Political Economy* 3(4): 541–64.

Nederveen Pieterse, Jan (1998) 'My Paradigm or Yours? Alternative Development, Post-Development, Reflexive Development', *Development and Change* 29(4): 343–73.

Robertson, Roland (1987) 'Globalization Theory and Civilizational Analysis', *Comparative Civilizations Review* 17: 20–30.

Robertson, Roland (1994) *Globalization: Social Theory and Global Culture*, 3rd edn. London: Sage.

Robertson, Roland and Lechner, Frank (1985) 'Modernization, Globalization and the Problem of Culture in World-Systems Theory', *Theory, Culture and Society* 2(3): 103–17.

Schuerkens, Ulrike (2001) *Changement social sous régime colonial: du Togo allemand aux Togo et Ghana indépendants.* Paris: L'Harmattan.

Schulz, Manfred, ed. (1997) *Entwicklung: Theorie – Empirie – Strategie*, Festschrift für Volker Lühr. Hamburg: Lit.

Sklair, Leslie (2001) *The Transnational Capitalist Class*. Oxford and Malden, MA: Blackwell.

Strassoldo, Raimondo (1992) 'Globalism and Localism: Theoretical Reflections and some Evidence', in Zdravko Mlinar (ed.) *Globalisation and Territorial Identities*, pp. 35–59. Aldershot: Avebury.

Sztompka, Piotr (1993) *Sociology of Social Change*. Oxford: Blackwell.

Tetzlaff, Rainer, ed. (2000) *Weltkulturen unter Globalisierungsdruck. Erfahrungen und Antworten aus den Kontinenten*. Bonn: Dietz.

Tomlinson, John (1991) *Cultural Imperialism: A Critical Introduction.* London: Pinter.

UNESCO (1996) *The Cultural Dimensions of Global Change: An Anthropological Approach.* Paris: UNESCO.

Warnier, Jean-Pierre (1999) *La Mondialisation de la culture*. Paris: Éditions de la Découverte.

Waters, Malcolm (1995) *Globalization*. London and New York: Routledge.

PART I. SYSTEMATIC COMPARISONS ACROSS EMPIRICAL CASE STUDIES

3

Culture, Identity and Hegemony: The Body in a Global Age

Lauren Langman

The current sociological interests in identity reflect the increasingly problematic nature of subjectivity. Traditional *Gemeinschaft* societies, with strong social ties and stable worldviews, provided their members with a clear, fixed and unambiguous identity. However, with the rise of rational commerce, greater division of labor and growth of cities, social mobility became possible; social bonds became attenuated and dominant ideologies and understandings were questioned. Identity became problematic as options increased (Baumeister, 1986). Industrialization accelerated these trends. With consumerism came a number of fantastic identities, available at a price. By the end of the 20th century, popular culture valorized ideal-ized bodies as sites of commodified forms of health, beauty and fashion promising glamorous identities and ecstatic sexuality (Langman, 1993). This encouraged various forms of consumption in which commodified pleasures of the body provided a proliferation of identities defined by consumption, lifestyle and/or fandom.

Contemporary globalization, with its time-space compression and plural-ization of life-worlds, has again impacted the social, cultural and subjective to foster transformations of identity. Globalization creates forces that both homogenize and differentiate identity. For Castells (2000), identities in network society may serve to (1) legitimate the status quo, (2) resist society, or (3) articulate new projects. Furthermore, global consumerism fosters (4) certain ludic identities expressed in spectacles, games and hedonistic life-style that become moments of hegemonic process. Identities as self-referential cultural narratives and integral moments of self are articulated in the routine presentations and performances that embodied subjects enact in the quotidian, but so certain submerged identities are also realized in various liminal sites. The problematics of contemporary identity can be seen in various debates over hegemony, resistance, social fragmentation, identity politics, or youth cultures.

Culture, Ritual and Identity

Reflexivity enables people, individually or collectively, to articulate identities: narratives of self tell a story of who one is, where one has come from and what makes one distinct from another. Narratives of identity typically begin with mythical roots of origin, legends that link the past with the present to establish a distinct people and ensure its continuity over time. Ancestral myths may often include stories of gods and heroes who personify cultural ideals and values. Cultural identities are not just collections of myths and stories, but scripts that are expressed in the ritual performances that sustain solidarity and affirm distinctive roles and personae. The orderly performances of the quotidian require that certain identities remain submerged, either through repression or isolation. However, as Nietzsche (1999), Durkheim (1965) and Victor Turner (1966) suggested, societies bifurcate experience into realms of structure and anti-structure. There is a quotidian of the normative and episodic moments of the liminal. Even though social controls limit thought and conduct for the sake of preserving the regularities of social life, there are anti-structures, liminal sites of resistance, inversion and repudiation, where social norms can be safely flaunted (V. Turner, 1966). These episodic expressions in liminal times allow articulations of otherwise submerged identities and tabooed desires in highly ritualized forms. Moreover, these episodic identities serve to maintain social stability through controlled violations of the cultural order.

These anti-structural releases can only exist for fleeting moments in marginal, interstitial, or even imaginary sites which tolerate the expressions of acts, feelings and identities that are usually forbidden or are taboo. Such realms provide spaces of freedom, equality, spontaneity and role reversals. As transitory, encapsulated realms of agency, with their own codes of conduct, inversions of norms and proscribed acts of transgressions of official codes are tolerated, even celebrated. In the western world, restrictive imperatives of the Apollonian structure foster anti-structural counter-responses such as the spontaneous frenzy of the Dionysian cults (Nietzsche). The alternative realms of the West have included the chiliastic, millenarian and the carnivalesque. As discussed in this article, American football/Superbowl, the Rio Carnival and body modification exist as liminal domains of ludic indulgence. Such liminal moments can provide certain individuals access to usually submerged identities through which they experience an alternative reality (Bloch, 1986). But the liminal also serves to secure the hegemonic structure.

Identity and the Body

The body, whether working (Marx, 1978; Weber, 1996), lusting (Freud, 1989), playing (Huizinga, 1955), celebrating the sacred (Durkheim, 1965), or being civilized (Elias, 1978), has long been a central element of the social. Durkheim (1965) was among the earliest observers to illustrate the relationship between identity, ritual and the body. Totemism was the most elementary form of religion, a set of beliefs and practices regarding the sacred and profane that granted people a common identity based on lineage. The specialness of the totem as the progenitor of the clan and a collective self-representation was celebrated in dramatic rituals that affirmed solidarity and celebrated the clan's common lineage within an 'imagined community' based on kinship. Rituals united people into a community, a church. Rituals, as scripted performative moments and enactments of embodied identities, were located within a complex system of song, dance and a number of restricted dietary and sexual taboos. Ritual performances, with their frenzied bodily indulgences and close physical proximity, kindled strong emotions that evoked a collective energy which came over the celebrants as they joined together in common songs, dance and ecstatic frenzy. These rituals evoked an emotional contagion that dramatized the power of the sacralized society, reinforced social solidarity and celebrated collective identities based on lineage.

For Durkheim, the body was also a site of basic social classifications. These categories are marked not only on the body, but inscribed through ritual practices such as circumcision, scarification, tattooing, or piercings that are associated with gender, birth, sexuality, or rites of passage. Despite the differences between pre-modern and modern peoples, Durkheim's analysis of representations and rituals still offers profound insights. While social relationships, commitments, attachments and identities might tend to wane over time, in order to endure and reproduce itself, a society (or a sub-culture) must continually renew its bonds of solidarity and affirm its collective identity. Every society creates emotionally gratifying rituals in which people come together at times and places deemed sacred and special that are distinct from the profane or ordinary and that dramatize the power of the social.

Recent sociological discussions on identity, embodied desire and corporal subjectivity have renewed academic interest in the body. Foucault's (1977) analysis of the disciplining of the body, as a means of inscribing identities and control, has found a receptive audience (Grosz, 1994). The work of Bryan Turner (1996), Mike Featherstone (1991) and Chris Schiller (1993) made the body a central focus of sociological study. With globalization, questions of identity imbricate bodies that may be nationalized, gendered, racialized, eroticized, surveilled, disciplined and decorated. Every culture is interested in body images and practices. These may include ideals of beauty, rules and norms of cleanliness, culinary manners and bodily exposure and display. These norms influence how the body is experienced in everyday life, and how it is celebrated in ludic rituals. An individual's self-identity begins with gendering, racializing and locating the body in an age-graded status system. Fashion, dress and adornment are important badges of identity since they locate the actor either inside or outside a particular group. Therefore, social constructions of embodiment and bodily action are intrinsic components of cultural identities transformed by global forces.

Hegemony, Resistance and Cultural Rituals

While Durkheim (1965) showed how religion celebrated and sustained the power of the society, for Gramsci (1992), the power of collective rituals sustained the political power of elite segments of the society: its historic blocs. Hegemony, the production of spontaneous assent to domination, depended on the ideological control of culture by intellectuals allied with historic blocs. The control of representations and understandings rendered ruling-class interests normal and natural while critique was demoniacal, pathological, bizarre and immature. But hegemony at the level of culture required individual subjectivity with an elective affinity for hegemonic worldviews and values that sustained rule. In most societies, various people in charge of socialization, such as parents, teachers, religious leaders, and of late, the mass media, attempt to colonize desire, consciousness and identity (Langman, 2000; Giddens, 1992). Social rituals provide the stages where socialized performative identities can be carried out to sustain solidarity and secure social reproduction by providing individuals various emotional gratifications such as attachments to others, recognition and a sense of empowerment.

Structures of domination foster resistance. But domination is often cloaked so that effective counter-strategies may be shunted to realms where they are neutralized. As Habermas suggested, legitimacy crises could migrate to subjective realms of identity and motivation. The same social structures that impose external constraints also foster alternative realms apart from the restrictions of the quotidian. In our global age, when consumerism is hegemonic (Sklair, 2001), consumer culture provides spaces for transgression. The spectacle, an extraordinary public event or display, has long been part of complex societies. But in the current age, a typical form of spectacle is the mass-mediated carnival. The carnival emerged in feudal Europe as an expression of peasant folk culture (Bakhtin, 1968). It created liminal spaces for the ludic that granted feudal peasants pleasurable release. Carnivals were times and places of inversions, sanctioned deviance and reversals of norms. It stood opposed to the official feasts and tournaments that celebrated the power of the elites, who were instead parodied, mocked, hectored and ridiculed. Moral boundaries from the political to the erotic were transgressed. Carnivals expressed the Dionysian that Nietzsche claimed was suppressed by restrictive Apollonian domination. Whereas most spectacles were sponsored by elites, carnivals generally arose from the people. Today, mass media have joined the spectacle with the carnivalesque to create a carnival culture of the grotesque that has fostered a migration of subjectivity away from political economy, critical reason and concerns with the social, towards personal lifestyles, ludic identities and emotional gratifications. This is evident in various rituals of cultural consumption such as football and soccer games, as well as rock concerts, cyber-porn and extreme forms of bodily adornment like tattoos, piercings and scarification. The mass production of transgressive identities based on privatized hedonism, fun, games and forbidden pleasures has also been a strategy that maintains rule.

To explore the relationships between globalization, identity rituals and embodiment, I would like to consider three different celebrations of the body: Carnival in Rio, American football and extreme body modifications (piercings, tattoos). These collective affirmations of identity serve to valorize difference and inclusion in the face of global trends to homogeniz-ation. Each of these forms of celebration of the body affirms a distinct, local identity apart from the global, while at the same time they have become commodified spectacles. Carnival celebrates an egalitarian erotic of bodily indulgence and illusory luxury. Extreme body modification marks a rejec-tion of modern global society by urban primitives who disdain both the corporate nature of football and the sporadic carnival as ersatz escapism. Yet it is the most globalized. They turn transgressive identities into a year-round festival of inversion. Superbowl, carnival and body modification can thus be understood as body rituals that provide otherwise forbidden pleasures celebrating distinctly different expressions of identity that clearly express difference from the Other. Each of these radically diverse rituals of embodied identity, rooted in earlier eras, has been transformed by globaliz-ation. Each can be understood as an adaptive response that provides people with various emotional gratifications. However, such ludic identities stand apart from the quotidian since they celebrate fantastic escapes in encapsu-lated 'dreamworlds', or they openly reject modernity by simulating a return to pre-modern life. Yet, each sustains hegemonic processes insofar as sanctioned deviance sustains the dominant moral codes and the class system.

Carnival of Rio

The early Portuguese explorers described Brazil as a sexual paradise, an erotic Eden without modesty or restraint: 'There was no sin south of the equator' (DaMatta, 1991). South European Catholicism was tolerant of the sensual and allowed a space for bodily pleasures, desires and indulgence in the flesh. The mythological origins of Brazilian identity begin with free and easy relations between (male) colonials, indigenous tribes and slaves that included the sexualization of master–slave relations. The pre-colonial legacies, traditions of indigenous tribes and Portuguese settlers melded with that of African slaves to define a unique cultural mythology of a happy people free of inhibitions and free of racial prejudices (Freyre, 1956).

By the late 18th century, the Carnival of Venice had become a ribald festival for Italian elites. Carnival was brought to Brazil as part of their efforts to modernize and Europeanize their culture. Yet, carnival was transformed in the New World as it became the major cultural ritual celebrating Brazil's unique identity. Incorporating the folk cultures of its indigenous people, medieval Europe and West Africa, Brazil's carnival expresses alternative experiences and legacies rooted in the social history of the poor as opposed to the official history celebrated by elites in state festivals, such as Independence Day. It applauds the historical continuity and distinctiveness of the unique montage of Brazilian society. But it is the poor of the *favelas*, samba schools, carnival associations and block organizations that own Brazil's carnival, not the elites.

In the 1830s, carnival was celebrated in the home with family and neighbors. Later the carnival *de rua* (street) or *clube* (ballroom) appeared. Brazilian society sharply divides the home and the street. The home ideally is a world of order, calm and control, whereas the street is the site of passion, freedom and even danger. Carnival is a spontaneous, spectacular, public nocturnal celebration that takes place in the streets and plazas where the boundaries of performer and spectator are blurred. During carnival, the poor lay claim to public spaces and the night, thereby repudiating the ordinariness of home, work, job and church where the everyday worlds of dominance, order and restraint are located. It is a time and site of vibrant play and merrymaking. Carnival is not a spectator sport viewed at a distance. Massive crowds fill the streets to drink, dance, sing, shout, prank, flirt and sometimes make love (Linger, 1992). Carnival demands that the celebrants be in constant immediate physical, often erotic contact with each other. Boundaries are blurred as spectators become performers, and performers become spectators. All who view and participate in carnival become swept up by its music, passion and excitement. Revelry abounds, barriers fall and there are inversions of norms. In the polysemic liminal antistructures of ironic inversion and sensual indulgence, everyone has a good time.

Dreamworlds of Fulfillment

To the normal world of work, carnival is play; to the hierarchy of gender and control, there is an equality of desire as women initiate eroticism as equals. To the norms of constraint, indulgence is the rule. Carnival creates realms of emotions and experiences apart from the typical. Thwarted desires are fulfilled. As a *festa popular*, it values life over death, joy over sadness and the poor over the rich. It is an intersubjectively shared framework for ritual performances that dramatize both real and fantasized identities elsewhere negated. It is a respite from the woes and anxieties of 'normal' lives. Carnival provides a time for community, recognition and dignity which are rarely found in the daily lives of the impoverished. The poor can find 'microspheres of empowerment', where the janitor may be a great dancer, the maid a fine singer and the factory worker a songwriter-musician. Brazilians leave aside their hierarchical, repressive society to live more freely and individually. Indeed, in the context of carnival, we can now understand sexuality and aggression as realms of empowered selfhood and expressions of agency.

Self-esteem comes from one's position on the social ladder while resentment is fueled by conditions of hierarchy and domination that deny dignity and respect. Resentments quickly accumulate in lower reaches of the society because socially and politically incapacitated individuals most suffer from the arbitrary exercise of power. In this system, the ability to withstand impositions by others and, conversely, to impose one's will on them acts as a pre-moral affirmation of the self. Negative energy can be released in carnival, which makes the release of feelings one of the central moments of Brazilian identity. *Briga*, a disposition for aggressive displays to defend honor that often leads to injury and murder, is an expression of violent *desabafar*, smothered resentments and frustrations. The perilous consequences of storing bad emotions can be avoided by means of controlled release of internal pressures in many ways, including drinking, dancing, shouting and relatively open displays of aggressive and sexual impulses. Such emotions can be expressed within the limits permitted by carnival without danger of rupturing cordial interactions and the social order (Linger, 1992). Aggressive rituals, as forms of empowerment, grant subordinates symbolic equality through sublimated releases such as throwing cornstarch, water, confetti, or mud on one another and on superiors. Thus, carnival acts 'like a restorative ritual, at once signals a problem and resolves it' (Linger, 1992: 23–5). In this way, doing carnival repairs the self and provides a degree of recognition and, in turn, dignity, honor and power to those who otherwise have so little.

Fantasies of Equality, Dreams of Wealth

Carnival evolved out of the social conditions of subordination. The patriarchal legacy of the colonial era shaped race, class and gender systems and created sharp dualities between men and women, and between masters and slaves that have persisted. Given Brazil's structural position in the world economy, gross inequalities of wealth, race and gender persist. Carnival is a festival of the poor who live in the *favelas* that teem with the unemployed, and those who work in low-wage service jobs that cater to the affluent. The poor suffer indignities and degradations in their ordinary dealings with superiors, e.g. obeying rituals of subordination and deference. Poor people receive brutal treatment by state authorities that provide little relief/welfare. Paramilitary death squads kill poor youths. Therefore, carnival is a momentary release from the not so hidden injuries of social class. The rules of erotic propriety, modesty, gender relations, sobriety and deference are suspended as the millions of poor become 'rich' for four days.

Carnival as a liminal site of sanctioned transgression provides alternative realms of freedom from oppressed labor, patriarchy and coerced sexuality. It is a Dionysian moment of compensatory liminality that repudiates the dominant culture and celebrates an alternative egalitarian erotic that comes from the people who are the entrusted caretakers and producers of the event. There are no constraints of race, class, or gender. During carnival, the poor inhabit alternative realms apart from the squalor and hardship of their usual lives. They can imagine themselves kings and queens ruling kingdoms of fantasy. Carnival is a symbolic dissent; a joyous expression of outrage against injustice by the weak and scorned that have been degraded by the powerful, but it is not an overthrow of the structure of inequality (DaMatta, 1991). It provides a kind of ritual irony, a safety valve for release from the established order, not a mastered irony in the creation of a new order and new values (Brown, 1987).

Carnival is a time of ironic inversions and reversals of normal hierarchies: the poor can experience luxury as they dress in fantasized splendor and, for a moment, be dukes and ladies, or rogues and villains. Men dress as women, women as men. The elaborate dress, masks and costumes of carnival symbolize a conjunction of domains, syntheses of the person, their roles and who or what they would like to be. Whether erotic, grotesque or absurd, the party clothes and fantastic costumes (*fantasosias*) of the samba parade stand as inversions, reversals of what are usually separate identity domains. Identities, roles and categories that are typically separated are brought together; thief and cop, prostitute and lady of the house, transvestite and macho all dance together (DaMatta, 1991). Everyone is joined together into one big family; class, race and gender boundaries are momentarily overcome. Though Brazil has the greatest inequality in Latin America, the intermingling of classes is quite typical – during carnival. That carnival is a fantasy does not nullify its psychocultural force. At the end of carnival, the poor look forward not to social change, but to next year's carnival. Thus carnival, while episodically repudiating cultural norms, serves to secure the enduring hegemony of the social and political arrangements that create the condition that make sure carnival takes place and continues to be needed, rather than to foster a just society.

Realities of Eros

Carnival creates an anti-structure of ludic equality that empowers women and grants them erotic agency. Carnival celebrates the sensual in a society of otherwise repressive patriarchal values. Women move out of their culturally prescribed domains into the public spaces usually reserved for men. The carnival valorizes female sexuality in relatively egalitarian mass festivals. Female modesty and reserve, typical of everyday life in the home, wane as exhibitionism and desire become 'normal' aspects of carnival. Women in highly revealing clothing are rarely aggressively approached, while the otherwise macho men appear timid. The revealing clothing is typical, but this is more a celebration of the aesthetics of femininity and female empowerment than prurient voyeurism or exhibitionism. The desiring woman flaunts her erotic body and takes center stage in the streets, parades and ballrooms. These symbolic acts move the private realm of the household into the public sphere, where the public and private are temporarily blended into one realm. 'The naked, seductive women mark the transformation of public space into one big house' (DaMatta, 1991: 106). Sexual indulgence is permissible when the restraints of ordinary norms and social conventions are suspended. While relaxed sexuality takes place, carnival is not a sex orgy in the streets. Egalitarian, anonymous sexuality in a masked form is part and parcel of carnival as inversion.

Carnival as Commodity

Carnival, as a ritualized celebration of a liminal identity, rooted in Brazil's myths of origin, has moved into the contemporary world. This identity has been transformed by commodification in global markets. Perhaps, this started when Sartre's 'Black Orpheus' introduced Brazilian carnival to the wider world just as modern globalization was emerging and international tourism began to grow. In the 1990s, the lure of carnival, transformed by advertising and public relations campaigns in a celebration of erotic license, became a 'precious' commodity, a desirable tourist attraction drawing people from all over the world. Although the roots of carnival were in medieval Europe, in the era of globalization what had begun as a pre-Easter holiday in a 'remote' part of the world has become a multi-billion-dollar business event, and marker of cultural identity. Rio became a primary destination for sex-tourism, especially during carnival. As a liminal site for inversion, it attracts gays from all over the world, especially since drag queens, cross-dressers and fantastic costumes are a typical aspect of carnival. Travel agents joined with samba schools in order to provide affluent tourists with samba lessons, carnival choreography and a place in the parade, or on the floats that provide an entry into dreamworlds. So today, Europeans, Americans and Asians sing, dance and march with the poor. This juxtaposition empowers both.

Brazil has valorized carnival as both a means of attracting tourists and, at the same time, emphasizing the uniqueness of its distinct identity in a McWorld of Benetton identities. As the Southern core economies became integrated into Mercosur, the regional trade blocks, and commercial and travel barriers further eroded, there was more and more celebration of carnival as difference. At the same time, in the face of globalization and its tendencies to homogenize identities, Brazil has emphasized its identity as an easy-going, fun-loving people, especially comparing itself to its neighbors Argentina and Chile. And with the body rituals of carnival, its celebration of the fantastic and the erotic, a uniquely Brazilian identity stands apart from a globalized world of ever more homogeneity.

Celebrating American Capital: Superbowl as Identity

Competitive sports and games celebrate the abilities and bodies of champions as exemplars of the group's values of skill, loyalty and teamwork. Athletic training, schooling of the embodied self, instills identification with particular organizations, schools, teams, or even nations. While few people are professional athletes, sporting events serve as entertainment, commerce and affirmations of loyalties. But more important, much like religious rituals, sporting events can be seen as a celebration of identities. While many sporting events are places where nations can compete against each other, e.g. soccer and Olympic games, some sports are clearly associated with particular nations, e.g. cricket, sumo wrestling, bakshi or America's version of football. While football is rooted in European festivals of Lent, games of soccer and rugby, it has become a uniquely American game that has come to celebrate a general allegiance to a distinctively American masculine identity that sets them apart from others in a globalized world where cultural differences narrow and where there is greater uniformity of thought and action. The annual Superbowl has become the most popular celebration in America, eclipsing Independence Day and even Christmas.

Saving American Masculinity

American identity is rooted in the aggressive aspects of American charac-ter, embedded deep in the Puritan sensibility: a hostility to untamed nature and a more explicit urban tempo (Cummings, 1972: 104). A crucial moment of both early Puritanism and later 'muscular Christianity' was the increas-ing economic power of the male as an individual economic actor as opposed to clan, family, or guild. However, this economic power came at the price of highly disciplined behavior in the marketplace or in bureaucracies. Protestantism reflected the world of masculine asceticism that displaced female emotionality. With growing urbanization and industrialization, as men left farms for cities, the nature of their work changed, as did the roles of women. Greater numbers of women began entering colleges and the workforce. The New Women, more assertive and androgynous, raised new questions and rekindled old anxieties about gender identity and passivity (Oriard, 1993; Dworkin and Wachs, 2001). There arose a growing fear of effeminacy among the upper middle and elite classes. Industrialization and the factory system had severed work from home and craft. So people increasingly turned to sports for a positive sense of self (Cummings, 1972).

Amateur athletics were promoted to foster the values of discipline, teamwork and aggressiveness that were required by the industrial order, as well as a strong, masculine identity (Schwartz, 1997). Football, as a violent competition between teams of males seeking territorial power and control, was foretold in the earliest moments of American culture (Langman, 1992). Football became organized into a college sport with formal rules for the elite few who went to universities like Harvard, Princeton, Columbia, or Yale, where college football served to affirm a heroic masculinity. It was believed that young, college-educated football players would become the business, professional and political leaders of the future (Oriard, 1993: 211).

The growth of football as an elite sport was aided by the efforts of one of the first Yale players, Walter Camp. He saw football and corporate life as essentially equivalent to some principles of management in which player positions are organized on the basis of function and ability. Football, as a gentlemen's sport, quickly spread from Eastern colleges to urban sandlots (Schwartz, 1997). Thus, it is not surprising that football first emerged among the new national elites as they were attempting to forge an inclusive national identity that would valorize masculine aggression during the period of brutal industrialization during and after the bloody Civil War.

Industrialization and the expansion of leisure time as well as the growth and commodification of spectator sports brought large crowds together for sporting events. For much of the 20th century, baseball, a working-class game, was the national pastime. By the late 1960s, football games were watched on television and had growing audiences who were not college educated. American football eventually became a lucrative business, the culmination of which is the Superbowl – the most widely celebrated annual event of American popular culture, with over 100 million viewers and global corporations paying some $500,000 for a 30-second TV commercial spot. To achieve such popularity, the Superbowl taps long-standing cultural legacies and deeply rooted desires. It both draws on and reproduces the historical construction and performance of identities in an age of globalized consumption. The Superbowl has become both a reflection of American culture and a unique expression of American (male) identity (Langman, 1992).

Assertive Masculinity

The devotion to football and its cultural power derives from the collision of the modern and anti-modern with a dialectical embrace of competing notions of manliness. For middle-class males in the 19th century, the new industrial and commercial order meant a redefinition of work in terms of mental rather than physical activity, and uncertainty about the masculinity of mental work. Physical power became a mark of the lower classes, while rationality in industry kept it tied to middle-class definitions of masculinity. Football represented a union of the physical and the mental that was difficult for middle- and upper-class men to find elsewhere in modern America

(Oriard, 1993: 201). Whether in football or in war, the violence of men in combat is not irrational, specific goals are bound by rules. Well-planned strategies and practiced tactics serve to bond males together and provide them with recognition and a sense of empowerment. The planned, yet still mystical bonding of males through the pain and violence of war or football, with their heroic masculinities and struggle for victory, overcomes separation and alienation, and for brief moments provides wholeness and completion. As Bataille (1997) might suggest, violence enables the transcendence of the mundane through a descent into excess and degradation. Football acts as a catharsis in which the domination over and symbolic castration of the Other displace violence from everyday life and preserve the social order.

Male players use instrumental aggression to combat each other, while cheerleaders foster a solidarity through the shared male gaze of the powerful warriors and the males, who identify with them, and the women, who desire them, thereby reproducing gender domination. Thus while most men are not overtly violent to each other and do not abuse their wives or children, domination through violence is valorized through the football player who acts out the erotic/aggressive fantasy desires of many spectators and implicitly reinforces the gender privileges of males, their monetary advantages, institutional power and feelings of superiority. Football can be seen as a will to violence and refusal to accept bourgeois civility that remains encapsulated within the substantive rationality of society. But repressed violence must be released, even if symbolically, lest it return as self-hate. Football violence is subjected to rules that make it a site between 'the unreason of desire and the rational order of civilized society . . . As a form of character ethics, football inculcates a virile asceticism of fortitude and discipline that will serve men well in the society at large in much the same way as does the military' (McBride, 1995: 82).

Football in consumer capitalism is both an economic enterprise and an ideological mirror of the system. In this sense, football is an alternative realm of male teams engaged in violent territorial competition. The game as spectacle stands in dialectical opposition to the quotidian of corporate life, where violence is neutralized. Thus, football is a boundary maintaining male subculture that mythically glorifies hyper-masculine identities. It is not abstractly understood as a cultural ritual, but as the occasion for 'real men' to get together and express who they truly are.

War on the Athletic Field

Just as Barthes (1957) saw wrestling as an allegory of good vs evil, American football can be seen as an ideologically constructed myth of disciplined, instrumentally oriented warriors ready to go to war. Walter Camp not only compared football to business but also to war (Oriard, 1993). Teams were like platoons; lines were engaged in hand-to-hand combat; the players in the trenches were directed by 'generals', called coaches, whose locker rooms resembled war rooms. The groans, screams, blood and injuries, stretchers and medics simulate a battlefield. 'It is an aggressive strictly regulated team sport fought between males who use both violence and technology to win monopoly control of property for the economic gain of individuals within a nationalistic, entertainment context' (Rapping, 1987: 84). Thus, war and commerce, as rationalized combat, find their ultimate ritual performance in the Superbowl that celebrates the male warrior/spectator and affirms that they are *real men* who enjoy violence and power (McBride, 1995). Football valorizes the phallic aggression of war but without actual death and destruction. Whereas wars eventually end, the Superbowl confirms aggressive identities and constantly renews them in celebrations of violent male performances.

Superbowl is a celebration for American men that affirms often submerged phallic, aggressive masculine identities. Following Bataille (1997) and Girard (1977), the Superbowl allows the taboos against in-group violence to be sustained, the ritual sacrifice of the enemy enables both the experience of the taboo and its transgressions. Primitive violence is subsumed under rational codes that carefully locate combat within a clearly measured site. It occurs at definite times and places, regulated by strict rules in which technological rationality attempts to control the violence of war and commerce in simulated fashion. In modern armies, the shoulder supports the rifle and rocket launcher, and in football, it throws the 'bomb' or 'missile'.

The ideal football hero is a hyper-real male warrior in armor joining a long legacy of warriors fighting over territory. The football player moves from civilian to warrior as he dons his helmet, massive padded shoulders and extensive body armor – icons of masculinity that exaggerate male angularity and musculature (Oriard, 1993). He joins with the centurion, gladiator, armored knight and samurai, seeking victory in violent combat on the field of battle. But football spares the spectator the unpleasant reality of war, while simulating its primary emotions in the safer spectacle of sports. The teams with their totemic emblems (uniforms, mascots, names) enact rituals of solidarity that draw in the spectators and bring all together to affirm an inclusive group identity of warrior males and their cheering female consorts.

Phallic Worship

In America's traditional gender ideology, assertive masculine power stands above and against feminine passivity. As a cultural fiction that recreates the psychological dynamics of war, football is a phallic aggressive male struggle for the exclusive possession of the phallus. It reiterates the boundaries of the homoerotic community by defining sexual differences based on victorious winners and vanquished losers. Whereas the defense attempts to sack the quarterback and strip the ball, the quarterback attempts to penetrate the defense through the use of his surrogates – the ball carriers and receivers. When the defense is successful, the siege undergoes transformation. The offense becomes the defense (ball-less), and the defense is now the offense in possession of the ball/phallus. Although the defense is in the more vulnerable position, as if a female, the defensive players attempt to reverse this disadvantage by acting with even greater aggression.

These warriors with big shoulders are juxtaposed against the slight bodies of female cheerleaders. Masculine power reigns, female passivity is elided, and phallic identity is affirmed, sustaining male solidarity. Communities of pride and dignity are created in observing violent combat that cements male bonds through misogynist denigrations of women and the conversion of the enemy into 'pussies'. America frustrates community, attachment and dependency, and thus abhors those who embody these qualities, for example women and traditional peoples. Whatever else, football affirms that men are not the women they fear and desire (McBride, 1995: 164). While football employs the aggressive arm, players and fans have an ambivalent obsession with breasts – not for warmth, nurturance, intimacy, connection, or relationships. Hyper-masculine football valorizes breasts to contrast gender difference and affirm masculinity. The larger the breast, the greater the visual difference between real men and real women. The castrated woman can never be a true and equal buddy who bonds through violent territorial games, but she does serve as the perpetual anti-fetish whose very existence as a curvy castrata celebrates the superiority of penis power (Irigaray, 1985).

Breasts are objects of a male gaze that empowers the voyeur through visual domination. Pom-poms can be understood as exaggerated symbolic breasts that also serve to affirm hyper-masculinity as difference. A woman is not a person but a pastiche of breasts and orifices to be penetrated, dominated and denigrated, thereby dramatizing masculinity as superior. While some women may find male violence erotic and desire submission to the warrior, the female Other can never enter the sacred temple of the phallus and delight in its rituals of violence. Sports knowledge has become a central trope of identity for real men, which differentiates them from women, children and 'effete intellectuals'. Typically, males gather around the television set, bond through the consumption of intoxicants and the exchange of sports talk laden with frequent obscenities and a sexual imagery of phallic power and domination by penetration and degradation.

American Particularism

American society, from its earliest moments, has been particular in its toughness and violence against native populations and French colonizers, born of revolution. Given these legacies, it is not surprising that football would eventually become its most popular team sport. Superbowl as mass spectacle began in the era that gave rise to modern feminism and globaliz-ation. Much like its 19th-century origins, it valorizes heroic masculinity when male realms (work, politics) face encroachment by women. Moreover, in the global age, when a mass-mediated popular culture can be found anywhere, and rock stars are everywhere, football remains a distinct articu-lation of American identity now intertwined with global consumerism. Global corporations compete to peddle their goods to the viewers.

The Superbowl part, as expression of heroic masculinity in fantastic form, has become the highlight of the annual cycle of popular culture, the most important ritualized celebration of America's particular identity. Men gather in living rooms, dens, game rooms, or television rooms to cheer, curse and consume a great deal of beer. Dutiful women prepare foods, serve beer, and some even try to understand how men can find joy watching the warriors battle. Otherwise subdued, moderate men, watching the game with others, articulate the otherwise subdued and submerged identities of the aggressive male hero.

Modern Primitives: Globalization and the Production of Surplus People

One of the main consequences of globalization has been to radically trans-form local economies, occupational systems and the structures of opportunity. With technological innovations in production, job export and import substitution in the advanced societies, there have been major trans-formations of the workforce. For the majority of semi-skilled workers, there are fewer opportunities for social mobility and higher standards of living. Instead, there has been growing underemployment, especially in the expan-sion of low-skilled service work, temporary work and contingent labor. Thus, we see what might be called the production of 'surplus populations'; large numbers of youth complete school, yet their job prospects are dim. Insofar as the status systems in western capitalist societies have been based on occupational attainment, we have seen the proliferation of identity-granting alternative subcultures of meaning that provide members with recognition and dignity. Just as delinquent youth or avant-garde bohemians create alternative subcultures that stand as alternatives to mainstream society, body modification has become the basis for a plurality of identity granting, emotionally satisfying subcultures of resistance and opposition.

Fashion as Identity

In every society, people dress and adorn themselves according to social conventions. This has been based on categorical status such as age, gender, occupation, or some other indication of social rank. In modern societies where status is attained and hence more problematic, people use public displays of self to differentiate themselves from others and indicate inclusion within a subculture of status, occupation, or value orientation (Simmel, 1950). Fashions and adornments act as markers of identity that tell others who one is and who one is not. Clothes, adornment and appearance have thus become statements of cultural capital as well as cultural resistance and opposition to values and norms of the dominant society. Appearances can be seen as replicating class/culture conflicts in the larger society. From the sans-culottes to the all-black attire of anarchists, bohemians, or contemporary Goths, certain styles of dress and adornment become expressions of personal lifestyles that articulate oppositional identities.

Through Simmel's (1950) writings, we see the function of vanity, wherein the adorned individual accentuates his/her personality by wearing jewels and metals, which simultaneously invokes both admiration and disdain from others. The individual distinguishes and amplifies him-/herself in the view of, and at the cost of, others. However, to be extraordinary is not simply a matter of exhibiting the material objects themselves; it is a display of its more-than-appearance value. Simmel writes, 'it is not something isolated; it has roots in a soil that lies beyond its mere appearance, while the unauthentic is only what it can be taken for at the moment' (Simmel, 1950: 342). Various styles of dress, coiffure and ornamentation valorize the vulgar, the obscene and the grotesque. Wilson (1987) suggests that the 19th-century dandy was the archetype of anti-fashion; sporting an oppositional style was designed to shock and to demonstrate hostility toward the conformist majority. Therefore, statements of identity, fashion and adornment become important declarations of opposition, rebellion, resistance and confrontation.

The Body as Identity

During the past few decades, along with and due to globalization, we have seen a globalized proliferation of body modifications as fashion statements. Growing populations of youth, and many not so youthful, adorn themselves with a variety of studs, rings, posts, and tattoos. Contemporary expressions of adornment use decoration of the body as a template upon which aesthetic sensibilities are inscribed and through which identity is articulated. There are today certain extremes of body modification that radically transform the body into a medium of identification and art, actively defining and exhibiting one's membership as a 'modern primitive' living in a liminal anti-culture of modernity. The more extreme piercings and markings are an expression of contempt for the dominant culture and repudiation of mainstream society, as well as valorizing the grotesque as a method of generating a reaction of disgust and fear – style aimed to shock (Wilson, 1987). Sanders (1987: 395) notes: 'The tattoo is both an indication of disaffiliation from conventional society and a symbolic affirmation of personal identity.' Some split their tongues, growing numbers so decorate their genitalia. These distinctive markers of self that so clearly repudiate dominant styles and tastes, point to growing resistance to the consequences of globalization articulated as a cultural rebellion within certain youth cultures.

Adolescence is a stage in the life-cycle in which young people typically seek autonomy, if not rebellion from parents, replete with disdain of parental values and lifestyles as they quest their own, independent identity. While at one time body modification was considered quite deviant, it is now so common as to be ordinary, to be a fashion statement that has entered the mainstreams of society. Perhaps one-third of youth are likely to have some form of body piercing and quite often a tattoo. Nevertheless, the extremes of body modification push the limits from stylish to transgressive. We are of course referring to multicolored hair, multiple rings and studs, and various implants such as horns or furrows. Much like Brazil's carnival as a liminal time and site for transgression, extreme body modification is an inversion of what is 'normal'. What is ordinarily prohibited is celebrated, e.g. the lower body, whose orifices and products were foul, vile, and repugnant. But whereas carnival is an annual celebration, body modification is a permanent transformation.

Modern Primitives – Transgression as Identity

Various expressions of extreme body modification can be understood as articulations of identities of resistance that reject the repression and con-formity intrinsic to modernity and by so doing, attempt to recapture the carnivalesque of a pre-modern Dionysian lifestyle through embrace of the grotesque. Many of those who have had some sort of extreme body modifi-cation regard their markings as a rejection of the sterility and emptiness of modernity and see themselves as 'modern primitives' (Vale and Juno, 1989). In other words, body modifications can be understood as a statement of active disdain and rejection of dominant culture through embrace of a decivilizing process that promises to restore a lost moment of repression dis-carded, desire unbound and authenticity regained.

In western culture, forms of body modification such as tattoos, scarifica-tion and piercings have typically been regarded as a regression to primitive practices. In the Judeo-Christian context, tattooing and modifying the body are regarded as transgressive. According to Leviticus 19:28: 'You shall not make any cuttings in your flesh on account of the dead or tattoo any marks upon you.' Yet, in other non-western cultures, body modifications are considered sacred or magical. The unmarked body is a raw, inarticulate and mute body. It is only when the body acquires the marks of civilization that it can begin to communicate and become an active part of the social body (Vale and Juno, 1989). While tattoos, piercings and other forms of extreme body modification are not considered civilized modes of communication in mainstream western culture, they are indeed social.

In many age-graded societies, dramatic rites of passage mark the transition from one stage or status to the next (van Gennep, 1960). Body modification is an essential ritual for entry into the communities of 'modern primitives' that celebrate transgressive identities, the markers therefore delineate passages to the in-group that dramatize its boundaries. Many of these rituals involve various painful body modifications. Such practices fulfill a universal human function in providing a rite of passage as a cultural drama as well as providing the means by which members proclaim their various social affinities (Holtham, 1992). As Holtham notes, 'what seems evident is that in traditional societies, rituals of body modification practices connect people and their bodies to the reproduction of long established social positions whereas in the industrialized West body piercing seems to serve the function of individuating the self from society' (Holtham, 1992). Body modifications become an important element of transgressive identities and a profound lived experience through their incorporation into lifestyles of resistance within a community of meaning in a globalized world where social ties and shared values are becoming ever more problematic.

Insofar as modifications can be seen as initiation rites into a community of meaning, as passages to a higher status identity, they are eagerly sought by the initiate and celebrated by the community. Psychological research has suggested that the more painful and dramatic initiation rites are, the more highly rated and evaluated are the group: any group whose entry requires suffering must surely be worth entering. Body modification is a dramatic means of entry into certain subcultures and identification with a particular group as well as a matter of fashion.

The Cultural Transformation of the Pubic Sphere

The body, long the center of the private realm, has become the template upon which aesthetic sensibilities are inscribed. Inversion, indeed transvaluation is nowhere more evident than in the decorations and modifications of the genitals, that were once private and hidden through shame. The pubic has become public and its adornment a basis of personal pride. Such adornments may include rings, studs, posts, tattoos, reshapings, surgical modifications and saltings, injections of saline solutions that grossly enlarge and distort. These body adornments are proudly shown off among members of the alternative community and proudly displayed on websites. For Simmel (1950), the original purpose of covering the genitals was to call attention to sexual parts by adorning them. Only later did shame emerge as a means of social control. Following Simmel, for certain cultures of resistance, not only making the private public, but calling attention to one's genitals by means of adornment, can be seen as a repudiation of civilization and its repressive morals and constraints.

In the English language, the word 'primitive' was first used by the Catholic church to refer to the pure beginning of its own religion ('primityve churche of Christ').Yet, in the 20th century, the term acquired a negative connotation, used to describe non-western appearances and activities. Western Europe and Euro-America espoused the ideology of progress, where heterogeneity threatened humanity's unitary ascent to greater knowledge, sophistication and goodness. Thus, primitive became a powerful label used to describe the ignorant, barbaric and uncivilized (Vale and Juno, 1989). Cultural differences were seen as various stages of development, with the West representing the most developed and advanced of all. Cultural diversity was stamped out and replaced by refinement, enlightenment and 'civilized behavior'.

Compensatory Gratifications

Postmodernists argue that we are now in an age without grand narratives; the modern social order has imploded into a plurality of subcultures and decentered subjects. But we argue that capitalism, in its global form, remains the grand narrative of our time. The fragmentation of the social is rooted in the class structure, the division of labor and the proliferation of segmented markets, producing a plethora of goods and a pluralization of life-worlds based on consumer subcultures and/or lifestyle enclaves that sustain a multitude of identities. The traditional sources of stability in people's lives, their community, their workplace and even families have been attenuated. In an unstable world, extreme body modification, as a badge of modern primitivism becomes an act of identification and empowerment where people are able to reclaim their body in a way that cannot be mediated by others. In a world without job security and predictable careers or enduring relationships, there is a sense of permanency with a decorated body. Thus, to accentuate one's personality, and to become extraordinary, allows one to take control of one's existence and thereby impose stability. Thus the 'modern primitives', as an identity-granting carnivalesque community, provide an alternative realm that rejects the dominant culture and provides its members with a number of compensatory gratifications. But unlike carnival, it is not temporary.

With body modification, the body itself has been turned into a work of art in which agency confronts normative disciplinary practices to recreate a personal aura in an age of virtual reproduction. The individual becomes a sort of artist by transforming his or her body into a piece of art. The piercings and tattoos can be understood as expressions of agency in which the body itself has become a medium for the articulation of liminal identities that valorize the grotesque, the bizarre and the vulgar. Consequently, to adorn and to modify the body is a choice that reclaims agency. Modifications and styles that are clearly visible and seeking attention ensure that one is looked at. For Sartre, to be looked at was to be rendered powerless, to be made an object, whereas for the 'modern primitive', to command the gaze and the grotesque does command view, is to have power over the Other.

Whether the gaze invokes disgust by the mainstream, or acceptance by the subculture, to be viewed as different is to gain empowering recognition.

Walter Benjamin (1968) argued that art, when mechanically reproduced, lost its unique qualities imparted by the artist. He saw that mechanical reproduction enabled a democratization of culture and pluralization of interpretation. Jessica Benjamin (1992), in her psychoanalytic approach to female masochism, suggested that women endure pain and humiliation in order to gain recognition. In her analysis of the fictional *The Story of O.*, she described how the heroine voluntarily submitted to sexual servitude and degradation to gain recognition and personhood. Benjamin suggests that it speaks to real issues that many women face today. If we join the Benjamins, we can see that for men or women, to decorate one's body is to claim authorship and reclaim an embodied authorship of self. Although this may involve pain, the pain is an expression of agency, recognition and inclusion. Insofar as global capital has displaced many from the contracting cultural mainstream, the pain of modification becomes a way of authoring one's own pain. Seeking pain rather than being pained turns passivity into activity by controlling pain and the impressions that modifications make on Others.

The Globalization of Body Modification

Sailors who voyaged to Polynesia, Hawaii, New Guinea or New Zealand in the 19th century adopted the tattoo. By the later part of the century, it had become a common urban art form among the working classes, often an implicit statement of assertive masculinity or a tribute to a loved one. In the late 1960s, it was sometimes embraced by hippie counter-cultures as a transgressive repudiation of middle-class norms of propriety. Indeed a number of women got tattoos; often a flower or butterfly was put in places that only a lover might see. Such tattoos were marks of empowered femininity and a political statement rejecting traditional bourgeois erotic norms in that small tattoos were meant to be seen. Much like carnival, youth festivals and music concerts like Woodstock often included a great deal of nudity and sexuality. Of course, the heavy use of drugs like marijuana and psychedelics like LSD enhanced the interaction of adolescent hormones and social pressures toward transgression.

By the mid-1980s, as globalization led to the deindustrialization of much of Europe and the US, many young people began to get pierced. For example, large numbers of men, in part to protest against patriarchy, began to wear an earring. Body piercing in more extreme forms started to become popular among gay communities. By the late 1980s, body modifications were found in most of the cities of the developed world, a world that we noted was undergoing economic restructuring. But by the mid-1990s, as the Internet allowed ease of communications between people worldwide, and the popular culture of the developed world had spread almost everywhere, or should we say, the reach of the American cultural industries was universalized, the youth cultures of America and England became the desirable alpha models for youth in other countries. Further, bands such as the Beatles, the Rolling Stones or Jefferson Airplane became part of the popular cultures wherever a number of people could afford the records and tapes. Soon, with the growth of disaffected youth cultures, we began to see imitation and identification. The embrace of body modification spread to many parts of the world, Latin America, Japan and the Philippines. This is not to ignore many cultural barriers such as Islamic countries, Israel (Orthodox Jews prohibit tattoos), or those vast regions of the world where people are more concerned with survival than projecting an image. Besides many have had body modifications before they were stylish: for example, tattoos in the South Pacific, circumcision in Muslim countries, or female genital mutilation.

Conclusion

Globalization, with its new forms of production, transportation and universalized mass media, has led to major cultural changes and thus transformations of identity. Popular culture, as the ideological expression of globalized consumer society, encourages new identities and lifestyles based on material and cultural consumption. Some identities wane, and others are transformed. Superbowl in America, the carnival of Brazil and body modification can be seen as ritual performances that celebrate embodied identities otherwise submerged. Each of these three celebrations of identity was shaped by specific historical material factors and cultural logics that were transformed by globalization. Each can be seen as ludic articulations that allow, if not encourage that which is usually constrained. Each fulfills usually suppressed desires. These rituals thus illustrate that the transformation of identities rooted in social histories is affirmed in solidarity-maintaining rituals; many such identities are often submerged, especially those that might oppose the dominant values; social stability often rests on the episodic and/or marginal nature of such identities; these identities are often articulated in the liminal anti-structures of the society, in ludic realms in which the articulation of resistance, opposition and the transgressive are shunted from the structures of power and thereby neutralized; and finally, often lost in many discussions of identity, greatly depend on the body.

In his now famous analysis of the birth of tragedy, Nietzsche (1999) argued that behind the Apollonian religious cults of harmony and self-discipline stood the Dionysian, which celebrated bodily indulgence in wine, song, dance and frenzied passion. For Freud (1989), 'rational civilization demanded guilt-based renunciation of instincts'. And for Max Weber (1996), such rationality was manifested in ascetic Protestantism, disciplined work, bureaucratic administration, even rule-bound music and sports. Reason stood apart from, if not opposed to affectivity and hedonistic indulgences of traditional society and its carnival culture. Norbert Elias

(1978) complemented Weber in showing that a 'civilizing process' mediated between sociocultural changes and internalized controls. Rituals of manners and politeness fostered constraints upon the body and impulsivity, suppressing the carnival and recasting its vulgarity, grotesqueness and sensuality as the denigrated and excluded Other. Weber noted that the repression of bodily desire, sublimated in work that was akin to a religious calling, led people to endless productive effort and thereby allowed them to accumulate far more than they needed for immediate consumption. But the move from an industrial society to a consumer society has required the relaxation of restraints in order to allow consumerism to flourish. Thus, while repression enabled the spirit of capitalism to flourish, those spaces of indulgence allowed the repressed to return.

Capitalism fostered impulse gratification as a marketing tactic that eroded constraints to spend money. Promises of forbidden pleasures have become integral aspects of mass marketing. Consumerism now depends on the production and diffusion of carnivalesque dreamworlds, fantastic realms that promise and often provide more pleasurable moments of bodily gratification than does the constraining rationalized quotidian. Consumption, as sites of otherwise denied pleasure, freedom, agency and *joissance*, serves to sustain late capitalist society. These anti-structures, liminal sites for the forbidden, as repressive desublimations, sustain the dominant cultural system. In this sense, the Superbowl celebration, carnival and body modification are all aspects of hegemonic processes in which identities realized in cultural consumption sustain hegemonic social relations.

Carnival is now globally diffused as a commodity that provides emotionally gratifying identities in the new liminal spaces of capitalism. As the capitalist system produces ever more inequality, we see a carnivalization of the modern world, which promises Dionysian pleasures that mask and sustain growing inequality. These pleasures can be found in the Superbowl, the Carnival of Rio and modified bodies throughout the global world. Each in their own way can be seen as performative celebrations of ritualized identities and as providing subjects with a variety of gratifications. At the same moment, each can also be seen as sustaining the hegemony of the global system.

If carnival is the dream of joining the (upper reaches) of the dominant society, Superbowl can be seen as the celebration of the dominant American political economy in fantastic form, and the extreme body modifications of modern primitives articulate a resistance to global society. Brazil celebrates the erotic (female) body in a fantasized realm of equality; football celebrates the violent body of the male warrior in simulations of team warfare, while modern primitives use transgressive body modifications to mark the rejection of modern society. On the other hand, modern primitives, through their body modification rituals and communities of resistance, reject the very repression and sexism that fostered carnival. Instead of episodic gratifications in encapsulated realms, they make resistance a permanent stance through a return to imagined localities of an earlier time and place.

Much like carnival celebrants, modern primitives gain a variety of compensatory gratifications through transgression. These transformations of embodied identity, locating selfhood in realms of privatized hedonism, as moments of hegemonic process, insure that there will be no transformations of the global political economy that fostered these rituals of self.

Bibliography

Bakhtin, Mikhail (1968) *Rabelais and His World.* Cambridge, MA: MIT Press.

Barthes, Roland (1957) *Mythologies*, trans. Annette Lavers. Paris: Seuil.

Bataille, Georges (1997) *The Bataille Reader.* Malden, MA: Blackwell.

Baumeister, Roy F. (1986) *Identity. Cultural Change and the Struggle for Self.* New York: Oxford University Press.

Benjamin, Jessica (1992) *Bonds of Love: Psychoanalysis, Feminism and the Problem of Domination.* New York: Pantheon.

Benjamin, Walter (1968) *Illuminations.* New York: Harcourt, Brace and World.

Bloch, Ernst (1986) *The Principle of Hope*, 3 vols, trans. N. Plaice, S. Plaice and P. Knight. Oxford: Basil Blackwell. (Orig. pub. 1959.)

Brown, Richard Harvey (1987) *Society as Text, Essays on Rhetoric, Reason, and Reality.* Chicago, IL: University of Chicago Press.

Castells, Manuel (2000) *The Rise of the Network Society.* Malden, MA: Blackwell.

Cummings, Ronald (1972) 'The Superbowl Society', in Ray Browne, Marshall Fishwick and Michael T. Marsden (eds) *Heroes of Popular Culture*, pp. 101–11. Bowling Green, OH: Bowling Green University Press.

DaMatta, Roberto (1991) *Carnivals, Rogues and Heroes.* Notre Dame, IN: University of Notre Dame Press.

Durkheim, Emile (1965) *The Elementary Forms of the Religious Life.* New York: Free Press.

Dworkin, Shari Lee and Wachs, Faye Linda (2001) 'Size Matters: Male Body Panic and the Commodification of Masculinity in Mainstream Health and Fitness Magazines', paper presented to the American Sociological Association, Anaheim, CA.

Elias, Norbert (1978) *The Civilizing Process.* New York: Pantheon.

Featherstone, Mike (1991) *The Body: Social Process and Cultural Theory.* London: Sage.

Foucault, Michel (1977) *Discipline and Punish: The Birth of the Prison*, trans. Alan Sheridan. New York: Pantheon.

Freud, Sigmund (1989) *Civilization and its Discontents.* New York: Norton and Norton. (Orig. pub. 1930.)

Freyre, Gilberto (1956) *The Masters and the Slaves (Casa-Grande and Senzala): A Study in the Development of Brazilian Civilization.* New York: Knopf.

Giddens, Anthony (1992) *Modernity and Self Identity.* Stanford, CA: Stanford University Press.

Girard, René (1977) *Violence and the Sacred*, trans. Patrick Gregory. Baltimore, MD: Johns Hopkins University Press.

Gramsci, Antonio (1992) *Prison Notebooks*, ed. Joseph A. Buttigieg, trans. J.A. Buttigieg and Antonio Callari. New York: Columbia University Press.

Grosz, Elizabeth A. (1994) *Volatile Bodies: Toward a Corporeal Feminism.* Bloomington: Indiana University Press.

Holtham, Susan (1992) 'Body Piercing in the West: A Sociological Inquiry'; available at: www.bmezine.com

Huizinga, Johan (1955) *Homo Ludens. A Study of the Play-Element in Culture.* Boston, MA: Beacon Press.

Irigaray, Luce (1985) *Speculum of the Other Woman*, trans. Gillian C. Gill. Ithaca, NY: Cornell University Press.

Langman, Lauren (1992) 'From Pathos to Panic: American Character Meets the Future', in Phillip Wexler (ed.) *Critical Theory Now*, pp. 165–240. London: Falmer Press.

Langman, Lauren (1993) 'Neon Cages: Shopping for Subjectivity', in Rob Shields (ed.) *Lifestyles of Consumption*, pp. 40–82. London: Routledge.

Langman, Lauren (2000) 'Identity, Hegemony and the Reproduction of Domination', in *Marx, Weber and Durkheim*, pp. 238–90. New York: Gordian Knot Press.

Linger, Daniel (1992) *Dangerous Encounters*. Stanford, CA: Stanford University Press.

McBride, James (1995) *War, Battering and Other Sports*. Atlantic Highlands, NJ: Humanities Press.

Marx, Karl (1978) 'Economic and Philosophical Manuscripts of 1844', in Robert C. Tucker (ed.) *The Marx–Engels Reader*, 2nd edn, pp. 66–125. New York: W.W. Norton.

Nietzsche, Friedrich Wilhelm (1999) *The Birth of Tragedy and Other Writings*. New York: Cambridge University Press.

Oriard, Michael (1993) *Reading Football*. Chapel Hill: University of North Carolina Press.

Rapping, Elayne (1987) *The Looking Glass World of Nonfiction TV*. Boston, MA: South End Press.

Sanders, Clifton (1987) 'Marks of Mischief: Becoming and Being Tattooed', *Journal of Contemporary Ethnography* 16(4): 395–432.

Schiller, Chris (1993) *The Body and Social Theory*. London: Sage.

Schwartz, Dona (1997) *Contesting the Superbowl*. London: Routledge.

Simmel, Georg (1950) *The Sociology of Georg Simmel*, trans. Kurt H. Wolff. New York: The Free Press.

Sklair, Leslie (2001) *The Transnational Capitalist Class*. Oxford and Malden, MA: Blackwell.

Turner, Bryan S. (1996) *The Body and Society: Explorations in Social Theory*. Thousand Oaks, CA: Sage.

Turner, Victor (1966) *The Ritual Process: Structure and Antistructure*. Chicago, IL: Aldine.

Vale, Victor and Juno, Andrea (1989) *Modern Primitives*. San Francisco, CA: Re/search Publications.

Van Gennep, Arnold (1960) *The Rites of Passage*. London: Routledge and Kegan Paul.

Weber, Max (1996) *From Max Weber: Essays in Sociology*, ed. Hans Gerth and C. Wright Mills. New York: Oxford University Press.

Wilson, Elizabeth (1987) *Adorned in Dreams: Fashion and Modernity*. Berkeley: University of California Press.

4

'Ethnicity is Everywhere': On Globalization and the Transformation of Cultural Identity

Helmuth Berking

What can your nation do for you that a good credit card cannot do?' In posing this not wholly unironic question, anthropologist Ulf Hannerz is touching on a basic premise characterizing the contemporary discourse on globalization, namely the belief that, in the face of the transnationalization of commodity markets, financial markets and cultural markets, the 'national' is increasingly losing its significance as the master frame for the construction of collective identities and has become overlaid, undermined, or even replaced by deterritorialized identity formations. The stakes, however, are much higher, since the 'national' represents not only identities but our dominant form of sociation as nation-state organized societies.

It is in theses proclaiming the end of the nation-state (Appadurai, 1996a, 1996b; Bauman, 1995, 1996; Castells, 1996; Ohmae, 1995; Robertson, 1992; Ruggie, 1993; Rosencrane, 2001) or at least a significant loss of national sovereignty (Hannerz, 1996; Mathews, 1997; Sassen, 1991, 1996b) that theories of globalization find their common ground. Bearing in mind David Harvey's influential definition of globalization as a new round of 'time-space compression', we can note that this discussion is predominantly marked by spatial categories and scales, as well as by a general point of view that interprets 'globalization' as an inwardly contradictory dynamic of in essence spatially defined reconfigurations of politics, culture, society, gender, race and ethnicity. The range and depth of these ongoing processes of spatial reconfiguration are highly controversial. But to perceive the radical shift of all spatial scales and the corresponding organizational forms of social relations, we need only bear in mind that, in relation to the 'local', the 'regional' and the 'national', the 'global' is first of all and foremost a sociospatial scale. Referred to as the 'spatialization of social theory' (Feather-stone and Lash, 1995: 1; Soja, 1996; Massey, 1999), this 'geographical turn' in the social sciences has made itself felt in the categories and concepts which not too long ago seemed quintessential to mainstream social thought.

Against this background, the aim of the present article is to seek, in some measure, to reconstruct the globalization-related reconfiguration of social spaces, in particular, as far as a relocalization of national space is concerned.

The consequences of the idea of territoriality and territorial enclosure can best be studied with reference to the nation-state. First, I focus on the relational rearrangement of national space due to 'globalizing' forces. After briefly reviewing the principle of territorial sovereignty on which both nation-states as nationally organized societies and their depiction in the social sciences are based, I go on to describe some basic processes of globalization which directly relate to the form of organization of the nation-state, and are relevant to it, to the extent that they subvert the unity of territoriality, sovereignty and identity. Finally, I link these reconfigurations of national space with constructions of cultural identities which no longer appear to be set in an exclusively national frame but seem more and more to rely on and to play with strategies of 'ethnicization'. The question, then, is whether or not there is in fact a particular relationship between ethnicization and globalization.

I

The fact that we imagine the world we live in as a world of states points to the hitherto undisputed dominance of the 'nation form' (Balibar, 1991). What began with the Peace of Westphalia in 1648 and seems to be finding its preliminary climax in the postcolonial world of the beginning 21st century is the paradoxical universalization of an essential particularism (Wallerstein, 1996: 92; Robertson, 1995), namely the partition of the world into territorially bounded, in principle sovereign nation-states which tolerate neither a God above nor stateless zones below. The history of territoriality and the enforcement of the state's monopoly of legitimate violence is a history of wars between states and – often violent – colonization processes within nations.

The modern state is at once the most exclusive and quasi-natural framework, or as Immanuel Wallerstein (1996: 92) terms it, the 'primary cultural container', in which time passes and life happens, where people love and live, work and die, a container in which society, politics, culture and economy, each have their specific place and a specific history. The modern state constitutes the only form of a social-spatial organization of social relations in which all aspects of sociability, from the institutions of cultural hegemony to civil rights, from the mechanisms of redistributive justice to the monopoly on physical power, rest on the principle of *territorial sovereignty*. At the same time, the territorial model of the state established itself as the dominant epistemology, as a categorical state centrism, via a basic tenet of modern social sciences, namely that social relations are both organized and reproduced exclusively in territorially defined and spatially isomorphic entities (Brenner, 1999). State territory is thus the conceptual spatial unit which the social sciences use to constitute their objects: the economy as national economy, a sociology which analyses not 'society' but nationally organized society, a political science which perceives the nation-state as the main collective actor, and so forth.

Theories of globalization break with this categorical state centrism that regards the cartography of the global as identical with territorially bounded defined borders of nation-states. They seek to escape the dilemma, which John Agnew (1994) so succinctly designated as the 'territorial trap', by radically separating the 'global' and the 'national' as sociospatial scales, and by pitting global space as a deterritorialized 'space of flows' against the traditional 'space of places' (Castells, 1996: 378). What deterritorialization means is that we are increasingly faced with spaces not bound in territorial terms (the space of flows) and with forms of sociation defined in terms other than territorial (diasporic public spheres and translocalities) (Appadurai, 1996a, 1996b), the global effect of which is a systematic subversion of the principle of territoriality on which states, local cultures and collective identities rest.

II

Typical arguments adduced as evidence of the loss of meaning of the nation-state are based on three interlocking processes, mediated by the media-centred technological revolution of electronic communication: (1) the globalization of the economy, (2) the institutionalization of new transnational legal regimes and (3) the globalization of media and motion, of mobile images and people in motion.

The globalization of production, commodity markets and financial markets, thus the widely held thesis, eliminates the economic governance capacities of nation-states. Transnational corporations that are in possession of a global infrastructure are increasingly breaking their territorial links and seeking autonomy from national regimentation. In addition, they find themselves in a geostrategic position that, ironically, permits them to hold national governments to a declared policy of non-interference. As the logic of politics is reduced to the logic of the market, governments are no longer the masters in their own houses. 'The more that national states implement deregulation to raise the competitiveness of their nations and localities within them', Saskia Sassen (1996a: 42) points out, '. . . the more they contribute to strengthen transnational networks and actors.' State deregulation, however, goes hand in hand with the institutionalization of new regulatory regimes. The space of the global economy is structured both hierarchically and territorially. One need only think here of the concentration of global governance structures – corporate headquarters and the 'corporate service complexes' associated with them – in the so-called global cities (Sassen, 1991; King, 1990; Eade, 1997), or the invention of new tax and tariff regimes in the form of 'export-processing and free-trade zones'; or the worldwide integration of the stock and financial markets, to fully realize the extent of only a limited number of structural innovations whose paradoxical feature is that they are all 'grounded in national territories' (Sassen, 1996a: 13), without being exclusively subject to the principle of national sovereignty. To understand this reconfiguration of social spaces within territories defined by nation-states and the way in which the decentralization of state sovereignty is bound up with it, we need only cast a quick glance at the new legal regimes that are being used to regulate and control these spaces (see Sassen, 1996a: 12–13).

Even transnational corporations are in need of rules, iron-clad property rights and contract security. In short, they need a legal system that matches the spatial extension of the global economy and compensates for the territorially limited power reach of national sovereignty. Among the institutional innovations that appear essential for the operation of the global economy, there are two forms of organization that play a key role: private-sector arbitration boards (international commercial arbitration) – 'the leading contractual method for the resolution of transnational commercial disputes' (Sassen, 1996a: 14) – and, once again, private, bond-rating agencies like Moody's Investors Service and Standard and Poor's Ratings Group, which now steer both capital flows and the investment strategies of both transnational corporations and national governments alike (Sassen, 1996a: 14–15). The power resources of these organizations are not only beyond the reach of national territorial sovereignty, they are also crystallization points for non-national sovereignties, which again put on the agenda the basic motives of the theoretical discussion on democracy: accountability and legitimacy.

However, the picture of the transnational configuration of regulatory regimes, tentatively described by Rosenau (1992) as 'governance without government', remains incomplete so long as we fail to consider the active geostrategic roles played by leading industrialized countries as authors of various globalization scripts (see Panitch, 1996). They write scripts directing the action of international institutions, among them the International Monetary Fund and the International Bank for Reconstruction and Development. They have formulated the General Agreement on Tariffs and Trade, set up the World Trade Organization, vigilantly watching that the outcomes remain controllable. To speak against this backdrop of the end of the nation-state seems to be as absurd as it is dangerous. But still, this 'internationalization of the state' (Panitch, 1996: 85) affects the pillars on which territoriality and sovereignty rest, inasmuch as it sets the stage for institutionalized forms of the articulation of sovereignty in denationalized spaces. In short, not only is the unity of territoriality and sovereignty identified for centuries with the nation-state breaking apart, the elements and sources of power of what we imagine to be national sovereignty are being reallocated and rearranged in sociospatial terms. Or as Jan Nederveen Pieterse (1995: 63) puts it: 'Thus, state power remains extremely strategic, but is no longer the only game in town.'

The second central line of argument concerning the decline of the nation-state refers to new trends towards transnational jurisdiction. While the economic dimensions of globalization are primarily spelled out in terms of a division between territoriality and sovereignty, the discussion over new legal regimes focuses on the relation between sovereignty and identity.

For the last two decades, a new development has been taking shape that sees the institutional formulation of international human rights regimes colliding with legal institutions typical of the nation-state. Since human rights, in pointed contrast to the legal category of citizenship, can neither be conferred nor distributed on the basis of criteria of affiliation, such rights cast a shadow of doubt on the principle of national sovereignty. At the same time, human rights are also bound up with a gradual devalorization of civil rights as the decisive material substrate and legal space on which national identities are institutionally based. Since citizenship and the civil rights it entails, define a privileged space of legitimate membership, human rights, which are enforced by the same institutions of the nation-state, necessarily deflate the hierarchical distance between 'us' and 'them'.

Though already conceptualized in the founding documents of the American and French Revolutions, the international career of human rights guarantees began only in 1948 with the UN Universal Declaration of Human Rights, which was followed two years later by the European Convention on Human Rights. Ratification and supplementary protocols were another few decades in the making, and only then was an effective corpus of legal instruments actually available. All these are, like deregulation agreements, international treaties whose paradoxical effect is that they strengthen the hand of non-governmental actors. In the case of human rights regimes, this means that the principle of individual rights is incorporated in an international legal system hitherto regulated by guarantees of national sovereignty and self-determination. 'The concept of nationality', Sassen (1996a: 97) writes, '. . . is being partly displaced from a principle that reinforces state sovereignty and self-determination . . . to a concept emphasizing that the state is accountable to all its residents on the basis of international human rights law. The individual emerges as the object of international laws and institutions.' And, in this arena, too, the state is no longer the only game in town. Individuals and groups, even illegal immigrants, now possess rights that they can claim from the state in which they live, or in any other state as well. In terms of basic economic, social and cultural rights, citizenship has lost much of its significance. Among other things, this is graphically illustrated by diasporic transnational communities: the services and rights guaranteed by states are dues no longer only to citizens but to all people – which, not accidentally one must add, feeds the hate and the xenophobia of those who see themselves as the better citizens. Loyalty and national identity, it might be argued, no longer pay, and the implementation of values based on a normative acknowledgement of institutionally defined goals is becoming a risky business for the state.

The third line of argument, not only relevant for the 'new geography of power' (Sassen, 1996a: 5), but also especially important to the 'new geography of identity' (Yaeger, 1996), we are interested in here is based on concepts of cultural globalization. Theories of cultural globalization share with the earlier described, more or less political-economy-oriented approaches, a critique of categorical state centrism, and an emphasis on sociospatial reconfigurations, which are primarily conceptualized as deterritorialization processes. These approaches are coming more and more to see national space as a 'leaking container' (Taylor, 1994: 157), too, but without attributing any exclusive explanatory value to economic dimensions of globalization. Of equal central importance, moreover, are motion and mediation, migration and media (Appadurai, 1996a, 1996b; Hannerz, 1996), inasmuch as they make globally available both deterritorialized images, scripts, identity options and deterritorialized forms of community.

Neither the global flow of cultural artefacts, nor worldwide population movements stop at the borders of nation-states. *Baywatch* finds its devoted audience in Kyoto no less than in Moscow, or Mexico City. Asian martial arts, popularized by the movie-industry, deliver a new framework for reshaping images of western masculinity. Evita-Madonna runs through gender-specific imaginations all over the world; the voices of Islamic fundamentalism can be heard in Berlin as clearly as they can in Istanbul or Karachi.

III

But there are not only images and scripts but people: immigrants, refugees, UN Blue Helmets, specialists of every colour, managers and tourists, who in the global here and now are transcending the borders of local cultures. The interplay of migration and mediation evokes those translocal and transnational communities, which in the form of 'diasporic public spheres' (Appadurai, 1996a: 10) are radically challenging the unity of national territoriality, sovereignty and collective identity as we once imagined them to be. To the concept of diaspora (Hall, 1990; Safran, 1991; Gilroy, 1993; Cohen, 1997; Clifford, 1997; Anthias, 1998; Mitchell, 1997), originally restricted to classic cases of violent expulsion and territorial resettlement, first of the Greek, then the Jewish and finally the Armenian communities. We have to attribute special importance, inasmuch as this concept is now applied more or less to all ethnic groups living outside their original territory. This semantic shift from ethnic group to diaspora implies three different changes of meaning. Unlike the informal communities known from ethnic neighbourhoods, some of which vanish over time into the melting pot, diasporas are (1) intentional political and cultural organizations, which (2) are dedicated to special interest policies, i.e. a struggle for recognition of their identity at the transnational and subnational levels, and (3) whose particular sociospatial quality is that they are located simultaneously within particular states and outside any state; in short, diaspora means forms of community not defined in territorial terms as well as a source of power emerging out of transnational spaces that are no longer fixed within the boundaries of nation-states. 'Diaspora', Khachig Toeloelyan (1996: 4) notes, 'are the exemplary communities of the transnational moment'. Cuban exiles, for instance, represent a sociocultural formation that extends from Madrid to Miami and beyond, and uses its distinct cultural and political institutions to seek to directly influence politics in Havana (see Toeloelyan, 1996: 4–28). The Indian diaspora extends from Sydney to the Silicon Valley. It is in a diverse and direct way implicated in the political-religious disputes of both India and its host countries. Moreover, without the Jewish diaspora in the United States, the geopolitical landscape of the Middle East would definitely look very different. One could go on with these examples, but what is more important is that within these diasporic public spheres, we can glimpse an articulation of the silhouettes of a trans-national form of sociation which offers a good point of departure for a study of the crisis symptoms besetting the nation-state.

The end of the nation-state, so the thesis goes, is first of all, the end of the hyphen between nation and state (Appadurai, 1996b). The reason why, in the global here and now, these two terms are diverging, is the fact that for the first time in the history of the modern state, they are developing distinct relations to territoriality and territory. While the state, and only the state, remains insolubly bound up with its original territoriality and sovereignty, the close alignment between territory and national identity appears to be losing force. States are no longer exclusively able to guarantee the territorial organization of markets, life-worlds, identities and histories. In the global 'market for loyalties' (Price, cited in Appadurai, 1996b: 48), they are forced to compete with a bewildering diversity of providers of ethnic, racial, scientific, feminist, fundamentalist, spiritualist identity options, and among these, religious formations are only the most significant examples of deter-ritorialized identity constructions that now form the basis of transnational loyalties (see Appadurai, 1996b: 49).

As state and nation diverge, or more precisely, as the holy unity of state-bounded territoriality and territorially defined collective identity dissolves, relations between state and society are shifting. Power, responsibilities, and scopes of action once monopolized by the state, are now being bestowed on and demanded by individuals and groups. This gives rise to new self-regulatory regimes within societies. This is a dynamic which potentially makes possible both 'gains' and 'losses' in civility (Berking, 1996a) – although under present conditions, its connotations appear to be primarily negative. We are faced with an arbitrarily expandable number of mini-ethnicities that design their cultural identities via the ethnicization of social conflicts. In this historical moment in which the modern state is – by no means totally voluntarily – backing off from the inner colonization of society, the internal ethnicization of society seems to become the most promising mode available to society to self-regulate its identity problems. It is not only Mr and Mrs Everyman that are 'searching for a center that holds' (Bauman, 1995: 140–1), but the social sciences suddenly discover their predilection for communities as a (postmodern) form of sociation, one which, only three decades ago, they had self-confidently doomed to oblivion as a regressive historical relict.

But what is it that makes ethnicization so attractive as a strategy of power and identity politics? Why are we so eager to gamble away these civilizational gains that might result from reflexive 'self-relations' and alterations in stocks of cultural knowledge? Under what circumstances are narratives of exclusion framed in the light of a 'cultural fundamentalism' (Stolke, 1994) which damns the other by recognizing its difference that permits to maintain their definitional power of the actual? The conventional wisdom we are faced with here is a typical reaction to increasingly bitter struggles for a piece of the economic pie. But such explanations do not shed any light on the problem why these reactions, and not others, are seen as holding a promise of success.

IV

Confronting these questions, I would like to offer some cultural-sociological conjectures, guided by the background premise that the ethnicization of social conflicts is merely a byproduct of a larger trend of cultural globalization as a process which affects the very mode of identity constructions inasmuch as it appears to encourage *the ethnicization of cultural identities*.

The global circulation of cultural artefacts is leading to a permanent de- and recontextualization of spatially bound cultural knowledge, lifestyles, etc. This means that while integrated in global circulation, they are at the same time permanently (re)defined by an incorporation of images and scripts from this field. However, when belief systems, worldview structures and identities come to function as mirrors of all other belief systems, worldview structures and identities, the symbolic universe of local cultures loses its ontological aura as an unquestioned fact. This may entail the spread of cultural relativism and necessitate the generation, protection and stabilization of inner convictions against competing interpretations; the inner spaces of social groups, once kept together via strong identifications and the internalization of collectively shared values, all of a sudden appear as fragile, as those categorizations of the 'other' which in-groups inevitably need in order to secure identity and difference. In short, cultural identities and cultural difference are more and more experienced on an everyday level, as socially *constructed*, which means they become consciously accessible and extremely useful as power resources in the daily struggle for social advantages.

These attributions guaranteeing difference that potentially transform every single other into the Other, are at present assuming the guise of politics (Neckel, 1994: 48). This applies for the traditional arenas of power struggles in which governments, parties and political entrepreneurs more and more often mobilize (and form) 'their' audiences through 'ethno-national' invocation; this, however, also applies to those arenas of sub-politics in which cultural identities are politically constructed in the first place.

The demands of moral, cognitive and ethnic minorities for recognition and legitimate representation of their particular feature, presented in the framework of 'nationality', 'ethnicity', 'race', 'gender' and 'sexuality', supply the potentially mobilizing motivational dynamics for group conflicts, which are currently increasingly overlaying the class-related problems of capitalist societies (see Berking, 1996b). It is not by chance that 'politics of identity' constitute a form of symbolic mobilization which, consciously and in an emancipatory manner, breaks with seemingly universal demands for justice and equality in favour of the particular. What is at stake for these forms of emancipatory politics are fundamental experiences of injustice, contempt and cultural – i.e. ethnic, gender-specific and sexual – stigmatization, and, therefore, a strategy which aims at transforming the dominant model of cultural representation. The risk inherent in this mode of universalization of the particular, strengthened by 'the global valorization of particular identities' (Robertson, 1992: 130), is not only that it systematically undercuts sociostructurally induced disparities; what appears even more momentous is the tendency to create new 'totalizing fictions' (Somers and Gibson, 1994: 55), in which a single category, for instance 'gender', determines all other attributions signifying identity. Totalizing fictions run counter to the logic of identity constructions, which appears to be infinite.

There seems to be a self-contradictory dynamic at work here: the clearer the contours of the project of identity, the lower the chances of mobilizing people; this causes a predicament for collective actors, who may want to guarantee at the same time the space needed for inner differentiation, and to mobilize the greatest possible external consensus. Presupposing that identity policies, emphasizing primarily reflexive self-relations and changing stocks of cultural knowledge, both mirror and represent a mode of being in the world which demands of individuals and groups permanently and constantly to perform the enormous feat of *convincing themselves that they are convinced*, we can easily understand the use of these totalizing fictions as an emergency brake against incessant expansions of contingency. Acknowledging the constructed character of cultural identities, however, constitutes the *emancipatory potential* of these protest formations, which are reversed into their opposite exactly at the moment in which this knowledge is negated in favour of chances for political mobilization. The ethnicization of cultural identities that then takes place, has to do with the psychologically enigmatic process of 'forgetting something deliberately' (Offe, 1996: 268). Ethnicization in this context needs to be understood as the process of the affirmation of difference, a process in which ascriptive features are (re-)essentialized and the reflexive mode of constructing difference or identity is consciously abandoned, 'deliberately' forgotten.

In the struggle for recognition, the advantages of ethnicization seem self-evident. Ethnicization promises a continuation of categorical belonging and creates islands of identity in the sea of contingency while also opening up political space for the construction of foe images of the highest intensity. An increase in intensity can serve as an affirmation of identity. Yet, the risky dynamic involved in constantly having to convince yourself that you are convinced does not cease at this point. What is deliberately forgotten is always in danger of being remembered by third parties, and it is exactly this precarious psychosocial situation in which, as soon as 'second-order' essentialisms come into play, violence enters the stage as an ultima ratio against failing permanence.

Let me briefly report on the construction of a totalizing fiction which will shed some light on the local conditions under which problems are contextualized which, at first glance, have no significance for the local actors themselves. The data are taken from a group interview with seven boys and eight girls – ninth graders of a high school in an East German village – that I conducted in June 1992 as part of a community study. The study focused on everyday life experiences before, during and after the fall of the Wall; on the way in which these students were dealing with German unification. The interviewees talked about the awkward feelings that their first visit in West Berlin evoked; they complained about the cultural desert that shaped village life once socialist youth organizations had collapsed; they reported on the dramatic changes of their family lives due to extraordinary unemployment rates; on their own resignation in view of their job situations, etc. Once the issue of foreigners was addressed, the discussion immediately became excited. Russians and Poles, literally the only foreigners these students might have been in contact with over the years, were of no interest. 'The Russians, they are really pathetic, they live in caves nowadays.' Instead the 'Turk' became the emblematic figure of all kind of ascriptions. 'The Turks', shouted Paul, 'they come over here, file their application, which takes five years, and while they're waiting, they produce another seven kids; then they have to stay here and get all their money from the state.' 'Okay, I'm not only talking about the Turks, but about all these jerks, these fucking asylum-seekers.' The fact that there was not a single 'real' Turk to be found within at least 90 kilometres did not change the power of imagination, which was kept going by rumours – street traders who cheated their way into the homes, criminal offences by foreigners who did not even exist, rapes that never took place, etc. 'You never know whether you're going to get home safe. The fear . . . the fear is about the girls', Marcel explained, and he was right. The construction of the 'Turk' is a male topic. The female interviewees either withdrew from the discussion, or answered back at the boys: 'Hey, man, you look like a Turk yourself, so you'd better shut up.' Group dynamics play on adolescent gender wars and male fantasies over threatened masculinity. 'I don't know how you can talk like that as a girl, how you can say that they [Turkish boys] look sweet; I don't really know how you can say that, man, they'll take you down to the taiga and sell you off into the desert.' To add some authority to this narration, one youth, Olaf, attributed it to the local pastor: 'He told us so, and therefore it must be true.' Nicole heard a similar tale: 'After their marriage, my aunt and her husband travelled to Turkey and they met there one of these camel traders, who wanted to buy my aunt for about 10 camels.'

Taiga, desert, camels, Turks, rape, prostitution – here we have images, rumours and second-hand information that owe nothing to personal experience or to the local life-worlds of those who entrap themselves in an imagery of adolescent adventure literature. The consequence, however, is that this makes of the very far, the very near: the Turk is already knocking at the front door.

The devaluation of local experience articulated here is one of the typical effects of what John Durham Peters (1997) has characterized as our mass-media-related 'bifocal' worldview. Mass media, these totalizing-image-representation machines, offer access to a world which would otherwise, and in view of our limited local experience, not be available. But these totalizing images archive a kind of coherence that systematically devalorizes local knowledge and experiences as in some way fragmentary. 'I may see blue skies, but the satellite picture on the TV news tells me a huge storm is on its way' (Peters, 1997: 81). Totalizing images undermine the authority of the local. The images of the Turk, which East German kids constructed, expresses one of the local variations of the general discourse about the xenophobia of that time. The obvious absence of any coherence in this local narration shows the efforts that have to be made before you become familiar with a completely unfamiliar theme. And indeed, this topic was put on the agenda and kept going mainly from outside, as I learned later. The two male group leaders were weekend 'rightists', who were heavily engaged in a youth club in another town, which was taken over by the FAP, one of the most militant right-wing organizations at that time. The Turk these former East Germans encounter is exactly the representation of the Turk which the rightists had brought to the east of Germany. The Turk becomes *the Turk* only by identification with those who while representing the Turk as *the Turk*, represent themselves as the only true Germans.

V

Once ethnicized cultural identities have reached the institutional level of collective actors, the struggle for recognition turns into a merciless fight for territorial presence. Then we find, as in the new German state that once constituted the German Democratic Republic, 'liberated national territories'. Public spaces are symbolically sealed off, and violence serves as the means of last resort to enforce entrance and exit rules. Meanwhile, the politicization of ethnic enclosure, the politics of ethnicity which – at least until now – is in Germany mainly focused by the ethnic majority, has, in the US, reached its highest point of fragmentation and segregation in the society as a whole. Anyone can play! Indeed, everyone must play.

Furthermore, we have binding linguistic rules which encourage narratives of exclusion of a quite different manner, since they concur with potential sanctions. In art and literature, in science as well as in the inner spaces of ethnic groups, the rule applies: only in the self-representation of your own group can you expect to receive the seal of legitimate representation. Cultural artefacts of whites on blacks, of men on women, of heterosexuals on homosexuals, and vice versa, seem to stigmatize racially, or sexually, or both (see Heller, 1994). African-Americans are better off avoiding white friends and white neighbourhoods; women who do not identify with/reveal themselves to be feminists have almost no chance to be hired at an institution of higher learning; Hispanic youngsters are pushed into educational and second-language programmes irrelevant for their social existence as Americans; Indian immigrants are considered white in some school districts, while being categorized as an ethnic minority in others – a difference substantial in terms of 'entitlements'; Asian-Americans fight for a curricular recognition of a tradition that was created by the efforts of the American Census Bureau; and I, myself, had to sign a US labour contract to learn that I belong to the race of Caucasians, a taxonomic location that is of no effect in my Westphalian home town, but which has many, quite different consequences in American society.

The institutionalized forms of racism that Agnes Heller (1994) has referred to as 'biopolitics' are at once a precondition and a result of this identity-related mobilization unfolding around territoriality and socio-spatial control. The Italian Lega Nord (and certainly the breakup of Yugoslavia) is one of the most significant examples of ethno-regional identity politics in the European realm (see Schmidtke, 1996). Chicago, an agglomeration consisting of about 67 ethnic neighbourhoods – and which enjoys the reputation of being the most segregated US big city – has recently contributed another variant. Since the beginning of August 1997, the area around North Halsted Avenue has been presenting itself as the first officially recognized gay neighbourhood in America. Symbols and flags in the universal colours of the 'gay pride rainbow' mark and redefine social space, according to the sexual preferences of some of the area's inhabitants, which leads to a situation of not only new lines of conflict with the religious right, but also with traditionally ethnic neighbourhoods such as Greektown, Chinatown, Pilsen, Germantown and so forth, who vehemently polemicize against being put on the same footing with a mere sexual lifestyle (see *New York Times*, 27 August 1997).

At the other end of the ethnic reconfiguration of urban spaces, we have the ghetto, a sociospatially fixed, place-bound institution of racist exclusion which is kept up not through the expression of ethnic affinity or 'choice', but through outside pressure and violent defence of the 'colour line'. Economic destitution, endemic violence, drug abuse and antisocial behaviour are only a few of the typical features condensed by the majority of American society almost emblematically in order to form the figure of the black man as a rapist, as the drug dealer or gang-member, and of the black woman as 'a teenage welfare queen'. And do not the facts themselves speak the language of moral decay?

Such interpretations and images of decay, which take up an important space in public discourse, make us forget that these enclaves of poverty and terror are a product of urban planning, local politics and government pro-grammes (Venkatesh, 2000). Loic Wacquant (1994) has shown with refer-ence to Chicago's South Side, that ghetto inhabitants are systematically barred from access to the job market and to basic institutions of urban infra-structure. But what connects the enclaves of poverty and terror with those typical identity-motivated redefinitions of urban spaces? Until now, we have been talking about tendencies of the ethnicization of cultural identities and a context in which the ghetto apparently does not fit. As a 'place of decay', the ghetto represents for mainstream society the outmost outside. It is this imagination of a territorially limited evil, a 'locus of evil', that forces its exclusion. Thus, it is no accident that the ghetto has simultaneously become the exemplary frame of reference for a discourse which is gaining social power, that on the 'new urban underclass' (Wilson, 1987; Jenks and Peterson, 1991; critically: Gans, 1996; Katz, 1993; Aponte, 1990), even in Europe. What is at stake in this frame of reference is no longer an uncov-ering of the interplay of race, class and poverty, but motivations, the defi-cient norm and value orientations of those who live there (Wacquant, 1994: 232–3); what steps into the place of the analysis of those social and power-structural context conditions is the thesis of the context-generating power of individual failure. Were one to accept the perspective of its constructors, the new underclass would now have to be seen as populated by those who have been marginalized, because of their habitual incapabilities and social pathologies, which means that they must rightly be excluded and kept apart from participation in the social intercourse of mainstream society; they are 'misfits', who finally can be treated with no reference to the basic standards of civilized behaviour (see Offe, 1996: 275).

The construction of the new underclass – a concept that meanwhile appears to have been given up by the social sciences because of its theoretical poverty – is still given a lot of attention in public and social policy discourses and feeds a social imagery that goes beyond the ethnicization of cultural identities by reaching into communally shared knowledge. And it is this *wahlverwandtschaft* geared to subjectivization and particularization among the taxonomies and identity constructions dear to the social sciences that now provides politicians, scientists, managers, the average Jills and Jacks, with motives and justifications to undermine ethnically the insti-tutionalized standards of civilized behaviour. We cannot contradict those who object that internal ethnicization, as a self-regulatory mode of modern societies, represents no more than a cynical variation of a globally induced multiculturalism, seen as gaining the day *à la longue* without alternatives in sight. But we must assume that the sociospatial reconfiguration of national space in ethnic terms does not necessarily result in social relations of recognition, but instead goes hand in hand with narratives of exclusion which do not at all strengthen the self-regulatory potentials of societies still organized around the principle of the nation-state.

VI

That all three dimensions of globalization described here affect the form of the modern nation-state is beyond doubt. Equally beyond doubt, however, should be the conclusion that what we are faced with here is not so much the end of the modern state but rather a significant reconfiguration process of the relation between state, territoriality, sovereignty and identity. This new geography of power is inclusive and yet rediversified in a sociospatial way. This geography knows many agents who act simultaneously in local, regional, national and global contexts and organization structures. This geography necessitates not only elementary deterritorializations, but equally elementary reterritorialization processes with respect to cultural identities and local and transnational forms of communities. Thus, the new geography of power lies neither completely outside nor below the modern nation-state, even though the latter is increasingly losing its social-integrative functions, and it is turning from the nation-state to the state. This state, unburdened by its mode of implementation of values, one could argue, still functions, but no longer integrates. Were this the case, we would be dealing with a constellation unanticipated in the literature of the social sciences; states, then, may survive as formal organizations, but without having to fulfil the primary condition of their own functioning, namely to be recognized by their specific social base as a meaningful and practical institution (Offe, 1991). The power source for this outcome is, and will remain for the time being, the state monopoly of legitimate violence.

Bibliography

Agnew, J. (1994) 'The Territorial Trap: The Geographical Assumptions of International Relations Theory', *Review of International Political Economy* 1(1): 53–80.

Anthias, F. (1998) 'Evaluating "Diaspora": Beyond Ethnicity?', *Sociology* 32(3): 557–80.

Aponte, R. (1990) 'Definition of the Underclass: A Critical Analysis', in H. Gans (ed.) *Sociology in America*, pp. 117–37. Newbury Park, CA: Sage.

Appadurai, A. (1996a) *Modernity at Large.* Minneapolis: University of Minnesota Press.

Appadurai, A. (1996b) 'Sovereignty without Territoriality', in P. Yaeger (ed.) *The Geography of Identity*, pp. 40–58. Ann Arbor: The University of Michigan Press.

Balibar, E. (1991) 'The Nation Form: History and Ideology', in E. Balibar and I. Wallerstein (eds) *Race, Nation, Class*, pp. 86–106. London and New York: Verso.

Bauman, Z. (1995) 'Searching for a Centre that Holds', in M. Featherstone, S. Lash and R. Robertson (eds) *Global Modernities*, pp. 140–54. London: Sage.

Bauman, Z. (1996) 'Glokalisierung oder Was für die einen Globalisierung, ist für die anderen Lokalisierung', *Das Argument* 217(38): 653–64.

Berking, H. (1996a) 'Solidary Individualism: The Moral Impact of Cultural Modernization in Late Modernity', in S. Lash, B. Szerszynski and B. Wynne (eds) *Risk, Environment and Modernity*, pp. 189–202. London: Sage.

Berking, H. (1996b) 'Lebensstile, Identitätspolitiken und Gestaltungsmacht', *Gewerkschaftliche Monatshefte* 8: 488–93.

Brenner, N. (1999) 'Beyond State-Centrism? Space, Territoriality, and Geographic Scale in Globalization Studies', *Theory and Society* 28(1): 39–78.

Castells, M. (1996) *The Rise of the Network Society.* Cambridge, MA: Blackwell.

Clifford, J. (1997) *Routes: Travel and Translation in the Late Twentieth Century.* Cambridge, MA: Harvard University Press.

Cohen, R. (1997) *Global Diasporas: An Introduction.* London: UCL Press.

Eade, J., ed. (1997) *Living the Global City.* London: Routledge.

Featherstone, M. and Lash, S. (1995) 'Globalization, Modernity and the Spatialization of Social Theory: An Introduction', in M. Featherstone, S. Lash and R. Robertson (eds) *Global Modernities*, pp. 1–24. London: Sage.

Gans, H. (1996) 'From "Underclass" to "Undercast"', in E. Mingione (ed.) *Urban Poverty and the Underclass*, pp. 141–52. Oxford: Blackwell.

Gilroy, P. (1993) *The Black Atlantic.* London: Verso.

Hall, S. (1990) 'Cultural Identity and Diaspora', in J. Rutherford (ed.) *Identity: Community, Culture, Difference*, pp. 222–37. London: Lawrence and Wishart.

Hannerz, U. (1996) *Transnational Connections, Culture, People, Places.* London and New York: Routledge.

Heller, A. (1994) 'Die Zerstörung der Privatsphäre durch die Zivilgesellschaft', *Ästhetik und Kommunikation* 85/6: 23–35.

Jenks, C. and Peterson, P., eds (1991) *The Urban Underclass.* Washington, DC: The Brookings Institution.

Katz, M., ed. (1993) *The 'Underclass' Debate.* Princeton, NJ: Princeton University Press.

King, A.D. (1990) *Global Cities.* London: Routledge.

Massey, D. (1999) 'Power-Geometries and the Politics of Time-Space', Hettner Lecture II, University of Heidelberg.

Mathews, J. (1997) 'Power Shift', *Foreign Affairs* 76(1): 50–66.

Mitchell, K. (1997) 'Different Diasporas and the Hype of Hybridity', *Environment and Planning D: Society and Space* 15(2): 533–53.

Neckel, S. (1994) 'Gefährliche Fremdheit', *Ästhetik und Kommunikation* 85/6: 45–9.

Nederveen Pieterse, J. (1995) 'Globalization as Hybridization', in M. Featherstone, S. Lash and R. Robertson (eds) *Global Modernities*, pp. 45–68. London: Sage.

Offe, C. (1991) 'Die deutsche Vereinigung als "natürliches Experiment"', in B. Giesen and C. Leggewie (eds) *Experiment Vereinigung*, pp. 37–61. Berlin: Rowohlt.

Offe, C. (1996) 'Moderne "Barbarei": Der Naturzustand im Kleinformat', in M. Miller and H.G. Soeffner (eds) *Modernität und Barbarei*, pp. 258–89. Frankfurt am Main: Suhrkamp.

Ohmae, K. (1995) *The End of the Nation State.* New York: Harper.

Panitch, L. (1996) 'Rethinking the Role of the State', in J. Mittelman (ed.) *Globalization: Critical Reflections*, pp. 78–94. London and Boulder, CO: Westview Press.

Peters, D.J. (1997) 'Seeing Bifocally: Media, Place, Culture', in A. Gupta and J. Ferguson (eds) *Culture, Power, Place*, pp. 75–92. Durham, NC: Duke University Press.

Robertson, R. (1992) *Globalization.* London: Sage.

Robertson, R. (1995) 'Glocalization: Time-Space and Homogeneity-Heterogeneity', in M. Featherstone, S. Lash and R. Robertson (eds) *Global Modernities*, pp. 25–44. London: Sage.

Rosenau, J. (1992) 'Citizenship in a Changing Global Order', in J. Rosenau and O. Czempiel (eds) *Governance without Government: Order and Change in World Politics*, pp. 1–29. Cambridge: Cambridge University Press.

Rosencrane, R. (2001) *Das globale Dorf, New Economy und das Ende des Nationalstaates.* Düsseldorf: Patmos.

Ruggie, J. (1993) 'Territoriality and Beyond: Problematizing Modernity in International Relations', *International Organization* 47(1): 139–74.

Safran, W. (1991) '"Diasporas in Modern Societies": Myths of Homeland and Return', *Diaspora* 1: 83–99.

Sassen, S. (1991) *The Global City.* Princeton, NJ: Princeton University Press.

Sassen, S. (1996a) *Losing Control? Sovereignty in an Age of Globalization.* New York: Columbia University Press.

Sassen, S. (1996b) 'The Spatial Organization of Information Industries: Implications for the Role of the State', in J. Mittelman (ed.) *Globalization: Critical Reflections*, pp. 33–52. London and Boulder, CO: Westview Press.

Schmidtke, O. (1996) *Politics of Identity.* Sinzheim: Pro Universitate.

Soja, E. (1996) *Thirdspace.* Cambridge, MA: Blackwell.

Somers, M. and Gibson, G. (1994) 'Reclaiming the Epistemological "Other": Narrative and the Social Constitution of Identity', in C. Calhoun (ed.) *Social Theory and the Politics of Identity*, pp. 37–99. Cambridge, MA: Blackwell.

Stolke, V. (1994) 'Kultureller Fundamentalismus', in R. Lindner (ed.) *Die Wiederkehr des Regionalen*, pp. 36–63. Frankfurt am Main: Suhrkamp.

Taylor, P. (1994) 'The State as Container: Territoriality in the Modern World-System', *Progress in Human Geography* 18: 151–62.

Taylor, P. and Knox, P., eds (1995) *World Cities in a World System.* Cambridge: Cambridge University Press.

Toeloelyan, K. (1996) 'Rethinking Diaspora(s): Stateless Power in the Transnational Moment', *Diaspora* 5(1): 3–36.

Venkatesh, S.A. (2000) *American Project: The Rise and Fall of a Modern Ghetto.* Cambridge, MA: Harvard University Press.

Wacquant, L. (1994) 'The New Urban Color Line: The State and Fate of the Ghetto in Post Fordist America', in C. Calhoun (ed.) *Social Theory and the Politics of Identity*, pp. 231–76. Cambridge, MA: Blackwell.

Wallerstein, I. (1996) 'The National and the Universal: Can There Be Such a Thing as World Culture?', in A. King (ed.) *Culture, Globalization and the World-System*, pp. 91–106. Minneapolis: University of Minnesota Press.

Wilson, W.J. (1987) *The Truly Disadvantaged.* Chicago, IL: Chicago University Press.

Yaeger, P., ed. (1996) *The Geography of Identity.* Ann Arbor: University of Michigan Press.

5

Multiple Modernity, Nationalism and Religion: A Global Perspective

Willfried Spohn

Introduction

Since the breakdown of Communism, we have been witnessing a worldwide and often parallel revival of nationalism and religion. This development had already started earlier with the Islamic revolution in Iran, the religious and nationalist counter-movements in the Soviet bloc, the new nationalism in the developed West as well as the emergence of forms of religious nationalism in many parts of the non-western world. But only with the collapse of the Soviet empire in the second world as well as the demise of socialist and Communist movements in large parts of the third world, the parallel development of nationalism and religion has spread on a global scale. This parallel development appears in different phenomena like the growth of ethnic nationalism, the revitalization of religion, the strengthening of religious fundamentalism as well as the connection between religion and nationalism in various forms of religious nationalism (Marty and Appleby, 1987; Beyer, 1994; Bielefeldt and Heitmeyer, 1998; Haynes, 1998; Jürgensmeyer, 1993). This is also the background of Samuel Huntington's (1996) well-known, though contested thesis (Müller, 2001) that the new world order of the 21st century will be characterized by growing conflicts along the fault-lines of civilizations and embedded national and cultural identities.

For the social and political sciences, this worldwide parallel development of nationalism and religion has come as a surprise, challenging the received disciplinary frame theories and analytical orientations. The common theoretical foundation, though questioned by Marxist and postmodernist counter-currents, has been the modernization paradigm assuming with modernization, social differentiation, individualization, national integration, democratization of national societies and also the decline of religion (Müller and Schmid, 1995; Zapf, 1971). As a consequence, the development of nationalism was to be expected, but rather in a civic and secular form than as a combination of ethnic and religious nationalism (Casanova, 1994; Smith, 1998). From that perspective, the contemporary parallel growth of nationalism and religion presents a basic theoretical dilemma for the still predominant mainstream positions in the political and social sciences. This dilemma is even more obvious since the transformation research on post-Communist Central and Eastern Europe as well as the developmental sociology in non-European societies have been accompanied by a renaissance of the modernization paradigm (Bönker et al., 2002; Müller and Schmid, 1995; Dube, 1990).

In order to solve this dilemma, globalization theories – often inspired by Marxist and postmodernist counter-currents to the modernization paradigm – have promoted an alternative approach. In a critique of the nation-state framework of the modernization paradigm, the predominant globalization theories attempt to explain national phenomena primarily as a consequence of the growing impact of global forces or the emergent globality of the current world (Albrow, 1998; Beck, 1998; Loch and Heitmeyer, 2001). From that perspective, the main features of the modern age in the form of nation-states, national economies, cultures and societies are structurally transformed by the growing impact of economic global forces, transnational political structures and a global secular culture. As a consequence, the present worldwide revival of ethnic nationalism and religion, religious fundamentalism and religious nationalism is primarily seen as a defensive reaction against the forces of globalization or the emerging world system. Thus, the parallel global growth of nationalism and religion seems to be the general rule of the day, whereas the formation of civil and secular forms of nationalism as in western and particular Western European societies appears to be rather the exception.

From my own comparative, historical-sociological perspective, both macro-paradigms share a common methodological bias: they essentialize either the nation-state system or the global system and directly correlate within each unit political, socioeconomic and cultural phenomena and dimensions, instead of considering the local, national and transnational macro–micro linkages, relations and interactions (see in a similar critical direction, Arnason, 1990; Robertson, 1992). In such a one-sided system perspective, modernization theories falsely generalize from the Western European experience of secular nationalism in the modern era, instead of considering the varying religious foundations and components in Western and Eastern European nationalism. Inversely, globalization theories falsely generalize from the current phenomena of ethnic and religious nationalism in the non-western world, instead of considering the simultaneous phenomena of secular and civic forms of nationalism. In between, so to speak, I propose to analyse and explain the current growth of ethnic and religious nationalism particularly in the non-western world as the consequence of multiple forms of modernity, modernization and democratization (Eisenstadt, 1999a, 1999b, 2000; Knoebl, 2001; Spohn, 2001) in reaction to the former worldwide imposition of state secularism either by western liberal or eastern socialist regimes.

In the following, I would like to substantiate this historical and comparative sociological approach by (1) outlining a multiple modernity perspective on the relation between nationalism and religion; (2) reconsidering

European exceptionalism of secular nationalism; (3) exemplifying my approach to the rise of ethnic and religious nationalism in the non-European world; and (4) concluding with some summarizing remarks on the impact of globalization on the worldwide rise of ethnic and religious nationalism.

Multiple Modernity, Nationalism, Religion and Secularism

In light of the worldwide revival and strengthening of ethnic and religious nationalism, one basic premise of the conventional modernization paradigm has become particularly questionable: the assumption of the general and universalizing evolution of a civic and secular form of national integration, nationalism and national identity. In a nutshell, the modernization paradigm assumes that the modernization of traditional societies is constituted by a bundle of core processes such as nation-state formation, social differentiation, individualization, capitalist development, political democratization and secularization (Alexander, 1994; Müller and Schmid, 1995; Zapf, 1971). From that perspective, with the dissolution of ethnic communities and religion as constitutive for traditional societies through these modernization processes, national integration, nationalism and national identities in modern societies are shaped by civic and secular forms. Accordingly, the growing worldwide development of modernizing societies in the context of the present globalization processes should be accompanied by a parallel movement towards civic and secular forms of nationalism (Smith, 1975). This theoretical assumption seemed to hold for the spread of secular regimes in the previous decolonization period, but is no longer tenable for the present period of a global growth of ethnic and religious nationalism (Andrian and Apter, 1995).

An alternative solution to this theoretical dilemma is offered by globalization and world-system theories, rejecting the evolutionist and nation-state-centred premises of the modernization paradigm. Two main varieties of globalization and world-system approaches can be distinguished: globalization and globality as a consequence of modernity, on the one hand, and as a principal break with modernity, on the other. In the first version presented, for instance, in the globalization and world-system approaches of Michael Mann (1991) and John Meyer (1997), globalization is seen as a multidimensional generalization of the western model of modernity and, with it, the dissemination of the nation-state, capitalist production and the homogenization of national cultures. Here, the spread of ethnic and religious nationalism is seen as a part of the conflicting process of nation-state formation with a secular culture in the context of widespread multi-ethnic and religious cultures and low degrees of democratic pluralization. But similar to the modernization paradigm, the problem remains why the imposition of a state secular culture is accompanied by a rise rather than a decline of ethnic and religious nationalism.

In the second version as formulated for instance in the world-system theories of Niklas Luhmann (1984) and Immanuel Wallerstein (1999), the generalization and institutionalization of the western model on a global scale fundamentally change the conditions of each nation-state. In the world-system theory of Wallerstein or Chase-Dunn (1989), the present rise of ethnic and religious nationalism is seen as a political and cultural counter-reaction to the socioeconomic core–periphery hierarchy of the capitalist world system. In the version of the communicative world-system theory of Niklas Luhmann, developed particularly by Peter Beyer (1994), the main tendency is the development of social differentiation on a global scale, provoking as before in the western cases a counter-reaction of non-western religions against the segmentation of the religious realm. In both theoretical variants, however, the relationship between the world system and the many nation-states remains unclear and thus the question has to be put why in the present phase, and not before, a worldwide rise of ethnic and religious nationalism is occurring.

Another macro-sociological alternative I follow here in order to solve the theoretical dilemma of explaining the global rise of ethnic and religious nationalism in the contemporary period offers the concept of multiple modernity as developed particularly by Shmuel Eisenstadt's (1999a, 1999b, 2000) comparative civilizational approach. Here, the mainstream evolutionary premises of modernization, globalization and world-system theories that western modernity in the present period is generalizing and universalizing on a global scale are questioned. Instead, it is presupposed that western modernity is only one among other types of modernity evolving in the various civilizations of the world. The concept of multiple modernity thereby assumes that traditions are not simply dissolved by modernization or globalization, but rather that particularly religious and imperial traditions remain constitutive dimensions of modern societies. On the one hand, religious traditions either in the form of axial-age civilizations – a term taken from Karl Jaspers – such as Judaism, Christianity, Islam, Buddhism or Hinduism or in the form of non-axial age civilizations such as Japanese Shintoism or other particularistic religions are of crucial importance (Eisenstadt, 1987b, 1992a). On the other, the imperial traditions that often, but not always, combine with axial-age civilizations are of crucial importance (Eisenstadt, 1994). According to Eisenstadt, these religious and imperial traditions are reconstructed and shape, despite evolving processes of secularization and imperial decline, multiple programmes of modernity and multiple processes of modernization.

Regarding the contemporary global rise of ethnic and religious nationalism, the concept of multiple modernity has three major implications. First, in a parallel to the recent criticism of the widepread modernist approaches in nationalism research, it is assumed that not only political-civic, but also ethnic-primordial components remain constitutive dimensions of modern national identities and modern forms of nationalism (Smith, 1986, 1998). Instead of presupposing that, with the formation of modern nation-states the ethnic bases of national identity and nationalism are replaced by political and civic dimensions, it is assumed that ethnicity, though continually reconstituted and reconstructed, remains a crucial component of modern national identity and nationalism. Accordingly, the ideal-typical distinction between two basic types of nationalism, a political-civic western type and an ethnic-cultural eastern type, is problematic. Rather, national identities and nationalisms vary in their combinations of ethnic-primordial and political-civic components (Greenfield, 1998; Brubaker, 1998).

Second, the concept of multiple modernity, in a parallel to the recent criticism of the secularization thesis in the sociology of religion (Bruce, 1992; Casanova, 1994), presupposes that religion, despite the various forms of secularization, remains a constitutive basis of national identity and nationalism. In the recent sociology of religion, the modernization-*cum*-secularization thesis assuming an evolutionary decline and dissolution of religion by modernization processes has come increasingly under attack. Of course, it is not denied that, along with modernization in western societies, secularization processes in the form of the institutional separation between church and state, the decline of religious commitment and the development of secular culture have played a major role. At the same time, however, it has become evident that the secularization processes do not dissolve religion, but they develop in different patterns combining religious and secular components and proceed in oscillating movements of secularization and desecularization (Martin, 1978; Lehmann, 1997). Recent studies on the relation between religion, nation-building and nationalism have started to question the modernist assumption that nation-state formation and modern nationalism dissolve religion and religious identities by secular forms of national identity. Rather, religion and religious identities are transformed by nation-building and collective identity formation and remain a constitutive component of modern nations and national identity (Armstrong, 1982; Hastings, 1997; Hutchinson, 1996). Instead of assuming a general evolutionary trend towards secular nationalism or national identity, nationalisms and national identities combine in varying forms religious and secular components.

Third, the concept of multiple modernity assumes that in the contemporary global era an intensification of interactions between differing civilizations with varying combinations of ethnic, national, political, civic, religious and cultural components takes place. This assumption contrasts with the generalizing premise of a growing global dissemination and reproduction of the western model of the secular nation-state and nationalism as in the modernization versions of globalization theories, or the opposite generalizing premise of a growing ethnic and religious counter-reaction as in the world-system versions of globalization theories. Globalization processes are not to be seen simply as a growing dissemination and imposition of western market capitalism, democratic nation-state and secular culture, but rather as multiple, though hierarchical and uneven, encounters of varying types of modernities in their economic, political, religious and secular cultures on a global scale (Robertson, 1992). Western modernity and its globalizing dissemination are not simply coterminous with the universal model of secular modernity, but are shaped by specific forms of capitalism, democracy, predominantly Christian as well as Christian-based secular cultures. Non-western varieties of modernity are not simply an adaptation of non-western civilizations to western modernity, but an incorporation of western impacts and influences in non-western civilizational dynamics, programmes of modernity and modernization processes (Eisenstadt and Schluchter, 2000). As a consequence, an explanation of the contemporary global rise of ethnic and religious nationalism has to consider the internal dynamics as well as external forces of nation-state and national identity formation within the various civilizations on the globe.

Nationalism, Religion and Secularization in Europe

In a sense, the model of secular nationalism, as formulated in classical sociology and generalized in mainstream modernization theory, reflects the European experience of nation-building and nationalism or more precisely the French revolutionary form of a secular nation-state and nationalism, which served as a model for most modernizing European nation-states. The French model institutionalized the separation between church and state, the formation of a secular national culture as well as the privatization of religion and, on these foundations, French nation-state formation combined with a secular or laicist nationalism and national identity. Classical sociology recognized the structural affinity between religion and secular nationalism in their affective, symbolic and normative binding force and so interpreted nationalism as secular religion (Durkheim), substitute religion (Weber, Sombart) or ideology (Marx, Mannheim). In synthesizing classical European sociology, modernization theory then saw modern nationalism in the context of democratic nation-states as a form of secular national identity, though preserving as civil religion some remnants of religion.

This model of secular nationalism or secular national identity indeed grasps a variety of structural developments and features of European modernity. The modernization of European societies was accompanied by deepening processes of secularization: in institutional terms as a growing separation of state and church as well as in cultural terms as a general decline of church membership, religious practice and belief. These secularization processes went hand in hand with the formation of secular nation-states, secular institutions of education and socialization as well as secular national and civic cultures. At the same time, however, this secular model of national identity neglects or underrates the continuing importance of the religious foundations and components of modern nationalism and national identity in Europe (Baron, 1960; Davie and Hervieu-Léger, 1996; Davie, 2000). In all European cases, even in the French one, the church or churches remain important institutions and actors in the nation-state; religious cultures and values exert a continuous influence on national cultures; national and state symbols retain religious components; and national identities continue to entail not only secular and secular religious, but also religious forms of identification (Hastings, 1997). Accordingly, also in the European cases, national identity formation is characterized by religious–secular combinations rather than a mere replacement of religious by secular components.

The model of secular nationalism and national identity, in addition, neglects the considerable variations in the combinations of secular and religious components in European nationalism and national identity formation. In combining laicist with Catholic components, the French case of national identity formation has some structural similarities with other Catholic countries in Western and Southern Europe such as Spain, Portugal, Italy or Austria, though the weight of the secular components in these Catholic cases differs (Spohn, 2003). By contrast, the cultural construction of national identity in predominantly Protestant Great Britain has some structural similarity to other Protestant cases in Scandinavia in forming a rather pluralist Protestant national identity with a differing weight of secular components (Colley, 1994; McLeod, 1999; Soerensen and Strath, 1997). As well, confessionally mixed cases like Germany, the Netherlands or Switzerland integrate Protestant, Catholic and secular components in different configurations (Haupt and Langewiesche, 2001; Spohn, 2003). On the other side of the continent, most East Central, South Eastern and Eastern European countries were characterized in their pre-Communist phase by strong impacts of religion on national identity formation, then in their Communist phases by a rift between secularist and religious features and now in their post-Communist phase by a general restrengthening of the religious components (Spohn, 1998, 2002). A general evolutionary model of secular nationalism or national identity formation cannot account for these considerable variations in European modernity.

As an alternative theoretical approach to the religious–secular variations of national identity formation in Europe, the concept of multiple modernity starts from the specific features of the European civilization in a comparative-civilizational perspective (Eisenstadt, 1987a). Of crucial importance, here, are the general institutional and cultural foundations of the European civilization in the Roman empire and its adoption of Christianity and with the decline of the Roman empire and the expansion of Christianity, the formation of the structural and cultural pluralism of the European civilization. European structural pluralism, on the one hand, developed as a result of the political-institutional division of the Roman empire, its territorial relocation from the Mediterranean South to the continental North and its fragmentation into multiple political centres around aristocratically integrated ethnic groups. On this basis, multiple states and finally modern nation-states developed, but in different time zones of imperial decline and political centre formation. Following Stein Rokkan (Flora, 1999) and Ernest Gellner (1994), four main zones of state formation can be distinguished: the

Western European early organic, the Western Central European late unifying, the East Central European late-late peripheral and the Eastern empire contracting nation-state formation zone.

European cultural pluralism, on the other hand, was based on the Christian synthesis of Jewish, Greek-Hellenistic and pagan traditions and the differentiation of Christianity in different religious main types: Western Latin and Eastern Greek Christianity and again the subdivision of Western Christianity in Catholicism and Protestantism and Eastern Christianity in its Byzantine and Russian centres. Christianity formed a crucial general foundation, since the Middle Ages, of the evolving connection between political centre formation, ethnic community building and cultural-linguistic homogenization. First, Christianity contributed to the decline and disintegration of the Roman empire through the division between religious and secular power and its replication of this power division in the multiple political centres and its church institutions (Graubard, 1998). Second, Christianity provided with the Jewish-biblical concept of the chosen people the model for an ethnically based form of political community building (Hastings, 1997). Third, Christianity with its egalitarian-individualistic ethos as constitutive for the Protestant reformation but also developing in Catholicism and Orthodox Christianity was a major vehicle for the translation of the Latin and Greek Bible into vernacular languages and thus the cultural homogenization of nations (Hastings, 1997). On these foundations, national identities in Europe were generally shaped by Christianity, though in different institutional forms and cultural contents according to its main religious types.

These originally close relations between Christianity, ethnic groups, states and collective identities were then transformed with the development of the modern nation-state, the democratization of political regimes, the homogenization of national cultures, the change in state–church relations as well as the generation of secular cultures through the impact of enlightenment. However, these structural and cultural processes did not simply replace the Christian foundations of collective identities, rather they transformed the religious components and added secular components to collective identity formation (van der Veer and Lehmann, 1999). The evolving varying combinations of the religious and secular components in collective identity formation in Europe depended on the different secularization patterns in the main types of Christianity, on the one hand, and the main types of state formation, on the other.

Following David Martin's (1978; see also Casanova, 1994) general theory of secularization, I assume that the more pluralistic organized religion is, the less marked cultural secularization is, and inversely, the more monopolized organized religion is the more pronounced cultural secularization is. Accordingly, Protestant pluralism results in rather weak cultural secularization, though again with typical differences between the more pluralistic Calvinist and the more monopolistic variety. In this context, national identity formation is marked by a secularizing Protestant pluralism rather than laicist secularism. The Catholic monopoly leads to a strong secularist tendency, but with an organicist countermove. Here, national identity has to bridge this religious–secularist divide. The mixed pattern with predominant Protestantism and subdominant Catholicism results in an asymmetric secularization pattern: high in its Protestant part and low in its Catholic part. In this context, national identity has to bridge the Protestant and Catholic dualism as well as the religious–secularist divide. The Christian Orthodox caesaropapism is even more monopolistic than Catholicism, but more state-bound and with a higher tendency towards state secularism and lower societal secularism. National identity has here to bridge the religious and secularist cleavage.

At the same time, however, these various secularization patterns and their impact on the composition of national identities are modified in the different state formation zones. In the Western European zone of early organic nation-state formation, the formulated relations between secularization patterns and national identity appear in their purest form. The Protestant part of Great Britain and Scandinavia is characterized by a pluralizing Protestant, increasingly secular national identity, whereas the Catholic part of France, Spain and Portugal integrated in their national identities a sharp clerical–anticlerical divide combining strong secularist with weaker Catholic layers. In the Western Central zone of long-lasting imperial impacts and late unifying nation-state formation, the imperial component has an additional effect (Spohn, 2003). In the predominantly Protestant, but confessionally mixed case of Germany, national identity formation bridged the Catholic–Protestant and religious–secularist divide, resulting today in religious and secular components; whereas in the Catholic cases of Austria and Italy the Catholic–secularist divide has been weaker and the Catholic components stronger against the secularist components than in Western Europe.

In contrast to Western and Western Central Europe, the East Central European zone with peripheral, late-late nation-state formation lacked for a long time period independent statehood and state churches and therefore the secularization process as well as the religious–secularist division characteristic of monopolistic forms of organized religion were considerably weaker (Spohn, 1998, 2003). Already in the pre-Communist era, the various Christian religions were closely linked to peripheral nation-building, nationalism and national identity formation, whereas the secular and secularist components were much less influential. In the Communist period, a secularist ideocratic regime was established, partially superimposed from outside by the Soviet Communist empire, partially by domestic secularist-Communist elites. As a consequence, religion, nation-building and nationalism fused even more and hence the breakdown of Communism was characteristically accompanied by not only a revival of nationalism but also a strengthening of religion and religious nationalism (Ramet, 1998). In the Eastern European empire-contracting zone with tsarist Russia, finally, the evolving state reform of autocracy and imperial nationalism was connected with a strong anticlerical and secularist movement against Orthodox Christianity. On this basis, in the Soviet Union Marxist-Leninist ideocracy replaced Orthodox caesaropapism, yet this totalitarian state secularism was unable to promote also societal secularization. On the contrary, it provoked a strong religious and nationalist revival now breaking through in post-Soviet Russia (Stoelting, 1991; Spohn, 2002).

In sum, the evolutionary model of secular nationalism, as presupposed in mainstream modernization theory and renewed again as frame theory of post-Communist transformation research only partially corresponds to the varying constellations of nationalism, religion and secularization in Europe. As I argued, it neglects the religious, particularly Christian foundations of European ethnogenesis and nation-building, it also abstracts from the religious components of European modern nationalism and it overlooks its considerable variations in the religious and secular components. Only in contemporary Western Europe, though with limits and exceptions, are the secular layers in national identities progressing, but in varying constellations with Christian, Catholic or Protestant components and different Catholic and Protestant colours of secularity. In post-Communist Eastern Europe, by contrast, the religious, Catholic, Protestant and Orthodox components in national identity have been intensifying as a countermove to the previous Communist state secularism though again in varying secular–religious configurations. Of crucial importance for these varying constellations of nationalism, religion and secularism in Europe are the civilizational foundations, the forms of state formation, nation-building and democratization as well as the type of religion and the related secularization pattern.

Nationalism, Religion and Secularism in the Non-European World

The conceptualization of European modernity as a specific type of modernity with varying modernization constellations of national identity formation, religion and secularization also opens a comparative-civilizational perspective for the differing constellations of national identity formation in other civilizations and civilizational modernization contexts. From such a multiple modernity perspective, it is needed to analyse the specific modernization dynamics in the non-European civilizations; their imperial legacies and religious cores; the intra-civilizational forms of state formation, nation-building and democratization; the different forms of religious transformation and secularization; as well as the impacts on these civilizations through the interactions with European and western modernity in the eras of colonialism and postcolonialism. From this perspective, I argue that the present worldwide rise of ethnic and religious nationalism in non-European world regions is to be seen as a corollary of the global quest for national homogenization and democratization against the elite imposition of a secular (either western liberal or eastern socialist) nation-state model in predominantly multiethnic and religious, only partially pluralized and secularized societies. I confine myself in all superficial brevity to a comparative outline of this thesis.

I begin with the Americas, as historically formed settlement societies from predominantly European origins in largely destructive, but also reconstructive interactions with the ancient civilizations of indigenous peoples and with recently growing immigration from also non-European parts of the world. Against this background, North America and Latin America should not be seen as derivatives of western modernity either in a developed or a developing variety, but as specific civilizations with their own developmental dynamics and trajectories (Eisenstadt, 2000). In North America, the United States developed as the first nation on the British model of a Protestant pluralistic constitutional democracy, but broke with the traditions of the aristocratic monarchy and the established church (Lipset, 1996). British Protestant denominationalism and sectarianism became generalized, the evangelical-missionary components strengthened and state and religion separated (Martin, 1978; Casanova, 1994). Within this institutional-cultural framework, the rapidly growing immigrant populations with their different religious traditions, various types of Protestantism, then Catholicism, Judaism, recently also Islam and other world religions, followed this model of ethnically based denominational communities. As a result, institutional secularization has been very high, and cultural secularization very low. On these foundations, American nationalism developed within a multiethnic, multireligious, civic collective identity, though retaining generalized evangelical, civil-religious and civic-democratic features (Eisenstadt, 2000). In this context, the recent conspicuous rises of Protestant fundamentalism and African-American Islamism should be seen as intensifications of ethno-religious identities, but by no means as changes in the basic multireligious and civic form of American national identity.

In Latin America, by contrast, the historical frame conditions were created through the colonialization of the ancient American civilization by Spain and Portugal in a combination of formal state imperialism and the Catholic universal church (Burns, 1990; Wiarda, 1992). This close connection between state and church supported not only the development of oligarchic-authoritarian regimes, but also a high monopolization of organized religion and on these double bases one could expect a reproduction of the European Latin-Roman pattern of secularization with a strong secularism, an organicist reaction and a nationalism integrating this religious and secularist divide (Martin, 1991). This was also the case for the strongly liberal-secularist anti-colonial movements that led at the beginning of the 19th century to the formation of independent nation-states. However, three clusters of factors distinguish the formation of Latin American nationalisms in their religious and secularist components from the Catholic countries in Western and Southern Europe. First, the national independence movements were carried primarily by secularist elites, influencing only to a limited degree the middle and lower social classes (Wiarda, 1992). Second, under the roof of the postcolonial oligarchic regimes and the still powerful Catholic church and on the basis of growing multiethnic and multi-racial immigrant populations, the internal processes of state formation and nation-building remained weak. Under these institutional and social frame conditions, the processes of ethnic-religious pluralization throughout the 20th century were strong and those of cultural secularization remained weak. Certainly, the revolutions in Mexico, Nicaragua and Cuba established secularist regimes, but they were typically not able to secularize popular Catholicism (Levine, 1986). Instead, two major tendencies of religious pluralization evolved in the contemporary period: the differentiation of Catholicism by the impact of social-Catholic liberation theology and the conversion to evangelical Protestantism, in particular Pentecostalism (Beyer, 1994; Martin, 1991). On this basis, the Latin American authoritarian-populist road to democratization is connected with a more pluralistic-religious than secular process of national identity formation.

Whereas postcolonial nationalism and national identity formation in the Americas developed within two different Christian institutional and cultural frameworks, those in the Islamic civilization showed very different features. The Islamic civilization from North Africa, the Near and Middle East to Southern and South-East Asia came along with the economic, military and scientific rise of Europe under increasing pressure of the European colonial powers. As a result, the imperial centres in the Islamic civilization, the Ottoman, the Persian and Mogul empires declined and large parts of the Islamic civilization came under formal colonial rule particularly by France, Great Britain and Russia. In this context, anti-colonial and later, after independence, postcolonial nationalisms and national identities developed, oriented to the European models but crystallizing within the modernizing dynamics of the Islamic civilization (Lewis, 1968; Huff and Schluchter, 1999). Of particular importance here is the Ottoman-Turkish case as the most powerful imperial centre of the Islamic civilization (Lewis, 1968). As an empire-contracting nationalism, modern nationalism in Turkey shows some similarities to Russia, but differs as regards the Islamic components. In the declining Ottoman empire, there emerged a European-oriented modernization movement attempting to complement the Arabic high language with vernacular Turkish and to reform the Islamic legal structure and educational system in a western secular direction. With the breakdown of the Ottoman empire and the Kemalist revolution, the emerging Turkish nation-state combined with Turkish ethnic nationaliza-tion and secularist transformation of the legal and educational systems and banned Islam to the private sphere (Mardin, 1989). However, this state sec-ularism was imposed from above and had to be secured by the military not only against a more radical socialist secularism but also a growing religious politicization of Muslim society. In the context of a liberal-authoritarian regime and after the delegitimation of socialism, the present tendency is a continual strengthening of Islamic political currents, but in the direction of conservative-democratic parties rather than Islamic fundamentalism. Thus, with deepening participatory democracy, Turkish national identity is integrating a growing Islamic component into the hegemonic secularism (Bazdogan and Kasaba, 1997).

In contrast to the Ottoman-Turkish empire, the other parts of the Islamic civilization often became colonized by the European powers and differed therefore in the formation of postcolonial nation-states and emerging nationalisms. Originally, confronted with the success of the European model of the modern nation-state and its role as a reform model in the Ottoman empire, the emerging nationalism in the Islamic world was also shaped by secularist liberalism. However, with the colonial politics of the European colonial powers, liberal-secularist nationalism turned into a more radical anti-colonial secularist socialism. In the context of the East–West conflict, there emerged authoritarian socialist-secularist regimes with the support of the Soviet Union, on the one hand, and traditionalist-patrimonial regimes with the support of the United States and Western Europe, on the other (Keddie, 1969; Beinin and Stork, 1997). This elite secularism, carried by intellectuals educated either in the West or in the Soviet Union, became first challenged by a more radical western Marxism, but was replaced after its delegitimation by a growing political-nationalistic mobilization in various Muslim societies. Islamic nationalisms thereby oscillate between more pragmatic and more totalitarian orientations, but Islamicist fundamentalism has gained a growing influence (Al Azmeh, 1993). In this spectrum of rising religious nationalism, the Iranian Islamic revolution is rather the exception than the rule (Arjomand, 1993). So Iran, originally a separate imperial centre based on minority Shiism, was spared formal colonial rule and then combined an autocratic regime with a radical western liberal secularism. These conditions were favourable for the success of an Islamic nationalism establishing a constitutional-parliamentarian theocracy with growing liberalizing tendencies. But in most other cases, the authoritarian-secularist, either traditionalist or socialist regimes are increasingly challenged by rising Islamic nationalism with varying repression and incorporation policies. Therefore varying mixtures of secularist, Islamic and national identities within liberalizing authoritarian nation-states may be expected.

The Jewish civilization, as noted earlier, was the birthplace of the concept of a religious nation that through its transposition into Christianity became the religious foundation of nation-building and nationalism in Europe. Despite its dispersion all over the world, the Jewish diaspora was held together as a religious nation, but due to its diasporic existence, more in the sense of an ethnic-religious than national-religious community (Eisenstadt, 1992b). Modern Jewish nationalism or Zionism, in striving for and rebuilding a Jewish nation-state, was a reaction to modern European nationalism and its inability – either in its secularist or its cultural versions – to incorporate the Jewish community, as in the United States, in a religious pluralist framework. But Jewish nationalism, directed at the emancipatory, liberal and socialist currents of European enlightenment and rejecting the ethnic-religious legacy, was predominantly secular rather than religious. Only with the foundation of the state of Israel – after the Holocaust, the

immigration of non-European Jewry and the threat of Arab nationalism –
did religious currents in Jewish Zionism resurface and Judaism become
established as a privileged state religion (Eisenstadt, 1987c). As a reaction
to this monopolistic religious position or low institutional secularization,
however, the cultural secularization process in Israeli society has been
rather marked, despite the high internal religious diversity of Judaism. At
the same time, this Jewish state conception as well as the Arab nationalistic orientation of the Palestinian minority contributes to the radicalization
of the ethno-nationalistic conflict between the Jewish and Palestinian populations in Israel (Dieckhoff, 1998). In this context, the fundamentalist
currents on both sides gain more weight. But despite this, Israeli national
identity contains both civic-secular as well as diverse ethnic-religious
currents.

Whereas in Israel the Jewish and the Islamic civilization meet in a nationalistic stalemate, in Africa Christianity and Islam, in the context of postcolonial multiethnic states, are involved and often in conflictive ways in
multiple processes of nation-building and national identity formation
(Haynes, 1998). Except for the early existence of the Egyptian Coptic and
Ethiopian Orthodox churches, Christianity, more as Catholicism than
Protestantism, expanded in Africa as a result of European colonization and
missionary endeavours. Though the Catholic and Protestant churches were
closely linked to colonial regimes, Christianity became in large parts of
Central and Southern Africa indigenized, fusing with religious traditions
and shaping popular religiosity. Islam had already spread in pre-colonial
times in Northern and Central Africa and became, particularly in the form
of popular Sufism, newly invigorated as part of the anti-colonial, anti-
Christian movement. With the decolonization after the Second World War,
Christianity as well as Islam became an integral part of postcolonial nation-
state formation, since both religions were better prepared to bridge the
multiethnic divisions in the newly independent states than the particularist
ethno-religious traditions. Postcolonial states were predominantly authoritarian, either following the western liberal-secular or the eastern socialist-
secularist model. Although the Christian churches as well as Islamic
religious communities attempted to accommodate with these authoritarian
states, they formed an integral part of populist-democratic movements
against them. State secularism, therefore, did not translate into cultural
processes of secularization, rather it became increasingly confronted by
religious and populist-democratic forms of ethnic and national identities.
Again, however, the different religious forms of Christianity and Islam
mattered. In the case of Christianity, religious differentiation and pluralization are supporting processes of political liberalization and democratization (Comaroff and Comaroff, 1991; Marx, 1997). Such as in Latin America,
the spread of Protestant sects, particularly Pentecostalism, is important
(Martin, 1999). In the case of Islam, Islamicist fundamentalist movements
have become more influential, aiming at the institutionalization of religious
law and theocratic government (Haynes, 1998). In the multiethnic setting of

most states, the strengthening of religious identities often goes hand in hand with an intensification of ethnic identities rather than with the formation of an overarching religious and pluralist national identity. Particularly conflicting are those cases where Christianity and Islam encounter each other in the same state.

The Indian civilization is characterized, similar to the European civilization, by a cultural pluralism of universalist religions (Eisenstadt, 1987a). Apart from predominating Hinduism, Buddhism was first to gain influence, then Jainism and Bhagavata, later Islam and finally Christianity as part of European and particularly British colonialism. A structural pluralism was typical, but the political development until the formal establishment of British imperial rule was characterized by centralization rather than fragmentation. In a sense, British colonial rule finalized Indian empire-building, though Indian dependence was accompanied by the division of British India in the Indian Union and Pakistan on the cultural foundation of the two dominant religions, Hinduism and Islam. The independence movement under Gandhi had still been characterized by religious pluralism under the roof of a secular-civic conception of the state. After independence, an increasingly closer relation between nationalism and religion developed, in India with Hinduism and in Pakistan with Islam (van der Veer, 1996, 2001). The development of nationally oriented religions and religious nationalism played a particular role in this cultural transformation of the two universalist religious traditions of Hinduism and Islam. As Peter van der Veer (van der Veer and Lehmann, 1999; van der Veer, 2001) has demonstrated, this cultural transformation was due to the impact of British Protestantism, particularly in its Methodist-evangelical variety, on the Indian elites, the anti-colonial nationalist movement and the reconstruction of Hinduism and Islam. As a consequence, after independence, in both states evolved a growing pressure on religious nationalism towards religious-national homogenization and, with it, an intensification of the conflicts between both nations. Certainly, in India as well as in Pakistan, secular-pluralist elite nationalism remains hegemonic, but at the same time, on both sides, it is increasingly challenged by popular religious nationalism.

Finally, some remarks on religion and nationalism in Eastern Asia, China and Japan. The Chinese axial-age civilization developed on the basis of the oldest and most long-lasting ancient empires and was shaped by three major religious traditions: Confucianism, Taoism and Buddhism (Eisenstadt, 1994). The decline of this ancient empire began with the rising impact of European colonial rule that also combined with an increasing expansion and influence of Christianity and enlightenment. The Chinese anti-colonial revolutions followed the western model of the secular nation-state, first, in a liberal-secular version, and then, under the influence of Marxism-Leninism, in a socialist-secularist version. The foundation of the People's Republic of China not only reconstructed the empire, but also institutionalized Maoist ideocracy, suppressing the Chinese religious traditions as superstition. But after the self-inflicted catastrophe of the Cultural

Revolution in Communist China and along with the increasing impacts of economic modernization, a new quest of meaning emerges, a renewal of religious traditions, particularly of Buddhism and Confucianism as well as a revitalized expansion of Christianity (Weiming, 1999). Thus, Communist ideocracy is transformed into an imperial-secular roof allowing for an increasing religious pluralism. In contrast, the Japanese non-axial civilization, due to its insular condition and national homogeneity, was able to preserve its sovereignty in the face of the European colonial powers. Its religious core was not structured by a universalist religion, but rather by a syncretistic combination of Buddhism and Confucianism with its own particularistic tradition of Shintoism. But, as Shmuel Eisenstadt (1996) has argued, it was precisely this combination of state autonomy, homogeneous nation-building and particularistic religious tradition that enabled Japan to incorporate selectively the western modernization model and to embark on a self-defined modernization path. As a consequence, Tokugawa religion with its neo-Confucianist ethic, Shintoist symbolism and Buddhist legitimization of the emperor remained an integral component of the modern Japanese state and national identity (Bellah, 1964). Certainly, after the defeat of Japanese militarism, the American model of liberal democracy and secularism came to be imposed, but this state secularism is not co-terminous with a western form of institutional and cultural secularization. On the contrary, despite the emergence of some more radical religious-sectarian and secular-Marxist currents, Japanese national identity remains predominantly defined by its own particularistic religious traditions (Arnason, 1987; Robertson, 1992).

Conclusion

In a *tour d'horizon* through the various world civilizations and regions I have tried to substantiate the general argument that the contemporary global rise of nationalism and religion, often in a combined form of religious national-ism, has to be seen as a reaction to the previous authoritarian imposition of the Western European model of state secularism – either in its western liberal or eastern socialist variety – in differing civilizations with predominantly religious and often multiethnic societies. This global intensification of religious and ethnic nationalism cannot be interpreted, as the mainstream modernization paradigm is tempted to assume, as a transitional phase to the western model of civic and secular national identity formation. Nor can it simply be seen as a general defensive reaction of non-western societies to the intensifying forces of western-dominated forms of economic, political and secular-cultural globalization. Rather, as I have tried to demonstrate, the contemporary rise of religious and ethnic nationalism is part of multiple modernization processes in different world regions, multiple constellations of nation-state formation and democratization as well as religious change and secularization in different civilizations in the present global era.

From this multiple modernity perspective, the European form of civic and secular nationalism and national identity formation as the model for the modernization paradigm and political modernizers is indeed exceptional, but at the same time, it has to be specified in its religious foundations and religious components. As indicated, even the most secularized Western European types of national identity are generally based on Christian foundations and shaped by the specific nationally predominating form(s) of Christianity. In this sense, they have to be seen as specific combinations of religious as well as secular components rather than as variations of a general secular model of nationalism and national identity. From that perspective, the alter ego of the western model, the American one, is characterized by a quite different form of a generalized religious, civic national identity in the context of a multiethnic and multireligious immigrant society. Conversely, the Eastern European imitations of the Western European model are characterized by different forms of peripheral and empire-contracting nationalisms with stronger religious components that, after the imposition of an atheist ideocracy, resurface in the current post-Communist phase.

In other civilizations and world regions, there has been, along with processes of modernization and often decolonialization, a general evolution towards state formation and nation-building, but on substantially divergent religious and often multiethnic foundations: in Latin America predominantly liberal democracies and temporarily authoritarian regimes combined with oligarchic elites and monopolistic Catholic churches in multiethnic immigration societies; in the Islamic civilization, strongly authoritarian states with secular regimes in a western liberal and eastern socialist variety dominated the scene on the foundations of traditionally religious and often multiethnic societies. In the civic-liberal but not fully secularized state of Israel, the Jewish civilization is in a fundamental nationalistic conflict with the Palestinian Muslim minority. In Africa, Islam and Christianity represent crucial and sometimes conflicting religious forces in the cultural homogenization in multiethnic postcolonial states. In India and Pakistan, civic but religiously pluralistic nation-states emerged from colonial British India, but with strong tendencies on both sides towards an exclusive Hindu and Muslim national identity. In China, an imperial nation with a Marxist ideocracy superimposes a multiethnic society with Confucian, Taoist, Buddhist and Christian traditions, whereas in Japan a civic-secular democracy incorporates the Confucian, Buddhist and Shintoist traditions. In a gross generalization, in all these non-European and non-western cases, modernization, state formation and nation-building combined with an authoritarian imposition either of liberal-secular or socialist-secular regimes. Thus, the continuing search and struggle for liberalization and democratization on a global scale is mostly directed against authoritarian state secularism by mobilizing religious and often ethnic identities. This is the major cause of the intensification of religious and ethnic nationalisms all over the world.

In these multiple constellations of modernization and democratization connected to the mobilization of religious and ethnic nationalisms in their pluralistic as well as fundamentalist varieties, the contemporary intensification of global forces plays an important role. In all parts of the world, they intensify interactions as well as conflicts between different civilizations, religions and secular cultures. However, it would be misleading, as the westernization versions of globalization theory tend to assume, to see the global rise of religious and ethnic nationalism only as an anti-modern, transitional phase on the road to a western civic-secular type of national identity. It would as well be misleading, as the postmodernist and world-system versions of globalization theory presuppose, to interpret the global rise of religious and ethnic nationalism as an anti-global, anti-western defence of threatened traditional societies with their religious and ethnic identities. Rather, as I have tried to demonstrate, it should be seen as a phase-specific result of the democratic, liberalizing and often populist contestation of authoritarian-secular regimes in the context of processes of state-formation and nation-building in non-European societies and their own multiple forms of modernity and paths of modernization.

Bibliography

Al Azmeh, Aziz (1993) *Islam(s) and Modernities.* London: Verso.

Albrow, Martin (1998) *Abschied vom Nationalstaat.* Frankfurt am Main: Suhrkamp.

Alexander, Jeffrey (1994) 'Modern, Anti, Post, and Neo: How Sociological Theories have Tried to Understand the "New World" of "Our Times" ', *Zeitschrift für Soziologie* 23(1): 1–28.

Andrian, Charles and Apter, David (1995) *Political Protest and Social Change.* New York: New York University Press.

Arjomand, Saïd, ed. (1993) *The Political Dimension of Religion.* New York: SUNY Press.

Armstrong, John (1982) *Nations before Nationalism.* London: Routledge.

Arnason, Johann (1987) 'The Modern Constellation and the Japanese Enigma', *Thesis Eleven* 17(1): 4–40.

Arnason, Johann (1990) 'Nationalism, Globalization and Modernity', in Mike Featherstone (ed.) *Global Culture*, pp. 185–204. London: Sage.

Baron, Salo (1960) *Modern Nationalism and Religion.* London: Macmillan.

Bazdogan, Serif and Kasaba, Resat, eds (1997) *Rethinking Modernity and National Identity in Turkey.* Seattle: University of Washington Press.

Beck, Ulrich (1998) *Was ist Globalisierung?* Frankfurt am Main: Suhrkamp.

Beinin, Joel and Stork, Joe (1997) *Political Islam.* Los Angeles: University of California Press.

Bellah, Robert (1964) *Tokugawa Religion.* Glencoe, IL: Free Press.

Beyer, Peter (1994) *Religion and Globalization.* London: Sage.

Bielefeldt, Heiner and Heitmeyer, Wolfgang, eds (1998) *Politisierte Religion.* Frankfurt am Main: Suhrkamp.

Bönker, Frank, Müller, Klaus and Pickel, Andreas, eds (2002) *Postcommunist Transformation and the Social Sciences: Cross-Disciplinary Approaches.* Lanham, MD: Rowman and Littlefield.

Brubaker, Rogers (1998) 'The Manichean Myth: Rethinking the Distinction between "Civic" and "Ethnic" Nationalism', in Hans-Peter Kriesi, Klaus Armingeon, Hannes Siegrist and Andreas Wimmer (eds) *Nation and National Identity: The European Experience in Comparison*, pp. 55–72. Zurich: Rügger.

Bruce, Steve, ed. (1992) *Religion and Modernization.* London: Routledge.

Burns, Bruce (1990) *Latin America.* Englewood Cliffs, NJ: Prentice Hall.

Casanova, José (1994) *Public Religion in the Modern World*. Chicago, IL: Chicago University Press.

Chase-Dunn, Christopher (1989) *Global Formation*. Oxford: Oxford University Press.

Colley, Linda (1994) *Britons: Forging the Nation, 1707–1834*. New Haven, CT: Berg.

Comaroff, Joan and Comaroff, Jane (1991) *Of Revolution and Revelation*. Cambridge, MA: Cambridge University Press.

Davie, Grace (2000) *Religion in Modern Europe*. Oxford: Oxford University Press.

Davie, Grace and Hervieu-Léger, Danièle, eds (1996) *Les Identités religieuses en Europe*. Paris: La Découverte.

Dieckhoff, Alain (1998) 'Israel: The Pluralization of a National Identity', in Hans-Peter Kriesi, Klaus Armingeon, Hannes Siegrist and Andreas Wimmer (eds) *Nations and National Identity: The European Experience in Comparison*, pp. 217–34. Zurich: Rügger.

Dube, So (1990) *Modernization and Development: The Search for an Alternative Paradigm*. London: Sage.

Eisenstadt, Shmuel Noah (1987a) *The European Civilization in Comparative Perspective*. Oslo: Scandinavian University Press.

Eisenstadt, Shmuel Noah, ed. (1987b) *Kulturen der Achsenzeit* I. Frankfurt am Main: Suhrkamp.

Eisenstadt, Shmuel Noah (1987c) *Die Transformation Israels*. Frankfurt am Main: Suhrkamp.

Eisenstadt, Shmuel Noah, ed. (1992a) *Kulturen der Achsenzeit* II. Frankfurt am Main: Suhrkamp.

Eisenstadt, Shmuel Noah (1992b) *The Jewish Civilization: The Jewish Historical Experience in Comparative Perspective*. New York: SUNY Press.

Eisenstadt, Shmuel Noah (1994) *The Political System of Empires*. New Brunswick, NJ: Transaction.

Eisenstadt, Shmuel Noah (1996) *The Japanese Civilization: A Comparative View*. Chicago, IL: Chicago University Press.

Eisenstadt, Shmuel Noah (1999a) *Fundamentalism, Sectarianism, and Revolution: The Jacobin Dimension of Modernity*. Cambridge, MA: Cambridge University Press.

Eisenstadt, Shmuel Noah (1999b) *The Paradoxes of Democracy*. Baltimore, MD: The Johns Hopkins University Press.

Eisenstadt, Shmuel Noah (2000) *Die Vielfalt der Moderne*. Weilerswist: Velbrück Wissenschaft.

Eisenstadt, Shmuel Noah and Schluchter, Wolfgang, eds (2000) *Early Modernities*. Daedalus.

Flora, Peter (1999) *Die Theorie Stein Rokkans*. Frankfurt am Main: Suhrkamp.

Gellner, Ernest (1994) *Civil Liberties*. London: Penguin.

Graubard, Stephen, ed. (1998) 'Early Modernities', *Daedalus* 127(3).

Greenfeld, Liah (1998) 'Is Nation Unavoidable? Is Nation Unavoidable Today?', in Hans-Peter Kriesi, Klaus Armingeon, Hannes Siegrist and Andreas Wimmer (eds) *Nations and National Identity: The European Experience in Comparison*, pp. 37–54. Zurich: Rügger.

Hastings, Adrian (1997) *The Construction of Nationhood: Ethnicity, Religion and Nationalism*. Cambridge, MA: Cambridge University Press.

Haupt, Gerhard and Langewiesche, Dieter, eds (2001) *Nation und Religion in der deutschen Geschichte*. Frankfurt am Main: Campus.

Haynes, Jeff (1998) *Religion and Global Politics*. London: Longman.

Huff, Toby and Schluchter, Wolfgang, eds (1999) *Max Weber and Islam*. New Brunswick, NJ: Transaction.

Huntington, Samuel (1996) *The Clash of Civilizations*. New York: Simon and Schuster.

Hutchinson, John (1996) *Modern Nationalism*. London: Routledge.

Jürgensmeyer, Mark (1993) *The New Cold War? Religious Nationalism Confronts the Secular State*. Cambridge, MA: Cambridge University Press.

Keddie, Nikki (1969) 'Pan-Islam as Proto-Nationalism', *Journal of Modern History* 41(2): 17–28.

Knoebl, Wolfgang (2001) *Spielräume der Modernisierung*. Weilerswist: Velbrück Wissenschaft.

Lehmann, Hartmut, ed. (1997) *Christianisierung, Dechristianisierung, Rechristianisierung*. Goettingen: Vandenhoek und Ruprecht.

Levine, David, ed. (1986) *Religion and Political Conflict in Latin America.* Chapel Hill, NC: Duke University Press.

Lewis, Bernhard (1968) *The Emergence of Modern Turkey.* Oxford: Oxford University Press.

Lipset, Seymour Martin (1996) *American Exceptionalism.* New York: Norton.

Loch, Dieter and Heitmeyer, Wolfgang, eds (2001) *Schattenseiten der Globalisierung.* Frankfurt am Main: Suhrkamp.

Luhmann, Niklas (1984) *Religion und Gesellschaft.* Frankfurt am Main: Suhrkamp.

McLeod, Hugh (1999) 'Protestantism and British National Identity, 1815–1945', in Peter van der Veer and Hartmut Lehmann (eds) *Nation and Religion: Perspectives on Europe and Asia*, pp. 44–70. Princeton, NJ: Princeton University Press.

Mann, Michael (1991) 'The Nation-State. Developing, Diversifying, Not Dying', in *States and Wars*, pp. 156–83. London: Macmillan.

Mardin, Serif (1989) *Religion and Social Change in Modern Turkey.* Oxford: Oxford University Press.

Martin, David (1978) *A General Theory of Secularization.* Oxford: Oxford University Press.

Martin, David (1991) *Tongues of Fire.* Princeton, NJ: Princeton University Press.

Martin, David (1999) 'The Evangelical Protestant Upsurge and its Political Implications', in Peter Berger (ed.) *The Desecularization of the World*, pp. 37–50. Grand Rapids, MI: Erdman.

Marty, Martin and Appleby, Scott, eds (1987) *Fundamentalisms Observed.* Chicago, IL: Chicago University Press.

Marx, Anthony (1997) *States, Nations and Race.* Cambridge, MA: Cambridge University Press.

Meyer, John (1997) 'The Changing Cultural Content of the Nation-State: A World Society Perspective', in George Steinmetz (ed.) *State and Culture*, pp. 123–44. Ithaca, NY: Cornell University Press.

Müller, Hans-Peter and Schmid, Max, eds (1995) *Sozialer Wandel.* Frankfurt am Main: Suhrkamp.

Müller, Heiner (2001) *Das Zusammenleben der Kulturen.* Frankfurt am Main: Suhrkamp.

Pollack, Detlef, Borowik, Irena and Jagodzinski, Wolfgang, eds (1998) *Religiöser Wandel in den postkommunistischen Ländern Ost- und Mitteleuropas.* Würzburg: Econ.

Ramet, Sabrina (1998) *Nihil Obstat.* Boulder, CO: Westview Press.

Robertson, Roland (1992) *Globalization.* London: Sage.

Smith, Anthony (1986) *Ethnic Origins of Nations.* Cambridge, MA: Cambridge University Press.

Smith, Anthony (1998) *Nationalism and Modernism.* London: Routledge.

Smith, Donald (1975) *Religion and Political Modernization.* London: Routledge.

Soerensen, Oystein and Strath, Bo, eds (1997) *The Construction of Norden.* Oslo: Scandinavian University Press.

Spohn, Willfried (1998) 'Religion und Nationalismus. Osteuropa im westeuropäischen Vergleich', in Detlef Pollack, Irena Borowik and Wolfgang Jagodzinski (eds) *Religiöser Wandel in den postkommunistischen Ländern Ost- und Mitteleuropas*, pp. 87–120. Würzburg: Econ.

Spohn, Willfried (2001) 'Eisenstadt on Civilizations and Multiple Modernity', *European Journal of Social Theory* 4(4): 499–508.

Spohn, Willfried (2002) 'Transformation Process, Modernization Patterns, and Collective Identities: Democratization, Religion and Nationalism in Germany, Poland and Russia', in Frank Bönker, Klaus Müller and Andreas Pickel (eds) *Postcommunist Transformation and the Social Sciences: Cross-Disciplinary Approaches*, pp. 199–218. Lanham, MD: Rowman and Littlefield.

Spohn, Willfried (2003) 'Nationalismus und Religion. Ein historisch-soziologischer Vergleich West- und Osteuropas', *Politische Vierteljahresschrift.*

Stoelting, Erhard (1991) *Nationalitäten und Religionen in der UdSSR.* Berlin: Elefant.

Van der Veer, Peter (1996) *Religious Nationalism: Hindus and Muslims in India.* Princeton, NJ: Princeton University Press.

Van der Veer, Peter (2001) *Imperial Encounters: Religion and Modernity in India and Britain.* Princeton, NJ: Princeton University Press.

Van der Veer, Peter and Lehmann, Hartmut, eds (1999) *Nation and Religion: Perspectives on Europe and Asia*. Princeton, NJ: Princeton University Press.

Wallerstein, Immanuel (1999) *The Essential Wallerstein*. Washington, DC: American Press.

Weiming, Tu (1999) 'The Quest for Meaning. Religion in the People's Republic of China', in Peter Berger (ed.) *The Desecularization of the World*, pp. 85–102. Grand Rapids, MN: Erdman.

Wiarda, Howard, ed. (1992) *Politics and Social Change in Latin America*. Boulder, CO: Westview Press.

Zapf, Wolfgang, ed. (1971) *Die Theorien der Modernisierung*. Cologne: Kiepenheuer.

6

Structural Change in Western Africa as a Legacy of European Colonialism: The Labour System in Ghana and the Ivory Coast

Ulrike Schuerkens

Introduction

Since the 1960s, the phenomenon of social change in the countries of the South has been a particular discussion topic of social scientists. A great variety of approaches can be found. These approaches began in the 1960s with the theories of modernization of Anglo-Saxon origin. In the 1970s, the theories of dependency followed, developed by intellectuals from Latin America. During the same period, theories of structural change and a structural-functionalist approach were developed. In the 1980s, theories began to refer to disconnection or endogenous development, as developed by UNESCO.

Today, it seems that this research situation needs a more profound approach, which takes into account current theoretical and empirical levels of the social sciences. Previous research has shown that progress in this research field can only be obtained when more general aspects and preferably theoretical aspects are tackled.[1] It seems interesting to concentrate one's approach on the concepts of structure and time, and to analyse their relevance for the countries of the South.

If we examine the temporal and structural aspects of development, we have to ask if a general structure of development exists in the South, and in particular, in Africa south of the Sahara. One of our fundamental hypotheses is to emphasize the internationalization of some structures, the more or less conscious acceptance of western models or parts of them by large groups in Africa south of the Sahara. In these countries, this meant the mixture between autochthonous models and one or more models crossing national frontiers. Colonization – interpreted according to an interactive understanding – had an important influence on the structural change of the autochthonous social systems, which had contact with different colonial powers since the end of the 19th century. Change induced by various colonial politics consisted of introducing a formal educational system, paid labour and a bureaucratic system. Despite great differences between autochthonous groups, we can today find elites who support a rather identical development in their own respective countries. Although colonial interventions came from outside the different countries, changes of the autochthonous societies had to be adapted to this model originating from another social system which had had an increasing influence since the beginning of the 20th century. The integration of different elements from this system with those of the autochthonous societies happened slowly and gradually. Today, no groups remain which are not influenced by structures of western models. The sort of change which occurred was dependent on the different autochthonous systems. These societies resisted in different ways and/or changed important aspects of their social systems necessary for their survival, despite the growing influence of the predominant model of development. At the same time, these autochthonous societies let very different cultural models inside their particular societies coexist; models which maintained and maintain ambivalent links with social structures imposed from outside national societies.

At this point, the element *time* becomes an instrument for the analysis of changes which took place in these societies. The transformation of a social system never concerns all elements at the same time: several elements change in the initial phase, and force other elements to change until the emergence of another structural model can be observed. In the case study presented in this article, we find a social structure which seems to be characteristic of the development of the societies of the South. Since the 1940s, Africa south of the Sahara has been living this structural change with more or less intensity according to social systems or groups. Thus, the problem of social change is linked to an analysis which concerns the interaction of two rather different cultural systems since the beginning of the 20th century, and, at the same time, the factor *time* allows the explanation of numerous phenomena resulting from this interaction.

Such an approach requires the utilization of other research methods. In order to illustrate the disharmonies and frictions within African societies, it seems important to consider elements which result from the interaction of these societies with western societies. The first analyses in this direction have been done,[2] but they are still marginal, and, above all, they do not represent detailed studies of the problem, because of the fact that they examine either the change of the autochthonous society, or the problem, without looking for a theoretical explanation. If we maintain that the interaction of African societies with societies of western culture led to the emergence of a new type of social system, despite the strong influences of former colonial powers, we are constrained to analyse this development by observing relevant development policies and the change of autochthonous societies.

I think it makes sense to examine the sort of interaction which took place between individuals, groups and societal structures in a process of structural change. In this case, individual life-stories can be considered to be the expression of a conflict between two structures.[3] During the interaction which took place in the colonial period, two different social systems confronted one another. Actions were related to two concepts of society. They reflected frictions and disharmonies between different value systems. An analysis of change underlines the fact that, at a particular moment, a given structure no longer represents a value system which can be accepted. This structure may no longer be adapted to social reality. If, furthermore, the way of reproduction of actions changes, structures which are no longer advantageous become problematic and have to be changed.

During the analysis of transformation processes of societies and, in particular, processes linked to colonization, this phenomenon can be observed in an astonishing way. Colonization – considered as a gradual process of change, and as the development project of a powerful group – brought about, in a rather short period of time, a fundamental restructuration of social systems of African societies. In particular, French colonization can be considered as an example of such processes of transformation. The systematic introduction of an economic, political, social and cultural system different from those of the African societies, implied that the colonial powers succeeded in introducing their structures and in reaching their objectives.

An analysis of social change which took place inside the African groups has to consider the influence of the western culture on these social systems, and the phenomenon of social change resulting from the interaction between both. This analysis is rather complex and surpasses theories of modernization, which privilege a development in direction of the western model without considering particular elements of a given society. Furthermore, it surpasses dependency theories, which tried to explain this change by the external influence of an uneven economic world system. Only an analysis which takes into account these three dimensions will show the social relations and the particular character of change during the colonial period and its effects on actual processes of change.

In general, social scientists using this approach consider reasons, forms and possible directions of social change. They reflect on the interest of society's members to assemble knowledge about past, present and future by taking into consideration the fact that it is nearly impossible to explain history completely or to make more than general predictions of future events.

Change can be found and analysed in rather limited groups, in processes of transformation, which are of varying lengths and of varying character, and, if the factor *time* is considered, as short- or long-term change or as continuous or non-continuous change. The sociological explanation of change is related to the structure which changes and to elements which cause this change. The analysis of social change tries to show conditions and factors which cause the movement of a society from one particular situation to another.

Two problems can be found here. On the one hand, elements must be established which are at the origin of change, and, on the other, original and final situations of transformation processes must be characterized. To tackle transformations means that the sociologist or the social anthropologist has to consider all aspects of a social system which form a given structure, mechanisms of selection for different actions and the possibility of resulting actions.

Processes may be represented by unique structural characteristics which structure a sequence of events. A social process can only be explained and characterized by the isolation of significant elements which form a given structure, and by an analysis of their relations.[4] A particular moment of a transformation process can be demonstrated by linking several elements and their mutual relations. The change of a given structure or the appearance of two different structures represents various periods of social history. Without the concept of structure, social processes and history in its particular aspect of development cannot be understood.

The approach of Teune and Mlinar,[5] which has influenced my research, tried to include these aspects in a theory of social change. Because of the fact that this conceptual model can be considered as a heuristic framework, I present in the following paragraphs some of its important aspects. Both scholars underline that they present a theory which takes into consideration societies of the South and the North, their past, their present and their future. According to them, development is a characteristic element of all social systems. It is defined by a growing diversity of systemic components, and a further integration of these or other components. Social development takes place between the poles of diversity and integration: the extreme point of integration means that the stability of different components of a system is so high that a continuous development, because of the rigidity of the structure, is no longer possible. The development of a system depends on the interaction between *diversity* and *integration*, which indicates the particular situation of the social system.

According to the authors, *integration* is the degree of probability of a change of characteristics of a specific system, which is caused by the change of its elements (Teune and Mlinar, 1978: 43). *Diversity* as a structural particularity of a system can be deduced from the distribution of the characteristics of a system's elements (Teune and Mlinar, 1978: 35). This is the stage of non-identity of the system characteristics. Thus, social development is a process which links the levels of *integration* and *diversity* (Teune and Mlinar, 1978: 44). The growth of these levels means the direction of social development. However, possibilities of disintegration or stagnancy are not excluded.

The transformation of a system happens at the moment when the system has attained its limits of *diversity* and *integration*. Then, a new principle of integration of a society appears, which, at the same time, represents a transformation of the system and its characteristic structures.[6] Furthermore, the degree of development depends on the quantity of system elements, which means that a higher variability of system elements permits a larger systemic change. This process can be imagined in the following way: at a particular instant, a new element is introduced; this element raises the diversity of the system, but reduces its level of integration; different components of the system accept the new element. The probability that a new element is produced accrues. The process which I describe here begins a new cycle with the creation of another element (Teune and Mlinar, 1978: 72). Therefore, each new element reduces the degree of system integration and raises, at the same time, the total number of its elements. The new element has to be integrated in the system. During this movement, it changes the links between the different elements. The degree of integration rises according to the degree of development of the system (Teune and Mlinar, 1978: 74ff.).

The Concept of Time and the Analysis of Social Change

When we return to the conceptual scheme of evolution,[7] we find that the development which took place during the colonial period was conceived by making use of evolutionary ideas. The procedure of France is interesting insofar as this country believed in a development in the direction of a particular model. It is evident that this sort of development led in the decades of French colonization to frictions, breakups and anomic situations. Forty years after the rapid decolonization of most of the countries of Africa south of the Sahara, it is agreed that this development follows a westernization pattern (Godelier, 1995: 169, 175), without the disappearance of certain cultural elements of African groups. The problem which has now to be tackled is the urgent duty to describe this sort of development, which was conceived and practised by countries such as France and Great Britain, and its unforeseeable effects, which were caused by elements of the cultures of the African groups interacting with western models. Today, the question is no longer to find possible ways of development, but actual tendencies must be emphasized, and secondary effects must be analysed.

In the case of countries of the South, these transformations were introduced by different colonial powers. The creation of a difference came from outside the social systems of African groups and had to be incorporated in existing social systems. These processes were undertaken with the aim to begin a transformation process, which started during the colonial period and could no longer be reversed some decades later. If one takes into consideration that the societies of Africa south of the Sahara were confronted with societal structures very different from their own structures, one can imagine the effort made in order to maintain social functions of values originating from two cultural systems, which referred to different social structures. The resulting disharmonies and frictions find their expression in what we now call development problems.

Consequences for the Research on Social Change

This more or less theoretical discussion obliges me to insist on several necessary elements of an analysis of processes of social change which the countries of the South have been living through. It seems to me that an analysis which uses concepts of the approaches of the 1960s through to the 1990s is no longer possible (Schuerkens, 1995a). My approach demonstrates that we have to reconsider the concept of structure, and, in particular, the transformation of a structure during a given time period. In the case of societies of the South – at least a large part of Francophone and Anglophone Africa south of the Sahara – this means that changes which take place can only be explained by the interaction of two very different societal structures since the beginning of the colonial period. In this situation, it is evident that the structures of dominant groups could be accepted more easily. However, they confronted the social structures of African groups. In the earlier years, until the 1940s, the coexistence of these two structures was possible despite their differences. Since the 1940s, the dominant structures of the model originating from outside the African social systems were implanted. They met with autochthonous structures, which had to react. In the early part of the colonial period, the survival of these social systems could often be noted. Actors ignored that some social elements had less and less influence, or even that these elements prevented a 'normal' functioning of social systems (Schuerkens, 2001a). When these disharmonies became obvious, scholars and development experts began to speak about breakups and underdevelopment. However, these concepts can rarely explain real situations. They indicate facts, without clarifying reasons.

I have shown so far that the issue of development has to be tackled alongside other concepts in order to explain problems, to see their origins and to suggest possible outcomes which would help to overcome situations often considered as dramatic. This means that we have to consider African cultures and their influences on a development which can no longer be conceptualized as if it could be reversed. This change should permit African societies to develop harmoniously while accepting structures introduced from outside their social systems.

In this sense, I underline the diversity of possible developments and the universality of some structures which met with the social structures of African groups. The diversity of a transformation is realized at a particular point, originating from the acceptance of, the desire for, or the refusal of an interaction. However, the actual multiplicity of cultures does not mean the same variety of development. Change in an interactive world has to accept local particularities, but should not be reversed to emphasize, for instance, the authenticity of a particular culture. Multiculturalism will continue all over the world. Yet, the actual tendency is one of an existing universality, which is difficult to demonstrate because of large local differences.

The Glocalization of the Labour System in Ghana and the Ivory Coast

In this part of my article, I show how social transformations introduced by the former colonial powers Britain and France have interacted with local African structures in Ghana and the Ivory Coast since the 1950s. I demonstrate that the autochthonous systems slowly changed because of contacts between different structural systems. One of my hypotheses consists of showing the character of internationalization of the labour system and the acceptance of western models by a great part of the populations in Africa south of the Sahara. The analysis of these two countries reveals that a particular interlinking took place: the colonial intervention came from abroad, and African societies had to adapt a model imposed by actors coming from very different social systems.

My aim consists in demonstrating how the introduction of different structural parameters has been reflected by individuals and groups. An actor lives in a particular period, and the dominant patterns of this period have an influence on him or her. An analysis of two life-stories collected in Ghana and one collected in the Ivory Coast shows different aspects of this transformation of the labour system, frictions and cleavages.

The Ivory Coast and Ghana were influenced by rather different colonial approaches. The Ivory Coast was influenced by an approach based on the French colonial model, which was characterized by the systematic introduction of French patterns to be adapted by local elites to African social, cultural, political and economic systems. France tried to change African institutions slowly, but the gulf between French and African structures meant a rapid confrontation of two very different systems. From the 1950s, the Ivory Coast was exposed to important change in its social, political and economic systems. Slowly, the country was introduced into world history. The elites accepted transformations linked to French interests. In the 1980s, the country experienced a crisis of its economic and political institutions, which demonstrated the difficult coexistence of African and western elements.[8]

Great Britain introduced political institutions in its colonial territories and permitted African societies to develop their own social systems. Nevertheless, due to the interaction of rather different groups, the African cultures experienced important processes of social transformation.[9] Since the colonial period, a national elite had been created, privileged because of its educational status, its professions and its wealth. Since 1957, Prime Minister Nkrumah tried to establish a 'socialist' system in Ghana. At the end of Nkrumah's period, the situation in the country was one of financial crisis. In the 1980s, the International Monetary Fund implemented an adjustment programme. Workers and the poor had to support the difficult conditions imposed by this programme. During the last few years, Ghana's economic situation has improved, but in comparison to the Ivory Coast, the country's GDP is much lower.

The transformation of the labour system in the two countries shows a diversification due to globalizing processes in the economic sphere. A new labour system appeared, which was influenced by international economic parameters.

Quantitative and qualitative data were used in this research. Census data and sociodemographic data were used to describe aspects of the labour systems of the two countries. The life-history method was used to reconstruct changes on the individual level. I selected older men (between 50 and 60 years), who had experienced the period of structural transformation of the labour system in a rural or urban context. I chose people with rather different profiles regarding salary, profession and social prestige. This procedure allowed me to study the labour system this group of more senior men had experienced during the last 20–40 years.

I used an interview guide to structure discussions, but I encouraged free associations too. Thus, I was able to cover a wide range of topics: the memory of the group related to the colonial period and the first years after the independence of the two countries; the transformation of their professional tasks due to the interaction of different labour systems, professional careers, earnings, etc.

During summer 1995, I collected about 50 life-stories, in the suburb of Taifa in Ghana's capital Accra, and in two suburbs (Marcory and Koumassi) in Abidjan, the major port city of the Ivory Coast. I was interested in illustrating the life-experiences of these men, which quantitative methods cannot reveal. Most of the life-stories were collected at the home of the interviewees or at their workplace, if, for instance, they possessed a small shop. The interviews took 45–110 minutes, with a median of 60–70 minutes. The life-stories enabled me to reconstruct the professional history of these men, their situation as retired people, various aspects of their marital life and their relationship to their children. Sometimes, the stories let me look in on the lives of men who had owned a farm and/or a house. Several life-stories revealed information relating to the economic, political and social history of the country, and, thus, to the structural constraints that this group was exposed to.

What about the labour system of the two countries? At the beginning of the 20th century, almost the entire population of both the Gold Coast (as Ghana was then called) and the Ivory Coast were peasants, and so one can imagine the great differences which would some decades later appear in these people's lives. Paid labour was introduced in these regions in the 1920s. In the 1950s, the workers in the north of these countries would only work away from their home villages for a year at most, if at all. To settle in the south of these countries was not yet a big attraction. The principal aim of these men was to gain some money during periods of low activity.

In 1975, 74 percent of the working population in the Ivory Coast lived in a rural area and only 26 percent in an urban area. In 1985, 60 percent worked in a rural area and 40 percent in an urban area. In 1988, 63 percent of the active population worked in agriculture and 12 percent were traders.

Workers, craftsmen and drivers accounted for about 13 percent of the active population. The other groups were rather small: 4 percent worked in public services; 3 percent were professional people; 3 percent were white-collar workers. In the same year, 15,000 persons received a pension (Schuerkens, 2001b: 50–8).

In Ghana, the census of 1984 gave information about the population according to different sectors of the economy: more than 3 million people worked in agriculture; 900,000 worked in industry; 130,000 people worked in public services; 130,000 people in trade; 220,000 people described themselves as technicians. In 1989, 70 percent of men were self-employed; 27 percent worked for an employer (Schuerkens, 2001b: 71).

From these data, we can conclude that a very different labour system had been introduced during a rather short time period. The group of men relating their life-stories had had to accept new norms and values. The life-stories – as we show later – revealed conflicts and new configurations, as well as the meaning of these changes. Over a period of no more than a few decades, a profound restructuring of African societies had been undertaken. The life-stories demonstrate colonial and neocolonial logics, and a way of life influenced by the creation of a new structural model. They reveal stereotyped situations, professional trajectories and patterns of conduct which can be found, with some variations, in western countries, too.

The Life-Stories

In order to show the local life-world of these men, I would like to present, first, two life-stories which I collected in Ghana. They illustrate traditional functions in a modern context. The first person, Nana Kwabena, was married to two wives in the customary way. He had seven children, who were between 27 and 35 years old. His children's formal educational levels were not high: they occupied jobs like taxi-drivers. His daughters were married and their husbands were taxi-drivers or small-scale traders. Kwabena could not read or write. His father had been a farmer. Kwabena himself worked as a farmer in his home village, but he emphasized during the interview that he also worked selling his crops: cocoa, coffee and palm nuts. He did not earn much money through this activity. Nevertheless, he employed two workers on his farm of two acres (Schuerkens, 2001b: 143–5).

His wives were both traders. One of them sold cold water and other small items. The other woman sold mats and baskets. Kwabena had managed to build three houses at a time when the prices were still low, houses where his family was now living. He did not want his family to rent houses. His children had bought items of furniture like armchairs, stools and tables. But, he stressed: 'The children do not have much money and nor do I have money. We are all poor and struggling. I must struggle to provide furniture for my visitors [to sit on]. The market is not helpful. People are not buying now. So we do not have money.'

He was elected chief of Taifa because in 1971 he was the first person to settle there. The inhabitants of the local area trusted him. He will be in this position until he dies, when another local man will be elected chief. Kwabena's role is subordinate to that of the chief of the whole city of Accra, but his responsibilities as district chief included, for instance, ensuring his local streets and area are kept clean. In his eyes, to be a chief was a prestigious position; he was not being paid at all. Kwabena told us about his role as chief: 'God has given me the talent to control people and I am happy with that. It's the work of God. I have a peaceful life and honour as a chief.' His activities meant he could receive gifts of goods. For instance, after our discussion, I was asked to buy him two bottles of beer. His only problem is that he did not have much money. Nevertheless, he did not think of himself as poor: 'If I don't owe anybody anything, I think I am okay.'

The second person I want to introduce was a traditional chief and a merchant (Schuerkens, 2001b: 145–7). Nana Michael was 46 years old when we interviewed him in 1995. He had two wives: he married one of them in church, and the other one in the traditional manner. He had four children: one was 25 years old and was studying medicine. The other three children were 10, 14 and 16 years old and were still going to state schools at the time of our fieldwork. Nana Michael himself had attended a state school for 10 years. Then he started a job, so he could get his driving licence and become a driver. He found his first job through the help of a relative. Seven years later, he decided that the profession of driver was no longer what he wanted. He told us: 'You can be a driver for somebody. When one's son goes to school, he will come out with a great profession, but you still remain a driver.' This argument led him to want to improve his situation. He informed his employer that his salary was too small. His employer's brother decided to lend him some money, which Nana Michael used to buy his first car. He employed a driver to take passengers between Accra and Lomé. After two years Nana Michael was able to pay back the money he had been lent. Ten years later, he owned four vehicles: two taxis and two mini-buses taking 15 and 19 people. He employed four drivers and four ticket sellers. A friend had lent him money to buy more cars, money which Nana Michael paid back promptly too. At the same time, he was the owner of a farm where he reared cattle and where he employed 25 people. With the money he made, he was able to build three houses.

His decision to leave his job as a driver appears to have been a good one. Nana Michael told us: 'I don't want to be rich and I don't want to be poor, because when you become rich you have no respect and when you are poor, [you may feel so desperate] at times, you may want to commit suicide. I want to be in between. If I can feed myself and pay my children's fees, I am okay. I don't want to work as a labourer. But my education will not allow me to become a minister.'

In 1986, at the death of his uncle, he inherited the position of traditional chief. For two months, he dedicated himself to learning the duties of a chief: how to speak in public, how to wear the traditional clothes, etc. His uncle had been a policeman, but he had owned, as Nana Michael in his turn, several houses and cars. Nana Michael's functions consisted, for instance, in settling disputes between couples or in assisting at funerals. These festivities were very costly, but they were linked to his position. With his numerous professional activities, he had enough money to exercise them correctly. However, Nana Michael's rather low educational level contributed to the fact that he did not abandon his rather modest lifestyle regarding clothes and food for instance.

The following life-story is from Abidjan in the Ivory Coast (Schuerkens, 2001b: 84–9). Claude G. was 68 years old in 1995. He was married and had 12 children, of whom one was a secretary, another an employee at a post-office and another an accountant. In the 1940s, he had attended primary school. At the age of 18, he began work in the dispatch department of a French company. Some time later, after an initial period of training, he became an accountant. Not happy with his salary, he moved to a better-paying company, where he stayed for 30 years until his retirement. After several years, he attained a managerial position immediately below the French expatriate employees, and was thus one of the few managers of his age in the Ivory Coast. His salary was high and his pension was very good in comparison to other pensioners. During his working life, he was able to buy two houses in Abidjan. His father and mother had been peasants. He was their only child to go to school and he achieved a better professional and financial level than his brothers and sisters. He has helped and still helps his siblings financially and in other ways, for example helping them in the construction of their houses. In this way, he continued to link two contexts: the world where he earned his living and which assured a comfortable pension, and his traditional African environment, which would not have accepted Claude G., the only one of his kin who had achieved professional success in the modern economy, spending his money on just himself, his wife and children. Instead he used his resources to help other people, a characteristic which may have influenced his ongoing financial success. Furthermore, he believed his situation as a pensioner would only be assured when all his children could guarantee their own livelihoods. He was proud of his success, but he was not presumptuous. Claude G. was interested in maintaining good relations with his extended family and his former colleagues. In fact, he had adopted a set of ethics which he had learnt during his career as one of the highest-paid African employees in any French enterprise and which he could combine with the obligations originating from his African kinship.

In general, I found that the professional situations of these older men were characterized by a rising mobility. The fathers of these men had mostly been small- or medium-scale farmers. Often, their sisters and brothers were still working on farms. Some individuals had experienced social mobility, but in no way the majority of family members.

A new professional life, regulated by criteria still unknown in the 1950s and 1960s, had been accepted due to schooling and/or professional activities. The men interviewed found social stability in their families or in their marriages. The strong links between husbands and their wives were astonishing, but they show that these older men need emotional security. In many cases they were married to only one wife and said that they wanted to stay in this relationship until death. In both countries, these men formed the first generation of retired employees. In their marriages, they tried to find a form of stability which their working life no longer guaranteed. Most of our interviewees' wives worked as traders in the informal sector. Relations between parents and children showed that familial ties were strong and they enjoyed leisure time with their families.

Another interesting topic to come out of the life-stories is that these older men were eager to build their own home during their working life. Building a house is considered an important marker of success and assures spatial stability. How much the construction cost depended on the men's professional situations. The time spent on this task was long: it would often take about 10 years before the house was built and the family could live there. Our interviewees were proud of their houses, and they allowed them to stay in an urban area after their retirement.

Through the life-stories[10] there emerge different sorts of answers to the structural transformations of the labour system. The economic system of both countries began to change in the 1920s, but only in the 1940s and 1950s did these changes became structurally significant. Since independence in the 1950s and 1960s, the globalization of the labour system has become more and more central for most of the African population. The life-stories brought very different answers to given situations. The individual could adapt to structural transformations in different ways. These differences could be explained by the personal labour situation. We could not find any differentiation between the men we interviewed themselves, but only between large economic sectors, such as agriculture, industry and the informal sector. This fact indicated a rather limited social integration of the labour system.[11] Actors had to find answers to new situations: their traditional system could no longer assist them. Furthermore, we found that differences in social origins played a secondary role: intellectual and social capacities could influence given solutions. If one had a successful farmer for a father, to be rich was no disadvantage. But in most cases, it was not possible to speak of the transmission of social privileges. Structural factors such as the level of unemployment, the restructuration of the economic system or the importance of the informal sector influenced the life-stories. Our analysis showed that the professional instability experienced rendered difficult each professional project. Often, and even more so in Ghana, the years spent in a professional school influenced neither the professional history nor the salary of these men.

In the Ivory Coast, the men were often fatalistic. Life was considered difficult, a fact which became a norm, due to the great number of actors concerned. However, these men considered their life as rather unique: they did not participate in collective actions. Often psychological adaptations could be found, such as to resign oneself to the situation or to become depressed. Nevertheless, the life-stories were rather different. It was difficult to find a common structure. People could only be differentiated into similar groupings by their general link to an economic sector, such as working in the primary, secondary or tertiary sector. This type of differentiation might be replaced in the next generation of retired men by differentiation according to social stratum. Conflicting situations which can actually be found in individual life-stories may then contribute to differentiate between individual actors and may indicate different hierarchical groups. The life-stories indicate that actors learned in a rather short time period new patterns of socialization and new professional activities.

I found that the lives of farmers were seldom characterized by material aspects, which would link these people to a monetary economy (Schuerkens, 2001b: 205–7). During the last few years, low prices of produce had had an influence on the life of these peasants, as had expenditure linked to children's schooling and to medical needs. The number of workers on what were often long-established farms was reduced too. These farmers form strong and close ties with their labourers: they work with them throughout their lives, supervising and coordinating their tasks. Yet the productivity of these men is rather low. Often, only the fact of inheriting a large farm, or having money through having had a second job in the city would differentiate these peasants. But such differences are only quantitative. The working attitudes of these peasants are similar. Some years previously, it had still been possible to build their own homes with the money earned from harvests. But in 1995, farmers were complaining their earnings were at no more than subsistence level.

It is interesting to consider common characteristics among these peasants' life-stories. This group has experienced a rather similar form of economic transformation, and integration into a monetary economy. The activities of these peasants have not fundamentally changed during the last few decades. As a group, the parameters one might use to assess their lives are very different from those one would use for urban men. Not only are their incomes different from those of men working in the towns and cities, but they indicate a much lower level of differentiation too.

I tried to include the informal sector in my research (Schuerkens, 2001b: 209–11). This sector is applicable to several categories of actors: young people; those trying to integrate into the urban economy after a rural–urban migration; and those who have had to leave the formal sector of the economy, for instance after having been dismissed, or following retirement. These reasons explain why few people can be found who spend their entire active life in the informal economy. Often, this sector of the economy is only attractive for people looking for work after having left the rural or the formal economy. Workers in this sector are influenced by factors associated with the formal economy, such as monetary income and the specialization of tasks, but also by factors linked to traditional agriculture (domestic activity, a low number of workers and low incomes). Thus, this sector is situated between the two other sectors, and forms a sector of transition.

Conclusion

The comparative method used in my research leads me to conclude that the differences between colonial policies (British and French styles) and neo-colonial practices ('socialist' vs liberal policy) are not that important for the internationalization of the labour system. I have shown that the transformations which I analysed in both countries seem to be characteristic of the structural change of the labour system in countries of the South, and, in particular, in Africa south of the Sahara. The confrontation of African labour systems with systems influenced by the dominant economic system shows that there have emerged in urban centres social patterns largely influenced by western economies, even if the informal and the agricultural sectors would seem to be more dominant in countries of the South. It has become obvious that, over the last three or four decades, the labour system of these countries has accepted patterns that link these economies in an irreversible manner to the dominant economic model.

Research about transformations in the countries of the South should therefore no longer look for a structural direction of change. Instead, studies should be undertaken which tackle normal forms of social change. We need more descriptive studies about countries of the South, and even comparisons with other regional contexts in the South and in the North, for instance Eastern Europe. My research findings can be extended to other countries of West and Central Africa, such as Senegal, Cameroon, or Gabon. Countries of the Sahel, such as Mali or Burkina Faso, should be approached rather more cautiously however, because their contacts with western economies seem to have been more limited and patterns of change might be different. In conclusion, I would like to stress that it is necessary to study how structurally different labour systems combine with one another in various parts of the world.[12]

I am interested in demonstrating in these life-stories how professional mobility is adapted to the crises and frictions of the economic, social and political systems of African countries. Professional failure and disappointments, the restructuration of economic systems and the transformation of the informal sector are the long-lasting effects of structural transformations. The life-stories reveal that high levels of professional instability prevent people making professional and career plans. The actual life-world is characterized by structural determinants such as the level of unemployment and the irregularities of the labour market.

Finally, it should be pointed out that the transformation of the labour system did not mean a change *inside* African society, but a change *of* African society, insofar as a structural transformation of the labour system took place which had important effects on professional identities.[13] My research has indicated that important development problems of the countries of the South have been resolved in a specific manner. If this hypothesis is right, the most serious transformation problems are behind us, although they still need detailed description. Research on their development comes next to studies of social change. Even if the 'normal' progression of transformation processes is still beset by frictions and disharmonies, strategic problems will no longer be in the foreground. Next on the agenda may be to tackle synthetic approaches, and to undertake comparisons with other regional contexts.

Notes

I am grateful to the World Society Foundation (Zurich, Switzerland) for its generous support to this research project. I would also like to thank Jean Copans and Jonathan Friedman for their very helpful comments and constant encouragement.

1 See my book *Du Togo allemand aux Togo et Ghana indépendants. Changement social sous régime colonial* (Schuerkens, 2001a).

2 See my book *Transformationsprozesse in der Elfenbeinküste und in Ghana: Eine historisch-vergleichende Analyse des Verhältnisses von Lebensgeschichten und strukturellen Wandlungsprozessen* (Schuerkens, 2001b: esp. 23). For further examples, see Chanock (1985), Dirks (1987), Piault (1987), Pons (1988) and Ziegler (1988).

3 Thomas and Znaniecki (1918–29) demonstrated this structural conflict with their description of the life of a Polish immigrant to the USA.

4 See in this respect Helbling (1984: 95).

5 See Teune and Mlinar (1978: 9).

6 See for example Brock and Junge (1995).

7 See Eder (1988: 306) for a similar conception.

8 On the different colonial regimes, see Schuerkens (2001a).

9 By transformation I understand a structural change in a social system, for example in the labour system described in this article. I refer to change when I speak, for example, of value change, which can take place with or without the transformation of a given social structure.

10 See my book on transformation processes in the Ivory Coast and Ghana (Schuerkens, 2001b), where I present at great length these life-stories.

11 See on the concept of integration Peters (1993).

12 See as an example of this sort of research the books written by Cabanes et al. (1995) and Pries (1997).

13 See in this respect Godelier (1995: 178).

Bibliography

Alexander, Jeffrey C. and Colomy, Paul, eds (1990) *Differentiation Theory and Social Change.* New York: Columbia University Press.

Alexander, Jeffrey C. and Sztompka, Piotr, eds (1990) *Rethinking Progress, Movements, Forces, and Ideas at the End of the 20th Century.* London and Boston, MA: Unwin Hyman.

Appadurai, Arjun (1996) *Modernity at Large: Cultural Dimensions of Globalization.* Minneapolis: University of Minnesota Press.

Brock, Ditmar and Junge, Matthias (1995) 'Die Theorie gesellschaftlicher Modernisierung und das Problem gesellschaftlicher Integration', *Zeitschrift für Soziologie* 24(3): 165–82.

Brumann, Christoph (1998) 'The Anthropological Study of Globalization. Towards an Agenda for the Second Phase', *Anthropos* 93(4–6): 495–506.

Buchholt, Helmut, Heidt, Erhard U. and Stauth, Georg, eds (1996) *Modernität zwischen Differenzierung und Globalisierung. Kulturelle, wirtschaftliche und politische Transformationsprozesse in der sich globalisierenden Moderne.* Hamburg: Lit.

Cabanes, Robert, Copans, Jean and Sélim, Monique, eds (1995) *Salariés et entreprises dans les pays du Sud. Contribution à une anthropologie politique.* Paris: Khartala, ORSTOM.

Chamboredon, Jean-Claude (1983) 'Le Temps de la biographie et les temps de l'histoire. Remarque sur la périodisation à propos de deux études de cas', in P. Fritsch (ed.) *Le Sens de l'ordinaire*, pp. 17–29. Paris: Éditions du CNRS.

Chanock, Martin (1985) *Law, Custom and Social Order: The Colonial Experience in Malawi and Zambia*. Cambridge and New York: Cambridge University Press.

Copans, Jean (1988) 'L'Anthropologie des travailleurs du tiers-monde aujourd'hui' (in 'Les Nouveaux Enjeux de l'anthropologie. Autour de G. Balandier'), *Revue de l'Institut de Sociologie* 3–4: 275–83.

Copans, Jean (1996) 'Sociologie/anthropologie du travail/de l'organisation/de l'entreprise?', *Journal des Anthropologues* 66–7: 29–39.

Dirks, Nicholas B. (1987) *The Hollow Crown: Ethnohistory of an Indian Kingdom*. Cambridge: Cambridge University Press.

Eder, Klaus (1988) *Die Vergesellschaftung der Natur. Studien zur sozialen Evolution der praktischen Vernunft*. Frankfurt am Main: Suhrkamp.

Eder, Klaus (1990) 'The Cultural Code of Modernity and the Problem of Nature: A Critique of the Naturalistic Notion of Progress', in Jeffrey C. Alexander and Piotr Sztompka (eds) *Differentiation Theory and Social Change*, pp. 67–87. New York: Columbia University Press.

Friedman, Jonathan (1994) *Cultural Identity and Global Process*. London: Sage.

Godelier, Maurice (1995) 'L'Anthropologie sociale est-elle indissolublement liée à l'Occident, sa terre natale?', *Revue Internationale des Sciences Sociales* 47, 143(1): 165–83.

Hannerz, Ulf (1989) 'Culture between Center and Periphery: Towards a Macroanthropology', *Ethnos* 54(3–4): 200–16.

Harmsen, Andrea (1999) *Globalisierung und lokale Kultur. Eine ethnologische Betrachtung*. Hamburg: Lit.

Helbling, Jürg (1984) 'Evolutionismus, Strukturfunktionalismus und die Analyse von Geschichte in der Ethnologie', in *Diachronia. Zum Verhältnis von Ethnologie, Geschichte und Geschichtswissenschaft. Ethnologica Helvetica* 8: 83–102.

Ingold, Tim (1986) *Evolution and Social Life*. Cambridge: Cambridge University Press.

Kohli, Martin (1986) 'Gesellschaftszeit und Lebenszeit. Der Lebenslauf im Strukturwandel der Moderne', in special issue 'Die Moderne – Kontinuitäten und Zäsuren', *Soziale Welt* 37(4): 183–208.

Laszlo, Ervin (1989) *La Cohérence du réel. Évolution, cœur du savoir*. Paris: Gauthiers-Villars.

Lautier, Bruno (1987) 'Fixation restreinte dans le salariat, secteur informel et politique d'emploi en Amérique Latine', *Revue Tiers Monde* 110(38): 347–67.

McMichael, Philip (1996) *Development and Social Change: A Global Perspective*. Thousand Oaks, CA, London and New Delhi: Pine Forge Press.

Øyen, Else, ed. (1990) *Comparative Methodology: Theory and Practice in International Social Research*. London: Sage.

Peters, Bernhard (1993) *Die Integration moderner Gesellschaften*. Frankfurt am Main: Suhrkamp.

Piault, Marc, ed. (1987) *La Colonisation, rupture ou parenthèse*. Paris: L'Harmattan.

Pons, Philippe (1988) *D'Edo à Tokyo: mémoires et modernités*. Paris: Gallimard.

Pries, Ludger (1997) *Wege und Visionen von Erwerbsarbeit. Erwerbsverläufe und Arbeitsorientierungen abhängig und selbständig Beschäftigter in Mexiko*. Frankfurt am Main: Lang.

Robertson, Roland and Lechner, Frank (1985) 'Modernization, Globalization and the Problem of Culture in World-Systems Theory', *Theory, Culture and Society* 2(3): 103–17.

Schuerkens, Ulrike (1992) 'Le Travail au Togo sous mandat de la France, 1919–1940', *Revue Française d'Histoire d'Outre-mer* LXXIX (295): 227–40.

Schuerkens, Ulrike (1995a) *Le Développement social en Afrique contemporaine. Une perspective de recherche inter- et intrasociétale*. Paris: L'Harmattan.

Schuerkens, Ulrike (1995b) 'The Notion of Development in Great Britain in the 20th Century and Some Aspects of its Application in Togoland under British Mandate and Trusteeship', *Sociologus* 45(2): 122–39.

Schuerkens, Ulrike (2001a) *Du Togo allemand aux Togo et Ghana indépendants. Changement social sous régime colonial*. Paris: L'Harmattan.

Schuerkens, Ulrike (2001b) *Transformationsprozesse in der Elfenbeinküste und im Ghana: Eine historisch-vergleichende Analyse des Verhältnisses von Lebensgeschichten und strukturellen Wandlungsprozessen.* Hamburg: Lit.

Schulz, Manfred, ed. (1997) *Entwicklung: Theorie – Empirie – Strategie. Festschrift für Volker Lühr.* Hamburg: Lit.

Spittler, Gerd and Beck, Kurt, eds (1996) *Arbeit in Afrika.* Hamburg: Lit.

Sztompka, Piotr (1991) *Society in Action: The Theory of Social Becoming.* Chicago, IL: University of Chicago Press.

Sztompka, Piotr (1993) *Sociology of Social Change.* Oxford: Basil Blackwell.

Sztompka, Piotr, ed. (1994) *Agency and Structure: Reorienting Social Theory.* Amsterdam: Gordon and Breach.

Tetzlaff, Rainer, ed. (2000) *Weltkulturen unter Globalisierungsdruck. Erfahrungen und Antworten aus den Kontinenten.* Bonn: Dietz.

Teune, Henry and Mlinar, Zdravko (1978) *The Development Logic of Social Systems.* Beverly Hills, CA and London: Sage.

Thomas, William I. and Znaniecki, Florian (1918–29) *The Polish Peasant in Europe and America,* 5 vols. Chicago, IL: University of Chicago Press.

UNESCO (1996) *The Cultural Dimensions of Global Change: An Anthropological Approach.* Paris: UNESCO.

Warnier, Jean-Pierre (1999) *La Mondialisation de la culture.* Paris: La Découverte.

Watson-Franke, Maria Barbara (1985) *Interpreting Life Histories: an Anthropological Inquiry.* New Brunswick, NJ: Rutgers University Press.

Ziegler, Jean (1988) *La Victoire des vaincus. Oppression et résistance culturelle.* Paris: Seuil.

7

Glocalization of Law: Environmental Justice, World Bank, NGOs and the Cunning State in India

Shalini Randeria

This article delineates trajectories of the glocalization of law by examining the interplay between the World Bank, NGOs and the state in India. It maps the changing contours of legal pluralism and hybridization of law in which traditional norms, national laws and policies, World Bank standards as well as international human rights and environmental regimes are recast in a new landscape of what Santos (1995) has termed 'interlegality'. Empirical material from several World Bank financed infrastructure and biodiversity projects on the subcontinent is used to analyse the processes of the transnationalization of law and the diverse paths of its domestication. These projects highlight the clash between environmental conservation and human rights as well as between the right to livelihood of local communities, whose survival depends on their collective rights to commons, and a model of economic growth based either on state-led development or on privatization managed by the state. The first part of the article considers the paradoxical consequences of the World Bank supported biodiversity project for the protection of lions in Gujarat, western India. The second section deals with the network 'Campaign for People's Control Over Natural Resources', which is contesting the state–market nexus involved in privatization at the expense of the poor. The global success of the transnational movement against the Narmada dam, which, however, failed to translate this success into local gains for those displaced by the project, is the subject of the third section. The disappointing experience of civil society actors who filed claims on behalf of those adversely affected by World Bank projects before the Inspection Panel, an innovative transnational legal arena, which has failed to realize its potential so far, is discussed in the fourth part.

These case studies show a diversity of supra-state and non-state actors at work in varying alliances with one another at the local, national and supranational levels. But they also demonstrate that the state is not merely a victim of neoliberal economic globalization, since it remains an active agent in transposing it nationally and locally. The monopoly of the state over the production of law is certainly being challenged both by international institutions and by civil society actors, subnational as well as supranational

(Günther and Randeria, 2003). However, in contrast to the widespread diagnosis of the consequent decline of the state and a dismantling of its sovereignty, I argue in the final section that it would be a mistake to take this self-representation of states at its face value. We are faced not by weak, or weakening, states but by cunning states,[1] which capitalize on their perceived weakness in order to render themselves unaccountable both to their citizens and to international institutions (Randeria, 2001, 2003a).

Due to its salience in domesticating neoliberal policies, the state remains an important interlocutor for civil society actors challenging these policies or seeking to mitigate their effects. However, grassroot NGOs and social movements in India are not only engaged in a defensive struggle against the state and the World Bank for the protection of the rights of indigenous peoples and other local communities over common property resources but are proactive in formulating new norms weaving together traditional collective rights, national laws and international standards. Their struggle for environmental justice is being waged through broad-based political mobilization and media campaigns but equally through the increasing use of national courts and international legal platforms. The latter includes the Inspection Panel at the World Bank, whose very genesis owes a great deal to the transnational coalition against the Narmada dam in western India (Randeria, 2001, 2003a, 2003c).

An important dynamic in the local transposition of neoliberal globalization consists in a part transnationalization and a part privatization of the state which increasingly effaces, on one hand, the boundary between the national and supranational and, on the other hand, that between state and civil society. Both contribute to what I have elsewhere described as the new pattern of scattered sovereignties (Randeria, 2001). The resulting reconfiguration of the state includes the selective implementation by the state of norms and policies designed by supranational institutions like the World Bank and the IMF and imposed in the form of credit conditionalities (Moore, 2000) or of 'project law' (von Benda-Beckmann, 2001). The distinction between law and public policy becomes increasingly blurred as rule-making is increasingly placed outside the arena of legislative deliberation and democratic decision-making (Randeria, 2003b). But an analysis of processes of glocalization of law needs to go beyond unpacking the state in terms of its legislative, administrative and judicial institutions each with its own logic. It must also include both an analysis of the decentralization of the state and the devolution of powers to regional and local governments as well as to NGOs which have taken over many of the functions of the state. If the state at the national level has lost some of its powers, regional governments have gained in influence as they now negotiate directly with the World Bank and try to implement investor-friendly policies in a bid to attract domestic and foreign capital. Therefore, the dynamics of glocalization are best studied at the level of the different regional governments in India. Two of the case studies in this article discuss some of these transformations, therefore, using empirical material from the province of Gujarat in western India.

Given its centrality to the neoliberal restructuring of governance both within and beyond the nation-state, law provides an important vantage point from which to study some of these facets of globalization and the resistance to it. This article draws attention to the dynamics of exclusion and pauperization by focusing on struggles in the legal arena against land acquisition, involuntary displacement, environmental degradation, illegalities of state practices and the infringement of fundamental rights including the right to life and livelihood which links environmental action with human rights issues. An attempt is made to ground the analyses of the global in local processes and to situate local processes within a larger context of socioeconomic transformation as these are affected by the policies of nation-states and international institutions.

Social movements and NGOs in India have long been resisting a destructive and inhumane model of development. They have recently assumed salience not only as translators of national and international law at the local level but equally as channels for the assertion of customary collective rights over local commons in national and international fora. As mediators linking the global with the local, social movement and grassroot NGOs with transnational connections are an important interface between nation-states, supranational institutions and local communities. Their entry into the national legal domain has been facilitated by the growth of judicial activism and public interest litigation but it has not been without its costs in terms of protracted legal battles with uncertain outcomes and the risk of depoliticizing an issue in the legal arena. Despite their equivocal experience with state law courts and supranational instances, social movements and NGOs across the country continue to use this arena in their struggles for social justice. But after extensive consultations at the grassroots, they have also formulated alternative people's laws and policies on land acquisition, forests, rehabilitation or intellectual property rights in addition to holding public hearings on these issues (Randeria, 2001, 2003c). They have thus challenged not merely the monopoly of the state over the production of law but also its exclusive claim to represent the greater common good.

Contesting the Lion's Share: Pastoral Communities, Biodiversity and the World Bank

International organizations like the World Bank introduce into the national legal arena concepts and principles which may be seen as 'proto-law' as they do not have the formal status of law yet, but in practice often obtain the same degree of obligation. Moreover, through their credit agreements with the state, they also introduce what may be described as 'project law' as an additional set of norms. Similarly, concepts like 'good governance', 'co-management', 'sustainability', etc. have all been elaborated in various international treaties, conventions, protocols, though they are neither fully developed principles nor show internal coherence (von Benda-Beckmann,

2001). At the national and local levels, various sets of actors invoke them as competing with, or overriding, national laws, or use them to ground the legitimacy of national law as well as to advance claims against traditional rights and customary law.

Some of the paradoxes and contradictions of the possibilities of the co-existence of multiple and overlapping legal orders are evident, for example, in the controversy between environmentalist NGOs and the human rights groups which have been at odds with one another over the protection of the rights of lions versus those of pastoralists in the Gir forest in Gujarat. Whereas environmentalists champion the protection of wild life, human rights NGOs have been concerned with securing the livelihood and cultural survival of the pastoral communities in the area. The powerful NGO World-wide Fund for Nature-India (WWF-India), with its transnational linkages, draws its moral legitimacy as representative of global stakeholders in the environment. It has used its financial resources and media connections to make a case for the displacement of pastoralists who in its view endanger the survival of the lions. For example, as part of its campaign for the protection of biodiversity, it filed a case in the Supreme Court against the government of India for failing to implement national environmental laws and policies. Against such a narrow environmentalist agenda, which pits people's rights to commons against conservationist goals, human rights NGOs and the local people's movement, supported by a South Asian and South-East Asian human rights network, have mobilized for the protection of traditional rights of access to, and use of, natural resources based on the customary rights of the pastoral communities. But instead of relying entirely on local norms to make their case, they have also invoked the doctrine of public trust, borrowing from its elaboration in recent US court decisions on environment. They invoke the principle of the state as a trustee rather than as the owner of natural resources, which are seen to belong to local communities dependent on them. The US doctrine of public trust is thus used by civil society actors in India to challenge the validity of the continued reliance by the Indian state on the colonial doctrine of eminent domain, which secures its sole control of forests, water and mineral resources (Randeria, 2003c).

Issues relating to both biodiversity conservation and displacement have been at the centre of the controversy surrounding the eco-development project of the World Bank in the Gir forest in western India.[2] The Gir sanctuary and National Park are located in Junagadh district with a protected area covering 1412 sq. km out of which 258 sq. km constitute the National Park with restricted access and complete displacement of the local population. The protected area is the last intact habitat of the Asian lion in the wild with about 284 lions estimated to be living in the area. According to the Forest Department's own figures, there are 54 traditional hamlets of pastoralists (*nes*) with an estimated population of 2540 within the area demarcated for the sanctuary (Ganguly, 2000). These families, which belong to several Hindu castes of Rabari, Charan and Bharwad, including two

Muslim communities of Makrani and Siddi, raise livestock and sell milk products. They are collectively known by the occupational term Maldhari (owners of cattle).

In 1972, over 800 families of Maldhari were forcibly displaced from the area demarcated as the National Park. Six hundred of these families were resettled under an inadequate rehabilitation programme which gave them land in villages near the sanctuary. This half-hearted attempt to turn pastoralists into farmers failed due to the poor quality of land made available to families with no knowledge of agriculture and no access to inputs required for cultivation. Within a few years, many successful pastoralists selling milk and milk products over long distances were reduced to wage labour. In a survey conducted by the Forest Department in 1971, families living within the area demarcated for the sanctuary as a protected area were divided into those recognized as 'permanent', those deemed to be 'non-permanent' and those considered to be 'illegal'. Only 'permanent' residents were granted a so-called 'Maswadi' pass, which entitles them to live with their families and graze their cattle within the protected area. This completely arbitrary division of the Maldhari communities has created families and family members with differential rights to residence and to carry on their traditional livelihood. It has also ruptured the social fabric, making it difficult for those living outside the borders demarcated by the Forest Department to visit the sacred sites of their communities within the Gir forest. Daughters and sisters married into villages on the periphery of the sanctuary, for example, now have the status of 'tourists' and are required to pay for a daily pass to visit their natal kin living in the protected area.

The rights of the pastoralists to forest products, grazing land and water resources are sought to be overridden in the name of the greater common good by WWF-India and the state government of Gujarat. They argue that both the local ecological system and the lions are endangered by the traditional grazing methods, used for large herds of livestock as well as by the Maldhari's increasing demands for the provision of modern infrastructure and other facilities in the area (such as tarred roads, electricity, schools and health centres). Following the interim order of the Supreme Court in the case filed by WWF-India in 1997, the Collector of Junagadh issued a notice evicting the Maldhari families from the Gir sanctuary in view of the proposed conversion of the entire area into a National Park. Human rights NGOs and people's organizations in the Gir area have so far been able to prevent forced displacement as it contradicts the terms of the eco-development project agreement between the World Bank and the government of India. In terms of the overriding commitments accepted by the government of India in its agreement with the World Bank (World Bank, 1996), for the limited duration of the project and within the six biodiversity project areas, World Bank policies safeguarding the rights of indigenous peoples and protecting those affected by a project from involuntary resettlement prevail over state laws. However, it is far from clear whether these conditionalities will have any permanent or pervasive impact on national resettlement policy or environmental laws.

The Wildlife Protection Act drafted with the expert advice of the Smithsonian Institute (USA) in the 1970s and adopted by the Indian parliament has provisions for declaring certain areas as 'protected areas' for purposes of setting up national parks or wildlife sanctuaries. Aimed at environmental conservation, it also contains procedures which work in practice to the detriment of the rights of local communities in these areas. WWF-India has found an ally in the Gujarat government and the two have teamed up to protect the environment using national legislation, whereas human rights activists have found an ally in the World Bank, which is committed to the standards laid down in its own operational directives and policies which protect project-affected people from forced eviction and guarantee the traditional rights of indigenous communities. These rules also provide for a participatory resettlement and rehabilitation of families affected by a project in a manner which protects their living standards, earning capacity and production potential and further stipulates that these should not deteriorate as a result of a World Bank project. So that ironically, the displacement, envisaged by the Gujarat government and the WWF-India in consonance with national law, has been temporarily averted by NGOs invoking World Bank norms. As the displacement would have contravened credit conditionalities accepted by the government of India as signatory to the agreement with the World Bank, the federal government prevailed on the regional government to stop all forced eviction. But this fine balance is likely to last only as long as the World Bank project.

In order, therefore, to anchor people's rights to natural resources in a more permanent policy framework beyond the short-term validity of the project law of the World Bank, human rights NGOs have advocated more systematic changes. They would like a programme of joint participatory management of national parks and sanctuaries modelled on the Joint Forestry Management programmes in which local communities and the state act together to preserve the forests. These joint conservation programmes are premised on the assumption that local communities, especially indigenous people, are the best protectors of their environment. Having lived in a symbiotic relationship with nature for centuries, they are assumed to have a traditional way of life and alternative local knowledge which enables them to live in harmony with their environment. Apart from the tendency to romanticize indigenous people within a global, anti-statist environmental discourse which valorizes local knowledge (F. von Benda-Beckmann, 1997), a primarily ecological view makes people's access to commons contingent on their conservation skills and intentions (K. von Benda-Beckmann, 1997) rather than framing the question in terms of their rights to land, forests and water for their livelihood. It may thus freeze the cultures and lifestyles of these communities in time, so that an obligation to continue with their traditional way of life is a price they may have to pay for their non-displacement from their ancestral lands and forests. Demands by Maldhari communities in the Gir forest for modern amenities like electricity, or metalled roads linking their settlements (*nes*) with the markets for their dairy produce outside the protected area, are rejected by the WWF-India and the Forest Department in the name of wildlife conservation. What appears at first sight to be the autonomy to pursue their own way of life may turn out to be an obligation to do so, an 'enforced primitivism' (Wilder, 1997: 217) in the interests of biodiversity and the Asiatic lion.

Civic Alliances Contest State Control over Natural Resources

Human rights NGOs present a case for people's rights over natural resources which goes much beyond the highly limited protective approach to displacement outlined in the World Bank policy as well as the sympathy for the mere participation of local communities as conservationists in the global environmental discourse. An all-India network of NGOs has recently challenged the very basis of such a policy, and of national laws, which recognize only individual rights for purposes of compensation disregarding the collective rights of communities to access natural resources. The Campaign for People's Control Over Natural Resources is a large new nationwide coalition of NGOs, including one from Gujarat, which seeks to reassert and protect the collective customary rights of local communities (e.g. pastoralists, fishing communities, marginal and poor farmers, landless labourers and indigenous peoples) to land, water, minerals and forests. Apart from court battles, many of the NGOs involved in the new network have been involved in local mobilization and protest on these issues for several years.

The entire problem of access to and use of common property resources has acquired a new urgency due to policies of liberalization and privatization introduced by the Indian state under the directive of the IMF and the World Bank. The central government itself admits in the new draft National Policy for Rehabilitation of Persons Displaced as a Consequence of Acquisition of Land that economic liberalization and an increase in private investment will generate a greater demand for land as well as for mineral resources and reserves located in regions inhabited primarily by tribal communities. Yet instead of a just and humane rehabilitation policy, based on a process of consultation and respect for democratic rights of the displaced, which would take into account the ground-level realities and complexities of land use and traditional rights to commons, the new policy only seeks to ensure efficient expropriation and legal security in the interest of investors. Increasingly, 'wasteland', forest areas and coastal areas under special environmental protection through the Coastal Area Zonal Plan are being acquired by the state and made over to industries at nominal prices. That such iniquitous development destroys the traditional agricultural, pastoral or other patterns of livelihood of those who are forcibly displaced, economically marginalized and rendered assetless seems to be an acceptable price for inexorable industrial growth and progress. Here is where the 'enabling state', representing the sectional interests of the rich in the name of 'national interest', comes increasingly into conflict with those of its citizens living in poverty who are dependent on common property resources of land, water, forests for their survival. Paradoxically, voluminous new national and supranational environmental and human rights law goes hand in hand with the erosion of the collective rights of communities, their traditional access to the commons and their right to determine for themselves their own vision of good life. Ecologically sustainable agriculture or pastoralism, which is either at the level of subsistence or produces for the market without large-scale commercialization, finds no place in official plans and policies. In view of the capitalist development model shared by the state and the World Bank, 'backward' peasants, pastoralists and tribals are to be modernized through integration into the 'national mainstream' and the market economy. The promise of industrial wage labour is held out as a stepping stone to higher income and skills for setting up independent business, a mirage of mobility into middle classes which is no more than 'a myth inspired by wishful thinking' as Jan Breman in his trenchant critique of the 1995 World Bank Development Report has argued (Breman, 1997: 88).

Liberalization has meant a shrinking of state responsibilities but not a shrinking of the state apparatus, just as it has not led to less state interventionism but rather to state intervention in favour of capital (Randeria, 1999). Through a combination of legislative and executive measures, the Indian state has been seeking to undermine the access of local communities over their natural resources. As the Campaign for People's Control Over Natural Resources[3] has pointed out in its appeal in November 2000, the increasing pressure of privatization and industrialization under the neoliberal regime is eroding people's rights to minerals, land, water and forests, turning these common resources into sources for private profit. The Campaign has drawn attention to two extremely worrying recent developments in this regard: the proposed amendments to the Land Acquisition Act (1894) and the proposed amendments to Schedule V of the Constitution.

Of colonial provenance, the Land Acquisition Act (1894) (revised in 1986) enables the state to acquire land for a public purpose without recognition and protection of people's right to their natural resources and without consultation with them. The postcolonial state has so far used it to dispossess and displace some 30 million people for large-scale dams and irrigation projects, urban development schemes, wildlife parks and sanctuaries. Most of those forcibly evicted have been the rural poor and about 40 percent of the displaced belong to indigenous communities whose rights the government of India as a signatory to the ILO Convention 107 is obliged to protect. They have hardly received any adequate compensation in the absence of a national law or policy on resettlement and rehabilitation, which has been a long-standing demand of NGO networks, who have presented an alternative draft people's policy on rehabilitation for public discussion.

Under the new policies of economic liberalization, there has been a rapid increase in land alienation by the state on behalf of private industries and mining companies. Simultaneously, there has been an increase in both spontaneous, sporadic, unorganized local resistance to these developments as well as more organized protest through networks of NGOs and social movements throughout the country. As the Land Acquisition Act (1894) only enables the state to acquire land for a public purpose, the central government is now proposing to amend the law to allow confiscation of land by the state on behalf of private industry and to introduce only cash compensation instead of providing alternative land. Ruling in a case where farmers had challenged such acquisition, the Supreme Court recently defined the setting up of private industry to constitute 'public purpose' thus permitting land acquisition by the state for use by private companies. A network of NGOs has started a nationwide campaign to protest against the proposed amendments and has drafted an alternative new Land Acquisition Act. Challenging this redrawing of the boundary between the public and the private, they advocate a participatory process of legislative amendment and a right to information rather than the shrouding of these new laws and policies in secrecy.

In September 1997, the Supreme Court had given an important judgement restraining state action and upholding the rights of Adivasi communities (indigenous peoples) to life and livelihood and to land and forests in scheduled areas reserved for them by the Constitution. Responding to a case filed by Samata, an advocacy group for Adivasi rights in Andhra Pradesh on the issue of mining in scheduled areas, the Court had held that government, forest and tribal lands in these areas cannot be leased out to non-tribal or to private companies for mining or industrial purposes. It declared all such leases by various state governments to be null and void as they contravene Schedule V of the Constitution. It decreed that mining activity in these areas could only be carried out by the state Mineral Development Corporation or a cooperative of the tribals subject to it being in compliance with the Forest Conservation Act and the Environment Protection Act (SETU, 1999). The Supreme Court also recognized that under the 73rd Amendment to the Constitution, Gram Sabhas and Panchayats are competent to preserve and safeguard the natural resources of the community. Thus, once again, it reiterated the right of self-governance of Adivasi communities.

This landmark judgement, known as the Samata Judgement, was an important check on the illegal practices of the state, which encouraged an unchecked commercialization of land, forests and water. The Supreme Court dismissed the subsequent appeals by both the state and the Union governments, which tried to overturn this decision against an environmentally unsustainable and economically inequitable industrialization. Under pressure from multinational corporations and Indian industry, the Union government has been seeking avenues to circumvent the judgement. The Ministry of Mines proposed, for example, an amendment to Schedule V of the Constitution with a view to removing all restrictions on the transfer of tribal and government lands in scheduled areas. The proposed amendment of Schedule V was to be tabled in parliament in the winter session of 2000/1, and would have permitted land acquisition by the state on behalf of private companies not only for public purposes but also for engaging in production for private profit. The amendment did not foresee any participatory process in which public purpose could be determined jointly by those communities whose rights to land, forests, water, a traditional way of life and livelihood are to be affected adversely. NGOs and social movements, who had been demanding such a consultative process and guarantees of protection for many years, have succeeded so far in blocking the legislation from entering the national legislature.

Transnational Coalition against the Narmada Dam: Global Victories, Local Failures

Given the fact that more and more citizens are now directly affected in their daily lives by the working of international institutions and their policies, it is not surprising that they choose to address these institutions directly with their protests, bypassing the national parliamentary arena in an attempt to transnationalize an issue. The many ambivalences of this new transnational arena of an emerging global civil society are illustrated by the long drawn out struggle of the Narmada Bachao Andolan (Save Narmada Movement) in Gujarat, together with a network of national NGOs and transnational NGOs in Europe and the USA against the building of the Sardar Sarovar dam on the river Narmada. The World Bank was eventually forced to withdraw its financial support comprising some 18 percent of the costs of the dam and 30 percent of the expenditure on the canals. Highly detrimental to the environment, the project was originally expected to displace 70,000 people (an estimate which had to be officially revised to 120,000) from a submergence area of approximately 370 sq. km (Morse and Berger, 1992). The World Bank itself conceded that it was later discovered that the construction of the canal network of 75,000 km would lead to the eviction and resettlement of at least about another 120,000 people which had neither been planned for financially in the project nor been taken into account at the time of its appraisal by the Bank (Shihata, 2000).[4]

Protest among the displaced communities had initially concentrated on issues of just compensation for the loss of land and livelihood, fair resettlement and rehabilitation policies and their implementation. Transnational linkages with the campaign against multilateral banks led over time to a shift of agendas and priorities. Mobilization and strategic action came to be focused on the eviction of the World Bank from the valley just as grievances came to be articulated increasingly in terms of an environmental discourse with international legitimacy and translatability. Gradually a radical 'no large dams' agenda, for which there was growing transnational support,

eclipsed concerns about appropriate technological safeguards, displacement, equity and justice. The vocabulary of the movement as much as the
timing of local action was often determined by demands of the global arena
and transnational constituency building instead of seeking to work through
regional and national political institutions. Some of the complexities and
contradictions of the campaign involving several Indian NGOs, environmental rights groups in the USA, development aid groups in Europe
(especially Germany), Japan and Australia are explored in Jai Sen's (1999)
excellent ethnography of the struggle against the dam. It traces the emergence of a new modality of transnational social action, the transnational
advocacy network (Keck and Sikkink, 1998), and delineates how the
dynamics of local resistance came increasingly to be shaped by the choice
of the arenas of negotiation and the structures of the international institutions used as levers of power. As social movements and NGOs in the
South link up with powerful northern and especially North American
NGOs to use US Congressional hearings as a forum to put pressure on
multilateral development banks in general, and the World Bank in particular, in order to change their policies and reform their structures, they not
only reinforce existing asymmetries in power between the North and the
South but also lend greater legitimacy to these institutions. Leapfrogging
the national parliamentary arena, addressing the World Bank directly and
putting pressure on it through the US Congress and executive directors of
industrial countries further diminish the legitimacy of subaltern states in the
South.

The movement in the Narmada valley, and the transnational campaign
supporting it, led to several unintended long-term structural changes in
Washington, DC rather than in India. Jai Sen (1999) argues that paradoxically the campaign reduced democratic control over the structures of the
World Bank by increasing the control of the US Congress and the concentration of power of the major share-holding states of the North (G7
members control about 60 percent of the vote) over the staff of the World
Bank. However, the campaign also resulted in internal changes of control
and review mechanisms at the World Bank. Among the latter is the revised
information disclosure policy, which lays down that specific project information pertaining to environment and resettlement be made known to
those affected by the project prior to its appraisal (Udall, 1998). It also contributed to the setting up of the Inspection Panel at the World Bank, which
is discussed in the next section, as well as of the World Commission on Large
Dams, a forum for the negotiation of a new set of international ecological
and human rights standards for large dams in which all stakeholders participate (World Commission on Large Dams, 2000).

If the experience of Indian citizens at a transnational forum like the
Inspection Panel has been disappointing, as is shown in the next section, the
Narmada Bachao Andolan's failed attempt to seek judicial remedy in
the Supreme Court of India after the withdrawal of the World Bank from
the project exposed some of the limitations of the use of national courts as

arena for social justice as well. It has been as difficult to make an international institution like the World Bank conform to its own resettlement norms and environmental standards, as it has been to get judicial remedy against a state which has constantly flouted its own laws and policies. Despite a controversial and prolonged public debate in India, the issue has neither been seriously debated in the national parliament, nor have any legal or policy changes taken place with respect to mega dams, land acquisition, involuntary displacement, or resettlement and rehabilitation. The movement in the Narmada valley, which sought to radicalize the 'damn-the-dams' agenda into a critique of the ideology and practice of gigantism in developmental practice and to broaden policy which includes models of an alternative future, relying on small, local, autonomous projects, was caught up for years in the Supreme Court, negotiating technical matters like the height of the dam. The government could justify its inaction with respect to policy changes by pointing to the sub judice status of all the issues before the court. In retrospect, the withdrawal of the World Bank from the project may seem like a mixed blessing as under pressure from NGOs in Gujarat, some Bank staff and missions had sought to enforce rehabilitation policies and their implementation. The relative improvement in policies and their enforcement in Gujarat as compared to Madhya Pradesh and Maharashtra can be traced to this donor pressure.

The verdict of the Indian Supreme Court in October 2000 was a grave denial of justice as well as a severe blow to people's movements. Moreover, it raised fundamental questions about the limitations of the use of law courts by social movements in their struggle for social justice. It took the apex court six-and-a-half years to come to the conclusion that the judiciary should have no role in such decisions! The majority judgement dismissed all the objections regarding environmental and rehabilitation issues relying entirely on the affidavits given by the state governments. It merely asked the Narmada Control Authority to draw up an action plan on relief and rehabilitation within four weeks. As critics of the judgement pointed out, it is hardly probable that the state government will do in four weeks what it had failed to do in 13 years. The majority judgement, which praised large dams and their benefits for the nation, permitted not merely the construction of the Narmada dam but by questioning the *locus standi* of social movements as public interest petitioners, it also set limits on the future legal options for collective action by citizens against the state.

In its writ petition filed by the Narmada Bachao Andolan (NBA) against the union government in 1994, the movement had asked for a ban on the construction of the dam. It sought this judicial remedy under Article 32 of the Indian Constitution which guarantees every citizen the right to move the Supreme Court in defence of the enforcement of his or her fundamental rights. The NBA contended that the magnitude of displacement caused by the dam was such that a total rehabilitation of those whose land was to be submerged by the project was impossible. Since no adequate provision for resettlement and rehabilitation had been made by the state governments, or could even be possibly made, it asked for a ban on the construction because of the violation of the award of the inter-state tribunal which required this condition to be met prior to the building of the dam. More fundamentally, the NBA raised the question of who has the right to define the greater common good and according to which criteria. Whose interest may be defined as the national interest when the interests of the displaced collide with those of future beneficiaries? Can a merely utilitarian calculus (a larger number of potential beneficiaries as compared to the victims) be used to deny poor and vulnerable communities their right to life and livelihood? Is it legitimate for the state to declare one set of partial interests, those of the rich farmer lobby, industrialists and contractors, to be synonymous with the public good? The NBA thus challenged the very assumption that the state by definition acts in public interest and asked for an independent judicial review of the entire project, its environmental, economic and human costs. Besides raising the issue of the illegality of state practices (e.g. the absence of environmental studies which should have been conducted prior to the construction process as mandated by the Ministry of Environment), the NBA argued that the adverse human and ecological costs of large dams in general far outweigh their benefits.

In response to the petition, the Supreme Court had stayed further construction on the dam from 1995 to 1999 while asking for reports from the three state governments on the progress on the rehabilitation of 'oustees' as well as future provisions for them, along with expeditious environmental surveys and plans to overcome hazards. During the hearings in 1999, the counsels for the state government of Gujarat had asked the Court to give a clear signal in favour of the dam so that foreign investors would be encouraged to invest in it (Sathe, 2000). It is difficult to judge how much weight the argument carried in the Court's decision to allow construction to be resumed, although not much progress had been made on either rehabilitation or environmental assessment. But the argument reflects the priorities and concerns of the government of Gujarat, which chose to privilege the right to security of foreign investment over the fundamental rights of its own citizens.

It is also worrying that the Court refused to consider the general question of the utility of big dams on the grounds that policy matters were best left to the legislature and administration, while at the same time declaring them to be essential for economic progress. Premised on the doctrine of separation of powers, this advocacy of judicial restraint in not going into policy issues, so as not to trespass on administrative competence, came as a surprise and a disappointment, after more than a decade of judicial activism in general and five years after the admission of the plea by the NBA in particular. However, the Narmada judgement does not mark an anomaly in the apex court's history of judicial restraint in the context of public interest petitions challenging large developmental and infrastructure projects in the last decade. Rather, as Upadhayay (2000) points out, it is consonant with the inclination of the judiciary to insist on the executive taking decisions correctly as opposed to taking correct decisions. The Supreme Court has often left it up to the government to decide on the nature of public projects for an improvement in living standards of citizens, and to resolve conflicts of interest arising from contrary perspectives on development. Interestingly in cases of environmental protection, the court has taken a very different view. Neither technical expertise nor policy issues have led the court to apply judicial restraint when it has attempted to reconcile development with ecological considerations. It has sought to develop a rich environmental jurisprudence to compensate for administrative indifference but has preferred a defensive approach of non-interference in administrative decisions on infrastructure projects (Upadhayay, 2000). Whereas it has often relied on European standards and US legal precedents in cases of urban and industrial pollution in recent years, the Supreme Court refused to apply western norms in the Narmada case or to consider any of the substantial evidence on violations of environmental norms and human rights of indigenous communities documented in the Morse Report commissioned by the World Bank (Morse and Berger, 1992).

Decades of resistance by the victims of development in the Narmada valley, who have borne the brunt of state repression and violence, have not led to any rethinking on the basic issues raised by the movement: forced displacement and ecological destruction in the interest of industrial development, as well as the search for more environmentally sustainable and socially just alternative models of development which respect cultural diversity and the right of communities to determine their own way of life. After the World Bank pulled out of the financing of the Sardar Sarovar dam on the Narmada river, the government of Gujarat floated bonds to raise capital for it within the country and abroad. Attempts to attract multinational finance, which are removed from democratic control in any of the countries concerned, have continued for the Maheshwar dam on the river Narmada. Three German companies – Siemens, Bayerwerke and VEW – sought credits from German banks and guarantees for foreign investments and exports from the German government in order to supply machinery and know-how. They were forced to withdraw from the project after intense lobbying and pressure from German NGOs, who publicized the long history of state repression and human rights violations associated with the dam. But that may not be the end of the story. Disregarding continuing public protests in India and despite a sustained campaign by German NGOs safeguarding the enforcement of environmental and human rights standards in development projects financed by the state, or in credit guarantees for private investors underwritten by the state, the ruling coalition of Social Democrats and Greens in Germany underwrote the credits for the Tehri dam in an ecologically fragile Himalayan region. This was not only under pressure from German industry but its timing could lead one to conjecture that it was equally a gift to the government of India, as an important member of the global coalition against terrorism.

Governance Beyond and Within the State: The World Bank Inspection Panel

A major achievement of the transnational campaign against the Narmada dam was the establishment of an independent Inspection Panel at the World Bank in 1993. It was set up in response to pressure from NGOs for more transparency and accountability as well as to threats from influential members of the US House of Representatives to block further US contributions to the International Development Association (Udall, 1998). The Panel is by no means a full-fledged body for adjudication but provides a forum for an appeal by any party adversely affected by a World Bank funded project. The primary purpose of the Inspection Panel is to examine whether the Bank staff has complied with its own rules and procedures. Its influence on policy formation within the World Bank is probably limited (Kingsbury, 1999). Barring a couple of exceptions, claims before the Panel so far have only had limited success as Bank staff have usually teamed up with the borrowing country in question to deny any violations. Together they have subverted full-fledged field investigations by the Panel by hastily drawing up remedial action plans for the future. The larger and powerful borrowing countries have supported each other on the Executive Board of the World Bank in resisting investigations which they regard as an infringement of national sovereignty. So the Panel has been increasingly used by civil society actors as much to publicize the violation of international environmental and human rights norms by their own governments and to pressurize them into compliance as to seek remedy against the World Bank's non-implementation of its own operational policies.

Among the 17 requests entertained by the Panel till mid-1999,[5] two were related to projects in India: the National Thermal Power Corporation (NTPC) power generation project in Singrauli in 1997 and the eco-development project (of which the Gir project discussed earlier is a part) in the Nagarhole National Park in Karnataka in 1998 (Umāna, 1998). In both cases, it was alleged that the Bank management had failed to comply with its own policies on environmental assessment, indigenous people and involuntary resettlement. The request contending serious flaws in the design and implementation of the eco-development project was submitted by an Indian NGO representing indigenous people living in the Nagarhole National Park. It submitted that no development plans had been prepared with their participation as laid down in Bank guidelines because the project had simply not recognized the fact that they resided within the core project area. It argued that the forced displacement of the Adivasi communities from their forest habitat would not only disrupt their sociocultural life but also destroy their means of livelihood. Although the Bank staff denied any breach of policies and procedures, the Panel, after studying the written documents and a brief field visit, recommended that the Bank's Board authorize an investigation. The Panel felt that 'a significant potential for serious harm existed' (Shihata, 2000: 135), as key premises in the design of the project appeared to be flawed. In view of the meagre information available to the Bank staff, the Panel felt that Bank staff could not have been able to foresee during project appraisal how the project could harm the Adivasi population in the park. Rather than consultations with them prior to the project as required by operational procedures, Bank management stated that it was envisaged to ensure their participation in the implementation stage. Shihata, the then chief counsel of the World Bank and a senior vice-president, admitted that such an approach involved the risk of non-compliance with the World Bank policy of consultation and participatory planning, a 'feature [which], though apparent, was not explained at the time the project was presented to the Board for approval' (Shihata, 2000: 134)!

The Panel noted that in violation of the guidelines on involuntary resettlement, no separate indigenous people's development plan was prepared at the appraisal stage and no 'micro plans', through which individual families and groups in the protected area could express their needs and get financial support, were under preparation for the Adivasi families, 97 percent of whom wished to remain in the National Park (Umāna, 1998). Despite these findings, and the potential of serious negative impact of the project on the indigenous communities in the area, the Bank's Board decided not to authorize any investigation in 1998. Instead it merely asked the management, together with the government of Karnataka and the affected people, to address the issues raised in the Panel's report and intensify project implementation and microplanning. Given the long history of non-compliance with Bank guidelines both by its own staff and by the government of Gujarat in the Narmada dam, as amply documented in the Morse Commission report commissioned by the World Bank, the Board's decision is a cause of concern. Besides the power of the Bank staff, it reflects the success of executive directors from borrowing countries, including India, as a bloc in thwarting Panel investigations, which they regard as an infringement of their national sovereignty. Under these circumstances, NGOs continue to be sceptical about the independence of the Panel, its limited mandate and the difficulties of access to it for people affected adversely by World Bank projects all over the world (Udall, 1997).

In response to the request of the Panel for looking into the NTPC power generation project in Singrauli, the World Bank management conceded, for the first and only time in its history so far, its partial failure to implement some of the Bank's policies. It submitted to the Panel a detailed action plan of corrective measures agreed upon with the government of India. After a review of the records and a brief preliminary field visit, the Panel concluded that although the guidelines regarding indigenous people had not been breached, the possibility of serious violations by the Bank of policies and procedures relating to involuntary resettlement and environmental assessment need investigation. The Panel's investigations confirmed these violations and it noted in its report that the failure 'appear[ed] more serious than previously assumed' (Shihata, 2000: 132). The Indian government, however, denied permission to the Panel for a full field-based investigation into the complaints, leading the World Bank Board to allow only a desk review of the project. And the Panel watched helplessly as the World Bank remained inactive in the face of a backlash in Singrauli as reprisals against the villagers, harassment and intimidation by local police and project authorities increased.

One is rather surprised to learn from Shihata's account that after this the 'Management concluded that "valuable lessons were learnt" from intensive reflection on the request (in the NTPC case) and continued to place emphasis on the implementation of the action plan' (Shihata, 2000: 132)! A decade after the World Bank's and the government of India's serious violations of environmental and resettlement policies led to the withdrawal of the Bank from the Sardar Sarovar project, one is surprised by the poor institutional memory of the World Bank; its lack of responsibility, even in the absence of legal liability, towards those affected adversely by its projects; its infinite faith in the borrowing government's political will and capacity to implement environmental and human rights conditionalities; the lack of World Bank supervision of this implementation and more generally its continued insensitivity to the social and ecological costs of the kind of development it advocates and finances. Despite the failure of the government of India to issue a national resettlement and rehabilitation policy, the World Bank surprisingly continues to advance credits for development projects involving forced displacement. This raises doubts as to the World Bank's seriousness in ensuring compliance with its own credit conditionalities and operational policies. It is not as if the Bank as an institution has not learnt from its past mistakes. Many of the norms enshrined in policies reflect the experience of the Bank with the adverse effects of its earlier projects and are the result of sustained lobbying by, and consultations with, civil society actors and representatives of affected communities in many countries. World Bank standards often emerge from local sources and are then globally diffused to other international and bilateral development institutions and borrowing countries through their incorporation into Bank policies and practices. A good example of such a process is the norm of land for land compensation for those families being displaced by a World Bank project instead of the earlier cash compensation for land acquired by the state. This standard was introduced after the experience of forced displacement and the struggle against the Narmada dam. But instead of ensuring compliance with it, it is likely to be given up by the World Bank under pressure from borrowing governments and private industry.

Although the World Bank continues to claim immunity from legal liability for the adverse impacts of its projects, parallel to the setting up of the Panel, Bank management began to convert operational directives and policies which were binding on the staff into non-mandatory recommendations (or 'Best Practices') which would render them 'Panel-proof' by placing them beyond the jurisdiction of the Inspection Panel. So that instead of the existence of the Panel affecting greater compliance by the Bank staff with the institution's own standards, limited desk investigations by the Panel are already leading to a watering down of standards to make them conform to the Bank and borrower's common practice of non-compliance.

The Cunning State and the Paradoxes of Democratization

A plurality of norms at the national and international levels and their collision may not necessarily be detrimental to the protection of the rights of local communities. It could afford a space for states, if they are politically inclined to use it, to protect the rights of their vulnerable citizens. For example, it could give the Indian state an opportunity not to bring national patent laws immediately into consonance with the WTO regime on the ground that such a harmonization would contravene the other existing international conventions to which the state is also a signatory (Randeria, 2002a). The question is whether within the constraints imposed by processes of neoliberal globalization and its new institutional architecture, a state has the political will to use the available legal space to further and to protect the interests of the poor and marginalized sections of its population. Or does the national political elite gain instead by pointing to the shrinking capacity of the nation-state to choose policy options and enact its own legislation by laying responsibility for its laws and policies at the door of the World Bank, the WTO or the IMF and thus divest itself of political accountability to its citizens?

The new architecture of unaccountable global governance facilitates a game of what I have termed 'passing the power', in which international institutions claim themselves to be utterly powerless servants of their member states, and states in turn capitalize on their perceived powerlessness in the face of prescriptions from Washington, DC or Geneva (Randeria, 2001). This creates dilemmas for civil society actors for whom the state is both an ally and an adversary depending on the context. On the one hand, they need the state in order to protect the rights of citizens vis-a-vis multinational corporations and international institutions. On the other hand, civil society actors increasingly use the international arena and transnational space to bypass the state, as, for example, in the case of the anti-Narmada dam movement, in order to directly address supranational institutions whose policies directly affect the lives of poor citizens.

In contrast to much of the literature on globalization, which emphasizes the increasing marginality of the state and its retreat in the face of inroads by global capital, I have argued that the state, its laws and policies continue to play a pivotal role in transposing and shaping neoliberal globalization at the national and local level. Before multinational corporations can be granted licences to exploit natural resources in Schedule V areas eroding the rights of indigenous communities in India, or before private industry is allowed to displace local communities and threaten their very survival, the Indian state has had to amend its laws and policies on mining and minerals and to implement its unamended land acquisition policy of colonial provenance to acquire land for industry. It has permitted the setting up of private industries in areas inhabited largely by indigenous communities and granted mining licences, tax and labour law concessions and favourable terms of operation to corporations (Kumar and Shivalkar, 2001).

While recognizing the new constraints on the freedom of the state to design and implement their own laws and policies (e.g. the strong pressure from the World Bank to amend mining policy to facilitate private foreign and domestic investment in the sector), it would be a mistake in my view to accept the self-representation of the post-structural adjustment state about its own weakness in this regard. The government of India has definitely neither implemented all the policy reforms demanded by the World Bank and the IMF nor enacted all suggested legal changes. It has refused to allow the Inspection Panel to investigate complaints by Indian citizens adversely affected by World Bank projects, or to agree, for example, to the full convertibility of the rupee, and has complied with other conditionalities like deregulation of the labour market or privatization of state enterprises only partially, selectively or half-heartedly. Cunning states certainly have the capacity to decide which and how much of the remedies prescribed in Washington for the ills of the national economy should be administered to some sections of its population.

Contrary to the rhetoric of many globalization theorists and of political elites, the state is not being rolled back as a rule-making or rule-enforcing agency. In an age of scattered sovereignties, it has merely lost its monopoly over the production, adjudication and implementation of law, if, given the plurality of postcolonial legal landscapes, it ever had such a monopoly (Randeria, 2002a, 2003c). The World Bank's 1997 World Development Report, titled 'The State in a Changing World', reflects the new role of the state as envisaged by international institutions. The post-structural adjustment state is conceived of by them as an 'enabling state', as one arena of regulatory practice among others (Gill, 1999). The prescribed goal of 'good governance' entails restructuring of the state to ensure the 'reliability of its institutional framework' and 'the predictability of its rules and policies and the consistency with which they are applied' (World Bank, 1997: 4–5). The policies and rules themselves, however, are insulated from public deliberation and parliamentary decision-making resulting in a 'democracy without choices' (Krastev, 2002).

I have argued that despite its decentring and restructuring through the influence of international institutions and the market, the state remains an important albeit contested terrain in processes of globalization. All laments about the loss of state sovereignty to the contrary, legislative enactments, judicial decision-making and administrative (in)action will continue to affect the way processes of globalization are mediated, experienced and resisted in India. Grounding the experience of globalization in an empirical study of resistance against forced displacement and land acquisition as well as in struggles for the right to livelihood and for control over natural resources, enables the linking of everyday life in rural India to transnational flows of capital and discourse while contributing to an understanding of the specificities of local transformations and the power relations that shape them. As the case studies analysed here show, law is an increasingly important, if ambivalent, arena in which interpretations of environmental standards, human rights and the public good, the regulation of the environment or access to common property resources are contested. Surprisingly, however, the field of law continues to remain marginal to studies of globalization and resistance to it.

The empirical material from India demonstrates the uneasy coexistence of several contradictory facets of these processes. If financial and technical aid for the gigantic Narmada project is organized transnationally, so is the protest against human rights abuses, ecological destruction and state violence. The World Bank simultaneously advocates economic policies in support of privatization and advances credits for large dams and polluting industries, which infringe on environmental and human rights along with directives to uphold those rights. But states eager to follow its directives to create an enabling environment for capital are likely to be brought under the scrutiny of the Bank's Inspection Panel for non-implementation of environment conditionalities and failure to comply with rehabilitation standards. Paradoxically, a spread of supra-state governance and an increasing importance of law in social life goes hand in hand with the erosion of customary rights to common property resources. It may be easier, however, to protect these rights by invoking international norms and the World Bank project law or credit conditionalities rather than by relying on national courts and domestic policies.

The case studies in this article remind us that globalization as locally experienced is as much about state law and World Bank loans as it is about the risks of displacement, impoverishment and exclusion, about global discourses of biodiversity and the local politics of transnationally linked social movements. Any mapping of the changing contours of governance within and beyond the nation-state will have to trace these connections between local actors and global discourses, between micro-practices and macro-structures.

Notes

1 My thanks to Ivan Krastev for suggesting this term to me which describes the strategies of the subaltern state.

2 I am grateful to Varsha Ganguly and Ashok Shrimali (SETU, Ahmedabad) for their generosity in sharing with me their experience of the struggle against the displacement of Maldharis from the Gir forest in the context of the World Bank eco-development project and for giving me access to their material on the project and the campaign.

3 My thanks to Achyut Yagnik (SETU, Ahmedabad) for clarifying many of the issues raised in this article in the course of discussions about the network and the campaign as well as for providing me documents relating to it.

4 Estimates of the number of people to be displaced vary widely and are a highly contested issue between the state and the movement. Irrespective of these competing claims, the Indian

state has a dismal record of development-induced displacement and the failure to rehabilitate those forcibly evicted. Large dams alone have displaced 16–38 million Indians since 1947, 75 percent of whom are still to be rehabilitated (World Commission on Large Dams, 2000: 104, 108).

5 For a detailed analysis of the history of the Panel, its procedures and the cases before it, see Randeria (2001).

Bibliography

Aravinda, L.S. (2000) 'Globalisation and Narmada People's Struggle', *Economic and Political Weekly* 35(46): 4002–5.

Breman, Jan (1997) 'Labour Get Lost: A Late-Capitalist Manifesto. A Stylised Summary and a Critique', *Zeitschrift für Sozialgeschichte des 20. und 21. Jahrhunderts* 12(1): 83–104.

Ganguly, Varsha (2000) 'Impact of Displacement on Quality of Life of Maldhari (Pastoral) Women of Gir Forest', unpublished PhD thesis, South Gujarat University Surat.

Gill, Stephen (1999) 'The New Constitutionalism of Disciplinary Neo-Liberalism in an Age of Globalization', paper presented at the Heinrich Böll Foundation Conference 'Feminist Perspectives on the Paradoxes of Globalization', Berlin, 5–6 November.

Günther, Klaus and Randeria, Shalini (2003) *Recht im Prozess der Globalisierung.* Frankfurt am Main: Suhrkamp.

Keck, Margaret and Sikkink, Kathryn (1998) *Activists Beyond Borders: Advocacy Networks in International Politics.* Ithaca, NY and London: Cornell University Press.

Kingsbury, Benedict (1999) 'Operational Policies of International Institutions as Part of the Law-Making Process: The World Bank and Indigenous People', in Guy S. Goodwin-Gill and Stefan Talmon (eds) *The Reality of International Law: Essays in Honour of Ian Brownlie*, pp. 323–42. Oxford: Clarendon Press.

Krastev, Ivan (2002) 'The Balkans: Democracy without Choices', *Journal of Democracy* 13(3): 39–53.

Kumar, Navleen and Shivalkar, Shilpa (2001) 'Impact of Land Alienation on Adivasi Women and Children', paper presented at the Minority Rights Group (London) and SETU (Ahmedabad) seminar 'Development, Equity and Justice: Impact of Globalization on Adivasi Women and Children of India', Hyderabad, September (to be published by the organizers).

Mahadevia, Darshini (1999) *Economic Growth and Environmental Degradation: Case of Gujarat.* New Delhi: Research Foundation for Science, Technology and Ecology.

Moore, Sally Falk (2000) 'An International Legal Regime and the Context of Conditionality', unpublished.

Morse, Bradford and Berger, Thomas (1992) *Sardar Sarovar: Report of the Independent Review.* Ottawa: Resource Futures International.

Randeria, Shalini (1999) 'Globalisation, Modernity and the Nation-State', in Katja Fuellberg-Stollberg et al. (eds) *Dissociation and Appropriation: Responses to Globalisation in Asia and Africa*, Studie 10, Zentrum Moderner Orient Berlin. pp. 15–25. Berlin: Das Arabische Buch.

Randeria, Shalini (2001) 'Local Refractions of Global Governance: Legal Plurality, International Institutions, NGOs and the Post-Colonial State in India. Habilitation', thesis submitted to the Faculty of Political and Social Sciences, Free University of Berlin.

Randeria, Shalini (2002) 'Entangled Histories of Uneven Modernities: Civil Society, Caste Solidarities and Legal Pluralism in (Post) Colonial India', in Yehuda Elkana et al. (eds) *Unraveling Ties: From Social Cohesion to Cartographies of Connectedness*, pp. 284–311. Frankfurt am Main: Campus.

Randeria, Shalini (2003a) 'Protecting the Rights of Indigenous Communities in the New Architecture of Global Governance: The Interplay of International Institutions, Cunning States and NGOs', in Rajendra Pradhan (ed.) *Proceedings of the Conference of the Commission on Folk Law and Legal Pluralism*, Chiang Mai, April. Kathmandu: ICNEC.

Randeria, Shalini (2003b) 'Domesticating Neoliberal Discipline: Transnationalisation of Law,

Fractured States and Legal Pluralism in the South', in Wolf Lepenies (ed.) *Shared Histories and Negotiated Universals*. Frankfurt am Main: Campus.

Randeria, Shalini (2003c) 'Legal Pluralism, Fractured Sovereignty and Differential Citizenship Rights: International Institutions, Social Movements and the Post-Colonial State in India', in Boaventura de Sousa Santos (ed.) *Another Knowledge is Possible: Beyond Northern Epistemologies.* London: Verso.

Santos, Boaventura de Sousa (1995) *Towards a New Common Sense: The Paradigmatic Transition in Science Politics and Law.* London: Routledge.

Sathe, Satyaranjan Purushottam (2000) 'Supreme Court and NBA', *Economic and Political Weekly* 35(46): 3990–4.

Sen, Jai (1999) 'A World to Win: But Whose World is it, Anyway? Civil Society and the World Bank, the View from the "Front": Case Studies', in John W. Foster and Anita Anand (eds) *Whose World is it Anyway? Civil Society, the United Nations and the Multilateral Future*, pp. 337–90. Ottawa: United Nations Association in Canada.

SETU (Centre for Social Knowledge and Action) (1999) *Development, Equity and Justice: Adivasi Communities in India in the Era of Liberalisation and Globalisation*, Report on a Roundtable, 6–9 April 1998. New Delhi: Minority Rights Group.

Shihata, Ibrahim F. I. (2000) *The World Bank Inspection Panel in Practice*. Washington, DC: Oxford University Press.

Udall, Lori (1997) *The World Bank Inspection Panel: A Three Year Review.* Washington, DC: Bank Information Center.

Udall, Lori (1998) 'The World Bank and Public Accountability: Has Anything Changed?', in Jonathan Fox and David L. Brown (eds) *The Struggle for Accountability: The World Bank, NGOs and Grassroots Movements*, pp. 391–435. Cambridge, MA: MIT Press.

Umãna, Alvaro, ed. (1998) *The World Bank Inspection Panel: The First Four Years (1994–1998)*. Washington, DC: World Bank.

Upadhayay, Videh (2000) 'Changing Judicial Power: Courts on Infrastructure Projects and Environment', *Economic and Political Weekly* 35(43–4): 3789–92.

von Benda-Beckmann, Franz (1997) 'Citizens, Strangers and Indigenous Peoples: Conceptual Politics and Legal Pluralism', in René Kuppe and Richard Potz (eds) *Law and Anthropology: International Yearbook for Legal Anthropology* 9, pp. 1–42.

von Benda-Beckmann, Keebet (1997) 'Environmental Protection and Human Rights of Indigenous Peoples: A Tricky Alliance', in René Kuppe and Richard Potz (eds) *Law and Anthropology: International Yearbook for Legal Anthropology* 9, pp. 302–23.

von Benda-Beckmann, Keebet (2001) 'Transnational Dimensions of Legal Pluralism', in Wolfgang Fikentscher (ed.) *Begegnung und Konflikten Eine Kulturanthropologische Bestandsaufnahme*, pp. 33–48. Munich: Verlag der Bayerischen Akademie der Wissenschaften.

Wilder, Lisa (1997) 'Local Futures? From Denunciation to Revalorization of the Indigenous Other', in Günther Teubner (ed.) *Global Law Without a State*, pp. 215–56. Aldershot: Dartmouth.

World Bank (1996) *Staff Appraisal Report: India. Eco-Development Project*, Report No. 14914-IN, 3 August. Washington, DC: World Bank.

World Bank (1997) *World Development Report 1997: The State in a Changing World*. New York: Oxford University Press.

World Commission on Large Dams Report (2000) *Dams and Development: A New Framework for Decision-Making*. London: Earthscan.

8

Knowledge between Globalization and Localization: The Dynamics of Female Spaces in Ghana

Christine Müller

Current debates in sociology claim that knowledge is an important or even the major factor for present and future social change. Studies such as those on knowledge production in science in the western world (Knorr-Cetina, 1999) or on the production of expert knowledge in non-western countries (Evers, 1999) speak about a worldwide transition process towards knowledge societies. Evolution and entry into these societies become a global phenomenon which cannot easily be addressed in the ongoing expansion of new information and communication technology and the growing access to information in southern countries. The contemporary process can be described as a social and political restructuration and a new definition of relations between the North and the South. To date, this relationship is still grounded in the language of development. Regarding knowledge, the long-maintained asymmetries and dichotomies of a developed and a non-developed world and the implicit continuation of a one-dimensional transfer of knowledge from Northern development organizations to the South are challenged by an active politicizing of knowledge due to the establishment of separate structures and spaces of knowledge production forming new discourses and paradigms on development. The actors I refer to in this article are women in Ghana who have organized themselves at local, regional and national levels as well as cross-culturally/-nationally, framing an 'epistemic culture' on development, which in accordance with Knorr-Cetina (1999: 1) can be defined as a culture that creates and guarantees knowledge in practices, processes, structures and symbols and cannot be separated from other spheres of social life. My argument contradicts Giddens's assumption that globalization is a consequence of modernity and a product or project of the western world (Giddens, 1995: 214–15). In its further hypothetical reflection, this would lead to a homogenizing of knowledge, finally covering the globe within a single web of knowledge. The sources of dynamics within globalization processes are definitely local, situating knowledge-generation processes within specific local contexts. These local contexts are small microcosms which can be detected all over the world. Since local processes have a structuring effect on globalization, the interesting point of view is the interconnection between these micro-cosms constituting translocal processes along the 'fluid ends of relations between cultures' (Nederveen Pieterse, 1995: 62) and within the different levels of society, thus making globalization a relational product within a given society and between societies.

The discovery of the relevance of knowledge in the South in the sense of 'what know natives?' (Sillitoe, 1998: 203) has since its beginnings been attributed in social anthropology to detailed ethnographic descriptions of health, agriculture and ecology, out of which I only want to mention the studies of E.E. Evans-Pritchard on the ethnic group of the Nuer in Sudan or those of R.S. Rattray on the Ashanti in Ghana. These fruitful insights into the diversity of local forms of organization of knowledge were not recognized in the 1950s at the beginning of development cooperation. Development cooperation was supported by rhetorics of modernization, which were also reproduced by national organizations and agencies within 'developing' countries. Claiming imported and implemented knowledge during the process of modernization as superior to local knowledge had negative consequences and constructed a Janus-faced 'system of ignorance' (Hobart, 1993: 1), meaning that local knowledge was not considered valuable for development and as such was not only ignored, but the planning processes considered this knowledge as inappropriate insofar as they applied inadequate research criteria which were not of relevance for those who were supposed to develop. Similarly, the legitimation as superior prevented a process of self-reflection of development knowledge, which in many projects failed to be sustainable and valuable. Paul Richards (1985) exemplified discontinuities in an agricultural research situation in Sierra Leone along the 'interface' (Long, 1992: 6) between local and scientific knowledge and its changing conceptions.

To date, by sticking to the term 'local', many studies in social anthro-pology or in the context of development projects fall into the trap of an analytical restriction of knowledge as bound to an artificial cut-off place, continuing to construct the 'myth of a village community' (Albrow, 1998). Reality, however, changes rapidly. Both the academic context of knowledge production itself – where I situate myself – and the research area are socially embedded in a glocalized environment.[1] In order to react to the global creolization of cultures, social anthropology is challenged by a re-examination of its methodological perspectives and its theoretical definitions of categories such as nation, community and society. A social anthropo-logical understanding of local knowledge must be a first step to overcome the traditional mapping of knowledge as contained in a 'box'. By taking up the approach of a 'transnational anthropology' as proposed by Appadurai (1998: 48), our perspective is twofold: the analytical reflection on the academic production of knowledge on one hand, and the production of knowledge in the researched field on the other hand. Both production back-grounds are situated in transnational and cross-cultural contexts, urging for a methodological opening of the 'box'.

What now are the global relations constituted by translocal interactions I refer to? During the UN Decade of Women between 1975 and 1985, women took up the opportunity to organize themselves at the Women's World Conferences in Mexico 1975, in Nairobi 1985 and later on in Beijing in 1995, and to institutionalize the exchange in organizations, out of which several globally acting women's organizations evolved, focusing on topics such as health (ISIS International), law (WLD [Women, Law, and Development], Washington), environment (WEDO [Women, Environment, and Development Organization], New York), or development (DAWN [Development Alternative with Women for a New Era]). The permanent feedback to the real, living context in its worldwide extension is channelled along polycentric organizational structures which are either decentralized into regional offices or connected with other national/regional organizations. Knowledge production within these organizations is generated by mechanisms based on local–global cycles: life-world knowledge is transformed on a global level into common strategies and programmes. An additional source of knowledge is scientific knowledge, which is produced by being affiliated to a university or having one's own capacities of research. Besides these two dimensions, women are now creating their own approaches on development and realize them in projects and programmes. The most prominent and global approach is the empowerment approach of DAWN,[2] a research network consisting mainly of women in the South. It was first formulated at the UN Conference of Women in Nairobi in 1985. Women's lives are conceptualized within global economic, political and social relations (Sen and Grown, 1987). Empowerment is looked for in order to overcome unequal gender relations and to transform social institutions such as state, market and civil society. Power is not something which women can simply receive: they have to gain it, turning themselves into subjects of development and not mere objects. The approach did more than merely form a common basis for a vision among women's organizations. The fact that international relations between women, which started under the auspices of UN conferences, turned to a worldwide permanent collaboration and global networking structure in a North–South as well as in a South–South relationship is more important.

I would like to highlight the configuration of interconnectedness constituting these glocal relations. My starting point is at the local level: a small rural village in Ghana, where I collected data for my PhD between 1998 and 1999. One important aspect of translocal relations is the personal movement between different locations of interactions such as the Women's Forum in the regional and national capitals. The means of following up personally the different locations reveals that local interactions are still based on face-to-face communications, which are clearly distinguished from an Internet analysis, where the globe is squeezed into one screen. One's own mobility takes up the understanding of the formation of knowledge which flows across distances. The spatial formation of knowledge in social theory has been underestimated. The phenomenological approach of Alfred Schütz

(1962) as well as the constructivist approach of Berger and Luckmann (1966) emphasize the temporal structure of the life-world as the intrinsic property of consciousness (Berger and Luckmann, 1966: 26) and draw a peripheral interest in the spatiality of knowledge. I want to try to overcome the ongoing 'space-blindness' in the sociology of knowledge by using a differentiated analytical approach which emphasizes the generation process of spaces through local practices and the shaping of spaces through trans-local interactions. In addition, I refer to some historical and current events in order to complete an underlying time–space analysis framework. In the final section of this article, I focus on what is currently meant by talking about local knowledge, a term Clifford Geertz (1983) introduced to social anthropology and which has since had a rising career, finally entering the discourse of development policies.[3]

The Location of Action

The rural village in which I locate myself is not different from many other villages in the Brong-Ahafo region in southern Ghana. The region belongs to the most fertile agricultural areas of Ghana, also known as the food cradle of the country, with the cultivation of yams, cassava, maize, pepper and plantain. The production of cocoa drastically declined after a severe bushfire, in 1984, destroyed almost all cocoa plantations. Its regeneration has been prevented by annual human-caused bushfires. The hard and intensive work in agriculture as well as the processing of cocoa into food for consumption and for sale is mainly done by women.[4] After economic hardship during the 1980s, due to droughts and the implementation of structural adjustment and economic recovery programmes by the World Bank and the International Monetary Fund, leading to a privatization of companies and to rising prices of electricity, water and daily goods, the economy stabilized in the late 1990s. In the year 2000, a peaceful change with a new government set an end to the 16-year rule of the NDC Party and its president, J.J. Rawlings, who took over power in a coup d'etat, and who had governed since 1994 after democratic elections. Apart from interethnic conflicts between the Konkomba and Mamprussi in northern Ghana in 1994, and tensions in the Volta region along the borders to Togo, the country faces a stable political situation with a multi-party system and a plurality of associations, such as unions, displaying an active civil society. Women in urban and rural settings are organized in many different ways: based on jobs in the form of trading or market associations, based on religion, such as Muslim and Christian organizations and based on self-help aspects, such as the organization of the deaf/dumb women. In the history of Ghana, women's organizations played an important political role during the struggle against British colonialization at the beginning of the 19th century and up to 1957, the year of Ghana's independence. Collective military actions were organized by female heads of towns or villages, called queenmothers. Queenmother Yaa Asantewaa is still well known in the everyday history of the people (Arhin, 1983: 96). One specific feature of the ethnic group Akan, which covers a large region of southern Ghana, is the local social organization in 'traditional' institutions which are constituted by 'parallel' structures of male and female representatives existing in each family, and headed by the royal family with the chief and the queenmother.[5] The feature of 'parallel' structures does not only exist in Ghana, but at least in 20 other ethnic groups in Southern, Eastern and Western Africa (Lebeuf, 1963). In postcolonial Ghana, 'traditional' institutions as a whole lost their political relevance with the building up of a nation based on a socialist ideology and a modern bureaucratic-administrative system. Only recently have 'traditional' institutions in an ongoing process of decentralization regained local political relevance. The chief's palace is the major institution addressed by Ghanaians on matters such as the need for additional land, settlement of quarrels between individuals, discussion of political decisions, settlement of disputes with other towns, the changing of money and political representation during visits from higher ranking politicians or chiefs. In sum, it is a political, financial, representational and judicial institution. Within 'traditional' institutions, asymmetries between actors are articulated by female heads of families, the subqueenmothers, who up to now had no access to the meetings at the chief's palace.

Doing 'Reflexive Modernization'

'We are not too shy' had been the explanation of subqueenmothers in defending themselves and by supporting their claim for inclusion into the meetings at the chief's palace against the argument of shyness brought forward by the subchiefs, who claimed that they would invite the subqueenmothers, but they would never dare to come. The subqueenmothers' task is the regulation of disputes and responsibility for the youth within the family. Subqueenmothers are elected by family members according to criteria such as openness, patience, the way they talk to other people, their behaviour in public affairs and even how they walk. With their formal nomination, their clothes, hairstyle and behaviour change. Subqueenmothers are, in comparison to subchiefs, a new phenomenon, as the first woman was elected in 1985. All of them are much younger than the subchiefs, having an average age of 40 years. They replace the eldest women (*obapanyin*) within the family, who used to be responsible for the education of the female grandchildren and who transmitted their knowledge, based on the experiences of several generations, in various situations such as during farmwork or on the compound. Previous experiences and proven practices were transmitted from the past to the present. Copying and oral transmission were and still are the main media of knowledge transmission. Up to the middle of the 20th century, the transfer of knowledge was organized along the principles of seniority and gender. The eldest woman passed her knowledge to female grandchildren, and the eldest (maternal) man to the male grandchildren. The knowledge of these old women was socially legitimated and symbolically mediated through the constitution of 'spaces in-between' connecting the presented with the 'appresented' world. The 'app-resented' world, to borrow an expression from Alfred Schütz (1962: 343), is the world of religion, the consultation of gods in order to solve personal problems, or concepts of the natural world such as the prohibition to cross the river on Tuesdays. The 'appresented' world as a construction of symbolic universes is made visible through symbolic practices in the everyday world. The process of transcendence beyond the visible world refers back to the everyday world by giving a meaning to the symbolic and social order of society. In particular, elderly experienced women had a transformative effect on society: they undertook actions in situations of defence, prevention, edu-cation and in the solution of problems. They exercised social influence on the family and in the town. Yet their influence gradually diminished due to the influence of conversions to Christianity during the 20th century. Further-more, the important link between the old women in the family and the queenmother of the town was cut off as a result of the marginalization of the social and political position of the queenmother. The vanishing of female public spaces and their complete abolishment or reduction to private spaces explain why elderly women have currently lost their capacity of transmitting their knowledge to the younger generation. This was a process of delegitimation of knowledge, which competed with modernization and formal education. Nevertheless, some elements of their knowledge, for instance the storing of crops or the use of traditional medicines, are still valid and are practised even by the younger generation, although the gendered structure of knowledge transmission is now concentrating on their mothers as the major source of knowledge acquisition.

In a historical perspective, a shift can be observed from the *obapanyin* to subqueenmothers, from seniority status to symbolic habitus (Bourdieu, 1976: 170). Subqueenmothers are now trying to extend their spaces beyond the family context. In a first step, they wanted to participate in meetings in the chief's palace. In order to attain this aim, they organized in informal gatherings, which I only accidentally observed while relaxing in a shady corner on the side of a street. The final intention is not to change structures within 'traditional' institutions: the transformation of power hierarchies is a predisposition to regain symbolic spaces, which would allow action on social issues in the town. Those issues encompass the redefinition of old spaces, such as puberty rites, for instance, in response to the increase in teenage pregnancies. The rites are conceptualized as a form of communi-cation between subqueenmothers and young women living in town. They are used for sexual education and for the integration of knowledge about topics such as AIDS or the meaning of formal education. Another topic is the dried out stream, which was once a power source worshipped by women. Its consultation was prohibited by the chiefs. The riverside should be revitalized, according to these women, in order to make the water flow again. Major discussion topics of subqueenmothers focus on social and environmental issues, and they look for solutions. They bridge vanished symbolic spaces and fill them with new elements. The struggle of sub-queenmothers to enter the palace is, on one hand, against the queenmother of the town, who does not support their ideas of entering the palace, and, on the other hand, against the subchiefs and the chief. In the context of 'tra-ditional' institutions, gender is not a basis for solidarity and common interest among women. The division between royal and non-royal kinship establishes and manifests a hierarchical relationship.

The legitimation of the subqueenmothers to change the taken-for-granted world of 'traditional' institutions is based on two issues: first of all, on the fact that they constitute the direct link between people in the town and in the palace, and that they facilitate an exchange information in both directions. They argue,

> We want to attend the meetings, to get information, to listen to what is being said, and to influence the decisions. We can pass the decisions made on to the people in town. We can also make suggestions, we can help the men, especially when it comes to women's matters.

The second aspect is their common symbolic identity as *aberewa nyansafo*, the keepers of the knowledge and wisdom of old women, who, in former times, advised the queenmother at the palace. Both aspects have resulted in a shifting of boundaries with the effect of a 'partial collapse of representation' (Bourdieu, 1991: 126) because of the fact that the sub-queenmothers were finally able to appropriate the political space of the palace by convincing its members with the argument that they are the *aberewa nyansafo* and in this function can support the subchiefs and the decision-making processes.

The struggle of the subqueenmothers has been based on observing, exploring, analysing and discussing their own life-world. These women integrated the aspect of knowledge as a factor of social change to end past marginalization and to legitimate their own knowledge. With their change of rules and resources, and the altered meaning of social order, subqueen-mothers do nothing more than 'reflexive modernization' in accordance with Lash's (1994: 113–14) definition, which means criticizing existing processes and looking at the possibility of increasing their power. The aim of the politicization of knowledge is to gain social power, to redefine symbolic spaces and to react within the social world.

Bridging between old and new elements of knowledge in reacting to social issues is embedded in a translocal discourse on gender relations within 'traditional' institutions at a higher social level. In all regions of Ghana – apart from the two northern regions – subqueenmothers and queenmothers have organized themselves since 1994 in a Queenmothers' Association, founded by a subqueenmother. The organizational structures at district and regional level are based on democratic elections and dis-mantle the dispositions of 'traditional' structures. In the same manner as subqueenmothers who entered the palace at the local level, queenmothers tried to enter the Regional Houses and the National House of Chiefs. The chiefs rejected participation of the queenmothers by sticking to the argument of tradition, which they define as the long existence of a political system, and by considering the queenmothers to be housewives. A close look into the history of the political system reveals that the Regional House of Chiefs was established in 1961 and the National House of Chiefs in 1971. Both aforementioned arguments are used to restrict and to fix spaces and boundaries. The queenmothers refer in public discussions, such as seminars organized by the umbrella organization of all women's organizations in Ghana, the National Council of Women and Development (NCWD), to a different time frame when they use the word 'tradition'. Tradition is according to them a legitimation of their position within 'traditional' institutions, but it must correspond to a changing world which re-examines permanently the public responsibilities of its members. The chiefs within both Houses continue to stick to their arguments. However, a former president of the National House of Chiefs reviewed the discussion after the World Women's Conference in Beijing. He tried to address the gender balance within this institution.

With the assistance of the NCWD and the integration of scientific knowledge resulting from a study on 'Women in Public Life in Ghana' (ISSER, 1998),[6] the arguments of the chiefs were deconstructed. Research results on gender relations and concrete proposals how to change them became an integrated asset in the knowledge repertoire of queenmothers, who continue to put pressure on chiefs.

In meetings of the Queenmothers' Association at district and regional levels, old and new elements of knowledge are discussed. The diversity of topics ranges from breast-feeding and artificial imported baby food, to the discussion on puberty rites in connection with modern forms of family planning. At this stage, queenmothers suggested to the Ghanaian parliament to pass a law on rights which have proved their efficiency in several cases: 'There is a logic in cultural practice', as one subqueenmother said. The discussion on the law is ongoing. The integration of new forms of knowledge is taking place by constant collaboration with other women's organizations in common meetings and in mutual visits. Income-generating projects such as bee-keeping and the production of soap, launched by (sub)queenmothers as a reaction to the severe economic situation, are special concerns. The projects enable the women to earn an additional income as well as giving work opportunities for young women selling these products. Economic and social assistance created a solidarity among (sub)queenmothers, which extends the family context and kinship relations. The economic aim to secure and to maintain the production of subsistence follows the logic of a 'moral economy' (Elwert et al., 1983: 286) by assisting each other in coping with daily insecurities and uncertainties. This form of women's self-help initiative was observed by Eva-Maria Bruchhaus in other parts of West Africa. Through exchange visits to neighbouring countries, women developed sustainable and locally adaptable forms of technology, permanently innovating their flour mills and the production of vegetables, fruits and oil (Bruchhaus, 1988: 54). Innovation is carried on by individuals: one woman activist was experimenting with the drying of pepper in a self-developed solar-cooker in rural Ghana. She presented her results at a seminar for 'renewable energy' in Kumasi in 1998, which was attended by women from different parts of Ghana. This innovation was discussed in the Women's Forum in Accra, attended by more than a hundred women from different women's organizations. Knowledge thus does not only circulate from the urban to the rural parts, but also from the rural to the urban context. The movements of one queenmother, travelling as a member of the National Commission on AIDS all over the world, are different. She informs the association with her new knowledge. Thus women's organizations take over the function of a translocal 'social apparatus' (Schütz and Luckmann, 1975: 295), which accepts new elements of knowledge distributed by circulation. This practice permits permanent innovations.

The Women's Forum

Knowledge also interests the monthly Women's Forum, which was established in 1998 by the representative of the NCWD in the capital of the Brong-Ahafo region, Sunyani. The forum is conceptualized as a meeting to facilitate the exchange of knowledge and information. Every forum is addressed to one specific topic such as 'traditional' medicine, inheritance rights, education in vocational schools, or specific health aspects. Roughly 60–100 women coming from different women's organizations in the surrounding area participate. The forum starts with an introductory talk by a local expert (a policewoman, a medical doctor, etc.) followed by an open discussion. During lively discussions, women analyse their own life-world by identifying reasons for change. For example, they discuss the rise of disease by addressing its causes or the increasing mortality rate of women due to hypertension, which is attributed to the severe economic situation in the country and the multiple burdens women cope with.

Global discourses are brought down to the local level by being contextualized in local issues. This was best exemplified by the discussion of violence against women, a discourse of the women's rights movement worldwide, introduced by a policewoman bringing forward hard facts on a growing number of violent acts in the region during the year 1998, such as cases of rape, wife beating and other violent acts against women in the domestic and public sphere.[7] The policewoman argued that violence exists in different forms: it can have a physiological, psychological, economic, or cultural character, and can affect an individual in multiple ways. The participating women reacted to this issue by pointing out their own experiences or that of well-known cases. They proposed to take up strategies such as changing laws, organizing themselves, going into politics and using the media.

Whatever topic is discussed, women identify social, economic, political, or religious reasons, and critically examine the institution as well as gender constructs. The confidence in their own life-world is not taken for granted any longer: they identify and explain the 'pathologies of modernity' (Habermas, 1981: 554), and politicize old and new elements of knowledge. The forum turns into a space for conducting 'critical theory' (Habermas, 1981: 549), since the personal life-world becomes the methodological object of analysis. In a common process of discovery, the participants are sharing, analysing and reflecting their experience. The principle of this non-hierarchical form of participation has its roots in Paolo Freire's idea of adult education, realized by learning from each other and in order to induce social change (Butegwa and Nduna, 1995: 59). The NCWD representative leaves the interaction process in the hands of the participants, who furthermore have the power to suggest strategies. In this motivating approach, answers and comments are given by the audience. The process of finding self-defined possibilities for actions is left open. The strength of this form of interaction is to build alliances among women, aiming to explore and to take up further strategies. Networking becomes a method of strengthening the organizations. It was used by the NCWD representative who knew it from the paradigmatic approach of WiLDAF (Women in Law and Development Africa), to which I turn in the next section of this article.

The integration of the NCWD into the international context of women's organizations resulted in a change of politics in headquarters at Accra and decentralized offices, each located in one of Ghana's regional capitals. The organization was originally founded, in 1974, by the Ghanaian government as a national machinery for the advancement of women. It turned its policy away from the implementation of politics from above, to a channelling from below. The Women's Forum in Accra is another platform for the reflection on global discourses and international politics in connection with their own experiences. The creation of forums at both levels has led to new spaces for negotiating the diversity of women's life-world, to adapt politics, aiming at improving their lives by building up connections and networking within local organizations. Glocalization is not only constituted by flows of discourses and of knowledge, but by institutions which react by changing their structures, their policies and their methodological perspective. They focus on gender relations and no longer on women, isolated from the social context. By building its own capacities of development in the form of platforms, the NCWD opens a space for the articulation and exchange of knowledge, hybridizing elements of knowledge. The fact of sharing and negotiating their knowledge makes organizations and individuals independent from external knowledge.

Glocalized Practices: Networking and Bridging

Networking as a form of interaction among individuals and between organizations extends beyond the frontiers of Ghana. The interesting feature is not only the exchange of knowledge, but the spread of a method which makes the mutual exchange within the institutional structures of the formal women's organizations possible. The NCWD representative in Sunyani took it over from workshops of WiLDAF, Ghana, which she has regularly attended as a volunteer. WiLDAF is an organizational network working in 26 African countries and is unique in its pan-African extension. Examples of organizations on a transnational level are given by the South American Network CLADEM (Comité Latino-Americano y Caribe para la Defensa de los Derechos de la Mujer) founded in 1987 and the Asian network APWLD (Asian Pacific Women in Law and Development) founded in 1986. All three organizations concentrate on the issue of law and development, and stay via their headquarters in permanent contact with Women, Law and Development based in Washington. The idea of establishing a network on the African continent was taken up by six women from Kenya, Uganda, Ghana, Zimbabwe, Botswana and Senegal at the World Women's Conference in 1985 in Nairobi, who tried to establish a pan-African network. The formal founding took place in 1990 in Harare, Zimbabwe. Today, the network encompasses 500 organizational and 1500 individual members. The overall topic of WiLDAF is the issue of law as a legal and social construct and its importance for development. The broad defined legal framework is split into women's social, economic and political rights and the amendment of constitutions. The framework is open and flexible in order to integrate new issues such as globalization, trade and deregulation, environment, media and information, topics which were much discussed during the third general meeting at the Accra Conference Centre in July 1999, where more than 150 delegates met.

Communication on a pan-African level and beyond is realized by using the Internet for the distribution of information and of urgent letters. The Internet becomes a medium of 'shared politics' (Youngs, 1999: 66), used for lobbying national governments or international organizations, such as the European Union or the World Bank. In 1999, WiLDAF-Mauritius started a global campaign against the deregulation and liberalization of trade, following on the EU green paper, and fearing growing competition, exploitation and disempowerment, which clearly contradicts the passing of the Beijing Platform of Action by national delegations. Together with ENDA, an environmental organization in Senegal, and the European network WIDE (Women in Development Europe), located in Brussels, they lobbied during a discussion day with the European Commission in Dakar, Senegal. Through electronic media, women's organizations transform their real lives into the 'cultural politics of cyberspace' (Escobar, 1999: 32): the effect of the everyday physical world and culture is represented in a global extent, but the core force underlying the global agency still permits the defence of their localities.

The formal organization of WiLDAF is based on decentralized power structures, which avoid a homogenization of predicted policies from above and the encrusting of a growing network. The emphasis on decision-making processes and a policy design at the local level is an indication of the recognition of diversities of women's realities. From the pan-African level towards the local level, the common framework of WiLDAF is adapted step by step to the specific local context. The two female heads of WiLDAF-Ghana, both lawyers, select each year a new law which concerns women in the country, such as intestate law, which regulates the system of inheritance, marriage law, the law on the maintenance of children and violence against women. In collaboration with volunteers, these laws are permanently negotiated by the Queenmothers' Association, the market women, social welfare officers, teachers, nurses and community development workers. Laws are permanently negotiated, and both sides take further action to change them to the benefit of women or to take up measures to assist women. For example, a subqueenmother can assist a woman in the village with background information about where to bring forward a case on failed financial support from a divorced husband for his young son. Law is therefore not conceptualized as an isolated tool. Politics emphasize the support of a legal culture in three fields: (1) the legal structure (courts, procedures to exercise rights), (2) substance (e.g. customary law) and (3) culture (attitudes and behaviour). The importance of this pragmatic approach lies in the active appropriation of law as a tool of transformation by knowledge. One woman in the village explained:

> *NA:* Nowadays, men cannot cheat us. If my husband dies, I know that I can live in this house, even if I am his second wife. Everything we have in the room belongs to me. They will come to take it, but I know my rights, now we are educated and we know how to get our rights. It is not like in former times, when they drove you away and your husband's family took over. I can go to my family's house, but I know that everything here belongs to me.
>
> *CM:* How did you get to know?
>
> *NA:* They talk about it everywhere, in Sunyani, at the market, it comes on the radio, even in my shop.

WiLDAF is one example of how spaces are bridged by permanent interaction. Regarding this institutional level, the permanence of interactions follows a differentiation from a common framework on law at a pan-African level to local particularities and vice versa: an integration and homogenization of everyday local legal realities of women into the common framework. Along these levels, the personal networking for exchange is assisted by workshops, conferences, women's forums, meetings and the use of media.

The interweaving along the levels and even beyond the African continent indicates that women's spaces are not isolated from each other, but are overlapping along the interfaces of women's formal and informal organizations. These organizations can metaphorically be described as pillars of production, generation, articulation and politicization of knowledge. Networking, as the major feature of interaction, builds bridges between the pillars. Knowledge is circulated and distributed on and across these bridges. Within networking as a medium, knowledge flows across ethnic, national and state borders, bridging rural–urban distances. Networking is a practice which opens up and offers new ways of transforming gender relations and social institutions. Connections and interactions between the pillars are structuring and extending spaces towards the establishment of a global knowledge architecture, turning local agencies into glocalized practices.

The Local in the Global: Broken Horizons

Space is produced through agency, and the shaping of spaces also constitutes new forms of agency. The extension of space is structuring the dynamics of 'glocalization', whose driving force is self-organization (Robertson, 1995: 26). What is now meant by local? The starting point was the networking between the subqueenmothers, creating their own female space for social change. At the local level, knowledge is generated by previous and new experiences. New elements are embedded through translocal networking. The local organization of knowledge generation changes insofar as the world within its reach expands. The reach of knowledge is translocal, the validity – and this is the important aspect – remains local. Local refers to the aspect of validity whereas translocal characterizes the aspect of spatiality. The constitution of local–global linkage is not a direct one, it is broken into the multiple interludes between the different levels. Local particularities such as knowledge on environment, law, or rites do not vanish, even the opposite takes place: a redefinition. The content of knowledge becomes translated into discourses, agendas, or programmes. By these acts of translations, cultural particularities vanish. The creation of knowledge repertoires is dependent on the specific context. Since everyday knowledge is relevant for agency in the village, scientific knowledge becomes important in the (Sub)Queenmothers' Association and in the Women's Forum in Accra. The interesting empirical aspect is not only the constitution of local production of knowledge itself, but the interconnection and the dynamics between these spaces.

Knowledge generation and production have been practised under the aspect of transformation. This tendency draws our attention once more towards the importance of research. A Ghanaian professor who conducted a study on gender and forest management in northern Ghana as part of the WEDNET initiative,[8] being back at the university, theorized her empirical data and brought back the results by translating them into a practical language and by establishing contacts with women's organizations. In the double reflexive form, academic knowledge becomes a new type of hybrid knowledge, re-embedded into the original context, politicized and finally used as a tool for transformation. This form of knowledge production is not one-way, but it is embedded within a circle, which blurs the hegemonic forms of academic knowledge and the borders between academic and everyday knowledge.

The concern of knowledge as the basis of transformation is part of an exceptional book titled *Gender Training in Ghana* (Tsikata, 2001). Several Ghanaian academics and activists analyse here the impact of national and international politics on gender relations from a gender perspective in Ghana, but develop their own perspectives, too. They follow the paradigm of a politicizing knowledge in research, training and development politics. Their criticism is addressed to development agencies, which are still sticking to a depoliticized form of participation and the planning of programmes and projects by referring to the discourse of women and development. Part of their argumentation is that development programmes are not really aiming at the transformation of social relations, and thus remain fruitless. Participation in development cooperation must go back to the original meaning of the transformation of social relations: for instance gender training must follow an approach based on transformation. However, participatory approaches such as rapid rural appraisals and participatory rural appraisals, which are organized in a technical manner, are the dominant form of research on knowledge. Local knowledge is post-integrated into predefined concepts of development, reduced to be a source of information and a utensil for application, whereas western knowledge remains the 'world-ordering' knowledge (Hobart, 1993: 3). I argue against this mechanical reduction of local knowledge by drawing attention to the fact that the complexity of local knowledge encompasses issues of history, identity and politics which can hardly be separated from each other, making understandable that knowledge is not static, but is a dynamic social process.

A few northern researchers understood the approach of conceptualizing knowledge as a process. They repoliticized their research agenda, for instance by integrating local researchers from the beginning, reflecting on the gathered data and building up a common project (Wieringa, 2002). The approach of cross-cultural research and politics is still difficult, especially during fieldwork. It touches the crucial aspect of cross-cultural power relations. It is however a common understanding that knowledge is a process and that the reality of development is socially constructed (Berger and Luckmann, 1966). The politicizing of knowledge and the self-refexivity of the research process and context mean that the self and the other are not dichotomies but their life-worlds are interconnected. Other people put the question of an objective equalization, a mutual interrelatedness of one's own existence and those of other people (Schütz, 1962: 126).

Women in Ghana are not an exception when they formulate their own discourses and agendas on development. This is a sign of resistance against mainstream development politics and practices. Examples from other parts of the world such as Asia, Latin America or the Caribbean (Escobar et al., 2002: 28–36) indicate that women are now defending their local knowledge and their cultural environment. With the building up of globally organized networks and the use of them for local politics, women are now defining globalization from the global networks. Irrespective of other national and international development organizations and agencies, different development politics are appearing. Resistance and the establishment of one's own capacities of knowledge have the potential to change the knowledge order, locally and globally.

Notes

I want to thank all those people in Ghana who contributed to my work during long interview sessions, group discussions and day-to-day interactions.

1 The term 'glocalization' (Robertson, 1995: 26) combines the local with the global, opening the analytical perspective towards the interplay between both levels.

2 DAWN was created by a group of 22 women in Bangalore in 1984. It was first attached to the University of West Indies (Barbados) and is now organized in decentralized structures with regional offices in the Caribbean, Asia, Latin America, Africa and the Pacific.

3 For a critical analysis see Diawara (2000).

4 Roughly 70 percent of women in Ghana work in the agricultural sector (Tsikata, 1989: 75).

5 The differentiation is given by history: the first ones who settled in town received the black stools, a fact which legitimates their position. Apart from political privileges, the economic situation of members of the royal family often does not differ too much from other people's.

6 The study was conducted in collaboration with the Development and Project Planning Centre of the University of Bradford (UK), the Institute for Social Statistics and Economy Research (ISSER) of the University of Ghana (Legon) and the NCWD.

7 Statistics for the year 1998 indicate 42 rapes, 98 attempted rapes and 97 incidents of assault.

8 WEDNET (the Women, Environment and Development Network) was launched in 1989 and set up a research programme in eight anglophone and francophone countries with regard to women's knowledge in the management of natural resources. This approach combines scientific research with a policy agenda and the publications of *WEDNews* (Jommo, 1993: 158).

Bibliography

Albrow, Martin (1998) *Abschied vom Nationalstaat.* Frankfurt am Main: Suhrkamp.

Appadurai, Arjun (1998) *Modernity at Large: Cultural Dimensions of Globalization.* Minneapolis and London: University of Minnesota Press.

Arhin, Kwame (1983) 'The Political and Military Roles of Akan Women', in Christine Oppong (ed.) *Female and Male in West Africa*, pp. 91–8. London: Allen and Unwin.

Berger, Peter and Luckmann, Thomas (1966) *The Social Construction of Reality.* New York: Anchor Book.

Bourdieu, Pierre (1976) *Entwurf einer Theorie der Praxis.* Frankfurt am Main: Suhrkamp.

Bourdieu, Pierre (1991) *Language and Symbolic Power.* Cambridge: Polity Press.

Bruchhaus, Eva-Maria (1988) 'Frauenselbsthilfegruppen: Schlüssel zur Entwicklung aus eigener Kraft oder Modernisierung der letzten Reserve?', *Peripherie* 30/1: 49–61.

Butegwa, Florence and Nduna, Sydia (1995) *Legal Rights: Organizing Women in Africa.* Harare: WiLDAF.

Diawara, Mamadou (2000) 'Globalization, Development Politics and Local Knowledge', *International Sociology* 15(2): 361–71.

Elwert, Georg, Evers, Hans-Dieter and Wilkens, Werner (1983) 'Die Suche nach Sicherheit: kombinierte Produktionsformen im sogenannten informellen Sektor', *Zeitschrift für Soziologie* 12(4): 281–96.

Escobar, Arturo (1999) 'Gender, Place and Networks: A Political Ecology of Cyberculture', in Wendy Harcourt (ed.) *Women@Internet*, pp. 31–54. London: Zed Books.

Escobar, Arturo, Rocheleau, Dianne and Kothari, Smita (2002) 'Environmental Social Movements and the Politics of Place', *Development* 45(1): 28–36.

Evers, Hans-Dieter (1999) *Globalisierung der Wissensgesellschaft – Ansätze einer neuen Entwicklungstheorie*, Working Paper No. 310. Bielefeld: Sociology of Development Research Centre, University of Bielefeld.

Geertz, Clifford (1983) *Local Knowledge: Further Essays in Interpretative Sociology*. New York: Basic Books.

Giddens, Anthony (1995) *Konsequenzen der Moderne*. Frankfurt am Main: Suhrkamp.

Habermas, Jürgen (1981) *Theorie des kommunikativen Handelns*, Vols 1 and 2. Frankfurt am Main: Suhrkamp.

Hobart, Marc (1993) 'Introduction: The Growth of Ignorance', in Marc Hobart (ed.) *An Anthropological Critique of Development*, pp. 1–31. London: Routledge.

ISSER (Institute of Statistical, Social and Economic Research) (1998) *Women in Pubic Life in Ghana*. Legon: University of Ghana.

Jommo, Rosemary Berewa (1993) 'African Women's Indigenous Knowledge in the Management of Natural Resources', in Filomina Chioma Steady (ed.) *Women and Children First*, pp. 157–68. Rochester, VT: Schenckmann.

Knorr-Cetina, Karin (1999) *Epistemic Cultures*. Cambridge, MA and London: Harvard University Press.

Lash, Scott (1994) 'Reflexivity and its Doubles: Structure, Aesthetics, Community', in Ulrich Beck, Anthony Giddens and Scott Lash (eds) *Reflexive Modernization*, pp. 110–74. Cambridge and Oxford: Polity Press.

Lebeuf, Annie (1963) 'The Role of Women in the Political Organization of African Societies', in Denise Paulme (ed.) *Women in Tropical Africa*, pp. 93–120. London: Routledge and Kegan Paul.

Long, Norman (1992) 'Introduction', in Norman Long and Ann Long (eds) *Battlefields of Knowledge*, pp. 3–16. London and New York: Routledge.

Nederveen Pieterse, Jan (1995) 'Globalization as Hybridization', in Mike Featherstone, Scott Lash and Roland Robertson (eds) *Global Modernities*, pp. 45–68. London, Thousand Oaks, CA and New Delhi: Sage.

Richards, Paul (1985) *Indigenous Agricultural Revolution*. London: Hutchinson.

Robertson, Roland (1995) 'Glocalization: Time–Space and Homogeneity–Heterogeneity', in Mike Featherstone, Scott Lash and Roland Robertson (eds) *Global Modernities*, pp. 25–44. London, Thousand Oaks, CA and New Delhi: Sage.

Schütz, Alfred (1962) *The Problem of Social Reality, Collected Papers 1*. The Hague, Boston, MA and London: Martinus Nijhoff.

Schütz, Alfred and Luckmann, Thomas (1975) *Strukturen der Lebenswelt*. Neuwied and Darmstadt: Luchterhand.

Sen, Gita and Grown, Caren (1987) *Development, Crisis and Alternative Visions*. New York: New Feminist Library.

Sillitoe, Paul (1998) 'What Know Natives? Local Knowledge in Development', *Social Anthropology* 6(2): 203–20.

Tsikata, Dzodzi (1989) 'Women's Political Organisations 1951–1987', in Emmanuel Hansen and Kwame E. Nisin (eds) *The State, Development and Politics in Ghana*, pp. 73–93. London: Codesria.

Tsikata, Dzodzi, ed. (2001) *Gender Training in Ghana*. Accra: Woeli Publishing Services.

Wieringa, Saskia (2002) 'Women's Sexual Empowerment in Indonesia', paper presented at the EADI workshop, Rome, 15–16 March.

Youngs, Gillian (1999) 'Virtual Voices: Real Lives', in Wendy Harcourt (ed.) *Women@Internet*, pp. 55–68. London: Zed Books.

PART II. REGIONAL CASE STUDIES

9

Transnational Migration and Development in Postwar Peripheral States: An Examination of Guatemalan and Salvadoran State Linkages with their Migrant Populations in Los Angeles

Eric Popkin

Scholarly interest in transnational migration has emerged in the context of the massive population movements that have occurred in the current era of globalization. Changes in the international economy and the diffusion of space–time compressing technologies have created the conditions that intensify exchanges between immigrants and their places of origin. Immigrants pursue either individual or collective relationships with the country of origin for a variety of reasons including the difficulty in obtaining economic security in either sending or receiving societies, racial and ethnic discrimination in the host society, and/or a desire to assist in the socioeconomic development of communities of origin often neglected by home governments or destroyed by civil conflict (Basch et al., 1994; Popkin, 1997). Migrant-led transnationalism includes maintaining kinship and social networks across borders, sending or receiving remittances and the establishment of hometown associations that engage in collective community projects in the home region, among other activities (Goldring, 2002). The elaborate linkages between migrant-sending and receiving areas that emerge lead some analysts to conceive of transnational migration as a phenomenon that may go beyond individuals and households, incorporating entire communities (migrant and non-migrant members) into the globalization process (Basch et al., 1994; Levitt, 1998; Goldring, 1992; Rouse, 1987; R. Smith, 1995; Smith and Guarnizo, 1998; Portes et al., 1999). Transnational communities have three novel features: they are a product of global capitalism due to the labor demand from the North; they constitute a phenomenon distinct from the traditional patterns of immigrant adaptation; and they offer more opportunities for popular initiatives (Portes et al., 1999).

The density and complexity of such interactions across local spaces coalesce into a single sphere of social action, the transnational social field, which evolves as a newly constructed social space that straddles international borders (Rouse, 1991; Basch et al., 1994). As immigrants construct transnational social networks of obligations and assistance, home country elites respond by attempting to reincorporate the immigrants into the sending nation polity. Transnational social fields become consolidated in the context of the interaction between the transnational practices of immigrants ('transnationalism from below') and the transnational engagement of sending country elites ('transnationalism from above') (Smith and Guarnizo, 1998; Landolt et al., 1999).

My primary concern in this article is to examine the political dimensions of the transnational social field. I am interested in delineating the political and economic conditions that motivate peripheral nations to incorporate their emigrant population into the home country polity, given that the specific causal links between the contemporary global economic order and transnational political practices are seldom explored in detail in the transnational migration literature.[1] I am particularly interested in examining the conditions that lead to 'transnationalism from above' or state-led transnationalism in the Central American nations of El Salvador and Guatemala.[2] An inquiry into this issue also requires careful analysis of global cities, sites of capital accumulation. As Portes (2000: 167) has noted, 'the new transnational space of which global cities are nodes is created by sustained flows of capital, technology, information and people'. Portes also notes that these global phenomena are played out in local spaces and against backdrops of very local conditions and histories. Global economic forces are centered in, and at the same time transforming cities. Given this facet of globalization, I want to consider how Central American state-led transnationalism shapes immigrant politics in Los Angeles, the site of the largest concentration of Salvadoran and Guatemalan immigrants in the United States. The article specifically assesses Salvadoran and Guatemalan immigrant organizations in Los Angeles, which serve as transnational institutions that draw the attention of state actors in the home countries. An examination of the Salvadoran and Guatemalan cases enables me to consider the specific dimension of politically motivated migration and how countries of origin implement state-led transnational strategies given presumed tensions with segments of their respective emigrant populations. If collaboration occurs, does it facilitate the social, economic and political incorporation of previously disenfranchised populations leading to further democratization in the home country? Or do historical tensions further empower home states, legitimate them, and facilitate the implementation of strategies on home state terms? Does this engagement contribute to socioeconomic development in specific locales within El Salvador and Guatemala?

In this article, I argue that the nature of El Salvador and Guatemala's insertion into the global economy and the resulting adverse effects of neoliberal policies require these states to devote considerable resources to establish relationships with immigrant organizations and transmigrant elites in the United States. This need leads these states to attempt to alter US immigration policy so as to guarantee the ability of Guatemalan and Salvadoran immigrants to maintain their residence in the US. Although Guatemalan and Salvadoran immigrant organizations gain some leverage over the process of local development within the home country, these groups confront a range of obstacles in their effort to gain a greater voice in political and economic affairs in the countries of origin. In the Guatemalan case, immigrant organizations face serious obstacles in regions considered vital to Guatemalan state efforts to maintain security and political control as compared to communities located elsewhere. In the Salvadoran case, immigrant organizations achieve higher levels of authority in the sending communities due to considerable collaboration with municipal officials in the context of implementation of community projects, a finding that can be explained partially by higher levels of postwar democracy achieved in that country as compared to Guatemala. Finally, government policies that attempt to leverage international migration in an effort to promote productive development at the local level will likely falter in the longer term in the absence of state-supported macroeconomic policies aimed at reducing socioeconomic disparities in Guatemala and El Salvador. This shortcoming results in the maintenance of the traditional power structure and social hierarchies in these states. The data I rely on come from qualitative fieldwork completed in Los Angeles, El Salvador and Guatemala between 1993 and 2001 (Popkin, 1996, 1998; Popkin et al., 1997).[3] After a brief review of the literature on state-led political transnationalism, I examine Guatemalan and Salvadoran immigrant organizations in Los Angeles. This review facilitates consideration of Central American state-led transnationalism and the interaction between this process and transmigrant institutional involvement in the countries of origin.

State-Led Political Transnationalism: Migrant Autonomy or State Control?

In the past decade, increasing numbers of governments with sizeable migrant populations abroad including Haiti, the Dominican Republic, Mexico, Colombia, the Philippines, and Grenada have been actively promoting the transnational reincorporation of their migrant citizens into state-centered projects (Smith and Guarnizo, 1998; Dresser, 1993; Goldring, 1998; Guarnizo, 1998). As the links between these countries and their respective migrant populations have intensified, the home states have redefined themselves as deterritorialized nation-states (Basch et al., 1994; Glick-Schiller and Fouron, 1998). Such deterritorialized nation-states guarantee that their emigrant populations have responsibilities to and some rights within their country of origin. A number of states have allowed migrants to obtain dual nationality or citizenship status enabling them to live abroad but vote in regional and national elections back home. Additionally, these states have facilitated the possibility for elected representatives of the migrant populations to participate formally in national governments.

The policies adopted by home states toward their migrant populations can generate novel forms of human agency as many migrants attempting to diversify their linkages with the country of origin are now viewed as a strategic asset by the home state (Guarnizo and Smith, 1998). These conditions have led some analysts to emphasize the liberating character of individual or collective transnational migratory practices (Kearney, 1991). In his study of Mixtec migrant farm workers, for example, Kearney (1991) suggests that in spite of experiencing a high level of poverty these workers create autonomous spaces in southern California and Oregon where neither the US nor the Mexican state has access or control. Other scholars contend that one needs to caution against such celebratory analyses that privilege migrant autonomy. Although transnational migration enables some transmigrants (such as transnational entrepreneurs) to take advantage of the logic of globalization and advance their economic position considerably, it should not be viewed simply as a liberating phenomenon but rather as a dialectical process (Guarnizo, 1998; Smith and Guarnizo, 1998; Landolt et al., 1999; Popkin, 1999; Goldring, 2002). These analysts question immigrants' ability to challenge the economic, political and social hierarchies in which they are embedded. These studies suggest that the increasing priority of home states to establish linkages with their respective migrant populations leads the transnational social field to become a terrain in which new relations of domination can emerge out of the established power structures. In a number of studies examining Dominican, Mexican, Guatemalan and Salvadoran transnational migration, analysts have demonstrated how state policies toward their migrant populations limit the range of programs that migrant organizations can implement in sending regions and often benefit state development and political objectives (Guarnizo, 1998; Goldring, 2002). In his comparative study of Mexican and Dominican transnational migration, for example, Guarnizo (1998) argues that Mexican transnational elites in addition to Mexican state institutional representatives reproduced ruling party power and control as well as class hierarchies. This article intends to contribute to this debate within the transnational migration literature through an assessment of the home state–immigrant interaction in the context of postwar reconstruction and development in Central American migrant-sending countries. I now turn to an assessment of global political and economic conditions that motivate and drive state-led transnationalism in this context.

Globalization and State-Led Political Transnationalism

Trends associated with the post-1970s logic of capital accumulation have led to a growing incorporation of all parts of the world into a single system of production and investment. Capital is being channeled into key regions and global cities, while structural adjustment programs strip away formal employment opportunities and the needed infrastructure of transportation, education and health services from peripheral regions, deemed superfluous to the newly defined circuits of wealth (Glick-Schiller et al., 1995). These processes have prompted a change in the nature of global labor displacement and insertion (Gordon, 1988). Indeed, we have witnessed the increased flow of international migrants in absolute terms leading to a shift from bilocational to multilocational movement directed to global centers that play a significant role in capital accumulation (Sassen, 1991; Wilson, 1994). As other analysts have noted, international migration has served as an important mechanism of labor market adjustment for some peripheral countries, diminishing the labor supply and therefore acting as a safety valve for labor markets with restricted employment opportunities (Perez Sainz, 2000).

Yet, there are additional factors related to the global economy that have forced peripheral states to rely on their migrant populations. The institution of neoliberal policies which have accompanied global economic restructuring has led to increasing peripheral country dependence on foreign investment. Within Latin America and the Caribbean region, dependence on the US has increased due to US influence in international financial institutions that also dictate the range of policies available for countries in search of foreign investment. In their effort to renegotiate their insertion into the global economy, peripheral countries have developed export-oriented economies that emphasize assembly manufacturing, non-traditional agricultural production and services such as tourism. These policies have not led to trade surpluses and public deficits have continued. Given these conditions, migrant remittances fulfill a key role for securing hard currency in these countries and for the subsistence of low-income households (Itzigsohn, 1995, 2001; Portes et al., 1997; Guarnizo and Smith, 1998; Popkin, 1999). Scholars have also argued that peripheral nation policy-makers pursue neoliberal policies that drain local areas with the knowledge that international migration will increase leading to migrant remittance payments that will ensure political stability in these locales (M.P. Smith, 1994; Mahler, 1996; Guarnizo, 1998; Popkin, 1999).

Migrant-sending state efforts to forge linkages with their populations abroad become all the more important for peripheral nations in the Caribbean Basin region (Central America and Caribbean nations) given that this region has become functionally integrated on an economic, demographic, social, cultural and, to some extent, even political level with the US. This process began with the implementation of the Caribbean Basin Initiative by the Reagan administration and has been bolstered by the recent passing of the Trade and Development Act of 2000 that dramatically increases access to the US market for Caribbean Basin (and African) nations in line with provisions included in the North American Free Trade Agreement (NAFTA). US exports to the Caribbean Basin countries rose by more than 200 percent from 1983 to 1997, reaching $19 billion, almost $6 billion more than exports to China (Lowenthal, 2000). This figure is also higher than US exports to Argentina, Brazil, Russia, or the whole region of Eastern Europe and could increase substantially with the NAFTA parity legislation. The demographic reality of Caribbean Basin interdependence with the US is also significant. According to Lowenthal, immigration from Cuba, the Dominican Republic, Haiti and Jamaica accounts for 10, 12, 14 and 15 percent respectively of those countries' populations. Los Angeles has become as linked to Central America as Miami is to the entire Caribbean Basin region. In fact, Los Angeles is the second largest Salvadoran city, the first being the capital of that country, San Salvador. The Salvadoran government currently estimates the Salvadoran migrant population at 2.5 million with 2 million living in the US. The total national population in this country is 6 million, which means that approximately 29 percent of the Salvadoran population lives outside the national borders. Currently, immigrants from the region provide the largest source of foreign exchange to their home countries through remittances, leading these peripheral states to concern themselves with US immigration policies. But interdependence has also led to the escalation of social problems in the region such as crime and gang warfare facilitated in part by increased deportations from immigrant enclaves in the US.

Given this context, peripheral states in the Caribbean Basin attempt to leverage the migratory process in an effort to facilitate the consistent sending of critical monetary transfers (remittances) that serve as crucial contributions to the national economies. Specifically, home states attempt: (1) to create a potential force that can lobby those actors in the US and can make important decisions which influence economic conditions in the home country, (2) to develop a market within the migrant community for home country goods, (3) to stimulate migrant investment for private sector initiatives in the home country and (4) to generate migrant investment for government development projects in the home country.

There are conditions specific to El Salvador and Guatemala that motivate these nations to pursue state-led transnational strategies. As countries that have experienced devastating civil wars that ended in the early/mid-1990s (1992 in El Salvador and 1996 in Guatemala), El Salvador and Guatemala have both needed to implement large-scale reconstruction efforts in an era of limited foreign investment and inconsequential levels of reconstruction aid.[4] Both governments have instituted neoliberal policies emphasizing free trade. In the case of El Salvador, these policies included the slashing of the public sector, privatizing state-owned utilities and lowering barriers to foreign investment, laying off thousands of workers and aggravating the country's chronic unemployment problem. As an example of a positive result, however, government officials note that exports from the *maquiladora* sector have increased from $796 million to $2.5 billion over the past 10 years (Swedish, 2002a). While this has generated thousands of jobs in factories assembling products for export, most of these jobs do not pay a living wage and include few protections or benefits for workers. According to the United Nations Development Program, these policies have resulted in a huge gap between the rich and poor in El Salvador as the wealthiest 20 percent of the population has 18 times the income of the poorest 20 percent (Swedish, 2002a).

One of the primary reasons for continuing high levels of poverty in El Salvador and Guatemala is the collapse of the agricultural sector in those countries, which employs over 30 percent of each population. There is no single cause for the severe agricultural crisis; rather government neglect of rural development in the neoliberal era coupled with a series of events including natural disasters: hurricanes, floods and earthquakes, followed by drought have led to a major food crisis. These events were accompanied by a collapse of international coffee prices to their lowest level in 100 years in real terms. Given Central America's dependence on coffee exports, this development proved to be devastating, costing some 600,000 jobs according to the Inter-American Development Bank (2002). In April 2002, the World Food Program launched an emergency feeding program in Guatemala, targeting the country's malnourished children. According to the World Food Program Report, Guatemala has the highest rate of chronic malnutrition in Latin America 'affecting 47 per cent of children under five years of age' (World Food Program, 2002). At a regional conference of the United Nations Food and Agricultural Organization (FAO) in April 2002, FAO director Jacques Diouf suggested that a lack of government political will and shrinking resources dedicated to the farming sector have contributed to chronic malnutrition such as that which exists in Guatemala. According to Diouf, official development aid from industrialized countries dropped 43 percent in real terms in the 1990–9 period (Swedish, 2002b). Moreover, the FAO stated that farmers have problems with limited access to markets for their crops, a result in large part from market distortions and protectionist measures on the part of industrialized countries that hurt the agricultural economies of poor countries. Finally, the FAO contended that food insecurity is also rooted in the inequitable distribution of productive resources and income.

The deteriorating rural conditions have contributed to Guatemalan and Salvadoran state dependence on emigration as a strategy to assure a degree of social stability given the inability/unwillingness of these states to implement macroeconomic policies that would guarantee productive employment for large numbers of the population. The departure of large numbers of Salvadoran and Guatemalan citizens to the US relieves the home states from responsibility to reorient their policies and enables these states to depend on migrant remittances that allow their populations to survive. Additionally, the importance of remittance dollars to secure the balance of payments and to cushion against the adverse effects of stabilization and adjustment policies in the Central American nations becomes clear when we examine the dollar amounts of these transfers. According to recent estimates provided by the central banks in their respective countries, the amount of remittances totaled $1.92 billion in El Salvador and $584 million in Guatemala in 2001 (Orozco, 2002). It is interesting to note that the international financial institutions most involved in Central American development, the Inter-American Development Bank, the World Bank and the United States Agency for International Development, have recently acknowledged deficiencies in the rural policies they have promoted in the region in the 1990s, as revealed by several recent conferences on the issue. A simultaneous thrust by these institutions has been the promotion of strategies to reduce the bank and courier remittance transmittal fees to the Latin American and Caribbean region, a tacit admission of the huge dependence that regional sending countries have on this source of funding in the face of such a serious rural crisis (Multilateral Investment Fund, 2001).

Collective Transmigrant Initiatives: Guatemalan and Salvadoran Immigrant Organizations in Los Angeles

Guatemalan Immigrant Organizations

According to the 2000 census, 372,487 Guatemalans resided in the US as compared to the 268,779 recorded in the 1990 census. These numbers represent 38.6 percent increase over this 10-year period. Of this number, the 2000 census also reported that 118,069 Guatemalans resided in the Los Angeles area. However, there exists considerable controversy over the number of Central Americans recorded in the 2000 census, as Central American immigrant advocates allege that the census severely under-reported their numbers by grouping them into a category with other Latinos (McDonnell, 2002). Although asked to write a specific nationality on the census form after checking the 'other Spanish/Hispanic/Latino' box, 18 percent of Latino respondents did not specify a national origin in the 2000 census. One recent study by the Pew Hispanic Center contends that 186,500 residents of Guatemalan ancestry resided in the Los Angeles area, 58 percent more than the 2000 census tally of 118,000. Additionally, this study suggests that 340,000 people of Salvadoran descent were living in the Los Angeles area, 60 percent more than the 2000 census reports (Suro, 2002). Guatemalans are the third largest Latino group in Los Angeles after the Mexican and Salvadoran populations. The dramatic increase in the Guatemalan immigrant population in the Los Angeles region between 1980 and 1990 evolved due to the escalation of war and political violence. According to the 1990 census, 30 percent of Guatemalans who resided in the Los Angeles region at that time had arrived in the area between 1980 and 1984, years in which the civil war and government-directed repression aimed at the civilian population peaked (Lopez et al., 1996; Popkin, 1998). Although it is difficult from census figures to determine the number of indigenous Guatemalans (Mayan) in the Los Angeles region, estimates place the number at between 4000 and 10,000, a small percentage of the total number of Guatemalans in this region (Popkin, 1999).

In a study conducted in 1994/5, my associates and I identified 38 Guatemalan immigrant organizations in Los Angeles of which 33 were hometown associations (*fraternidades*) (Popkin et al., 1997). Hometown associations draw their membership from a particular community or region of the home country. Of the 33 associations identified, 25 had exclusive Latino membership and eight had only indigenous members. These associations engage in social and cultural activities often with the objective of supporting development projects in the sending community/region. These projects include support for health clinics, schools, scholarship funds for children, parks, street paving, potable water and reforestation. In order to implement these projects, several of the *fraternidades* work directly with counterpart organizations in the home community. In some cases, the migrant organizations actually facilitate the establishment of these structures in Guatemala. Some of these Guatemalan associations collaborate loosely and/or negotiate with the appropriate governmental officials for specific types of assistance related to the implementation of their projects. However, for the most part, Guatemalan *fraternidades* have declared their political neutrality and have attempted to maintain their independence from the political parties in the home country. Virtually all of the indigenous *fraternidades* channel their support for projects through religious institutions in the sending region that determine the nature of the projects. The dollar amount of each project can be quite significant and in some cases can reach over $50,000 or more.

Guatemalan associations have formed coalitions. Both the Latino and indigenous *fraternidades* are grouped in umbrella organizations. The Asociación de Fraternidades de Guatemala (AFG), a coalition of 21 Latino associations (predominately hometown associations), was formed in 1990 with the objective of coordinating some of the activities of member organizations and working toward a stronger unified Guatemalan presence in Los Angeles. This organization holds large fundraising events and distributes the receipts to the member organizations. Current collective projects include a youth leadership-training program. Within the Mayan migrant community in Los Angeles, the Comité Maya has been formed. This structure includes representatives from four of the Kanjobal and Chuj (the largest Mayan language groups to be represented in Los Angeles) hometown associations in Los Angeles. This organization serves as a vehicle to support each association's events, particularly the patron saint festivities, and to coordinate collective events such as the visit of a religious official from the home region. In addition to this committee, Mayan migrants from the same four hometowns have joined together in the Proyecto Pastoral Maya, an organization which focuses exclusively on religious training in collaboration with a division of the Catholic Bishops Conference in the US that works specifically with migrant communities.

Additional Guatemalan immigrant organizations include the Guatemalan Unity Information Agency (GUIA), a group that began its work in 1997 with assistance from the Guatemalan consulate in Los

Angeles. Relying in part on years of work conducted by the Salvadoran opposition in Los Angeles, GUIA constituted the first organization engaged in immigration services specifically targeting the Guatemalan population in Los Angeles. In addition, the group offers computer training and high school equivalent programs to local residents. In the late 1990s, the Guatemalan consulate in cooperation with leaders of GUIA and the AFG established the Comité Civico Guatemalteco, a group working to expand recently enacted dual citizenship legislation in Guatemala to include the right of Guatemalans abroad to vote in home country elections while in the US and to nominate immigrant candidates to run in elections for political office in Guatemala. Recently, a new organization, Guatemalteco Pro Voto, has emerged that has taken this charge. Several members of this group have formed a political party, URNA (Union de Reforma Nacional en Acción), that is seeking to run candidates in the next round of Guatemalan elections. A new development has emerged which concerns the arrival in Los Angeles of representatives of Guatemalan political parties seeking funds and support in the form of endorsements who likely will influence family members back in Guatemala. Finally, there exists a Guatemalan Political Action Committee (GUATEPAC) that has the objective of running Guatemalan candidates in local elections in Los Angeles.

GUIA participates directly in a national network, the Congress of Guatemalan Organizations in the United States, CONGUATE. CONGUATE includes representation from approximately 15 immigrant organizations in the US and currently is focusing on four issues: (1) soliciting funds from the Guatemalan government to maintain a working group that will advocate/lobby in favor of the interests of Guatemalan immigrants to US congressional members; (2) soliciting support from the Guatemalan authorities to have their consulates in the US issue identification cards (*matricula consulares*) to Guatemalan immigrants in the US that can serve as identification for use with social service agencies, local police forces, banks and motor vehicle agencies; (3) requesting that the Guatemalan government permit Guatemalan immigrants abroad to vote in home country elections from their locations in the US; and (4) requesting that Guatemalan consulates offer legal assistance through their offices in the US.

Salvadoran Immigrant Organizations

According to the 2000 census, 655,165 Salvadorans resided in the US of which 212,663 resided in the Los Angeles metropolitan area (Los Angeles, Riverside and Orange Counties). The national numbers represent a 15.9 percent increase from the 1990 level of 565,081. As mentioned in the previous section, many analysts and advocates for this immigrant community believe that these estimates are grossly low.

In our study of Central American immigrant organizations, my associates and I identified 28 Salvadoran hometown associations in the Los Angeles area. These organizations function similarly to those present in the

Guatemalan immigrant community as described previously. With technical assistance provided by the organization El Rescate, many of the associations have formed a coalition called COMUNIDADES (Communities Unified for the Direct Assistance of El Salvador). In September 1993, representatives of eight of the hometown associations came together and formed the organization in order to promote the social and economic development of the Salvadoran community in Los Angeles, to preserve the Salvadoran culture of this immigrant population, and to support the national reconstruction of El Salvador. Since early 1994, over 14 of the 21 Salvadoran associations identified in Los Angeles have participated in the COMUNIDADES meetings.

For many years before the emergence of the hometown organizations, Salvadoran immigrant organizational politics was dominated by two organizations, the Central American Refugee Center (currently called the Central American Resource Center, CARECEN) and El Rescate. Both CARECEN and El Rescate supported the opposition to the Salvadoran government, the Farabundo Marti National Liberation Front (FMLN), during the war in that country. By adopting a transnational strategy and sending party members to the US in order to mobilize constituents against US intervention in El Salvador, the FMLN obtained a considerable degree of support and collaborated with diverse institutions in this country, including agencies working on the issue of immigration. Although these organizations offered social services to Central American immigrants (primarily Salvadorans) during the civil wars, they devoted considerable resources to providing support to popular forces within El Salvador working to change the socioeconomic order. Since the end of the wars, these organizations have altered the focus of their work, emphasizing the incorporation of the Salvadoran immigrant community into US society. These organizations currently offer a range of programs including programs oriented toward youth, community development and social services to the Salvadoran community. In addition to these programs, CARECEN offers extensive legal services. Other organizations have emerged that also offer legal services to the Salvadoran community. These include ASOSAL, the Asociación Salvadoreña, formally CRECEN, a grassroots organization of Salvadorans initially linked to CARECEN, and PIPIL, formed after a spilt within the ASOSAL organization. CARECEN, ASOSAL and PIPIL provide legal counseling and representation of undocumented Central Americans attempting to legalize their status. These efforts have focused on working with Salvadorans (and some Guatemalans) eligible for asylum or stay of deportation through the ABC and NACARA programs.

Since the end of the war, other organizations focusing on the incorporation of Salvadoran immigrants in US society have emerged. SALEF (the Salvadoran American Leadership and Education Fund) promotes the civic education of Salvadorans who are new or potential US citizens and provides training for future political leaders from this community. Additionally, this organization coordinates voter registration drives and offers internships to

Central American students in the offices of Latino politicians. This group also offers scholarships to Central American and other Latino students entering college. SALPAC (the Salvadoran Political Action Committee), emerged in 1998 and promotes political candidates that support issues of importance to Central American immigrants including education, poverty and crime.

CARECEN became instrumental in the formation of a national coalition of Salvadoran organizations, the Red Nacional Salvadoreña Americana (the National Salvadoran–American Network [SANN]). This organization includes approximately 15 organizations from throughout the US and has the primary goal of representing the interests of Salvadorans in the US on a national level with an emphasis on lobbying Congress on behalf of legislation beneficial to the Salvadoran immigrant community. Currently, the organization is exploring its potential involvement in community development projects in El Salvador that require immigrant participation. The leadership of this coalition includes many Salvadoran leaders who worked to support popular organizations in El Salvador during the civil war.

Salvadoran and Guatemalan State Strategies: The Immigration Context and US Immigration Policy

In order to implement their policies with regard to their migrant populations, the Salvadoran and Guatemalan governments through their embassies in Washington and consulates have worked to obtain legal status for their migrants in the US. Thus, these states have been actively engaged in campaigns on behalf of the ABC migrant class seeking to legalize its status in the context of changes in US immigration law. The ABC program was based on a class action suit brought by the American Baptist Church allowing those who had been previously denied asylum during the 1980s (over 95 percent of Guatemalans and Salvadorans who applied) to reapply. ABC class members would have been eligible for suspension of deportation under rules in play prior to the passing of the 1996 Illegal Immigration Reform and Immigrant Responsibility Act. Prior to the 1996 act, suspension of deportation status, granted to those who had resided in the US for at least seven years and who could demonstrate that deportation would result in hardship, enabled recipients to apply for permanent residence status and eventually citizenship. The 1996 law discarded suspension of deportation status and replaced it with a new status, cancellation of removal, that extended the wait to 10 years and required applicants to demonstrate that their deportation would result in severe hardship for a family member who is a US citizen, a condition much more difficult to prove.

In essence, by advocating on behalf of Central American political asylum applicants, the Salvadoran and Guatemalan governments support these applicants' claim that they fled political persecution committed by the governments. This stance contradicts the claims made by the governments of El Salvador and Guatemala during the civil wars. At the time, these governments viewed those who fled violence as subversives with illegitimate claims for political asylum in the US. Due to the perceived importance of migrant settlement to further its own economic and political objectives, the Guatemalan and Salvadoran governments appear willing to support the migrant contention that they fled politically motivated violence, as several analysts have noted in the Salvadoran case (Mahler, 1998; Landolt et al., 1999; Popkin, 1999).

A coincidence of interests between the Salvadoran and Guatemalan embassies and consulates and their respective organized immigrant communities (CARECEN, ASOSAL, SANN, GUIA, CONGUATE) led to a degree of collaboration between these forces contributing to the passage of NACARA (the Nicaraguan Adjustment and Central American Relief Act), that reinstated legal options to enable Guatemalans and Salvadorans who arrived prior to 1990 (ABC class members) to apply for cancellation of removal under the pre-1996 suspension of deportation rules and to seek permanent residency. The act also granted Nicaraguans and Cubans who arrived prior to 1995 automatic cancellation of departure. After issuing draft regulations considered unfavorable to Central American immigrants eligible to apply for cancellation of removal due to 'extreme hardship', the Central American governments along with the Salvadoran and Guatemalan immigrant organizations lobbied for the more lenient regulations that ultimately gained approval. Given the discrepancy in the treatment of these groups as compared to Nicaraguan and Cuban immigrants, the Salvadoran and Guatemalan embassies have been working to pass new legislation that would grant these groups (along with Hondurans and Haitians) the same privileges offered to the Cubans and Nicaraguans (the Central American Security Act [CASA]).

In June 2002, GUIA, ASOSAL and PIPIL collaborated with a number of other Salvadoran immigrant organizations based in the US in the context of a new coalition, the Central American Immigration Task Force, and sent a delegation to four Central American countries to motivate members of congress and the presidents of those countries to coordinate their legislative advocacy efforts in the US more closely with the immigrant organizations. The fact that the Task Force met with the presidents of Guatemala, El Salvador and Honduras (who agreed to coordinate with the Task Force) suggests that these governments see this collaboration as beneficial to achieve their interests. Furthermore, subsequent activities are planned between GUIA and the Guatemalan government including the government's commitment to have its consulate declare an official day of the Guatemalan immigrant in Los Angeles and to send a high-level delegation to work directly with GUIA and CONGUATE in lobbying key US legislators in support of the CASA Act. Recent activity by the Guatemalan Embassy in Washington resulted in the establishment of a Central American caucus within the US Congress. Collaboration between the

Salvadoran immigrant organizations and their government has increased in the context of a campaign to support the extension of Temporary Protected Status (TPS) offered to Salvadorans following the earthquakes that ravaged El Salvador in 2001. This status enables Salvadoran immigrants who do not have legal status and who apply for TPS to remain in the US without fear of deportation. TPS status for Salvadorans was scheduled to end in August 2002, but intense pressure by the Salvadoran government and immigrant organizations in the US led to the recent 12-month extension of this status to qualifying Salvadorans.

Guatemalan State Interaction with Immigrant Organizations in the US

Guatemalan State Projects

During the PAN (Partido de Avanzada Nacional) government (1996–9), the Guatemalan ambassador to the US, William Stixrud, worked to establish relationships with migrant organizations in the US as part of a broader strategy aimed at leveraging migrant remittances for productive development in the sending country. Consular officials contend that migrant remittances to family members do not lead to long-term productive investment since recipients often spend these funds on housing, consumer items, health and educational expenses. These officials assert that the collective projects supported by migrant organizations in the US have enormous potential to contribute to longer-term growth of the Guatemalan economy. According to Ambassador Stixrud, 10 percent of all Guatemalan migrants in the US, or 100,000 individuals, are affiliated with an organization with co-nationals (hometown association, professional organization, etc.). To leverage this organizational strength in support of development initiatives in Guatemala, the Guatemalan Embassy in Washington initiated an elaborate program, Chapines Sin Fronteras (Guatemalans Without Borders), which encouraged collective migrant direct investment in business ventures in target sending communities. This program incorporated the Guatemalan government Ministries of Agriculture and Economics and a number of large private sector organizations including the Association of Exporters of Non-Traditional Products (AGEXPRONT), the Rural Bank of Guatemala (BANRURAL) and the Guatemalan Chamber of Industrial Manufacturers. The principal idea of the program was to generate financing from migrant organizations for a package of projects put together by the relevant actors in Guatemala. The Ministry of Agriculture and AGEXPRONT traveled with the Guatemalan ambassador to a number of communities in Guatemala that have large migrant concentrations in the US. After making these visits, the Ministry of Agriculture prepared agricultural development project proposals that could be presented to migrant organizations in the US. Migrant organizations were encouraged to invest in a BANRURAL account established with the Bank of America in major cities in the US and earmark their funds for the project of their choice. Migrant organizations would invest directly in BANRURAL certificates of deposit and receive 7.5 percent interest on their investments. In turn, BANRURAL, through its 160 branches throughout Guatemala, would offer loans at 10 percent interest rate to local producers to implement the projects in the prioritized communities.

The final stage of the program involved the marketing of the product in the immigrant community in the US, a step that necessitated the establishment of small companies run by immigrants in the US. In order to obtain the funds for start-up costs for the companies, immigrant organizations would sell stock to (or accept loans from) members of the specific immigrant community taking advantage of the social capital that comes from membership in these communities. According to the coordinator of this program for the Ministry of Agriculture, her ministry assisted these immigrant companies by taking care of the labeling and shipment of the product from Guatemala to the US, the Ministry of Economics assumed the responsibility for the promotion of the products in the US, and AGEX-PRONT captured funding from international financial institutions for product feasibility studies. This initiative clearly targeted expansion of non-traditional agricultural industrial development in Guatemala as championed by the ex-ambassador, a leader of ANCAFE, the coffee producers' association in Guatemala and CACIF, the private sector federation of Guatemala. Additionally, the program specifically leverages the migratory process to offer credit to small producers in Guatemala.

In order to launch the program, the Guatemalan Embassy organized two national meetings that included the participation of all of the relevant actors from Guatemala and representatives from immigrant organizations from at least six cities in the US. Moreover, the Guatemalan ambassador arranged a tour for the Guatemalan institutions to meet with immigrant organizations throughout the US in conjunction with the appropriate consulates. According to information provided by the Ministry of Agriculture, a pilot project supported by immigrant organizations in the New York area began in December 1999. Immigrant organizations in New York established a company, Chapin Import Incorporated, and selected two projects among a list of eight provided by the Ministry of Agriculture (marmalade and vegetable production). In Los Angeles, the project was promoted by the Guatemala–California Chamber of Commerce, the AFG and the Guatemalan Trade and Investment Office. Other cities expressed interest in launching similar projects. Groups have raised for this effort between $10,000 and $100,000 with migrant professional organizations in Chicago and New York, demonstrating the most potential in the short run.

Following the defeat of the PAN government in the 1999 Guatemalan elections, this project was turned over to a non-profit organization and has not advanced as envisioned by the former Guatemalan ambassador to the US and by others involved in the process. One reason that this project has not advanced concerns the complexity of the effort, given the multitude of players involved and the difficulty in coordinating actions between different government institutions and between these forces and Guatemalan immigrant organizations. Furthermore, the volume and quality of the goods produced in Guatemala were questionable according to some respondents. BANRURAL in Los Angeles failed to generate enough resources to back up the investments of Guatemalan immigrant organizations. Finally, national governments from the same political party rarely last more than one administration. Thus major initiatives such as Chapines Sin Fronteras suffer from this lack of continuity.

State-Led Transnationalism and Local Development in Guatemala: The Case of Santa Eulalia

Located in the Kanjobal region (one of 22 Mayan ethnic groups within Guatemala) in the northern department of Huehuetenango, Santa Eulalia suffers from extreme inequality in land ownership patterns that on a national level benefit Ladinos, who dominate the country politically and economically. Land shortages resulting from population pressures and long-term subsistence agriculture that led to environmental degradation and decreased productivity have contributed to intense land competition and conflict within the municipality of Santa Eulalia. The absence of opportunities for wage employment has forced most households to send some members to the southern coast for several months a year to harvest coffee or sugar. Since the mid-1980s, international migration to the US has largely replaced seasonal migration to the coast as the strategy relied on to secure household expenditures. International migration was fueled by the civil war that deeply affected this region and all indigenous regions of the western highlands.

As a result of its high level of organization in Los Angeles and its support of an extensive hospital and medical insurance program in Santa Eulalia, migrant representatives of this community in Los Angeles were approached by the Guatemalan ambassador and the local consul general in an effort to establish a number of development projects in that community. Both the ambassador and the consul general collaborated directly with the Comité Maya and arranged a visit to Santa Eulalia and several other Kanjobal communities. Accompanied by members of the Ministry of Agriculture, AGEXPRONT, the consul general of Miami and a representative of a Miami-based Mayan migrant organization returned with a number of proposals including those to initiate a community-run bank that could channel migrant remittances and offer loans for agricultural production projects, to develop a hydroelectric plant, and to implement several agricultural projects including non-traditional fruit production. Upon return, the consul general urged the Comité Maya to mobilize financial support for these projects among the migrant community in Los Angeles. In an effort to facilitate leadership development training of Mayan migrants associated with Comité Maya, the consul general requested assistance from AFG, who approached the Comité Maya and encouraged them to formally incorporate into the organization so as to benefit from the expertise of Guatemalan professionals with experience in non-profit management.

By engaging in dialogue with the consulate and AFG, the Mayan migrant organizations have more access to the Guatemalan state and home country institutions than individual members enjoyed prior to migration. However, this sense of empowerment became tempered by the lack of coordination between the different state entities involved in the project. In fact, subsequent competition ensued between the Ministry of Agriculture and AGEX-PRONT (who worked in the formally conflictive regions of the country in the context of a reconstruction project called Inversiones por la Paz), as both institutions wanted to initiate independent agro-industrial development projects in Santa Eulalia and thus maintained their contacts with the community. Both entities submitted proposals to the Inter-American Development Bank for funds to implement their respective (and similar) projects that would also rely on migrant investment. This outcome led leaders in Santa Eulalia to fear poorly executed development programs in their region. Thus, the future direction of these projects is unclear. Moreover, in spite of the possibilities generated by the increased attention on Santa Eulalia, new forms of accommodation to traditional elites have emerged. Rather than helping to facilitate the implementation of a community bank in Santa Eulalia (owned and run by community members), government officials encouraged BANRURAL to open a branch in that community so as to guarantee the channeling of future migrant funds into a structure exclusively controlled by the private sector. Residents of Santa Eulalia rely on this financial institution since no other structure exists in the community. This outcome points to the fact that Guatemalan private sector initiatives do not evolve from altruistic motives.

Some Mayan leaders in Los Angeles believe that stronger connections with the Guatemalan Embassy, the local consulate and AFG may help to build additional support for the hospital in Santa Eulalia as well as provide some degree of protection in the face of the anti-migrant onslaught in Los Angeles. However, the forging of these new connections has led to a debate within the immigrant community from Santa Eulalia concerning the appropriate degree of collaboration with Latinos. Some argue that all the activity that has occurred in Santa Eulalia has simply reproduced the inequitable ethnic relations that exist in Guatemala. The divisions that have emerged in this immigrant community certainly strengthen the hand of the Guatemalan government in their efforts to exert more influence in this region.

What is interesting is that the Guatemalan government has not specifically prioritized collaboration with other hometown associations in Los Angeles. A review of the projects supported by 11 additional hometown associations based in Los Angeles revealed the limited, if any, contact between these groups and the Guatemalan consulate or other government representatives affiliated with the Chapines Sin Fronteras program. This finding suggests that collaboration with Guatemalan immigrant business organizations, including the relevant chambers of commerce, is more a priority than immigrant hometown associations. Additionally, of these 11 hometown organizations, only one, Sanmartinecos Unidos (San Martin Jilotepeque, Chimaltenango), collaborated on any significant level with local government representatives in Guatemala in the context of implementation of the projects they supported. In this case, the municipal government of San Martin collaborated directly with the Los Angeles-based group in the construction of a community center. It appears that, at all levels, the Guatemalan government has simply neglected the work of many of the hometown associations in areas that were not highly conflictive during the war (as compared to the Santa Eulalia case). Thus, the hometown organizations have had considerable political space to implement their projects within Guatemala. Moreover, some of the leaders from these groups who have traveled to Guatemala in the context of these projects have gained a degree of power in these local communities that sometime extends to their counterpart organization or to family members in these localities. The counterpart organizations within these communities in Guatemala, however, are often not well organized, especially as compared to the Salvadoran hometown associations described in the following section.

Salvadoran State Interaction with Immigrant Organizations in the US

Salvadoran State-Led Transnationalism and Local Development in El Salvador

Whereas municipal government officials have neglected (or have not been approached by) hometown associations in the Guatemalan case, these officials and other institutional leaders are actively involved in the implementation of local projects supported by Los Angeles-based Salvadoran hometown communities. CASE-LA (Santa Elena) has developed the most sophisticated organizational relationship with a committee in the home community. This relationship evolved from a rather unique arrangement that involves a San Francisco-based hometown association that supports Santa Elena. The *directivas* of the California-based hometown associations decided that a committee should be formed in Santa Elena that could articulate the needs of the home community and maintain the formal relationship with each of their associations. Several members from the two *directivas* traveled to the home community and organized a meeting with 25 of the most respected members of Santa Elena in order to explain their work in California. This meeting resulted in the creation of CASE-Central, the core organization that facilitates the implementation of development projects in Santa Elena and maintains contact with the two organizations in California. The working relationship between the three associations has resulted in a rather significant role for the US-based organizations in the development process in Santa Elena. Each of the three associations functions independently but interacts with each other in the context of the implementation of a common work-plan. CASE-Central determines the specific priorities for development projects, however CASE-Los Angeles and CASE-San Francisco place limits on and provide some level of direction to the conception and implementation stages of these projects. Virtually all of the money for the specific development projects is generated by the US-based associations. These funds have resulted in the leverage that the Californian associations maintain in the development process. Since their inception in 1990, the US-based associations have sent up to $10,000 annually to CASE-Central for a variety of projects, including a children's park, sports facilities, and health programs.

The committee in the home community has used the significant financial and political backing of the California-based associations as leverage to lobby the mayor of Santa Elena to provide support for their projects. For example, several years ago, CASE-Central pressured the mayor to build a wall around the health clinic so as to encourage the continued shipments of medical supplies from the US-based associations. The US-based associations had previously stated their concern about the repeated vandalization of the clinic. The mayor agreed to a request by CASE-Central to obtain funds which would enable the completion of a children's park, as it became clear that the money generated for this effort in the US would not meet all the costs.

A second hometown association, ARLA (Ciudad Arce), established a different form of relationship with the home community by working directly with the mayor's office to implement projects in the community. Unlike the structure established by the hometown associations supporting Santa Elena, which empowers the committee in the home community, ARLA decided which projects it would support in the community of origin. In the past, all funds generated for development projects in the home community were sent to a bank account in Ciudad Arce. All withdrawals from this account required the signatures of the mayor and *directiva* members in Los Angeles. In recognition of the important role of the Los Angeles-based association in the affairs of the community, the mayor of Ciudad Arce traveled twice to meet with the organization in Los Angeles. On one of these occasions, he received a plaque of recognition for his work in the Salvadoran community, which he proudly pointed out to those who visit his office. Members of the association added that the presence of the mayor in Los Angeles contributed to the prestige of the association by communicating to the broader immigrant base from the home community that the work of the association is significant.

Several years ago, a conflict between ARLA and the mayor led the association to form a committee in Ciudad Arce that consisted of representatives of a number of institutions. According to members of the association, the conflict revolved around the construction of a children's park, the largest project supported by the association. During the construction of the park, the total amount of $10,000 for the project was sent to the community by the association. However, when several members of the association visited

Ciudad Arce to inspect the completed project, they found that it was not finished and that all the funds had been expended. They expressed their concerns to the mayor and threatened to inform the rest of the community in Ciudad Arce that funds had been misappropriated by the mayor's office. Apparently, the mayor saw to it that the project was completed promptly, since the threat to inform the community occurred during an election year. The relationship established between ARLA and the mayor of the community demonstrates a unique form of leverage used by an immigrant association to impact events in the home community. The association forced the mayor to be accountable and threatened to intervene directly in the political affairs of the community if their demands were not met.

The work of the Hospital Association of Nueva Guadalupe reveals another facet of how Salvadoran hometown associations can leverage Salvadoran government support for their projects in the home community. Since 1990, this association has sent a variety of medical equipment and supplies to the regional hospital located in the community and has collaborated with the director of this institution. Several years ago, the association intervened directly with officials of the Salvadoran government, including the wife of former Salvadoran president Cristiani, in an effort to obtain a vehicle that the hospital had requested from the association to transport medical equipment. Several weeks after the association contacted the government officials, such a vehicle arrived in the community. Similarly, a telephone line was installed by the national government in Nueva Guadalupe due to a request made from the Los Angeles-based association. This telephone line enabled a fax machine donated by the association to be used by the hospital to improve its communication capabilities. The ability of the association to leverage support from national government officials enhanced both its projection and its influence in the community of origin.

Salvadoran State Projects

Whereas the Guatemalan government launched a rather large-scale program that aimed to involve predominantly Guatemalan immigrant business organizations, the Salvadoran government has recently initiated a program that prioritizes collaboration with hometown associations and seems to acknowledge the success of these organizations in implementing local development projects. Through El Fondo de Inversión Social para el Desarrollo Local (FIDSL) and the Dirección General de Atención a la Comunidad en el Exterior of the Ministry of Foreign Relations, the Salvadoran government is attempting to leverage the international migratory process by establishing linkages with immigrant organizations in the US that are engaged in local development projects in their country of origin. By offering funds for projects supported by Salvadoran immigrant organizations abroad, the Salvadoran government hopes to enhance local development efforts in El Salvador through increased collaboration between the immigrant organizations and local and national government officials in

El Salvador. This program, Unidos Por la Solidaridad, is influenced by a similar program in Mexico that offers matching funds to local projects in Mexico initiated by immigrants abroad. In order to promote the program, the Salvadoran government has sent several delegations of government leaders to the US, including the vice-president of the Republic. In Los Angeles, the Salvadoran government has prioritized the work of COMU-NIDADES given the breadth and effectiveness of its work within El Salvador. In response to the new government initiative, COMUNIDADES has recently combined forces with El Rescate, the North American Integration and Development Research Center at the University of California-Los Angeles and the Fundación Centroamericana para el Desarrollo Humano Sostenible in El Salvador in order to obtain additional support from local and national government institutions within El Salvador but on its own terms. These organizations remain concerned about the motives of the Salvadoran government in this effort, believing that the government wants to extend its political influence in several municipalities in El Salvador through collaboration with the hometown organizations. Additionally, these organizations point out that the political party in control of the Salvadoran government, ARENA, has increased its recruiting efforts in southern California. The government has recently provided matching funds to three hometown organizations in Los Angeles, Paraíso de Osorío and San Juan Tepezontes in La Paz province and La Laguna in Chalatenango province. Each of the projects supported by the Salvadoran government received considerable funding (ranging from $50,000 to $100,000). Given the newness of this initiative, it remains to be seen how this collaboration will work out.

Conclusion

In this article, I have argued that Salvadoran immigrant hometown organizations have become incorporated into home country local development efforts at a higher level than their Guatemalan counterparts due to a more developed organizational structure in the communities of origin and a higher level of engagement with government officials. In the Guatemalan case, the government attempts to exert control in 'vital' regions that tend to be those having experienced the highest levels of political violence which contributed to the Guatemalan exodus in the 1980s. These regions are predominantly departments resided in by indigenous (Mayan) Guatemalans, the most disenfranchised group in the country. In other regions, considered less critical to postwar elite political control, state officials tend to neglect efforts by Guatemalan immigrant organizations to implement local development projects. Guatemalan state-led programs aimed at leveraging the migration process for development seem dictated by elite business interests striving to maintain inequitable socioeconomic conditions in the home country. In the Salvadoran case, there exists more dialogue between government ministries, and immigrant organizations, and a state-led program which aims to take advantage of the increasing power of new grassroots actors on the Salvadoran scene.

These findings say something about the differing levels of democracy achieved in El Salvador and Guatemala in postwar periods and reflect differences in the relative strength of the immigrant organizations in Los Angeles. During the war, Salvadorans had a stronger and more numerous nucleus of activists working in organizations in Los Angeles than the Guatemalans. Thus, one finds higher levels of institutional continuity among Salvadoran organizations and a larger proportion of Salvadoran activists involved in organizing efforts in the postwar 1990s (Hamilton and Stoltz Chinchilla, 2001). Several additional factors may explain the relative strength and endurance of Salvadoran immigrant organizations. As noted by Hamilton and Stoltz Chinchilla (2001), one factor is the climate of fear that permeates the Guatemalan immigrant community, a fear that may reflect the trauma resulting from a long history of repression in Guatemala and more recent experiences of violence and persecution. Furthermore, this immigrant community continues to be sharply divided between the Ladino and indigenous populations. Additionally, Salvadorans have achieved a higher level of democracy in the postwar period within the home country as revealed by the impressive electoral gains at the local and national level realized by the political party established by a former guerrilla organization (FMLN) and significant gains made in the demilitarization of Salvadoran society. These gains have not been realized in the Guatemalan case as evidenced by recent death threats made against human rights activists (Bounds, 2002). In spite of these gains in the Salvadoran context, the institution of neoliberal policies limits the potential inclusion of large numbers of citizens into the political and economic process. In both countries, dependence on remittances is necessary to stave off even higher levels of poverty in the absence of macroeconomic policies aimed at employing much higher percentages of the population.

We can expect to see continued collaboration between Central American immigrant organizations and the home states, particularly in the realm of US immigration policy. However, the post September 11 context presents new challenges to state-led transnationalism in this region, given increased pressure by the US government to curtail the flow of Salvadoran and Guatemalan immigrants to the US and the real possibility that more favorable US immigration policies are not likely to be incorporated into a future Central American free trade accord as in the Mexican case.

Notes

I am grateful to the Colorado College Social Science Research and Development Fund for their generous support to complete the research for this project and to Katharine Andrade-Eekhoff for her advice and assistance during the research process.

1 It is important to distinguish between the political transnationalism that emerges in the context of international migration and other forms of transnationalism. As discussed by

Itzigsohn (2001), one form of political transnationalism is seen in the action of indigenous movements that create alliances with NGOs in core countries or other indigenous movements across national boundaries in order to strengthen their cause (Brysk, 1996). Evans (2000) describes three forms of political transnationalism under his concept of 'transnationalism from below'. Networks of activists working on the issues of human rights, women's rights, or the environment constitute the first type (referred to as 'transnational advocacy networks' by Keck and Sikkink [1998]). A second form of transnational politics is transnational consumer/labor networks that organize against transnational corporate exploitation of third world labor, according to Evans. Evans suggests that the third form of transnational politics is the global labor movement promoting core labor standards.

2 I use the concept state-led transnationalism to refer to home country government strategies and programs that aim to leverage the international migratory process to achieve their own political/economic goals in a manner consistent with Goldring (2002).

3 Data for this article were acquired from a number of research projects that involved extensive qualitative fieldwork in Los Angeles and focused on Salvadoran and Guatemalan immigrant organizations and leaders in Los Angeles (Popkin et al., 1997). Additionally, qualitative work was conducted in three migrant-sending communities in El Salvador (Santa Elena, Ciudad Arce and Nueva Concepcion) and two migrant-sending communities in Guatemala (Santa Eulalia, Huehuetenango, and Chapas, Santa Rosa) (Popkin, 1998; Popkin and Andrade-Eekhoff, 2002).

4 Post-civil war economic assistance from the US to El Salvador and Guatemala is extremely low when compared to the major commitment made by the US, particularly in El Salvador, during the wars in the 1980s. For example, US military assistance to El Salvador exceeded $6 billion in that decade, given the Reagan administration's commitment to defeat alleged Soviet/Cuban efforts to extend their influence in the western hemisphere through support of Marxist-oriented guerrilla movements in the region.

Bibliography

Ayala, Edgar R. (1999) 'Guatemalans Voting Abroad: El Voto en el Extranjero', *Report on Guatemala* 20(4): 5.

Basch, Linda G., Glick-Schiller, Nina and Szanton Blanc, Cristina (1994) *Nations Unbound: Transnational Projects, Post-Colonial Predicaments, and Deterritorialized Nation-States*. Langhorne, PA: Gordon and Breach.

Bounds, Andrew (2002) 'Return of Guatemalan Death Squads', *Financial Times* 7 June: 8.

Brysk, Alison (1996) 'Turning Weakness into Strength: The Internationalization of Indian Rights', *Latin American Perspectives* 23(2): 38–57.

Dresser, Denise (1993) 'Exporting Conflict: Transboundary Consequences of Mexican Politics', in Abraham Lowenthal and Katrina Burgess (eds) *The California–Mexico Connection*, pp. 81–112. Stanford, CA: Stanford University Press.

Evans, Peter (2000) 'Fighting Marginalization with Transnational Networks: Counter-Hegemonic Globalization', *Contemporary Sociology* 29(1): 230–41.

Gammage, Sarah (1998) *La dimensión de genero en la pobreza, la desigualdad y la reforma macroeconómica en América Latina*. San Salvador: PNUD (Programa de Naciones Unidas para el Desarrollo).

Glick-Schiller, Nina and Fouron, Georges (1998) 'Transnational Lives and National Identities: The Identity Politics of Haitian Immigrants', in Michael P. Smith and Luis Eduardo Guarnizo (eds) *Transnationalism from Below: Communities-Identities Unbound (Vol. 6, Comparative Urban and Community Research)*, pp. 130–61. New Brunswick, NJ: Transaction.

Glick-Schiller, Nina, Basch, Linda G. and Szanton Blanc, Cristina (1995) 'From Immigrant to Transmigrant: Theorizing Transnational Migration', *Anthropological Quarterly* 68(1): 48–63.

Goldring, Luin (1992) 'Diversity and Community in Transnational Migration: A Comparative Study of Two Mexico–US Migrant Circuits', PhD dissertation, Cornell University.

Goldring, Luin (1998) 'The Power of Status in Transnational Social Spaces', in Michael P. Smith and Luis Eduardo Guarnizo (eds) *Transnationalism From Below: Communities-Identities Unbound (Vol. 6, Comparative Urban and Community Research)*, pp. 165–95. New Brunswick, NJ: Transaction.

Goldring, Luin (2002) 'The Mexican State and Transmigrant Organizations: Negotiating the Boundaries of Membership and Participation', *Latin American Research Review* 37(3): 55–99.

Gordon, David (1988) 'The Global Economy: New Edifice or Crumbling Foundation', *New Left Review* 168(March/April): 24–64.

Guarnizo, Luis Eduardo (1998) 'The Rise of Transnational Social Formations: Mexican and Dominican State Responses to Transnational Migration', *Political Power and Social Theory* 12: 45–95.

Guarnizo, Luis Eduardo and Smith, Michael Peter (1998) 'The Locations of Transnationalism', in Michael P. Smith and Luis Eduardo Guarnizo (eds) *Transnationalism From Below: Communities-Identities Unbound (Vol. 6, Comparative Urban and Community Research)*, pp. 3–34. New Brunswick, NJ: Transaction.

Hamilton, Nora and Stoltz Chinchilla, Norma (2001) *Seeking Community in a Global City: Guatemalans and Salvadorans in Los Angeles*. Philadelphia, PA: Temple University Press.

Inter-American Development Bank (2002) 'Inter-American Development Bank, World Bank and USAID Express Support as Central America Faces Coffee Crisis and Rural Development Crisis', Press Release, 5 April.

Itzigsohn, Jose (1995) 'Migrant Remittances, Labor Markets, and Household Strategies: A Comparative Analysis of Low-Income Households in the Caribbean Basin', *Social Forces* 74(2): 633–57.

Itzigsohn, Jose (2001) 'Immigration and the Boundaries of Citizenship: The Institutions of Immigrants' Political Transnationalism', *International Migration Review* 34(4): 1126–54.

Kearney, Michael (1991) 'Borders and Boundaries of State and Self at the End of Empire', *Journal of Historical Sociology* 4(1): 52–74.

Keck, Margaret and Sikkink, Kathryn (1998) *Activists Beyond Borders: Advocacy Networks in International Politics*. Ithaca, NY: Cornell University Press.

Landolt, Patricia, Autler, Lilian and Baires, Sonia (1999) 'From Hermano Lejano to Hermano Mayor: The Dialectics of Salvadoran Transnationalism', *Ethnic and Racial Studies* 22(2): 290–315.

Levitt, Peggy (1998) 'Social Remittances: Migration Driven Local-Level Forms of Cultural Diffusion', *International Migration Review* 32(4): 926–48.

Lopez, David, Popkin, Eric and Telles, Edward (1996) 'Central Americans: At the Bottom, Struggling to Get Ahead', in Roger Waldinger and Mehdi Bozorgmehr (eds) *Ethnic Los Angeles*, pp. 279–304. New York: Russell Sage Foundation.

Lowell, B. Lindsay and de la Garza, Rodolfo O. (2000) *The Development Role of Remittances in US Latino Communities and in Latin American Countries*, Final Project Report. Los Angeles: Inter-American Dialogue and Tomas Rivera Policy Institute.

Lowenthal, Abraham F. (2000) 'Latin America at the Century's Turn', David Rockefeller Center for Latin American Studies (DRCLAS), newsletter.

McDonnell, Patrick (2002) 'A Latino Census Recount', *Los Angeles Times* 9 May.

Mahler, Sarah (1996) *American Dreaming: Immigrant Life on the Margins*. Princeton, NJ: Princeton University Press.

Mahler, Sarah (1998) 'Theoretical and Empirical Contributions Toward a Research Agenda for Transnationalism', in Michael P. Smith and Luis Eduardo Guarnizo (eds) *Transnationalism From Below: Communities-Identities Unbound (Vol. 6, Comparative Urban and Community Research)*, pp. 64–100. New Brunswick, NJ: Transaction.

Montes Mozo, Segundo and Garcia Vasquez, Juan Jose (1988) *Salvadoran Migration to the United States: An Exploratory Study*, Hemispheric Migration Project. Washington, DC: CIPRA, Georgetown University.

Multilateral Investment Fund (2001) 'Remittances as a Development Tool', a Regional Conference, Inter-American Development Bank, Washington, DC, 17–18 May.

Orozco, Manuel (2002) 'Remittances to Latin America: Money, Markets, and Costs', paper presented at 'Remittances as Development Tool' Conference, Inter-American Development Bank, Washington DC, 26 February.

Perez Sainz, Juan Pablo (2000) 'Labour Market Transformations in Latin America During the 90's – Some Analytical Remarks', paper prepared for the Social Science Research Council Conference, 'Latin American Labor a Decade after Reforms', San Jose, Costa Rica, 10–11 July.

Popkin, Eric (1996) 'Guatemalan Hometown Associations in Los Angeles', *Central Americans in California: Transnational Communities, Economies, and Cultures*, Monograph Paper, No. 1, pp. 35–9. Los Angeles: Center for Multiethnic and Transnational Studies, University of Southern California.

Popkin, Eric (1997) 'Central American Transnational Migration: The Role of Los Angeles Based Salvadoran Hometown Associations in Community Development in El Salvador', in Mario Lungo (ed.) *Migración internacional y desarrollo: el caso de El Salvador*, pp. 191–234. San Salvador: Fundación Nacional para el Desarrollo.

Popkin, Eric (1998) 'In Search of the Quetzal: Guatemalan Mayan Transnational Migration and Ethnic Identity Formation', PhD dissertation, University of California-Los Angeles.

Popkin, Eric (1999) 'Guatemalan Mayan Migration to Los Angeles: Constructing Transnational Linkages in the Context of the Settlement Process', *Ethnic and Racial Studies* 22(2): 267–89.

Popkin, Eric and Andrade-Eekhoff, Katharine (2002) 'The Construction of Household Labor Market Strategies in Central American Transnational Migrant Communities', paper presented at the American Sociological Association Meetings, Chicago, 16 August.

Popkin, Eric, Arguelles, Lourdes, Desipio, Louis and Pachon, Harry (1997) *Diversifying the Los Angeles Area Latino Mosaic: Salvadoran and Guatemalan Leaders' Assessments of Community Public Policy Needs*. Los Angeles: Tomas Rivera Policy Institute and National Association of Latino Elected and Appointed Officials Educational Fund.

Portes, Alejandro (1995) *Transnational Communities: Their Emergence and Significance in the Contemporary World System*, Working Papers Series, No. 16, Program in Comparative and International Development, Department of Sociology. Baltimore, MD: The Johns Hopkins University Press.

Portes, Alejandro (2000) 'Immigration and the Metropolis: Reflections on Urban History', *Journal of International Migration and Integration* 1(2): 153–75.

Portes, Alejandro, Dore Cabral, Carlos and Landolt, Patricia, eds (1997) *The Urban Caribbean: Transition to the New Global Economy*. Baltimore, MD: The Johns Hopkins University Press.

Portes, Alejandro, Guarnizo, Luis and Landolt, Patricia (1999) 'Introduction: Pitfalls and Promise of an Emergent Research Field', *Ethnic and Racial Studies* 22(2): 217–37.

Rouse, Roger (1987) 'Migration and the Politics of Family Life: Divergent Projects and Rhetorical Strategies in a Mexican Transnational Migrant Community', Center for US-Mexican Studies, University of California, San Diego, unpublished.

Rouse, Roger (1991) 'Mexican Migration and the Social Space of Postmodernism', *Diaspora* 1(1): 8–23.

Sassen, Saskia (1991) *The Global City: New York, London, Tokyo*. Princeton, NJ: Princeton University Press.

Smith, Michael P. (1994) 'Can You Imagine? Transnational Migration and the Globalization of Grass-Roots Politics', *Social Text* 39(Fall): 15–33.

Smith, Michael P. and Guarnizo, Luis Eduardo, eds (1998) *Transnationalism From Below: Communities-Identities Unbound (Vol. 6, Comparative Urban and Community Research)*. New Brunswick, NJ: Transaction.

Smith, Robert C. (1995) 'Los Ausentes Siempre Presentes: The Imagining, Making, and Politics of a Transnational Community between New York and Ticuani, Puebla', PhD dissertation, Columbia University.

Stanley, William Deane (1987) 'Economic Migrants or Refugees from Violence? A Time Series Analysis of Salvadoran Migration to the United States', *Latin American Research Review* 22(1): 132–54.

Suro, Roberto (2002) *Counting the 'Other Hispanics': How Many Colombians, Dominicans, Ecuadorians, Guatemalans, and Salvadorans are There in the United States*, 9 May. Los Angeles, CA: Pew Hispanic Center.

Swedish, Margaret (2002a) 'El Salvador: Bush Visit Amounts to Very Little', *Central America/Mexico Report* 22(2): 6–7.

Swedish, Margaret (2002b) 'Central America: Hunger Spreads Throughout Region', *Central America/Mexico Report* 22(2): 7–8.

Taylor, J. Edward (1997) 'International Migrant Remittances, Savings, and Development in Migrant-Sending Areas', paper presented at the Conference 'International Migration at Century's End', Barcelona, 7–10 May.

Taylor, J. Edward and Zabin, Carol (1996) 'Migration and Development in a Conflict Zone: A Micro-Economic Perspective', paper presented at Allied Social Science Association Annual Meetings (North American Finance Association), San Francisco, 5 January.

Wilson, Tamar Diana (1994) 'What Determines where Transnational Labor Migrants Go? Modification in Migration Theories', *Human Organization* 53(3): 269–78.

World Food Program (2002) *Emergency Report*, No. 12, 22 March.

10

Particularizing the Global: Reception of Foreign Direct Investment in Slovenia

Nina Bandelj

Global Forces of Foreign Direct Investment

A key indicator of economic globalization is a tremendous increase in world foreign direct investment flows (FDI).[1] By the end of the millennium, FDI had reached a record of US$865 billion, marking a more than 20-fold increase since 1970. How does such an immense amount of global capital impact economic practices in local settings? And in turn, how do local reactions shape global investment forces?

To address these questions, this article examines FDI in one East European transition country, Slovenia. Foreign direct investment is advocated as a catalyst in the transition process, since it contributes crucially needed financial, managerial and technological resources for the restructuring of formerly state-owned enterprises. Its spillover effects on domestic firms additionally revitalize the national economies (Schmidt, 1995; K. Meyer, 1998).

Despite the alleged importance of FDI for the transition to capitalism, the empirical evidence shows that FDI into Slovenia has been consistently *smaller* than the average for the East European region. How can this be explained? Slovenia has a central location in Europe and an excellent communication infrastructure. It has a well-developed industry with a long tradition. Its economy is stable with the highest GDP levels and GDP growth among the East European countries. Its workforce is skilled, well educated and has a strong work ethic. Slovenia has been a traditional trade partner with the countries of Western Europe and also has strong trade connections with the emerging markets of South Eastern Europe. According to Standard and Poor's credit rating, Slovenia has a lower assessment of investment risk than the Czech Republic or Hungary (FIAS, 1998). All of these positive characteristics should make Slovenia an attractive investment location. However, the actual FDI levels are very modest and represent the lowest share in GDP among the East European countries. What explains this enigma?

This article proposes that we can understand FDI in Slovenia if we pay close attention to the interaction between global forces and local life-worlds, and examine the reception of FDI in Slovenia. In a review of globalization studies, Guillen (2001a: 235) emphasizes the importance of 'local variations and how agency, interest and resistance mediate in the relationship between globalization causes and outcomes'. Uncovering how local actors respond to global forces is especially important for a study of FDI. After all, FDI is a relational process. It involves an exchange between two parties in the transaction – the investor and the host. As such, it is inherently a process of a continuous negotiation between global pressures and local interests.

To study the reception of FDI in Slovenia, the first part of the article examines how the Slovenian state responds to global investment pressures by analyzing the FDI policies, regulations and official documents. Subsequently, qualitative evidence of actual foreign investment transactions illustrates the economic practice. The analysis shows that yielding to the universalizing pressures of neoliberalism creates convergence in the official foreign investment policies. In practice, however, economic actors involved in the foreign investment transactions resist and particularize the global processes on the basis of their network ties, political circumstances and cultural affinities. Overall, the study emphasizes the social and political embeddedness of economic processes and substantiates how the decoupling of formal policies and local practices sustains the coexistence of uniformity and diversity.

Local Forces of Domestic Ownership Protection

While the globalizing forces of world foreign investment are in full swing, the transition countries of Eastern Europe are also undergoing transformations of their political regimes, economic systems and state identities, which brings about concerns with nation-building and national interests. As Calhoun (1993: 212) writes, 'nationalism . . . appeared as the primary issue in the realignment of Eastern European politics and identity'. After all, with such a drastic rupture with the fall of Communism, these nation-states had to almost reinvent themselves *de novo*.

In addition, the national question was revived in Eastern Europe after the collapse of Communism, because the nation-building of many states in this region was incomplete (Caratan, 1997). For the last 200 years, the majority of the region has been under foreign rule, either of the Habsburg monarchy, the Ottoman empire or Tsarist Russia. After the Second World War, Communist regimes suppressed national identity questions to maintain multiethnic countries, again delaying the nation-building process. Thus, only in post-Communism, which resulted in the disintegration of multinational states, could nation-building proceed. In fact, after the fall of the Berlin Wall, nationalism was used as a tool of political mobilization and support in the New Europe, probably in its worst form by the Serbian president Slobodan Milosevic (Caratan, 1997: 287). After 1989, in a number of countries such as Croatia, Slovenia or Latvia, 'the rhetoric and symbols with the greatest electoral appeal were national[ist] ones' (Verdery, 1998: 294). While in the ethnically heterogeneous states such as Serbia, *nationalist* sentiments were asserted by the hegemony of the core ethno-cultural nation over the ethnic minorities, in the ethnically homogeneous states such as Slovenia the prevailing sentiments were *national*, carried by the process of nation-building.

Nation-building or the process of establishing an identity of a nation-state as an *imagined community* (Anderson, 1983) inherently limited and sovereign, reinforces the idea of a self-government whose highest priority is to preserve and protect the interests of the national community and that which defines its uniqueness. In such circumstances, a response to global foreign investment pressures is likely to be resistance to foreign takeovers of domestic firms and opposition to the establishment of foreign enterprises on domestic territories and their inclusion in domestic economies.

Evidence from the International Social Science Program, 1995 Module on National Identity Survey, substantiates domestic protectionist interests in Eastern Europe, including Slovenia. Answering whether foreigners should be allowed to own land in a respondent's country, respondents from Eastern Europe were more than twice as likely to disagree or strongly disagree with this statement, compared to those from Western Europe. On average, 70 percent of the sample from Slovenia was of that opinion. Additionally, these respondents were also significantly more likely to report feeling close to their home country, agreeing that it is important to be a citizen of their country and to speak its main language. They were more proud of their country's history and agreed that people should support their country even if the country is in the wrong or even when it leads to conflicts with other nations. Moreover, these respondents agreed that their country should limit the import of foreign products in order to protect its national economy. Understanding the prevailing public opinion among Slovenians about the involvement of foreigners in the domestic economy casts additional doubt that the reception of FDI in Slovenia could be a straight-forward and unproblematic process.

Institutionalization of FDI Policies

At the national level, FDI policies signal an official response of a country toward foreign investment. Content analysis of FDI provisions in Eastern Europe reveals that the official policies reflect the negotiation between two extremes: freely opening borders and providing incentives to foreign capital, on one hand, and closing borders and discouraging foreign invest-ment, on the other hand (UNCTAD, 1996). The one end of the spectrum is rationalized by neoliberalism and FDI's proclaimed benefits to economic growth. Namely, the prosperity of a transition country would be greatly facilitated with inflows of foreign capital, transferred technological and managerial know-how and the integration of a transition economy into the web of multinational corporations. The other end of the spectrum is fueled by the nation-building discourse, which emphasizes the preservation of national economies and cultural traditions, and is grounded in opposition to exploitation by the rich West.

Situating itself in-between the two poles, a state can adopt a variety of official measures that more or less regulate FDI, impose restrictions over it or actively encourage it. For example, states can strongly intervene in the economic activity of foreign investment if they review every FDI effort and require an approval for every transaction from a domestic state agency. By identifying sectoral restrictions, states can prevent the investment in those strategic activities that should be preserved under national control, such as natural resources, armed forces, or media. States can also regulate foreign investment by setting limits on repatriation of profits.

On the other hand, there are several ways in which states solicit foreign investment by offering incentives that render the locations on their national territory more attractive than alternatives in other countries. In particular, states can offer a variety of tax holidays, and tax breaks, or they can exempt investors from paying customs tariffs. Moreover, the privatization schemes in the transition countries can also facilitate FDI by giving foreign investors equal rights to domestic investors to buy formerly state-owned enterprises.

How did the Slovenian state decide which policies to adopt? The economic theory proposes that public action aims at utility maximization. States as rational and purposive actors select the policy alternative that will ensure the most efficient outcomes. Considering the strong emphasis on the benefits of FDI for the transition to capitalism, the economic perspective would most likely predict that the Slovenian state would open its borders to foreign investment and enact liberal FDI policies.

On the other hand, a sociological account would propose that the adoption of the FDI policies is a process through which a state institutionalizes its attitudes toward FDI. Because of the protectionist attitudes expressed in public opinion, supported also by formal nation-building processes accompanying the establishment of a new state, it is likely that the official Slovenian FDI policy would reflect the national protectionist attitudes and be restrictive toward or even discouraging of foreign investments.

In fact, the Slovenian policy, in 1992, was to require a registration at the district court for every FDI transaction. Deals with non-privatized companies were subject to the Slovenian Privatization Agency's approval. Wholly foreign-owned companies were not permitted in the military equipment field, rail and air transport, communications and telecommunications, insurance, publishing and mass media (Dunning and Rojec, 1993: 34). These are activities where protecting national ownership could be considered crucial for maintaining control over strategic assets. Moreover, the Slovenian privatization scheme favored domestic owners, especially employee and management buyouts, over foreign investors. Furthermore, control of individual companies was regulated by the provision that company directors had to be Slovenian citizens and that a majority of any board of directors should be Slovenian citizens (FIAS, 1998). The attitude of protecting national assets in domestic hands and discouraging foreign ownership seems to be institutionalized in these official measures.

However, by 2001 Slovenia has changed its FDI legislation significantly. By 1997, with the adoption and the amendments of the Companies Act, provisions were put in place to give domestic and foreign investors equal rights to enter and exit business, and to provide them both with equal investment protection. Specific approvals, previously required for each potential foreign investor, were abolished, so was the stipulation about the required Slovenian citizenship for company and board directors. With the enactment of the Foreign Exchange Act in 1999, the foreign exchange regime was liberalized. It now allows a free transfer of profits and the repatriation of capital. Slovenia has also changed its tax law, and is now ranked as one of the most tax-favorable countries in Europe, with the company income tax set at 25 percent (FIAS, 2000). Obviously, the Slovenian policies pertaining to FDI have liberalized substantially.

In addition, by 1998 the idea that FDI can importantly contribute to the economy's restructuring and development had gained ground in the official political discourse and state-level FDI promotion had increased. The official document, *Strategy of the Republic of Slovenia for Accession to the European Union*, stated that 'Slovenia will encourage and promote inward FDI by stable, transparent and non-discriminative regulations of FDI based on the national treatment principle and by instruments of the Trade and Investment Promotion Office of Slovenia' (Mrak et al., 1998). In 2001, the government adopted another official document, *Slovenia in the European Union – Strategy for Economic Development of Slovenia* (IMAD, 2001), which further reaffirmed FDI as an important factor in Slovenia's development process. Moreover, the Trade and Investment Promotion Office of Slovenia submitted to the National Assembly *The Programme of the Government of the Republic of Slovenia for Encouragement of Foreign Direct Investment 2001–2004*, which the Assembly passed in 2001. Why did such substantial changes take place in the official attitudes and policies related to FDI?

To understand the changes in Slovenian FDI policy over time, we have to go beyond the national borders and consider the global context. Scholars have substantiated that the last two decades of the 20th century have seen a rise in market deregulation and economic liberalization on a global scale (Lash and Urry, 1987; Albert, 1993; Przeworski, 1995; Campbell and Pedersen, 2001). While many economists see this neoliberal reform as an instance in which the market is finally freed to select out the most efficient policies (Williamson, 1985; Posner, 1986), sociological neo-institutionalists consider neoliberalism as a political project promoted by international organizations (Meyer et al., 1997; Carruthers et al., 2001).

Explaining where policy changes come from, sociological neo-institutionalists argue that actors adopt policies which are isomorphic with those already in existence (DiMaggio and Powell, 1991). In this process, actors follow collectively established myths and ceremonies rather than objectively rational actions (Meyer and Rowan, 1977). While the initial argument was developed primarily to explain the isomorphic outcomes within organizational areas, recent work has adopted this reasoning also for the processes at the nation-state level. 'Nation-states are more or less exogenously constructed entities – the many individuals ... who engage in state formation and policy formulation are enactors of scripts [supplied by global culture and associational processes] rather than they are self-directed actors' (Meyer et al., 1997: 150). In this vein, state action is not primarily oriented toward efficiency, as economists would have it, but external legitimacy. National policy-makers adopt policies that are defined as most legitimate, i.e. those that would enhance the cultural standing and membership of a particular society in the nation-state community (McNeely, 1995). Hence, the adoption of neoliberal policies by the Slovenian state could be viewed as a search for legitimacy and inclusion into the global community of nation-states and into the associational bodies that support it.

Indeed, since its independence, in 1991, Slovenia joined or applied for membership with most of the prominent international organizations, which all strongly advocate neoliberalism and the opening of national borders to FDI. In 1992, Slovenia became a member of the United Nations and consequently its Conference on Trade and Development, UNCTAD. In 1993, it became a member of the International Monetary Fund and the International Bank for Reconstruction and Development. In 1994, it joined GATT and consequently, in 1995, became a member of the World Trade Organization and its main agreements. Two years later, the European Agreement was signed which made official Slovenia's negotiations for accession to the European Union.

According to Meyer et al. (1997: 144), all these organizations contribute to associational processes which construct, legitimate and propagate worldwide models of action. Neoliberalism is the action mode of the contemporary global culture shaped by such associational processes. Global organizations exert formal and informal pressures on (aspiring) member states, such as Slovenia, to align their legislations with neoliberal institutions, promoting convergence in official economic policies worldwide. As an EU accession country, Slovenia also faced coercive pressures to change its laws and allow foreign ownership of land, which was initially prohibited by the Slovenian Constitution (Bandelj, 2001). Thus, adopting permissive FDI policies likely reflects yielding to pressures from the international community, rather than signaling a drastic change in attitudes toward foreign investment in Slovenia.

In addition, policies are also converging because of mimetic isomorphism (DiMaggio and Powell, 1991). East European states are often competing for FDI from the West. Hence, they constantly try to match the FDI provisions in other countries. For instance, officials in the Slovenian Trade and Investment Promotion Agency expressed their opinion that Slovenia should adopt additional incentives and further liberalize its legislation in order to compete for foreign investments with other East European states, such as the Czech Republic and Slovakia. These countries are continuously improving their investment climate and are providing additional incentives to foreign investors. Their peer states should follow suit.

Decoupling of Policies and Practice

Acknowledging that coercive and mimetic pressures dictated changes in official FDI policies, we need to consider that the adoption of policy measures as a consequence of isomorphizing with the external world would not necessarily yield the intended results and would exemplify the decoupling of policies and practice (Meyer and Rowan, 1977). Decoupling is likely when nation-states model formal rules on an external culture that cannot be simply imported wholesale as a fully functioning system. Furthermore, it is easier to adopt formal arrangements than to make them work effectively. There is also a difference between how well resource-rich actors may be able to assume a given posture as opposed to weaker actors of the periphery (Meyer et al., 1997: 151–2). Transition countries may emphasize formal structuration but do not make policies work effectively.

It is likely that formal regulations are bypassed in practice. That there are variations between official rules and investment practice was also suggested to me in an interview with a high-ranking official at the Central and East European Privatization Network. He pointed out that investment negotiations in Central and Eastern Europe are often done on a case by case basis at the organizational level whereby seriously interested investors can bypass some of the legal regulations set at the host country level. The state or local governments can also make special amendments for the investments they really want to attract.[2]

More generally, findings in economic sociology about risk reduction on a broad range of economic exchanges support an emergent generalization that in conditions of high uncertainty, people do not tend to rely on institutional guarantees (Uzzi, 1997; DiMaggio and Louch, 1998; Ingram and Roberts, 2000). Rather, they channel economic transactions through previously existing business or personal relations because this strategy may reduce uncertainty and costs, increase knowledge of the other party and third-party guarantees.

Hence, it is likely that processes of FDI allow for much negotiation and diversification at the practical level of business transactions, even though official policies establish a uniform response to global investors. In fact, the formally more liberal foreign investment policy did not increase the quantity of FDI inflows in Slovenia from 1997, even though FDI in Eastern Europe has shown an upward trend (UNCTAD, 2000). This quantitative evidence additionally suggests that practice is decoupled from formal regulations.

FDI Transactions in Practice

When examining the practice of FDI, we should pay attention to how economic processes are constrained and enabled by – or embedded in – three sets of forces (DiMaggio and Zukin, 1990). First, structural conditions are influential because economic actors are located in networks. Second, political alliances and power struggles shape economic activity. Third, cultural effects are reflected in how shared collective understandings and meanings shape economic strategies and goals.

Generally, we can conceptualize the economic process of FDI as a social process, shaped by networks, politics and culture (Zelizer, 1988; Emirbayer and Goodwin, 1994; Barber, 1995; Fligstein, 1996; Spillman, 1999; for a review see Smelser and Swedberg, 1994). Because of the social, political and cultural embeddedness of economic transactions, Slovenians can particularize the global investment process and differentiate between individual foreign investors. The following sections draw on the evidence from actual FDI transactions to explore how the reception of FDI attempts is shaped by network ties, political alliances and cultural affinities between potential investors and domestic hosts.

Networks

Economic transactions flow through interpersonal relationships and other social networks. Researchers have studied, for example, how people use networks in labor markets, consumption practices, or business-to-business exchanges (see Granovetter, 1974; DiMaggio and Louch, 1998; and Uzzi, 1996, 1997 respectively; for a review see Powell and Smith-Doerr, 1994). In foreign investment transactions, two types of networks might influence the acceptance of various foreign investment attempts: organizational networks between foreign firms and companies in a host country, and personal networks among affiliates of a specific host country and foreign investor firms. This suggests that those foreign investment efforts where the investor firm has pre-existent business or personal ties to the target host firm will be more likely realized than those without connections.

In fact, according to a survey of foreign investment firms in Slovenia (TIPO, 1998), prior business cooperation provided an impetus to invest for more than two-thirds of the representative sample of the Slovenian enterprises with foreign investment share. One-third of the surveyed companies also mentioned that the decision was initiated through a contact by a foreign firm or a host firm. Decisions based on market analysis were listed by less than 1 percent of the investors; and they were never listed as a sole reason for investment. As Rojec et al. write, 'a handful of large (for Slovenian circumstances) FDI projects . . . *as a rule* emerged out of previous co-operation between foreign investors and Slovenian companies' (Rojec et al., 2001: 10; emphasis added). Foreign investors who had long-term business connections with managers in the formerly state-owned enterprises had an advantage over those without networks. Through long-term business cooperation, both sides of the transaction had relatively extensive knowledge of the other and established trustworthy relations. In these circumstances, host firms were much more likely to accept foreign partners as investors in their firms and helped to successfully complete the FDI transaction.

Power and Politics

Organizational studies also emphasize the role of power and politics in structuring organizational activities (Fligstein, 1990; Fligstein and Brantley, 1992; Roy, 1997). Foreign investment in existing firms shifts ownership structures and consequently distributions of control over decisions and resources. This implies that, in order to maintain control, domestic firms would more likely agree to a foreign acquisition of a minority than a majority share.

The offer of an Italian bank to acquire a 100 percent ownership share in the Slovenian bank Koper is a case in point. Although the three corporate partners owning the majority of the bank's shares were willing to sell to Italians, the foreign investment attempt was publicly interpreted as an exercise of control by Italians over a region of Slovenia which was once accorded to Italians. A civil society initiative launched a public appeal on the front page of a major national newspaper:

> To the Slovenian government and Attorney General to protect its public, state and national interest and to disable the supervisory board of the Slovenian Port [a major corporate shareholder in the Koper Bank] to usurp a public good and to estrange strategic assets in the Koper Bank to Italians ... The Koper Bank has to remain in Slovene hands, since the inhabitants of the Primorska region do not want another Rapal contract.[3] (*Delo*, 9 November 2001: 1)

The Slovenian Port together with other corporate shareholders responded in a public advertisement titled, 'The Bank of Koper will remain in Slovenian hands' (*Delo*, 15 November 2001: 13), reassuring the public that even if the corporate shareholders sell their shares, 'banks located in Slovenia will remain Slovenian, they will conduct business in accordance with Slovenian law'. They also promised to keep a 30 percent share of the ownership and remain the decision-makers in the bank. In the ad, they also noted that 'the highest price is not the most important criterion in this bank transaction' and that they would not sell shares in the financial company Fidor, part of the Bank of Koper, which owned vineyards and agricultural land in the region.

Because of the public polemics about this foreign investment transaction, the National Bank of Slovenia took three full months to reach its decision about granting the investment approval to the Italians.[4] They finally granted the approval with the provision that the Italian investor's 62 percent share only translated into 32.9 percent of the voting power. The three corporate owners kept altogether 30 percent of shares and signed a binding agreement not to sell these shares for at least four years.

One could argue that Slovenians are simply reluctant to sell their banks, which they consider as strategic national assets. However, in another case, a French investor smoothly acquired a 100 percent ownership share in a similar bank. No public calls against the transaction were raised, nor was there any media discussion or outcry against the investment. Thus, the fact that in the case of Koper the investors were Italians was of crucial importance. Negative historical experiences resonated in the collective memory of Slovenians and raised issues of power and control.

Power struggles and local economic and political elites are also reported to intervene in the FDI transactions in post-socialist countries (Stoner-Weiss, 2000). Based on this observation, it seems likely that foreign investment attempts will reflect local political and business elites' interests in either maintaining domestic ownership or accepting foreign investment offers. The case of a Belgian FDI in a Slovenian brewery illustrates this political embeddedness. Once the Belgians had announced their takeover intentions and made a public offer to acquire the majority share, a competing offer was made by Pivovarna Lasko, a Slovenian company. Anton Koncnik, president of the Slovenian para-state-owned capital and indemnity fund SOD (Slovenska Odskodninska Druzba), which owned 12.2 percent of the brewery's shares, decided unilaterally, without consultation with the fund's board, to sell these shares to the Slovenian Pivovarna Lasko as opposed to the Belgians. It so happened that this person was associated with the Slovenian People's Party, a centralist conservative party, which favors protection of domestic ownership. The management of Pivovarna Lasko also had political allegiance to that party. The SOD's supervisory board, which immediately asked for Koncnik's resignation, politically reflected the liberal coalition government, pushing its agenda to increase FDI in Slovenia. Three members of the board, however, all deputies to the National Assembly from the Slovenian People's Party, were against the resignation (*Delo*, 11 January 2002: 4).

This case illustrates the political embeddedness of economic activity, which might be especially prevalent in post-socialist settings. Several observers of the transition in East Europe also find a strong overlap between the political and economic sphere (Staniszkis, 1991; Frydman et al., 1996; King, 2001). The region may exhibit a form of political capitalism, where private individuals appropriate state power to shape enterprise activity (King, 2001: 5). Moreover, certain foreign investment efforts are much more readily accepted than others because of political alliances, which allows differentiation between individual foreign investors and particularizes global FDI forces.

Cultural Affinities

Economic behavior is culturally embedded because shared collective understandings of economic actors, their strategies and goals influence economic outcomes (DiMaggio and Zukin, 1990). In the case of FDI, the influence of cultural ties on economic activity seems particularly likely because the exchange not only involves a transfer of foreign capital, but also a transfer of a lasting interest in an acquired company. This lasting interest implies a significant degree of influence by the investor on the management of the host company (Dunning and Rojec, 1993). Knowing that management practices are not universal but culturally specific (Boltanski, 1990; Guillen, 1994; Lamont and Thevenot, 2001), we can infer that conceptions of management and work organization might be discrepant between a host and an investor. On these grounds, hosts might be more welcoming to investments that they consider closer to their cultural values and practices, and resist those that are perceived as distant.

Thus, conceptions of nationality influence international economic transactions, leading to differentiation between investors on the basis of their country of origin. Such differentiation comes across in a remark made by one of my Slovenian informants, who commented about the differences between German and Italian investors:

> Germanic people and Germanic investments are perceived as precise, orderly, trustworthy. Against Italians, there are always some suspicions. That their money is dirty, that things will get messed up, that there is some iffy business involved, that these are unreliable people. While, on the other hand, Germans and Austrians are elevated and treated as hyperorganized, orderly, trustworthy.[5]

Such differentiation implies that investment flows are imbued with cultural significance; their place of origin is relevant to the host's willingness to accept them. Culture, therefore, integrally influences economic exchanges. But culture is not understood as consisting in psychological characteristics but as historically institutionalized cultural repertoires (Lamont and Thevenot, 2001). In this vein, investor's and host's cultures need not be *similar* for a successful transaction to occur as long as both parties conceive of each other, as members of particular national groups, in a way conducive to 'cultural matching' (DiMaggio, 1993: 127).

Cultural matching occurs when exchange parties envision the other as a likely partner in a transaction. According to DiMaggio (1993), when economic agents

> ... need to go beyond immediate strong ties, power and reputation for probity [become] less useful bases of assessment ... Under these conditions, [economic agents] are thrown back on sympathy as an assessment criterion ... Sympathy is constructed in part out of categories (like us/not like us) and in part out of ongoing interactions in which participants form strong impressions (confidence, distrust). (DiMaggio, 1993: 126–7)

Reception of an attempt by HouseCo, an American multinational corporation, to buy a majority share in Rotor, a Slovenian company, illustrates the importance of sympathy in economic transactions. As one of the involved Rotor managers commented, the HouseCo negotiators were arrogant and too confident in a successful transaction outcome. In addition, during the HouseCo's investment attempt, articles appeared in national and local newspapers about 'the American way of doing business', implying lack of care for workers and merciless downsizing, and they labeled the FDI attempt by the Americans as 'a hostile take-over' (*Delo*, 10 June 1997: 12). These were certainly not the grounds to develop sympathies between the two transactors. In fact, HouseCo withdrew its offer and later decided to invest in the Czech Republic where the transaction proceeded smoothly. On the other hand, within a year, Greil, a German multinational with long-term business ties to Rotor, quietly bought one part of Rotor. Germans established this company as a separate legal entity from Rotor. The decision to invest was promoted by a former top manager of Rotor who personally knew top executives at Greil and saw the buyout as an opportunity to secure himself a position in this new German-owned company, after he failed to get support in his candidacy for the chief executive position at Rotor.[6]

On the whole, the qualitative evidence from foreign direct investment transactions illustrates that, in practice, the reception of FDI efforts is not an unproblematic and straightforward process. Economic actors at investment locations sometimes show outright resistance to the foreign investment efforts, particularly when they do not have pre-existent knowledge of the potential investor, when they want to protect their positions of control, or when they have certain preconceptions about the investors based on their countries of origin. Furthermore, because economic processes are socially, politically and culturally embedded, the Slovenian actors can differentiate between individual foreign investors based on their pre-existent networks, political alliances and cultural affinities. Hence, in practice economic actors particularize the global investment process.

Coexistence of Uniformity and Diversity

Whether increasing international movement of capital, people and culture makes the world more homogeneous is one of the key issues in globalization studies (Lechner and Boli, 2000). Much empirical work conducted on the subject has found divergent results. Research in the world-society tradition found increasing convergence in institutional arrangements across countries and organizations (McNeely, 1995; Meyer et al., 1997). Other scholars reported that over the past decades national value differences persisted (Ingelhardt and Baker, 2000) and that in order to cope with globalizing forces, countries and organizations strive to be different and emphasize their unique economic, political and social advantages (Guillen, 2001b). With regard to the presence of multinational corporations, empirical evidence suggests that the foreign and the local interact to produce hybrid practices or creole cultures (Watson, 1997; Hannerz, 2000).

The present study of FDI reception in Slovenia substantiates that global processes encourage both convergence and divergence. This is in line with Zelizer's (1999) proposition that 'the economy operates at two levels: seen from the top, economic transactions connect with broad national symbolic meanings and institutions. Seen from the bottom, economic transactions are highly differentiated, personalized, and local, meaningful to particular relations. No contradiction therefore exists between uniformity and diversity; they are simply two different aspects of the same transaction' (Zelizer, 1999: 212).

Guillen (2001a: 235) identifies that, in fact, the divergent findings in globalization studies are 'primarily due to the various levels of analysis at which different researchers operate'. To deal with this issue, this study examined both the national-level policies and organizational practices. Therefore, it has not only illuminated how homogenization and diversification happen concurrently but it has also identified the processes that sustain their simultaneity.

The analysis of FDI policies in Slovenia traced how yielding to the global associational pressures, which promote the liberalization of world FDI, requires of the Slovenian state to adopt increasingly more liberal FDI policies and to uniformly open its borders to foreign investors. However, such convergence in official policies does not correspond to the actual attitudes toward FDI in Slovenia, which are grounded in nation-building processes. Moreover, in practice, economic actors use a variety of strategies to particularize individual investors and to resist certain foreign investment attempts while they accept others. Unlike formal policies, which align with universalizing neoliberal reforms, embedded economic practice in local settings results in a great variety of actions and, ultimately, in the particularization of global forces.

Notes

A previous version of this article was presented at the 35th World Congress of the International Institute of Sociology in Krakow, Poland, July 2001. I thank Jozsef Borocz, Alexandra Kalev, Ulrike Schuerkens, Willfried Spohn, Cesar Rosado, Frederick Turner, Bruce Western and Viviana Zelizer for their helpful comments and suggestions on previous drafts.

1 FDI is the investment made by an investor company from one country (the investor country) with the objective of obtaining a lasting interest and an active role in a company in another country (the host country). The lasting interest implies the existence of a long-term relationship between the investor and the host and a significant degree of influence by an investor on the management of a company in the host country. FDI can take the form of foreign acquisition, in which the investor obtains an equity share in an existing company in a host country. Greenfield investment, on the other hand, involves the investor's establishment of a new company, wholly foreign-owned or in partnership with investors from a host country (Dunning and Rojec, 1993).

2 Based on a personal interview, 10 January 1999.

3 The Rapal contract was signed between Italy and Yugoslavia in 1920, where one-third of Slovenian territory, the Primorska region, was accorded to Italians. The contract was reconsidered in 1947 with a peace treaty between allied and associated states with Italy, although a considerable Slovene minority remained on the Italian territory. (Note: the translations from Slovenian to English are by the author.)

4 A policy set by the National Assembly ordered that any privatization and foreign investment related to the banking sector in Slovenia had to get an approval from the National Bank of Slovenia.

5 Personal interview, 1 February 2002.
6 Based on the evidence collected from interviews with the management of Rotor (18, 24 and 25 January 2002) and news articles.

Bibliography

Albert, Michel (1993) *Capitalism vs Capitalism*. New York: Four Walls, Eight Windows.
Anderson, Benedict (1983) *Imagined Communities*. London: Verso.
Bandelj, Nina (2001) 'National Identity Encounters Globalization: How Culture Constrains and Enables Foreign Investment in Slovenia', paper presented at the Annual Eastern Sociological Society Meetings, Philadelphia.
Barber, Bernard (1995) 'All Economies are Embedded: The Career of a Concept and Beyond', *Social Research* 62(2): 388–413.
Boltanski, Luc (1990) 'Visions of American Management in Postwar France', in Sharon Zukin and Paul DiMaggio (eds) *Structures of Capital: The Social Organization of the Economy*, pp. 343–72. Cambridge: University of Cambridge Press.
Brubaker, Rogers (1996) *Nationalism Reframed: Nationhood and the National Question in the New Europe*. Cambridge and New York: Cambridge University Press.
Burt, Ronald (1992) *Structural Holes: The Social Structure of Competition*. Cambridge, MA: Harvard University Press.
Calhoun, Craig (1993) 'Nationalism and Ethnicity', *Annual Review of Sociology* 19: 211–39.
Campbell, John L. and Pedersen, Ove K., eds (2001) *The Rise of Neoliberalism and Institutional Analysis*. Princeton, NJ: Princeton University Press.
Caratan, Branko (1997) 'The New States and Nationalism in Eastern Europe', *International Politics* 34(3): 285–302.
Carruthers, Bruce G., Babb, Sarah L. and Halliday, Terence C. (2001) 'Institutionalizing Markets, or the Market for Institutions? Central Banks, Bankruptcy Law, and the Globalization of Financial Markets', in John Campbell and Ove Pedersen (eds) *The Rise of Neoliberalism and Institutional Analysis*, pp. 94–126. Princeton, NJ: Princeton University Press.
DiMaggio, Paul (1993) 'Nadel's Paradox Revisited: Relational and Cultural Aspects of Organizational Structures', in Nitin Nohria and Robert Eccle (eds) *Networks and Organization*, pp. 118–42. Boston, MA: Harvard Business School Press.
DiMaggio, Paul and Louch, Hugh (1998) 'Socially Embedded Consumer Transactions: For What Kinds of Purchases Do People Most Often Use Networks?', *American Sociological Review* 63(5): 619–37.
DiMaggio, Paul and Powell, Walter (1991) 'The Iron Cage Revisited: Institutional Isomorphism and Collective Rationality in Organizational Fields', in Walter Powell and Paul DiMaggio (eds) *The New Institutionalism in Organizational Analysis*, pp. 63–82. Chicago, IL: University of Chicago Press.
DiMaggio, Paul and Zukin, Sharon (1990) 'Introduction', in Sharon Zukin and Paul DiMaggio (eds) *Structures of Capital: The Social Organization of the Economy*, pp. 1–36. Cambridge: Cambridge University Press.
Dobbin, Frank (1994) 'Cultural Models of Organization: The Social Construction of Rational Organizing Principles', in Diana Crane (ed.) *Sociology of Culture: Emerging Theoretical Perspectives*, pp. 117–42. Oxford: Basil Blackwell.
Dunning, John and Rojec, Matija (1993) *Foreign Privatisation in Central and Eastern Europe*, Technical Paper Series, No. 2. Ljubljana: Central and East European Privatization Network (CEEPN).
Emirbayer, Mustafa and Goodwin, Jeff (1994) 'Network Analysis, Culture, and the Problem of Agency', *American Journal of Sociology* 99(6): 1411–54.
FIAS (Foreign Investment Advisory Service) (1998) *Slovenia – Promoting Foreign Direct Investment*. Washington, DC: FIAS.
FIAS (Foreign Investment Advisory Service) (2000) *Slovenia – Administrative Barriers to Investment*. Washington, DC: FIAS.

Fligstein, Neil (1990) *The Transformation of Corporate Control.* Cambridge, MA: Harvard University Press.

Fligstein, Neil (1996) 'Markets as Politics: A Political-Cultural Approach to Market Institutions', *American Sociological Review* 61(4): 656–73.

Fligstein, Neil and Brantley, Peter (1992) 'Bank Control, Owner Control, or Organizational Dynamics: Who Controls the Large Modern Corporation?', *American Journal of Sociology* 98(2): 280–309.

Frydman, Roman, Murphy, Kenneth and Rapaczynski, Andrej (1996) 'Capitalism with a Camaraderly Face', *Magyar Hirlap* 8 March: 9.

Granovetter, Mark (1974) *Getting a Job: A Study of Contacts and Careers.* Cambridge, MA: Harvard University Press.

Granovetter, Mark (1985) 'Economic Action and Social Structure: The Problem of Embeddedness', *American Journal of Sociology* 91(3): 481–510.

Guillen, Mauro (1994) *Models of Management: Work, Authority, and Organization in a Comparative Perspective.* Chicago, IL: University of Chicago Press.

Guillen, Mauro (2001a) 'Is Globalization Civilizing, Destructive or Feeble? A Critique of Five Key Debates in the Social Science Literature', *Annual Review of Sociology* 27: 235–60.

Guillen, Mauro (2001b) *The Limits of Convergence: Globalization and Organizational Change in Argentina, South Korea, and Spain.* Princeton, NJ: Princeton University Press.

Hannerz, Ulf (2000) 'Scenarios for Peripheral Cultures', in Frank Lechner and John Boli (eds) *The Globalization Reader*, pp. 331–7. New York: Blackwell.

IMAD (Institute of Macroeconomic Analysis and Development) (2001) *Slovenia in the European Union – Strategy for Economic Development of Slovenia.* Ljubljana: IMAD.

Ingelhardt, Ronald and Baker, Wayne (2000) 'Modernization, Cultural Change and the Persistence of Traditional Values', *American Sociological Review* 65(1): 19–55.

Ingram, Paul and Roberts, Peter (2000) 'Friendships among Competitors in the Sydney Hotel Industry', *American Journal of Sociology* 106(2): 387–423.

King, Lawrence P. (2001) *The Basic Features of Postcommunist Capitalism in Eastern Europe: Firms in Hungary, the Czech Republic and Slovakia.* Westport, CT: Praeger.

Lamont, Michèle and Thevenot, Laurent (2001) *Rethinking Comparative Cultural Sociology: Repertoires of Evaluation in France and the United States.* Cambridge: Cambridge University Press.

Lash, Scott and Urry, John (1987) *The End of Organized Capitalism.* Madison: University of Wisconsin Press.

Lechner, Frank and Boli, John (2000) 'Introduction', in Frank Lechner and John Boli (eds) *The Globalization Reader*, pp. 1–3. New York: Blackwell.

McNeely, Connie (1995) *Constructing the Nation-State: International Organizations and Prescriptive Action.* Westport, CT: Greenwood Press.

Meyer, John W. and Rowan, Brian (1977) 'Institutionalized Organizations: Formal Structure as Myth and Ceremony', *American Journal of Sociology* 83(2): 340–63.

Meyer, John W., Boli, John, George, Thomas M. and Ramirez, Francisco (1997) 'World Society and the Nation-State', *American Journal of Sociology* 103(1): 144–81.

Meyer, Klaus (1998) *Direct Investment in Economies in Transition.* Cheltenham: Edward Elgar.

Mrak, Mojimir, Potocnik, Janez and Rojec, Matija (1998) *Strategy of the Republic of Slovenia for Accession to the European Union: Economic and Social Part.* Ljubljana: Institute of Macroeconomic Analysis and Development.

Portes, Alejandro and Sensenbrenner, Julia (1993) 'Embeddedness and Immigration: Notes on the Social Determinants of Economic Action', *American Journal of Sociology* 98(6): 1320–50.

Posner, Richard (1986) *Economic Analysis of Law*, 3rd edn. Boston, MA: Little, Brown.

Powell, Walter W. and Smith-Doerr, Laurel (1994) 'Networks and Economic Life', in Neil J. Smelser and Richard Swedberg (eds) *The Handbook of Economic Sociology*, pp. 368–402. Princeton, NJ: Princeton University Press.

Przeworski, Adam (1995) *Sustainable Democracy.* New York: Cambridge University Press.

Rojec, Matija, More, Matej, Simoneti, Marko, Mrak, Mojimir, Svetlicic, Andrej and Mocnik, Mirjam (2001) 'Slovenia: FDI Review', Faculty of Social Sciences, Ljubljana, mimeo.

Roy, William G. (1997) *Socializing Capital: The Rise of the Large Industrial Corporation in America*. Princeton, NJ: Princeton University Press.

Schmidt, Klaus-Dieter (1995) 'Foreign Direct Investment in Eastern Europe: State-of-the-Art and Prospects', in Rumen Dobrinsky and Michael Landesmann (eds) *Transforming Economies and European Integration*, pp. 268–89. Aldershot: Edward Elgar.

Smelser, Neil and Swedberg, Richard, eds (1994) *The Handbook of Economic Sociology*. Princeton, NJ: Princeton University Press.

Spillman, Lyn (1999) 'Enriching Exchange: Cultural Dimensions of Markets', *American Journal of Economics and Sociology* 58(4): 1047–73.

Staniszkis, Jedwiga (1991) *The Dynamics of Breakthrough*. Berkeley: University of California Press.

Stoner-Weiss, Kathryn (2000) 'Foreign Direct Investment and Democratic Development in the Russian Provinces: A Preliminary Analysis', *Policy Studies Journal* 28(1): 96–113.

Swedberg, Richard (1997) 'New Economic Sociology: What Has Been Accomplished, What is Ahead?', *Acta Sociologica* 40(2): 161–82.

TIPO (Trade and Investment Promotion Office) (1998) 'Raziskava podjetij s tujim in mesanim kapitalom' [Research on Companies with Foreign and Mixed Capital], Ljubljana, mimeo.

UNCTAD (United Nations Conference on Trade and Development) (1996) *International Investment Instruments: A Compendium*, Vols 1–3. Washington, DC: UNCTAD.

UNCTAD (United Nations Conference on Trade and Development) (2000) *World Investment Report*. Washington, DC: UNCTAD.

Uzzi, Brian (1996) 'The Sources and Consequences of Embeddedness for the Economic Performance of Organizations: The Network Effect', *American Sociological Review* 61(4): 674–98.

Uzzi, Brian (1997) 'Social Structure and Competition in Interfirm Networks: The Paradox of Embeddedness', *Administrative Science Quarterly* 42(1): 35–67.

Verdery, Katherine (1998) 'Transnationalism, Nationalism, Citizenship, and Property: Eastern Europe Since 1989', *American Ethnologist* 25(2): 291–306.

Watson, James (1997) 'Transnationalism, Localization, and Fast Foods in East Asia', in James Watson (ed.) *Golden Arches East: McDonald's in East Asia*, pp. 1–38. Stanford, CA: Stanford University Press.

Williamson, Oliver (1985) *The Economic Institutions of Capitalism*. New York: Free Press.

Zelizer, Viviana (1988) 'Beyond the Polemics on the Market: Establishing a Theoretical and Empirical Agenda' *Sociological Forum* 3(4): 614–34.

Zelizer, Viviana (1999) 'Multiple Markets: Multiple Cultures', in Neil J. Smelser and Jeffrey C. Alexander (eds) *Diversity and its Discontents*, pp. 193–212. Princeton, NJ: Princeton University Press.

11

Disintegration and Resilience of Agrarian Societies in Africa – the Importance of Social and Genetic Resources: A Case Study on the Reception of Urban War Refugees in the South of Guinea-Bissau

Marina Padrão Temudo and Ulrich Schiefer

In 1974, Guinea-Bissau finally won its independence from Portugal after more than 10 years of armed warfare led by the PAIGC.[1] It was one of the last African countries to attain national sovereignty. In 1980, a military coup headed by a former guerrilla leader brought a nationalist faction to power, bringing the country into international headlines. Another attempted coup, in 1998, set off a military conflict that soon turned into a full-scale civil war, involving troops from neighbouring Senegal and Guinea-Conakry. Fighting began in the capital of Bissau, as the rival factions tried to win control over the city, but soon spread to the countryside. More than 200,000 civilians were forced to leave the town and to run for their lives. While the urban elite fled to Senegal and Europe, the population of the urban periphery could only turn to the countryside.

Such events indicate the instability of political institutions[2] in the face of disintegration of society. The stealthy advance of these processes of disintegration should not deter us from recognizing them as the deeper cause of the decay of social and political institutions. In Guinea-Bissau, these instabilities cannot be attributed to external political and military interventions,[3] which had led to civil wars in Angola and Mozambique, two other former Portuguese colonies in Africa. In Guinea-Bissau, the most important external influence on society was development cooperation, the effects of which remain however beyond the scope of this article. In our study, we try to understand some of the mechanisms which link an African central society, which depends for its economic reproduction on the global society as represented by the dissipative economy of development cooperation, to the agrarian societies it tries to dominate politically. We try to understand furthermore how the disintegration of the central society into warring factions aggravated by international intervention of different kinds influences the economic and social reproduction of local interethnic networks of agrarian societies and how these societies cope with the additional pressures put on them by rival factions of the central power elite who compete for control of the influx of development aid by manipulating social identities derived from the ethnic matrix.

Our case study[4] allows us a more limited, but at the same time more focused view of the interethnic network of agrarian societies in a remote province of Guinea-Bissau, which was exposed to additional stress by the spillover effects of a disintegrating central society, torn by a civil war with regional dimensions. Even this remote area was pulled into the maelstrom of disintegrating societies. In the first phase of the crisis, the rural societies under observation could manage the extra burden placed on their already precarious subsistence by the waves of urban refugees and could save these internally displaced people from a worse fate. However, the partial loss of economic, social and political cohesion they suffered as a consequence was a very high price to pay. The consequences of this 'crisis' will only become evident in a few years' time. It will be aggravated by the manipulation of ethnic factors by rival factions of the central society, which is already visible today.

These agrarian societies are formed on the basis of ethnic distinctions, living in interethnic networks which use natural resources in both complementary and competitive ways. However, their functional principles are already being only partially respected. The explosion or collapse of the central society will not leave them unaffected and may bring internal ethnic tensions into open conflict.

Agrarian societies in Africa – i.e. societies whose reproduction rests on a mostly rural economy – are exposed to different processes of disintegration following different rhythms and different paces. Wars cause sudden destructions, which can be easily observed but often hide underlying processes of a much slower – and often stealthy – nature. However, their medium- and long-term consequences may be much more destructive. We need to distinguish, on the one hand, between processes of destruction that cause damage to the productive capacity of the societies but which do not impair their potential for reconstruction, and, on the other hand, processes which cause an irreversible decline in their capacity of social reproduction.

Sometimes, social sciences seem to ignore the fact that social reproduction encompasses the sphere of production. When the central society enters a downward spiral, the peripheral agrarian societies are also drawn downward. In countries like Guinea-Bissau, the agrarian societies are the only social organizations with a productive orientation and an autonomous production, which do not depend on the secondary dissipative economy of development aid (Schiefer, 2002). The majority of the population still gains its livelihood in rural economies and mostly from agricultural activities. To study decisive changes, therefore, requires an agronomic perspective.

In this study, we analyse the disintegration of agrarian societies in southern Guinea-Bissau from the perspective of social reproduction, distinguishing between internal and external dimensions. By 'disintegration', we mean the loss of the internal capacity for social reproduction. This process can be observed in the dismantling of social institutions normally guaranteeing both: social reproduction and the maintenance of the economic potential. This can also be seen in the loss of the capacity to reconstitute social relationships after breakdowns. This phenomenon is accelerated by the erosion of the spiritual dimension.[5]

The reduction of the functionality of social institutions lowers the potential of a society to socialize the younger generation. This is accompanied by and shown in the rise of deviant behaviours such as alcoholism and robberies, which are often taken as indicators for early stages of processes leading to a state of anomie.[6] Where accelerated population growth coincides with the failure of social institutions to fulfil their proper functions, social disintegration is accelerated and may lead to over-exploitation of natural resources.[7] The loss of the external reproduction potential – which does not necessarily mean the disintegration of agrarian societies – becomes evident when observing the loss of trust in relationships between agrarian societies and the central society and between different agrarian societies. This can lead to the isolation of affected agrarian societies, which may be enforced from the outside or may result in a deliberate withdrawal. Under certain conditions, agrarian societies may even be able to stabilize their capacity of reproduction by dissociating themselves from a political, economic and social environment which is characterized by the breakdown of the central society.[8]

We hope that the analysis of strategies of resource use employed by local populations and the relationships they entertained with the internally displaced people from the urban areas, whom they welcomed and sheltered, may contribute to an understanding of the capacity for reconstitution inherent in agrarian societies, and provide some insight into the behaviour of rural societies – particularly those organized in different ethnic entities – in response to crisis situations. We used different long-term research methods which were complementary. In addition to the four largest ethnic groups, which form the majority of the population (the acephalous and mostly animistic [but also the Christianized] Balanta, the acephalous but Islamized Nalu, the Islamized Fula and Sosso), the study also included the Islamized Tanda, Dajacanca and Mandinga, as well as the mostly animistic Papel and Manjaco. The research adopted a 'social actor' perspective as developed by Norman Long (Long and Long, 1992).

Historical Review

For centuries, the societies under consideration here had been under consecutive heavy attacks from external forces. Centuries of slave wars, military conquest by the Portuguese,[9] enforced colonial export production, a comprehensive modernization drive initiated by the colonial power after the Second World War – which ended in the anti-colonial war – the war of independence, which caused a decline in the agrarian societies, postcolonial efforts to reconstruct the economy by means of central planning, and, at last, the liberalization of the economy and the overabundance of development aid offered by governmental as well as non-governmental organizations – all these large-scale historical onslaughts damaged these societies in various ways which defy quantification. One way of substantiating this claim is a close investigation of their strategies of agricultural production. Already weakened by these assaults and two consecutive bad harvests, the agrarian societies had to put up with an onrush of urban refugees driven by war. The way they handled this additional burden allows us to understand crucial dimensions of their resilience and potential for reconstruction because only in crisis situations do societies activate their underlying survival mechanisms which are normally invisible.

Social Resources: Solidarity as a Fundamental Principle of (Inter)Ethnic Organization

The present case study investigates agrarian societies in the area of the Nalu of Cubucaré, the *regulados* (chiefdoms) of Cadique and Cabedú. Comprising only 1142 sq. km, the peninsula of Cubucaré hosts a complex interethnic network with complementing and competing ways of using natural resources. These interethnic relationships form the basis of the hitherto largely peaceful coexistence of various agrarian societies belonging to different ethnic groups. At the same time, they interlink and separate these societies socially, economically and politically.

The Nalu were the first to settle in the peninsula, followed by consecutive waves of immigrants of different ethnic origin. The most important of these groups were the Balanta, the Fula and the Sosso. The ethnic matrix still is the fundamental principle of social organization.[10] Before the successful 'pacification' by colonial conquest, there was a spatial separation of the *chão* (ethnically uniform areas of settlement). All groups still acknowledge the primacy of the ethnic group which first settled in a specific area as the basic principle of their mutual relationships. Thus, the peninsula, as well as the larger region of Tombali, continues to be called the *Chão de Nalu* – the 'area of the Nalu'. At present, everyone is allowed to move freely in the region.

Relationships of solidarity and reciprocity regulate the rights and entitlements of individuals. People operate within the most fundamental social unit of the *djorçon* (unilateral descent group). The smallest units of social organization are *morança* (compounds), which usually comprise more than one nuclear family. Schiefer and Havik (1993: 22) define *morança* as a unit of co-residence, based on family relationships, taking the 'aggregate family in a wider sense as the centre of a complex aggregate of relationships which relate economic aspects of production, distribution and transformation to political and societal aspects (such as descent groups, clans, gender and age groups) and finally to the cosmological dimensions of a society'.

Every *morança* is founded through a ritual, which requires the consent of the lineage and contains one or more *fogão* (fireplaces), the number of which is not determined by the number of nuclear families resident in this *morança*. It is the *fogão* which represents the basic unit of the organization of production, processing, consumption and distribution. Individuals simultaneously belong to more than one group within a multidimensional network of relationships. All members of a *morança* take part in communal activities which guarantee social reproduction of the main subgroups (matrilinear or patrilinear families), basic cells (*morança* or *fogão*) and extended units (lineage and village). Furthermore, each individual performs economic activities for his or her personal goals. Depending on their prestige and negotiation skills, heads of families (*chefe de morança* or *chefe de fogão*) try to integrate common labour efforts of individuals or subgroups (Temudo, 1998).

Their authority dwindling, heads of the *morança* no longer manage to prevent seasonal or permanent migration of the young, thus allowing these subgroups to become increasingly autonomous. This autonomy covers longer and longer periods of time, as well as an increasing number of different activities. While the Balanta tradition strictly prohibited any activity other than rice production and cattle breeding (e.g. trade activities), it is quite common today that some of their children emigrate or devote themselves to trade. Thus, Balanta parents have begun to support the education of their children at schools.

In an attempt to avoid the youth's long-term emigration, the elders of the Islamized ethnic groups have begun to grant rights of individual production, autonomous marketing and even autonomous activities in the area of magic to the youth – which used to be strongly defended privileges of the older generation – allowing individual ownership over any income derived from these activities. Another strategy of elders is to lower the age when young people can marry. The elders can only do this by paying the dowry of the first and sometimes the second wife of their sons. As this strategy does not keep young men from emigrating after having founded their families, women and children are often being left behind and have to suffer a condition of economic dependence. Moreover, the *morança* lose their inner cohesion and their capacity to mobilize labour and generate income which can be invested for the benefit of the community.

Within the Islamized ethnic groups, the migration of men overburdens women as they are left with the sole responsibility for survival of families, while men, whose labour is necessary for food production, are absent. The situation of the Balanta is different. Here feeding the family with rice is the responsibility of men – concomitantly with a clear separation of tasks within the gender division of labour. If a man fails to honour these obligations, his wives have the right to leave him – which they frequently do (Temudo, 1998: Vol. 1–348).

The dwindling of the elders' authority also becomes evident in their failure to punish deviant behaviour, such as theft or robbery. This has led to a noticeable increase in the number of crimes. The rigorous traditional organization of the Balanta into age groups allowed an easy mobilization of labour within the *morança*. A grown-up male could only marry after going through certain rites of passage (*fanado*), the timing of which depended to a large degree on the economic situation of his *morança*. The independence war and emigration so damaged social norms and the authority of the elders that today there are many young men who are not initiated but who marry and set up their own *fogão*.

Decisive elements which contributed to the decrease of the working capacity of male Balanta were changes in alcohol consumption. Previously a prerogative of elders and restricted to special occasions (van der Drift, 1990: 102), there is nowadays an uncontrolled increase in the consumption of alcohol, particularly among the younger generation and fostered by the increase in the cultivation of cashew.[11] The forced exchange of rice for cashew nuts which was promoted by the government increased the difficulties to mobilize Balanta youths for rice production. They turn instead to the production of cashew which requires less physical effort and is not as dependent on the weather as rice production. The production of cashew offers an additional source of income to women, who take to cashew wine making. Thus, the introduction of the cashew culture reduced incentives for rice production.

Formerly, village people were organized into groups according to age and sex *(mandjuandade)*, which were important institutions of socialization and mutual aid. Informal mutual aid groups existed as well, usually made up of friends, who were men or women of the same age. One after the other, all the *morança* were provided with necessary labour by the *mandjuandade*, irrespective of the number of members of a *morança* who belonged to the working group. After harvest, the *mandjuandade* was paid in rice, which was used to organize a festivity for the group.

Only the Tanda have kept this form of solidarity alive. Today, all *mandjuandade* demand an improved diet, i.e. meals including either fish or meat, and, in addition, tobacco, cola nuts, alcohol (Balanta) and money. Nowadays, only advance payment of Balanta work-groups can ensure a timely start of work in the fields – which few people can afford before the harvest.

Despite fundamental changes in the organization of mutual aid for work in the fields, the principle of general reciprocity (Lévi-Strauss, 1949; Sahlins, 1974: 193) continues to define intra- and interethnic relationships. This reciprocity includes presents of food, loans of produce and money in times of crisis, offers of bed and food to travellers, a hospitable reception of friends and relatives, gifts of magic objects which protect their bearers against evil of all sorts, gifts of traditional medicine and help at work. Hospitality is unlimited in time and is never refused to relatives and friends, even if the family has not enough food for its own members. A guest is not obliged to participate in the work of the host family, while being free to pursue economic activities for his or her own benefit. When guests leave, members of the family will offer them gifts, usually food, seed or plants.

In these rural societies, it is unthinkable to demand payment for rice a relative asks for during harvest time, even if a family's stock is insufficient to cover its own needs. For this reason, producers who sow before the others and plant a high percentage of early maturing varieties, produce more for the community than for their own family. Quite often, they find themselves in situations where they have to ask for rice themselves to bridge times of shortage between harvests.

As gifts and loans are embedded in a network of solidarity and reciprocity, it is very difficult to claim repayment of loans from family members or friends, particularly when only small amounts are concerned – even if accumulated small amounts may reach considerable proportions. There are observable trends, however, which indicate a weakening of relationships of reciprocity (Temudo, 1998: Vol. I: 401). While different strands of solidarity and reciprocity are woven into the interethnic network of relations in all directions, the lack of a comprehensive consensus between the observed societies allows for a considerable number of conflicts. The main conflicts occur between Balanta and Nalu in the management of natural resources, while in the area of livestock management conflicts may surface between the Balanta and all other ethnic groups. In Cubucaré, the Balanta are the only cattle breeders. After independence, they ceased to herd their cattle properly, which led to permanent squabbles because unsupervised cattle break into fields and damage crops. According to customary law, anyone may seize and kill cattle caught when damaging crops. Depending on the damage done, he or she may keep part or even all of the meat. Frequent attempts by Balanta to change management rules of natural resources are another source of conflict, which concentrates in two areas. According to the contracts between Balanta and Nalu, which were negotiated at the time of the Balanta immigration and sealed by spiritual entities, Balanta may use only low-lying land close to rivers for the cultivation of mangrove swamp rice according to their own techniques, which include the construction of dykes. It was with these dams that they created fields separated from rivers, and virtually opened these areas for agriculture. Today, many Balanta want fields for rain-fed crops in the forest areas, too. Quite often, they simply occupy land without performing the mandatory rituals for the opening up of land for cultivation, which were traditional prerogatives of the Nalu. A second cause of trouble is palm-wine tapping, which ultimately leads to destruction of the African fan palm forests (*Borassus aethiopum*), the trunk of which is highly valued for the construction of the roofs of the houses. This tree has almost completely disappeared.

After the democratic multi-party elections in 1994, a political clash of interests between the mostly Islamized groups – who supported the PAIGC – and the Balanta became apparent, as the latter, almost without exception, voted for the Partido da Renovação Social (PRS), a party organized along ethnic lines. Election results made the PRS the main opposition party against the winning PAIGC. As their presidential candidate, Nino Vieira, won the separate presidential election by only a very small margin, suspicion of election fraud was widespread and the Balanta's tempers rose against the followers of the governing party. In Cubucaré, the Balanta conducted a kind of cold war by temporarily refusing direct exchange of rural products with other ethnic groups and by increasing the price of rice. These changes in the intra- and interethnic relationships find a correlate in the increasingly risk-prone changes in cultivation strategies which can be observed over the last decades.

Genetic Resources: Diversity as a Strategy for the Reduction of Insecurity

The resilience of the agrarian societies and of the interethnic network is based on the culture of rice – which in turn depends on the availability of genetic resources – and the rights to access to and control of other natural resources. Several reasons sustain this argument. While other societies developed their instruments (machines, technology), or produced comprehensive systems of work organization that allowed for a large-scale transformation of nature (irrigation works, transport infrastructures), the real productive potential of the societies studied here is only partially dependent on the organization of work. While the Balanta's organization capacity is sufficient to build and maintain irrigation systems of several villages, their traditions set strict limits on the level of technology and the organization of work: strict customary laws prevented the Balanta from engaging in any economic activity beyond the cultivation of mangrove rice. Because of these restrictions, the only field where these societies possess a potential for an increase in production and a better adaptation to changes in their natural and social environment is to be found in the culture of rice, the most important food crop in Guinea-Bissau since colonial times. We therefore take a closer look at this produce, and especially at the selection of rice varieties, which plays a crucial role.

The transformation of the Tombalí region into Guinea-Bissau's main rice-producing area was a consequence of the Balanta immigration during the 1930s, which brought mangrove swamp rice cultivation (*bolanha salgada*) into the area (de Carvalho, 1949: 312). Before this period, rice was grown in rain-fed cultivation (slash and burn) and in valleys flooded by rainwater (*bolanha doce*). Rice production systems follow an ethnic matrix. Leaving present dynamics aside, they can be described in a simplified manner: traditionally, the Balanta are cultivators of mangrove swamp rice, while the Fula and Tanda are cultivators of rain-fed rice. Employing one of these farming systems in varying proportions, the other ethnic groups can be placed between these two extremes. While mangrove rice cultivation still allows, as a whole, the production of a marketable surplus, today rain-fed production is in a crisis. The Cubucaré region still produces surplus rice. But while some producers sell their surplus outside the region, more and more families inside the region fail to meet their yearly requirements in rice from their own production. However, the period of undersupply is limited. Food shortage is mitigated by a complicated system of interethnic exchange mechanisms, which include an exchange of work as well as of other products for rice and a system of loans compensating for the specialization.

The Balanta concentrate on rice production and cattle breeding, while Islamized groups develop a much more diversified system of production. Especially women produce and process a great number of rural products and are active in trade. Women are the most important actors on local markets and in direct exchange transactions. They gain rice with these exchanges, which is a major contribution to the self-sufficiency of most Islamized families. Exchange of goods often involves a time lag that compensates for different harvest seasons in saltwater paddy production and rain-fed production. The most important crop is the peanut, which is given to the Balanta in October. They repay with rice after threshing the following April or May.

In rain-fed cultivation, the full consumption of early maturing varieties, which ripen during the hunger period, often leads to a loss of seeds for certain varieties, which then need to be substituted by other varieties. The social rules of solidarity and reciprocity allow close relatives and friends of a producer to do harvest work for a day on his field, taking home as much rice as they can carry on their head. This is not considered a loan. Only a second request would be considered a loan, which has to be repaid. During times of harvest of the early maturing varieties, some families stay with relatives for so-called courtesy visits (*fala mantenha*) – or send their children. Everybody can 'offer' to help with the harvest, even if the owner does not really need help, and get paid for this 'service' in rice.

It is customary in mangrove rice production that whoever has more seedlings than is needed for the transplanting, offers them to producers who do not have enough. This leads to the – involuntary – introduction of new varieties and field trials. The circulation of plants within and between *morança* is frequent, because producers often try to grow more seedlings than they will need, due to their risk-reducing strategy. Moreover, the independence war contributed to the introduction of new varieties into areas where rice production had been completely abandoned. Despite heavy fighting in the Cubucaré region in the 1960s and 1970s, the diversity of the gene pool and the system of selection of varieties were not impaired. Rice production was upheld throughout 10 years of fighting; the region supplied a substantial proportion of food for the fighters. At present, many of the traditional varieties identified by Espírito Santo (1949) in the 1940s can still be found in the region.

Many of the elder producers have a detailed knowledge of the geographical distribution of different varieties in the country. The maintenance of a large genetic diversity consciously and carefully spread over time and space is one of the bases of this crop system. Producers can adapt to changing climatic and market conditions by a different selection of varieties. Therefore, they can collectively and individually minimize their risk. Rice cultivation was a field where profound endogenous innovations took place, mostly in variety selection (Temudo, 1996).

The majority of the producers interviewed cultivates more than one variety, giving the following reasons: reduction of risk, increase of yield, a better utilization of the available labour when using varieties with different cycles, adaptation to different kinds of soil, adaptation to different irrigation conditions, diversity in characteristics and qualities of the rice produced. At present, the enthusiasm for experimentation among the Balanta seems to be diminishing. Only very few producers from this ethnic group try to estimate the productivity of the varieties they use in field trials. Even estimates of their yearly production are rare. During colonial times, the Balanta were considered to lack the capacity to look ahead, as they sold more rice than their harvest permitted and then had to buy back rice at very high prices (Ribeiro, 1988: 2, 1989: 254; van der Drift, 1990: 101). When compared to the standards reported by Espírito Santo (1949), the Balanta of today seem to have become less careful with the harvesting procedures and the storage of seed and produce. Only bigger producers still conduct intensive field trials with new varieties and maintain a greater genetic diversity. These producers still cultivate the old, long-established varieties with a long cycle and high yield, such as *atanha*.

Women of all ethnic groups boycott varieties with a red skin and small grain because they are difficult to husk manually. This led to the decline of long-established high-yielding varieties. The introduction of rice-husking machines, however, enabled some family heads to return to the cultivation of varieties such as *atanha*, *thom* and *aninha*. Formerly the only source of income to the Balanta, overall rice production fell dramatically, due to a reorientation towards other activities like the production of cashew nuts, which can be bartered for imported rice.

In rain-fed cultivation, there is still a great diversity of varieties with different qualities, and particularly with different vegetation cycles. On average, every producer grows three varieties (25 percent grow more than three, the highest observed number was seven); the majority grows two varieties (25 percent grow more than two, the highest number observed was five) in mangrove rice cultivation. In all, 27 criteria for the selection of varieties were identified, three of which farmers consider crucial for determining whether a variety will be 'rice of the family' or 'best rice': 'yield in the field' (as measured by volume), 'yield in the pot' (as measured by the increase in volume during cooking) and 'yield in the belly' (as measured by the duration of digestion). The most important reasons for the nearly complete rejection of all high-yielding varieties used in trials by DEPA (Departamento de Pesquisa Agrícola), in an attempt by the state and international donors to introduce high-yielding varieties in order to guarantee national food security, are a weak increase in volume in the pot (during cooking) and a short digestion time. These varieties had also been rejected because their taste was too good. The selection of less tasty varieties aims at a reduction of consumption, and, therefore, helps to increase food security. Several less tasty varieties are selected by some producers for times of rice shortage.

Research in 1999, 2000 and 2001 showed, however, that the share of varieties considered tasty had increased as compared to the preceding period. This might be read as an indication for the decreasing importance of rice self-sufficiency, which may be linked to the disaggregation of the units of reproduction. An increasing proportion of producers is now in a position to buy rice for consumption with money obtained by growing fruit. Other strategies are the direct bartering of rice against cashew nuts, or the exchange of rice against products produced and processed by women.

The field trials and the local knowledge regarding variety selection are based on criteria which enable risk reduction and adaptation to local agro-ecological conditions. These criteria include a complex knowledge of the management of uncertainty on which all agricultural production systems in regions with limited resources are based. Field trials with new varieties are conducted where there are reasons to expect that a new variety might perform better than the ones used, according to one or more of the criteria already mentioned. If the expectations are confirmed, the new variety is adopted. Only rarely does a new variety completely replace old varieties. Usually, a new variety is introduced gradually and not exclusively.

The combination of economic liberalization and development cooperation led to a weakening of the agrarian societies, which can be shown through a detailed analysis of the changes in social organization and in the management of natural resources. Contrary to the ritual invocations of success by development ideologists, the agrarian societies have been sliding downwards on a negative spiral since the beginning of the 1960s. The inner cohesion of these societies began to slowly disaggregate, while the inter-ethnic network of exchanges – essential for the survival of these societies – was also put under increasing pressure. As demonstrated earlier, this has had negative consequences for the agro-technical aspects of agricultural production.

In this already tense situation, the agrarian societies were tested again by developments which pushed their capacity for endurance, well proven throughout the past centuries, to its limits. We show how the agrarian societies tried to cope with the heavy burden of receiving refugees from urban areas and how this changed their work organization and resource management (rice cultivation). This is to be seen against the fact that the majority of the urban population owed their survival to the agrarian societies.

War and Social Resilience

In June 1998, a political and military conflict erupted in Bissau which affected the whole country. It was triggered by a conflict between two political figures: Brigadier-General Ansumane Mané and President Nino Vieira disagreed over alleged or real deliveries of arms to rebels of the Casamance region in neighbouring Senegal. One of the main causes for the conflict was severe dissatisfaction of the veterans of the war of independence with the politics of the president. A second major cause can be found in power struggles inside the PAIGC.[12] In the beginning, the armed conflict was more or less restricted to the capital of Bissau. Called in by the president, troops from the neighbouring countries of Senegal and Guinea-Conakry spread the war over the whole country.

During the war of independence, Cubucaré had become a 'liberated area' under the rule of the PAIGC. Therefore, the Islamized ethnic groups still supported the PAIGC and the president, in stark contrast to the Balanta. While the latter immediately took sides and supported the revolt of the junta led by Ansumane Mané, the other groups remained neutral and tried to stay out of the fighting which broke out in 1998–9. At the same time, they took a critical stance to the internal conflict of the PAIGC, and did not support the attempt to replace the charismatic president – and former war hero – Nino Vieira, whom they had helped into power. However, the invasion by foreign troops called in by the president changed the situation. Henceforth, only his closest followers supported the president.

At the outbreak of the fighting, the urban elite fled abroad, mostly to Europe, while the bulk of the urban population, about 200,000 people, fled to the countryside. In Cubucaré, most of the families interviewed (70 percent) took in refugees. Many of the refugees accommodated were friends or neighbours of relatives who lived in Bissau and had fled together with them. On average, each *morança* took in seven refugees, but in some cases, the number of people accommodated exceeded the members of the *morança* by far. The behaviour of the Balanta towards displaced urban refugees differed from that of other ethnic groups. They took in fewer refugees, one of the reasons being that the Balanta from the capital fled to and found shelter in Mansoa-Nhaccra, their region of origin, which was closer to the capital than Cubucaré.[13] While the number of refugees sheltered by Balanta *morança* was between a minimum of four and a maximum of 20, the Islamized groups each took in an average of nine and reaching a maximum of 28. The highest number of Balanta refugees were found in the *morança* of well-to-do families in the villages of Caboxanque and Cafine, well known for their lucrative rice production. Of the total 158 *morança* of the sample, only 50 did not take in any refugees, 34 of which were Balanta. This imbalance can be explained by the fact that fewer Balanta from the south had emigrated to the capital before the start of the last war.

When the refugees arrived, they possessed nothing but the clothes they were wearing – not even food. They were granted food and shelter without any expectation of compensation: they were simply accorded guest status. A considerable proportion of refugees, many of whom were children, did not participate in the work in the field, or in the collection of edible plants in the bush, or in the processing of rural products to be sold or bartered for food. There were even reports of refugees deciding to visit other families precisely on days of communal work for their host *morança* – which did not delight their host families. The same happened on days when food was especially scarce. Refugees 'whose bodies were still used to heavy work' did participate in the collective fieldwork, and, in 1999, requested personal plots, the produce of which they took home with them, together with the food they were given by their host as farewell presents, when they finally left to resume their lives in Bissau.

The conflict lasted for almost a year, and, with a few exceptions, the refugees only left after the restoration of peace. Men were the first to return, leaving their wives and children in the care of their hosts for an additional time period. The influx of urban people fleeing the war came at the worst possible moment for the rural population: at the beginning of the first agricultural season, after a year of drought. In this situation, the refugees had to be fed on the already scarce reserves which had been earmarked for paying the workforce in the fields. Aggravating the scarcity of food, the following agricultural season, in 1998, saw yet another drought, which mostly affected the mangrove swamp cultivation, and thus the Balanta.

International emergency food aid proved to be inadequate. The foreign troops allied with the president either tried to prevent the entry of food aid into the country, or appropriated supplies for themselves.[14] Yet another part was embezzled in the process of distribution. Many families in Cubucaré who had accepted to take in refugees did not receive any help at all, others received only very little help and at very irregular intervals, depending on the distance between their *morança* and the distribution centres. The quantity of food distributed did not match the figures quoted in the media. The food distributed comprised rice, oil and a wheat product originally intended for the preparation of rations for children. In contrast to what has been reported for other emergency operations, this porridge – which was alien to the population's food habits – was received well and was also eaten by adults. As late as April 2000, one could find misappropriated food aid rations for sale in rural markets.

During wartime, most of the trade routes had been partially interrupted – with the exception of the Gabú–Cacine route, which continued to function well – partly due to the good conditions of the road, and partly due to the boldness of the travelling traders. While some of the traders 'rented' vehicles from the military for the transport of their merchandise, the military in turn used the traders' vehicles for the transport of soldiers and supplies.

Owing to the bad conditions of the road, only very few traders reached Cubucaré to buy fruit. Therefore, producers had no choice but to carry their produce on their heads or by boat to Cacine whenever conditions forced them to obtain cash for the purchase of food. The border markets of the

Quitafine region never ceased functioning during the war, mostly because the traders from Guinea-Conakry provided the region with merchandise, whenever they managed to escape the frontier guards. While market activities were greatly reduced by war, direct barter activities soared, if the time invested in these activities is taken as an indicator. The most important actors in this field were women of Islamized groups, who invested much time and effort in the production and processing of rural products. They had to cover great distances on foot until they found a Balanta willing to trade in their produce for rice, which they could then use to feed their families. Among the Balanta, both men and women took to trading in alcoholic beverages (mostly sugar cane brandy), which boomed during the war. As Balanta women were not quite as successful in procuring food for their families, many family heads were forced to slaughter a cow, or a pig, and to either sell the meat, or trade it in for rice directly. Many Balanta had to borrow animals from friends of other ethnic groups, since the rules of the lineage safeguard the number of livestock by forbidding the slaughter of their own animals except for clearly specified purposes. For this reason, many Balanta came out of the crisis situation with debts they might have to repay on short notice.

In order to assure food security, different strategies were applied: they can be divided into nutritional and productive strategies. Nutritional strategies – well-known from the annual period of scarcity before the harvest – aimed at saving rice through changes in the composition and timing of food preparation. Different ethnic groups employed different and rather characteristic strategies. The Balanta prepared only one meal a day, called 'one shot' (*um tiro*) which was eaten in the afternoon. Only during work peaks, were two meals served. Sometimes, the rice was cooked with beans, eaten with palm oil, or mixed with pounded raw palm fruit (*bonton*), to enrich the meals, and to prolong the time of digestion.

The eating habits of Islamized groups are based on a more diversified food pattern (Temudo, 1998: Vol. I: 311–53). They saved rice by adding other foodstuffs: bananas, manioc, yams, sweet potatoes or beans was served, either in alternate meals during a day or every other day according to the supply situation and the consent of the family. To increase the volume, rice was either cooked together with sorghum, or with a lot of liquid (*badadji*). Very poor families skipped breakfast, but continued to feed their children in the morning. Islamized groups ate more wild plants, especially yams (Tanda and Nalu), but also other plants which are normally not eaten, even in times of shortage, for example *palmitos* (Sosso and Nalu) and mangrove fruits (Nalu and even Balanta).

Productive strategies consisted in increasing the production of root crops (manioc, sweet potato, yams and others) during the dry season of 1998. In the rainy season of 1999, production of rice and drought-resistant cereals (sorghum, millet and fonio) was also stepped up. In addition, direct sowing in the mangove fields (instead of transplanting) was applied in order to make better use of the scarce seeds.

Producers with enough seed and rice to feed the workgroups attempted – with some success – to increase the area under cultivation and to diversify cultivation. The mangrove rice producers also turned to rain-fed cultivation and to freshwater rice, while the rain-fed cultivators also turned to valley freshwater rice. Freshwater paddy cultivation was used to obtain early maturing rice. Following some natural indicators of a rainy year, many mangrove swamp rice producers also decided to plant long-cycle varieties, obtaining necessary seed from other producers.

The seed management system was not destroyed during the war. Only 12.2 percent of the mangrove rice producers consumed all of their seeds, 20 percent ate a part, while 67.8 percent did not use any of their seed for food consumption. Among the rain-fed cultivators, 56.6 percent declared that they had not eaten any seed, while 15.6 percent admitted having consumed all their stock.

Producers who had consumed all or part of their seed tried to obtain seeds by bartering for them with cola nuts, rice (husked rice or food aid rice), honey (for the preparation of a kind of honey brandy which is an essential part of payment of Balanta workgroups for cultivation of mangrove rice) or work. Mangrove rice producers often received free seedlings from other producers who had a surplus in their seedbeds. Producers in all cultivation systems received small amounts of seed from friends and relatives, which led to a mix of many different varieties in the same field. Of the four varieties distributed by relief agencies,[15] only one corresponded to the preferences of the producers: *banimalio* – which was not an improved variety. Using the criteria 'yield in the pot', 'yield in the belly' and 'length of the stalk', the other varieties were assessed as bad. Being varieties with short stalks, in fact, they did not withstand the high water levels caused by the heavy rainfalls of 1999 in freshwater and mangrove fields. This situation could have been avoided rather easily: all the relief varieties had been distributed for years, and a simple investigation into their levels of acceptance could have made the emergency relief effort much more efficient. Moreover, the distribution of the seed took place very late. Most producers reported that they failed to get a harvest from the seed they received. Some of them foresaw a bad harvest and decided to use the seed grain for food immediately.

Changes also occurred in the organization of cooperation. Forms of mutual aid which had been lost since the independence war were reactivated. In contrast to the Balanta, the workgroups (*mandjuandade*) in most of the Islamized villages did not ask for payment for their work. In some other cases, they accepted payment after harvest and lowered their prices considerably. Since food was scarce, each of the young men of a *mandjuandade* brought his own food for the working day from his *morança*. The owner of the field was only expected to provide a supplement to the rice staple they brought along. This was a considerable relief for owners, who often had already given up hiring workgroups, because of the high costs.

The worst supply situation occurred when the war was over, during the rainy season of 1999. The Balanta were relatively better off than other groups because many of them had cashew plantations and could barter the cashew nuts for rice. Islamized producers, however, found themselves in a dire situation as the season for selling fruit was already over, when their only way to earn cash income both for the purchase of rice and for investment consisted in selling bananas and oranges. Lacking cash, they could not buy from the travelling traders even during the ceasefire and after the end of the war. Instead they attempted to barter palm-oil for rice, but were forced to accept extremely low quantities of rice for their palm-oil. Part of the rice they traded originated from warehouses in Bissau, which the revolting Junta had confiscated. It was sold to the countryside by travelling retail traders (*djilas*). Therefore, people often said it was the traders who profited most from the war.

The relief aid given to the region by some local and international NGOs was rather limited. Its components were: distribution of seeds on a credit basis, provision of rice and beans to farmers' associations (who had only to pay transport costs), supply of rice at market prices through the grain banks of some women's organizations, a food-for-work programme for road maintenance funded by the World Food Programme (targeted mainly at keeping the roads free of vegetation) and a programme to increase the rice production in freshwater fields. During and after the war, there was not a single coordinated intervention by the NGOs. The most highly valued measures were sales of rice and beans at a symbolic price by farmers' associations, run by a foreign NGO linked to the Catholic church, and the road maintenance programme of a local NGO, which, however, reached only a few villages. The supply situation improved because Mauritanian traders, arriving in Cubucaré together with refugees, sold their merchandise at prices much lower than previous market prices. Some of them decided to settle in the region after they were driven from Bissau, where they had come to dominate the retail trade since the end of the 1980s.

During wartime, the emotional climate was characterized by a general feeling of solidarity. At the same time, hostilities between supporters and the opponents of the president, and between the secret services of both warring factions, sometimes flared up. The interethnic fabric of the countryside was deeply affected by the military confrontations of armed factions of the central society fighting for political predominance. The military successes of the revolting Junta had some important psychological effects on the interethnic network of the agrarian societies. Throughout the country, it seemed to allow the Balanta to feel much stronger than before. They felt less and less obliged to respect historical interethnic agreements which used to be the basis for the management of the natural resources. This was evidenced in the rising number of violations of formerly respected rules of conduct. Some Balanta are reported to have uttered threats against people from other ethnic groups. Should the Junta win the war, they would no longer tolerate the killing of their cattle when caught in the act of destroying other people's crops: 'We will kill people who kill our cows.' These threats remain a sore point in the interethnic relationships of the region.

Perspectives

The agrarian societies provided a comparatively safe haven from the outbreak of violence for those segments of the urban population who, unlike the urban elite, were not in a position to leave the country. Acceptance of displaced urban dwellers into rural family compounds made the construction of refugee camps unnecessary – camps which have often turned into rather permanent institutions breeding further violence in a number of countries. In the studied region, refugees were distributed over a large area, and more or less integrated into stable social relationships where they were given food and shelter, where they found solace in their miserable condition, and help in caring for their children and families. They got a first-hand experience of African solidarity, which provided them with an opportunity to participate in agricultural and other economic activities, and offered them the chance to gain an income of their own, which – together with the farewell presents of their hosts – assisted them in making a new start in the town after their return. It is remarkable that the agrarian societies did not only accept their own kin, but also friends and neighbours of their relatives.

As a consequence of these events, the relationship between city dwellers and rural populations underwent some important changes. It is probable that the return of the displaced urban population will offer future rural migrants better opportunities to migrate to the city, as they will be able to rely on a network of relationships recently created. In addition, some of these new links may have an effect on economic activities of rural populations, particularly the younger generation. Studying these effects may provide important insights into rural–urban relationships in general.

The wave of refugees from the city arrived at a difficult moment for the agrarian societies, after two consecutive years of drought. The already weakened and declining agrarian societies withstood this additional blow surprisingly well. The mechanisms of seed management survived without noticeable changes, keeping its most important function intact, namely to provide all producers with adequate amounts and varieties of seed. Even under this extreme pressure, intraethnic and interethnic relationships of solidarity largely ensured the availability of seed even for those who had been forced to eat part or all of their seed. Even during the food crisis in the rainy season of 1999, social relations and the work organization did not cease to function. In this crisis, even some old and supposedly lost forms of mutual aid were reactivated. Neither the seed distribution systems nor the distribution of early maturing varieties were monetarized. However, this rather positive assessment does not apply to the Balanta, who suffered most from the consecutive years of drought and the reception of refugees. They did not manage to convince their youth to use more solidary forms of mutual aid in their field work.

Some important conclusions may also be drawn for future international emergency relief efforts. The multiplicity of criteria and the number of decision levels involved in the selection of varieties, which could be observed at the compound level, call for some changes in the strategy for developing 'packages of technological options', which would increase the number of options for local producers, building on already existing local capacities for research in the field. Such packages might also be able to contribute to the improved food security often invoked by development experts (Temudo, 1996).

In contrast to older strategic orientations of agricultural development, local producers do not consider an increase in the yield per area unit their highest priority. The agronomists' earlier concentration on high-yielding varieties therefore needs to be reconsidered both with respect to future agricultural research and with respect to emergency aid and development cooperation. Instead, the diversity of genetic resources should receive greater attention. The erosion of genetic resources during times of war severely limits the potential for reconstruction of agrarian societies after war. Emergency relief could therefore make an important contribution to the reinforcement of local self-organization and the organization of local mutual aid. Rice is the most important staple crop in a number of West African countries, where genetic resources are kept in situ and are therefore susceptible to war and natural disasters (Richards et al., 1997). The fact that diversity of genetic resources in Cubucaré, the centre of rice cultivation in Guinea-Bissau, has not been affected by war is of the greatest importance for countries like Sierra Leone and Liberia, where wars caused an erosion of genetic resources (Richards et al., 1997).

The interethnic relationships, which are of crucial importance for peaceful cohabitation and for the survival of the population, were put under additional stress by ethnic aspects of the power struggle. These relationships also showed a remarkable resilience, particularly in the crisis situation of 1999. The long-term effects of these events remain to be studied in more detail.

We close by considering some of the effects of the fast processes of change which the Balanta experienced. The results of our research do not allow a definite conclusion concerning the question whether the processes should be seen as processes of disaggregation or rather as processes of adaptation to a changing environment. During the crisis, the Balanta suffered more than other ethnic groups because their mechanisms for food security are less elaborate and their sense of responsibility is comparatively less evident. Compared with other groups, they suffer more from growing debts owed to members of other groups. This trend could worsen, should there be further years of drought. This process of growing indebtedness does not only negatively affect their productive capacity, by contributing to a scarcity of seed and by seriously damaging their capacity to hire work-groups for cultivation, but also undermines the interethnic trust which used to be a firm base for the interethnic relationships and their material basis, namely the asynchronous exchange mechanisms.

'Debts do not grow old' was one of the comments offered by a producer with respect to the Balanta's difficulties to repay their debts incurred in 1997, 1998 and 1999. In the long run, however, these debts can only be borne and cushioned by the system of general reciprocity, if producers who granted loans do not need these payments to guarantee their own subsistence. There are no indications that agrarian societies will ever receive adequate compensation for their solidarity from the urban society – apart from scant and individual acts of assistance from people whom they helped during the crisis.

Overall, the 'city' has given little to the 'countryside', while many of its inhabitants received substantial help from the rural areas. To the extent that it even exists in an explicit form, the rural development policy is very unlikely to change as a result of recent events. Therefore, expectations that the rural population might entertain will remain unfulfilled, and the previous trend of a widening gap between urban and rural areas will probably continue. The relationship between agrarian societies and the central society is of crucial importance for the interethnic networks. War and the following victory of an ethnically based party (Balanta) in the elections have already changed the interethnic balance of power. First rifts between the Balanta and other ethnic groups have already become visible. So far, the urban-based political elite in power has not yet played the ethnic card to the full and has not yet openly applied strategies of ethnic division in the countryside. But our research shows clearly that the potential for interethnic conflicts exists – and that its destructive effects may surpass anything experienced so far.

The Balanta, notwithstanding the fact that they are the largest ethnic group, representing about 40 percent of the total population, and that they fielded the highest number of fighters, both in the independence war and in the last war, had been discriminated against and had been excluded from political power ever since independence. President Nino Vieira removed some of their most important representatives from powerful positions, some lost their life during and after a trial. The ethnic party PRS won the parliamentary and presidential elections because of the large number of Balanta they could mobilize, and because of the widespread dissatisfaction of the urban population of the capital with the PAIGC. The fact that large numbers of young Balanta warriors joined the troops of the revolting Junta in the last war and in its aftermath can only partly be explained by the lust for adventure which incited them to escape from the authority of their village elders for some time. This move can also be seen as an attempt to increase the Balanta's military potential through integration into modern fighting units and access to modern weapons. Predominance of Balanta in the present urban power elite is already provoking other ethnic groups to rally together – and they are likely to use Islam as the smallest common denominator for their anti-Balanta alliance.

While the relationships between acephalous ethnic groups and the political power elite require a proper study, the first effects of the Balanta power takeover can already be felt in the countryside. One of the most important research problems is to adequately take into account the time lag of these effects. It can be expected that effects of the influx of urban refugees will only be felt after some years. In a first reaction, agrarian societies seem to absorb strong impacts and try to restore their previous state of affairs resorting to a wide range of traditional mechanisms. However, this attempt can only be successful if their potential for reconstruction has not suffered irreparable damage, if they still have the strength and the resources required for self-repair. Mechanisms used to regulate the interethnic relations of power are of crucial importance. Unless the elders succeed in re-establishing a balance of power between different ethnic groups, a destructive potential may be unleashed which could devastate the whole country. Already, the election victory of the PRS changed the balance of power in the region observed. The Balanta have started to challenge some of the basic tenets of interethnic cohabitation. The other ethnic groups still play a waiting game: 'We are still listening, we want to see, if this is going to be a state for the cows [of the Balanta and a main cause of crop destruction] or for the people.'

Notes

This research project, 'The Disintegration of Agrarian Societies in Africa and their Potential for Reconstruction', was funded by FCT, Portugal (Project Praxis/P/SOC/1110/1998// Poctii/Soc/11110/98). Earlier research was funded by the Stiftung Volkswagenwerk and by the Deutsche Forschungsgemeinschaft (DFG).

1 Partido Africano da Independência da Guiné e Cabo Verde.

2 See Rudebeck (2001) for the best analyses of state and political institutions.

3 There were a few conflicts with neighbouring Senegal about off-shore oil and alleged or real support for independence movements from the Casamance which used the border area as hinterland. This led to some military clashes at the border.

4 The results of the case study were produced in a long-term research context starting in 1986 with the research project 'Agrargesellschaften und Ländliche Entwicklungspolitik' in Guinea-Bissau at the Institute of Sociology of the University of Münster, headed by Christian Sigrist and funded by the Stiftung Volkswagenwerk. Our research followed developments which invalidated the development paradigm and led to the research project 'Disintegration of Agrarian Societies in Africa and their Potential for Reconstruction' at the Centro de Estudos Africanos, Instituto Superior de Ciências do Trabalho e da Empresa (ISCTE), Lisbon, funded by the Fundação para Ciência e a Tecnologia (FCT), Lisbon. More recently, the problem of traumatized African societies comes to the fore. In the period between 1993 and 1996, Marina Temudo studied livelihood systems and processes of disaggregation of multi-ethnic societies on the Cubucaré peninsula in the south of Guinea-Bissau and interfaces of knowledge systems between agrarian societies and external institutions (Temudo, 1998: Vols I and II). In 1999, 2000 and 2002, she investigated the consequences of the 1998–9 war for the disaggregation processes of the agrarian societies and their survival strategies.

5 See Desjeux (1987: 102) and Atteslander (1995: 12).

6 Atteslander (1995: 13): 'Anomie as a classical term means normlessness, lawlessness, no sense of social identity, being "socially lost".' Schiefer (2002: 34) describes a concept of social collapse: 'Anomie is understood, in the notion derived from Durkheim, as a process that can be self-reinforcing. This "positive feedback" can lead to a situation where anomic processes further other anomic processes and the societies in question can be drawn into a downward spiral of social disintegration.'

7 See Bakema (1994: 9), for a discussion of the 'tragedy of the commons' of Hardin (1968).

8 See the case of the Kuvale in Angola (Duarte de Carvalho, 1999).

9 See Pélissier (1989).

10 For a non-essentialist definition of ethnic groups, see Sigrist (1994b: 47).

11 Even before the liberalization of the economy, trade organizations in the countryside were obliged to barter rice against cashew nuts, which for a short time received a high price on the world market.

12 For the underlying causes of this war, see Rudebeck (2001), Schiefer (2002) and the special edition of *Soronda* (INEP, 2000).

13 For factors influencing the selection of the refuge area, see the case study of Bolama/Bijago by Biai (2000).

14 Van der Drift (2000: 47): 'The Senegalese borders – vital to Guinea-Bissau's trade and humanitarian aid – were closed, starvation was used as an additional weapon to fight the Junta'.

15 A FAO (n.d.) report about the seed deliveries of the emergency relief only mentions three varieties: IR 15-29 (mangrove rice), *banimalio* (mangrove and freshwater rice) and Sahel 108 (rain-fed cultivation). Volunteers of the Cafale project, which received seed from Caritas, reported that their organization distributed two mangrove rice varieties, IR 15-29 and WAR 77. This explains why two local designations were used.

Bibliography

Atteslander, Peter (1995) 'Introduction', in special issue 'Anomie: Social Destabilization and the Development of Early Warning Systems', *International Journal of Sociology and Social Policy* 15(8–10): 9–23.

Bakema, Reint J., ed. (1994) 'Land Tenure and Sustainable Land Use', *KIT Bulletin* (Amsterdam): 332.

Biai, Justino (2000) 'O impacto do conflito na reserva da biosfera do arquipélago Bolama-Bijagós, Bissau', *Soronda* (Bissau) 7 (June; special issue): 175–201.

de Carvalho, Joaquim Pereira Garcia (1949) 'Nota sobre a distribuição e historia dos povos da área do Posto de Bedanda', *Boletim cultural da Guiné Portuguesa* (Bissau) 14(4): 307–18.

Desjeux, Dominique (1987) *Stratégies paysannes en Afrique Noire – Le Congo.* Paris: L'Harmattan.

Duarte de Carvalho, Rui (1999) *Vou lá visitar pastores.* Lisbon: Cotovia.

Espírito Santo, Joaquim (1949) 'Notas sobre a cultura do arroz entre os balantas', *Boletim cultural da Guiné Portuguesa* (Bissau) 14(4): 197–232.

FAO (Food and Agriculture Organization) (n.d.) *Fourniture d'urgence d'intrants agricoles aux populations affectées par la crise,* OSRO/GBS/901/SWE, Rapport final. Bissau: FAO.

Hardin, Garett (1968) 'The Tragedy of the Commons', *Science* 162: 1243–8.

Heimer, Franz-Wilhelm (1979) *Der Entkolonisierungskonflikt in Angola.* Munich: Weltforum.

INEP (Instituto Nacional de Estudos e Pesquisa), ed. (2000) *Soronda* (Bissau) 7 (June; special issue).

Lévi-Strauss, Claude (1949) *Les Structures élémentaires de la parenté.* Paris: Presses Universitaires de France.

Long, Norman and Long, Ann, eds (1992) *The Battlefields of Knowledge: The Interlocking of Theory and Practice in Social Research and Development.* London: Routledge.

Merton, Robert K. (1957) 'Social Structure and Anomie', in *Social Theory and Social Structure,* rev. edn, pp. 131–60. Glencoe, IL: The Free Press.

Oliveira, Olavo, Havik, Philip Jan and Schiefer, Ulrich, eds (1993) *Armazenamento tradicional na Guiné-Bissau.* Lisbon, Bissau and Münster: CP–COPIN (Centro de Pesquisa – Cooperativa de Investigadores).

Pélissier, René (1989) *História da Guiné,* Vols I and II. Lisbon: Editorial Estampa.

Ribeiro, Rui (1988) 'O arroz na mentalidade Balanta', *Boletim de informação sócio-económica* (Bissau) 2: 1–11.

Ribeiro, Rui (1989) 'Causas da queda de produção de arroz na Guiné-Bissau – A situação no sector de Tite, região de Quinara', *Revista internacional de estudos africanos* (Lisbon) 10–11: 227–65.

Richards, Paul (1994) 'Local Knowledge Formation and Validation: The Case of Rice in Central Sierra Leone', in Ian Scoones and John Thompson (eds) *Beyond Farmer First*, pp. 39–43. London: Intermediate Technology Publications.

Richards, Paul, Ruivenkamp, Guido and van der Drift, Roy (1997) *Seeds and Survival: Crop Genetic Resources in War and Reconstruction in Africa*. Rome: IPGRI (International Plant Genetic Resources Institute).

Rudebeck, Lars (2001) *On Democracy's Sustainability*. Stockholm: Sida-Studies.

Sahlins, Marshall (1974) *Stone Age Economics*. London: Tavistock Publications.

Schiefer, Ulrich (1986) *Guinea-Bissau zwischen Weltwirtschaft und Subsistenz. Transatlantische Strukturen an der oberen Guiné Küste*. Bonn: ISSA (Informationsstelle Südliches Afrika).

Schiefer, Ulrich (2002) *Von allen guten Geistern verlassen? Guinea-Bissau: Entwicklungspolitik und der Zusammenbruch afrikanischer Gesellschaften. Eine Fall-Studie zu Guinea-Bissau*, (Habilitation Thesis, University of Münster). Hamburg: IAK.

Schiefer, Ulrich and Havik, Philip J. (1993) 'Introdução', in O. Oliveira, Philip Jan Havik and Ulrich Schiefer (eds) *Armazenamento tradicional na Guiné-Bissau*, pp. 21–35. Lisbon, Bissau and Münster: CP–Copin.

Sigrist, Christian (1994a) *Regulierte Anarchie. Untersuchungen zum Fehlen und zur Entstehung politischer Herrschaft in segmentären Gesellschaften Afrikas*, 3rd edn. Hamburg: EVA (Europäische Verlagsanstalt).

Sigrist, Christian (1994b) 'Ethnizität als Selbstorganisation', in Reinhart Kössler and Tilman Schiel (eds) *Nationalstaat und Ethnizität*, pp. 45–55. Frankfurt am Main: IKO (Verlag für Interkulturelle Kommunikation).

Temudo, Marina P. (1996) 'A escolha do sabor, o saber da escolha: selecção varietal e segurança alimentar na Guiné-Bissau', *Revista de ciências agrárias* (Lisbon) 4: 69–95.

Temudo, Marina P. (1998) *Inovação e mudança em sociedades rurais africanas. Gestão dos recursos naturais, saber local e instituições de desenvolvimento induzido*, Vols I and II (unpublished PhD dissertation). Lisbon: ISA (Instituto Superior de Agronomia).

Van der Drift, Roy (1990) 'O desenvolvimento do consumo de alcool entre os Balanta-Brassa da aldeia de Foia no Sul da Guiné-Bissau', *Soronda* (Bissau) 9: 95–115.

Van der Drift, Roy (2000) 'Democracy: Legitimate Warfare in Guinea-Bissau', *Soronda* 7 (June; special issue): 37–75.

Wöhlcke, Manfred (1996) *Soziale Entropie*. Munich: Deutscher Taschenbuchverlag.

12

Paradise Lost? Social Change and *Fa'afafine* in Samoa

Johanna Schmidt

> But you see, the thing that's interesting is that, when they're out, out and about, they flaunt it. They flaunt it. But when they come back home, they do exactly what I do. So in a way they're still trying to keep that balance, I find. And I think once, when I see the queens basically going out for it, and not giving a shit about their family, and becoming capitalist minded and becoming independent, I think that's a sign of Samoa saying that it's becoming western.
>
> (Fa'afafine participant)

Introduction

Samoan *Fa'afafine* are biologically males who express feminine gender identities. The Samoan word fa'afafine literally translates as 'like' or 'in the manner' of – *fa'a* – 'a woman' – *fafine*, but there is no easy translation for the word as a whole. While some dress as women, not all do; while many have sex with masculine men, their role in this act is usually perceived as strictly 'feminine' and thus they do not easily fit into the category of 'homosexual'; while some undergo body modifying practices to more resemble women, neither those who do nor the group as a whole can be readily defined as 'transsexual'.

Information outside Samoa about the islands often includes mention of fa'afafine, and tends generally to stress their social acceptance. For example, the Lonely Planet guide for Samoa suggests that fa'afafine are 'very much an integral part of the fabric of Samoan society' (Talbot and Swaney, 1998: 29), while on the Radio Australia website section 'Charting the Pacific', it is asserted that they were 'traditionally' raised as fa'afafine if a family was short of female labour, but may now 'choose' to be fa'afafine and are supported in that choice (Radio Australia, n.d.). In the promotional material for the widely distributed Australian documentary *Paradise Bent: Boys will be Girls in Samoa* (produced in 2000) the director Heather Croall states that fa'afafine 'are accepted as part of Samoan culture' (Croall, n.d.).

I myself first saw *Paradise Bent* on video just prior to leaving for Samoa in 2000 as part of my PhD research investigating the impact of globalization and migration on fa'afafine identities.[1] Although I understood that fa'afafine were a somewhat marginalized population, I was somewhat reassured by Croall's depiction of their easy lives and approachable natures, as I myself had not yet met any fa'afafine, and I left feeling confident about undertaking research in Samoa.

A couple of weeks after my arrival, I delivered a seminar at the National University. The topic was fairly general, but I ended with a short summary of my own research, expecting interest, and maybe some debate about the politics of *palagi* (Europeans) researching Samoan topics. These reactions were evident, but, unexpectedly in such an academic environment, other responses to my work made it clear that there is a real fear that research such as mine will give the outside world the impression that Samoa is a 'gay paradise'. Initially surprised at this concern, it was explained to me as resulting from events such as the then recent screening of *Paradise Bent* on Australia's SBS television channel. My Samoan audience was fully aware that for many viewers, documentaries such as this may well be the entirety of their experience of Samoan culture. Research such as mine seemed to simply add to what they see as an 'unhealthy' preoccupation with what is, after all, a relatively small proportion of the Samoan population. It transpired during my fieldwork that this reaction was not an isolated incident. While often not so publicly voiced, this social ambivalence regarding fa'afafine is evident throughout Samoa.

I have come to appreciate this paradox of apparent cultural acceptance and very real social marginalization of fa'afafine as a consequence of a combination of 'traditional' Samoan culture and the impact of globalization on indigenous constructions, representations and understandings of gender and sexuality. At the time of writing, I am still actively engaged in this research, and this article represents my current understanding of this paradox and how it is related to the wider framework of Samoan culture and the changes it has undergone.

The Local Life-World of Samoan Fa'afafine

In order to provide a basis for the following discussion, I first briefly outline the processes by which gender was/is constructed in the 'traditional' Samoan context, before discussing recent shifts in this area. These shifts originate in the fact that Samoan identities are predominantly sociocentric and relational and occur as a series of contextual, situational and collectivist arrangements, in contrast to the more internal, egocentric and individualistic self of the west (Shore, 1982: 136, 195; Besnier, 1993: 312–13; Mageo, 1998; Dolgoy, 2000: 127–8). Membership of and service to *aiga* (extended family) and community are central components of Samoan subjectivity, and in the village context, gendering is largely achieved through particular labour contributions to aiga and village (Schoeffel, 1979; Shore, 1981; Poasa, 1992: 43; Mageo, 1998; Sua'ali'i, 2001: 161). Women labour in and around the home and the village, whereas men work in the plantations and fish outside the reef (Shore, 1982: 225–6; Holmes, 1987: 80).[2]

Fa'afafine are identified at an early age by virtue of their propensity for feminine tasks (Poasa, 1992: 43; Besnier, 1993: 296). The following description of early life at home in Samoa is entirely typical of most of my respondents.

> When I was young, I know I was like this. I do all the girl's work when I was young. I do the washing, and my sister's just mucking around, cleaning the house, but my job at home is cooking, washing, ironing – everything.

Families do not seem to equate this early preference for feminine labour with an eventual (homo)sexual orientation, and 'sexual relations with men are seen as an optional *consequence* of [being fa'afafine], rather than its determiner, prerequisite, or primary attribute' (Besnier, 1993: 300). I discuss shortly how the 'optional' nature of fa'afafine sexuality is currently in apparent flux. What I wish to emphasize here is that 'traditionally' fa'afafine have been and generally still are initially identified in terms of labour preferences.

The issue of fa'afafine sexuality in the 'traditional' context is an area in which understandings are complex and at times contradictory. One of the more common arguments is that fa'afafine operated as 'go betweens' for the socially separated young men and women. As an adjunct to this role, it is suggested that they were (and still are) for most boys the first significant point of contact with a feminine person outside their own families, and sex with fa'afafine is seen as 'learning to be with a woman' (St Christian, 1994: 183).

Yet, it is also apparent that fa'afafine would often marry women and have children. Some authors suggest that those who married would 'abandon the category' of fa'afafine and become 'formally male' (St Christian, 1994: 182–3; Dolgoy, 2000: 135). However, I have also heard stories of fa'afafine who married women yet remained fa'afafine. I suspect that these apparently contradictory assertions are related to the looseness and contextual basis of the concept of 'identity' in Samoa. A person who was consistently seen as fa'afafine, and who then married and adopted one of the positions of status which are generally only open to married men, may have simply shifted their gendered expressions in many public contexts, such as the village *fono* (council), to a more masculine enactment. They may have thus appeared to have 'relinquished' their fa'afafine identities, while at the same time continuing to undertake feminine labour in private domestic contexts.[3] However, regardless of whether those who married remained fa'afafine or not, it is apparent that in the past to be fa'afafine did not preclude the possibility of marriage and reproduction, an aspect of potential fa'afafine life-experience that appears to have changed somewhat in recent decades. In order to illustrate how globalization has impacted on this and other aspects of fa'afafine identities and experiences, I first outline how Samoan gender frameworks as a whole have reacted to Samoa's increasing westernization.

Processes of Globalization and Transformations of Fa'afafine Life-Worlds

The introduction of capitalism to Samoa contributed to an increasing individuation of the traditionally group-oriented indigenous society, as the ability to earn individual incomes made people less likely to pool resources with their extended families, and economic wealth became a dominant yardstick of success (O'Meara, 1993: 136–8). Furthermore, industrialization and western media bring with them capitalist ideologies such as 'personal freedom', discourses which privilege individual over family (Altman, 1996: 86), especially the extended family of Samoa. Changes in economic structures have subsequently impacted on the role of labour in Samoan gender frameworks. As Samoans increasingly shift to the capital of Apia or overseas in search of paid employment (Galuvao, 1987: 111–15; Shankman, 1993), the work that they do is itself likely to be gendered, but the money which they now contribute to the family is largely ungendered. Thus, within the family context, the product of labour is rendered gender neutral.

As labour is becoming less significant in relation to identity in general and gender specifically, the increasing influence of western culture also seems to have led to an emphasis on appearance and bodily expression as a primary marker of gender, as demonstrated in aspects such as clothing. The everyday wear of most Samoans, men and women, is a *lavalava* (sarong) and t-shirt (although the men's lavalava is worn a little shorter than the women's). However, in Apia, the younger Samoan women are beginning to wear short skirts and skimpy tops, while the young men favour a more hip hop 'baggy' style. This gender differentiation and the related increased emphasis on sexuality are even more marked in the nightclubs, where the dance floors come to resemble black American popular music videos with a sexual explicitness I saw in *no* other context in Samoa.

Such enactments of gender not only emphasize sexuality, but also rest on the body in ways that suggest a significant move towards concepts of 'individual expression' rather than the relative conformity that typifies the more relational nature of 'traditional' Samoan gender and identity. So, for example, village chiefs forbid women dressing in mini-skirts, trousers, or shorts not only because they are seen as undignified, but also because the adoption of such palagi customs is seen as a direct assertion of personal rights over *fa'aSamoa* ('the Samoan way', or Samoan culture) (Shore, 1982: 109).

Of course, these models are not absolute – what I am rather suggesting is that through changes in the political economy and the influence of western discourses, there has been a shift in emphasis in the enactment of gender from being relational and expressed through labour contributions to aiga, village, or other collectives, to being something more 'internal' and expressed through individually embodied sexuality.

For fa'afafine, as for Samoan women, these social and cultural changes similarly mean that the feminine labour role within the family is no longer as predominant as a gender marker. To be feminine is no longer primarily based on the labour one performs, but is more centred on who one has (or would have) sex with – i.e. men. As I have mentioned, there is evidence that historically fa'afafine may once have married women, but during my research I have seen no indication that the fa'afafine of today consider such marriage a viable option. I asked one respondent in Samoa in his forties, who does not present himself as overly feminine, whether he would like to have children, to which he responded:

> I don't think it's a question of 'like'. I thought, if you felt, you know, I mean, for me, if I was going to have children it means that I have to, you know, marry a girl, and that's not natural to me.

Another relatively feminine respondent in her thirties offered me proof of her self-perception of herself as a woman.

> Every time someone says to me 'Why don't you look at a woman?', you know, '. . . and maybe it will change your whole perspective about being fa'afafine', you know what I always . . . I never say any word, you know, I just let anyone that talks to me, because I understand that everyone has its own way of things and all that, and I, coming back home I always say to myself, 'My God, it will be a sin for me,' you know, 'I will be a sinner if I try to establish a relationship with a woman.' Because, you know, my feelings is a hundred per cent – OK? So it's like a woman who is forced to have a relationship with another woman – OK? I mean, I will cry. It will cripple me psychologically – OK? It will damage, you know, everything that I've done. To me it would be, you know, an embarrassing experience, you know, to have a woman in my life. So I will say that, um, yes, I am a woman, OK?

These respondents articulate the centrality of sexuality in the gendering of fa'afafine identities in contemporary Samoa, a centrality that then impacts on other aspects of fa'afafine identities such as self-presentation. In Apia, the increasing use by young Samoan women of more sexualized western signifiers of femininity is echoed by fa'afafine (Mageo, 1996: 602).[4] One informant stated that before western contact, fa'afafine were simply 'feminine boys', but exposure to western movies taught them that clothing, make-up and appearance in general could be used as more definitive signifiers of gender. The use of western cultural forms is also apparent in the adoption of palagi names by fa'afafine. Most Samoan names are genderless (Shore, 1982: 144; Mageo, 1992: 451), and many fa'afafine will take on European feminine Christian names, often choosing a name that is associated with a famous and glamorous woman, such as a supermodel or pop diva. Thus both name and clothing become signifiers of hyper-feminine, highly sexualized western gender constructs.

Westernization has also had an impact on contemporary fa'afafine sexuality in relation to social control. 'Traditionally', social control in Samoa is largely based on external constraints rather than internalized morals, a system which functions best in family and village environments, where there are no strangers and life is very public (Shore, 1982: 148, 179–81; St Christian, 1994: 74). Samoans who move to larger urban environments are less constrained by the continual presence of and monitoring by significant others that typify social control in the villages (Keene, 1978: 86–9). Thus urban fa'afafine who are encouraged by western discourses to express a particularly sexualized femininity experience less need to downplay this sexuality, which is, as I later explain, relatively unacceptable according to more 'traditional' Samoan perspectives.

The relative anonymity afforded by Apia also allows fa'afafine to more openly pursue the sexual relationships that, according to western discourses, construct and reinforce their femininity. Families often value the ability of fa'afafine to do both men's and women's work while generally objecting to the increasingly overt expressions of sexuality. This can be a considerable problem in a culture where adults frequently remain living with their aiga, even after marriage. Simple changes such as access to rental or job-related accommodation means that fa'afafine and their partners may no longer be constrained by family attitudes towards their sexual practices.

Contemporary Fa'afafine Sexualities

It is tempting to argue that as a result of the anonymity of urban contexts, the independence offered by wage labour and the introduction of western discourses of personal freedom and individual rights, there has been a liberation of fa'afafine sexualities that, until recently, were somewhat repressed, and indeed such an understanding is implicit in many fa'afafine discourses. However, rather than think of it as having been 'liberated', I suggest a more Foucauldian perspective (Foucault, 1981), that fa'afafine sexuality has been constructed differently over the years, and it is only now that Samoan understandings of gender have become woven together with western discourses that sexuality is seen as fundamentally constitutive of identity – especially (but not exclusively) fa'afafine identities.

The continual shifts wrought by these processes can be seen in terms of how fa'afafine uses of western discourses of homosexuality are currently in flux. Concepts of 'gay' and 'straight' have never really been relevant in Samoa, and there is no Samoan term for 'homosexual' (Mageo, 1996: 591; Shore, 1981: 209). It is generally acknowledged that young Samoan men frequently engage in sexual acts with each other, but only in the absence of available young women (Mead, 1943: 61; Mageo, 1992: 449–50; James, 1994: 54; Peteru, 1997: 215), and such 'play' is not condoned, or even really acknowledged, between adult men (St Christian, 1994: 170). Two masculine youths having sex are also careful not to mimic heterosexual positioning or actions (St Christian, 1994: 182), and thus neither adopts the 'passive' or feminine role that would put their masculinity into question. That such acts have little relation to an 'identity' is demonstrated by the fact that those involved will almost inevitably and unproblematically go on to have sexual relations with young women and eventually marry (Keene, 1978: 105).

The fact that for Samoans it is the nature of the sex act rather than the object which is the key factor (Altman, 1996: 81–2) is central to understanding sexual relations between fa'afafine and masculine men. Fa'afafine 'construct themselves as something akin to heterosexual, that is, women seeking intercourse with men' (Mageo, 1996: 616). In this process, they relatively unproblematically adopt the 'passive' feminine position, and thus sex between a man and fa'afafine is not a threat to the man's 'heterosexuality' (Shore, 1981: 210). Even though most fa'afafine have penises, in Samoa 'The sexing function of the genitals . . . is derived from what is done with bodies as a whole, rather than from any innate sexual quality of the genitals alone' (St Christian, 1994: 97). Thus the manner in which the fa'afafine body is enacted during sex causes it to become something other than 'male' (St Christian, 1994: 183). It is this perception of fa'afafine sexuality as feminine that leads to the current dominant understandings of sex between masculine men and fa'afafine as distinctly not homosexual. Such assertions of heterosexuality have become increasingly important as western discourses of homosexuality enter Samoan understandings of sexuality, and consequently fa'afafine also reinforce their femininity with the fact that they are only attracted to and receive sexual attention from *straight* masculine men.

The difference between Samoan and palagi understandings of sexual acts between two 'male' bodies was explained by one of my respondents.

> So with lots of these people that are in high positions, I think most of them have been with a fa'afafine before, you know. It's like the life in New Zealand, that once you go with a queen or something like that, you always end up to be a gay person or something like that, but the Samoan guys, they don't . . . you know, they started off young with the fa'afafine and then they always end up getting married and have families.

The fact that Samoan men tend not to stay in long-term relationships with fa'afafine is recognized by all parties as a consequence of fa'afafine inability to bear children (Mageo, 1992: 453; Dolgoy, 2000: 185). Creating families is a central social imperative for all Samoans (Holmes, 1987: 81; St Christian, 1994: 99; Sua'ali'i, 2001: 170), and 'un(re)productive' sexual activity is seen as somewhat antisocial (St Christian, 1994: 100). Thus, it is fairly inevitable that Samoan men will eventually leave their fa'afafine 'wives'. As one respondent said,

> Don't ever fall so gracefully, you know, so crazy on a guy, especially a non-gay or a non-bisexual guy, because that person will always go back and look for someone who will give them kids.

It appears that the inevitability of this abandonment is leading to further shifts in fa'afafine sexualities, which I believe is to some extent linked to changes in expectations regarding relationships, which again must be briefly contextualized. Private actions and desire receive little recognition with Samoan cultural institutions (Shore, 1982: 185), and the public nature of Samoan life is not particularly conducive to insular relationships. As children, Samoans learn to trust a group of people, but perceive interpersonal relationships as undependable (Ortner, 1981: 390; Holmes, 1987; Mageo, 1998: 56). Even marriage is more pragmatic than emotive, and it has been suggested that Samoan culture does not share the 'western folk tradition' of each person having one 'ideal mate' somewhere in the world (Keene, 1978: 116). Yet as a result of western media, fa'afafine are now increasingly exposed to the idea that life-long committed relationships are virtually a right – a concept they may find all the more attractive given that the increasing dissipation of extended families means they cannot necessarily rely on their nieces or nephews to care for them in old age. As a possible consequence of this, some fa'afafine seem to be adjusting their criteria for potential partners, and more than one respondent in Samoa expressed a possible preference for a gay or bisexual palagi man, because palagi men are more independent of their families, and because someone who identifies as gay is more likely to endure the difficulties of a relationship with a queen.

'Authenticity' and Contemporary Fa'afafine

Given that contemporary fa'afafine identities are now so firmly enmeshed with western discourses of gender and sexuality, questions may be asked as to the 'authenticity' of these identities. Can it really be suggested that the high-heel-wearing beauty pageant contestants who frequent Apia's bars, flouting Samoan sexual mores, can still be considered fa'afafine, or have they become brown drag queens? Again, discussion of this issue requires contextualization in relation to contemporary Samoan culture and society as a whole.

As a result of globalization and subsequent economic and cultural changes, Samoans are now a highly diasporic population. In contemporary times, it is unfeasible to think of either migrant or source communities as separate entities, when they are strongly linked by communication and travel (Macpherson, 1997: 95–6). Macpherson suggests that 'What is forming at the intersections of all this movement is some meta Samoan society and culture which draws freely on what passes for Samoan culture and practice in various localities. From this inventory of knowledge communities "draw down" those elements which are needed at different times to make conduct and practices seem intelligible and reasonable' (Macpherson, 1997: 96). Such a model also applies to what it means to be a fa'afafine Samoan, but it is apparent that aspects are also contributed to the 'meta fa'afafine' inventory from the 'imagined lives' that fa'afafine encounter in western media and, for various reasons, identify with (Appadurai, 1991: 198). To be fa'afafine entails what Bourdieu (1977: 72–3) referred to as a disposition towards relating to other males who act in feminine ways, such as the drag queens of popular film, the gay couples of American dramas and the transsexuals of medical discourses. These images and identities become resources on which fa'afafine draw, along with dancing the *siva*, caring for their grandparents and weaving mats, in constructions and enactments of their subjectivities. However, it is apparent that in some cases the contradictions between possible aspects of what might be considered a fa'afafine identity cannot be sustained. Thus in contemporary Samoa, for a fa'afafine to marry and have children would severely problematize their 'fa'afafine-ness' in ways that might not have been the case 50 years ago. Yet both the married fa'afafine of former generations and the contemporary fa'afafine who sees marriage as a contradiction to her sense of herself as feminine are, within their respective historical contexts, 'authentic'.

In a process that mirrors both wider social hybridization of western and Samoan culture and concepts, yet which is also specific to their situations, fa'afafine are retaining distinct identities while also developing a more political voice. Even as contemporary Samoans seek to 'disown' fa'afafine, many fa'afafine themselves draw on aspects of 'traditional' fa'aSamoa as a solid foundation on which to base themselves as sexual and gendered people. This can be seen in the adaptation of the western institution of the beauty pageant, which has been utilized by fa'afafine not only as a way of publicly displaying their feminine identities and skills, but also as a means of redeeming their reputations and claiming a location within Samoan society and culture. Not only do the pageants afford considerable entertainment for the audiences and thus provide a forum for the public performance which is an integral part of Samoan life and identity (Keene, 1978: 61), but the proceeds are also donated to the local rest home. This is in keeping with the ideology of fa'aSamoa that emphasizes distribution over accumulation of wealth (Ortner, 1981: 364), and the fact that it is through generosity that Samoans gain the 'social credit' that accords them prestige (Keene, 1978: 150–1).

The pageants also represent part of a wider incipient development of a form of 'identity politics' among Samoan fa'afafine. While this 'gentle social movement' (Dolgoy, 2000) echoes western queer politics in its attempts to counter social marginalization, this adaptation of identity politics is also occurring in a specifically Samoan way. More than one informant suggested that the formation of subcultures such as those they saw in the exclusive gay clubs of New Zealand created an artificial, exclusionary environment, suggesting that for fa'afafine, social isolation, even of a voluntary nature, is not desirable. It is important that fa'afafine assert their identities as *part* of wider Samoan society, maintaining understandings of the Samoan self as relational and sociocentric.

Furthermore, an overtly confrontational political movement would not be particularly Samoan, whereas the manner in which fa'afafine manoeuvre themselves into positions where they are likely to gain recognition from others, rather than demand it themselves, echoes the wider context of political culture and cultural politics in Samoa (Shore, 1982). In spite of suggestions that a flourishing and political gay or lesbian community in third world nations is evidence of the 'liberation' of same-sex sexualities (e.g.

Drucker, 1996), such a community in Samoa would be antithetical to the very 'Samoan-ness' on which fa'afafine identities are founded.

Understanding Fa'afafine through New Discourses

The manner in which western discourses have worked their way through Samoan understandings of gender and sexuality has impacted not only on how fa'afafine enact their identities, but also on how Samoans understand these identities. As Samoans are confronted by the 'new breed' of sexualized fa'afafine, they see more and more similarities with models of homosexuality they are increasingly encountering from overseas. Significant exposure to these notions of homosexuality has also coincided with HIV/AIDS awareness and the accompanying moral panic and this, coupled with a strong conservative Christian morality, has led to marked disapproval of anything that might be interpreted as homosexuality – the obvious target in Samoa being fa'afafine.[5]

As well as the incursion of western discourses into Samoa, attitudes towards fa'afafine are also influenced by western discourses *about* Samoa. In the experience of Samoans, discussion of sexuality in Samoan culture is usually a compounding of the process of making exotic and erotic the Pacific Islands that started with the voyages of Captain Cook (Jolly, 1997), continued with erotic Orientalist depictions of Samoan women (Taouma, 1998), and was firmly entrenched in the popular western imagination by Margaret Mead (Durutalo, 1992). Samoans are wary of anything that might perpetuate this exotic/erotic discourse, although it must also be recognized that in the case of the 'marketing' of Samoa, these discourses are often drawn on in a very 'managed' fashion, resulting in a perpetuation of the 'dusky maiden' imagery in Samoan tourist literature and performances. However, such 'management' is often not possible in the case of the fa'afafine who 'run wild' and flaunt their sexuality, and it is inevitably these more flamboyant presentations that the palagi tourists pick on, as the less overt fa'afafine in their lavalava and t-shirts blend into the general Apia population. Outside Samoa, travel writers are beginning to focus on fa'afafine as an 'attraction' in Samoa (e.g. Percy, 2002), and in the case of travel articles about Samoa appearing in gay publications (e.g. Miles, 2001), it appears that the fears of palagi fascination with fa'afafine resulting in Samoa becoming part of the gay tourist circuit are not unfounded. While in Samoa, I met a significant number of palagi men who, upon learning of my research interest, inevitably regaled me with raunchy stories of scantily clad fa'afafine attempting to pick them up in Apia's bars and clubs. For the average tourist or travel writer who visits Samoa for a week or two, these urban 'drag queens' are likely to be the only fa'afafine they meet – or notice – usually without realizing that their experiences provide an insight into a very small proportion of the fa'afafine population in a very specific context.

Academic literature on fa'afafine also tends to focus on sexuality (e.g. Shore, 1981; Mageo, 1992, 1996; Peteru, 1997), following western ideologies that sexual orientation is one of the most significant means of dividing people into classes (Whitehead, 1981: 94), and that the gendering of behaviour follows on from this classification. Again, this perspective tends to recognize only those who are overtly sexual as fa'afafine – or, alternatively, ascribes 'homosexuality' to fa'afafine who may be sexually inactive (McIntosh, 1999: 11). This preoccupation with sexuality of fa'afafine on the part of both tourists and researchers then feeds back in Samoan fears that Samoans will continue to be represented as an oversexed population.

Globalization and Marginalization of Fa'afafine in Samoa

Having detailed how shifts in gender construction and the globalization of western discourses have impacted on enactments and understandings of fa'afafine identities, I now return to the paradox I detailed at the outset of this article in order to bring together these threads and explain how fa'afafine in Samoa are both accepted *and* marginalized.

Fa'afafine are a part of everyday life in Samoa – they work in travel agencies, they serve in bars, and they shop in the local supermarkets without attracting undue attention. While blending into Samoan society without drawing attention to themselves, and offering the service to family and community that is expected from all Samoans, these fa'afafine go relatively unremarked. It is the more recent emphasis on sexuality, especially what is understood as 'deviant' sexuality, which most Samoans object to. For example, the brothers of some fa'afafine may exert pressure on them to alter their sexual habits, while making no attempt to make them conform to masculine gender roles in terms of labour (Poasa, 1992: 49). Such apparent hypocrisy makes more sense when it is remembered that the self in Samoa is understood as relational, contextual and multifaceted, and that Samoans assess a particular aspect or action of a person only in relation to the relevant context (Shore, 1982: 137–46, 181–2). Thus, a brother will always be part of the family, or a good travel agent will be patronized, while an overtly promiscuous fa'afafine will be condemned – even if they are the same person.

Contemporary Samoan attitudes towards fa'afafine sexuality partially originate in the Samoan valuing of conformity to social expectations over self-gratification (Shore, 1981: 195–6; Shore, 1982: 118, 156–8). Sexuality is strongly associated with the aggressive and selfish aspects of people that are contrasted with socially controlled and 'cultured' actions (Shore, 1982: 228–9), and any public display of sexuality will incur social disapproval. This is especially so for women, who gain their prestige from their embodiment of control (Shore, 1982: 232), and whose status tends to be relatively low in terms of their sexual and reproductive roles (Ortner, 1981: 394–5). Thus Samoan disapproval of the newly sexualized, western-influenced femininity of fa'afafine may be seen to emerge from an already existent cultural tendency to devalue sexuality in general and women as *sexual* beings in particular.

The situation in Samoa is thus far more complex than a simply misplaced homophobia originating in missionary values targeted at a traditionally accepted group. The lived experience of, and Samoan attitudes to, contemporary fa'afafine can be seen as a complex reaction to a complicated set of circumstances, which include the impact of globalization on the Samoan political economy, shifts in how Samoan gender in general is enacted, considerable changes in the construction and expression of fa'afafine identities, and the globalization of sexual discourses, together with the continued existence of 'traditional' (although modified) attitudes about gender and sexuality and understandings of the self. For increasingly sexual and feminine fa'afafine who are, however, actually 'men', an already existent cultural devaluing of feminine sexuality has intersected with the relatively recent disapproval of homosexuality, so that fa'afafine are in some sense damned as women *and* as men.

Conclusion

Fa'afafine identities in Samoa currently hang in the balance between *tradition* and *modernization*, between Samoan cultural discourses of family, respect and social status, and western discourses of the liberation of sexuality, individual freedom and the right to emotionally fulfilling relationships. Altman suggests that in non-western gay subcultures, there are two perspectives – rupture or continuity. He writes that

> ... for some there is a strong desire to trace a continuity between pre-colonial forms of homosexual desire and its contemporary emergence, even when the latter might draw on the language of (West) Hollywood rather than indigenous culture ... For others, there is a perception that contemporary middle-class self-proclaimed gay men and lesbians in, say, New Delhi, Lima or Jakarta have less in common with 'traditional' homosexuality than they do with their counterparts in western countries. (Altman, 2001: 88)

Fa'afafine in Samoa seem to walk a fine line between rupture and continuity, often identifying as gay and fa'afafine simultaneously as a means of adopting and adapting to aspects of globalized western cultures while maintaining and enacting identities through processes that are distinctly Samoan. These processes support Marcus's observation that while the globe is becoming more integrated, 'this paradoxically is not leading to an easily comprehensible totality, but to an increasing diversity of connections among phenomena once thought disparate and worlds apart' (Marcus, 1992: 321).

Much as the quote with which I opened this article eloquently illustrated the tension between traditional culture and global forces for fa'afafine in Samoa, it was another participant who concisely and cogently summarized the shifting and flexible nature of contemporary fa'afafine identities, generously providing me with a diagram and comment that fittingly concludes my discussion.

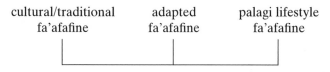

| cultural/traditional fa'afafine | adapted fa'afafine | palagi lifestyle fa'afafine |

To say that all fa'afafine are the same would deny the continuum or spectrum that exists. I believe we exist along this continuum during certain times of our lives – it's dynamic most of our lives and then when we find our niche in this continuum we then claim that niche for that time.

Notes

Parts of this article, and its original informing concepts, initially appeared in 'Redefining *Fa'afafine*: Western Discourses and the Construction of Transgenderism in Samoa', published in *Intersections: Gender, History and Culture in the Asian Context* (available at: wwwsshe.murdoch.edu.au/intersections/issue6/schmidt.html). I would like to thank the editors for their permission to use this material, and their support with my inaugural publication from this research. An initial version of this article was presented at the XVth World Congress of the International Sociological Association in Brisbane, Australia, 2002, and I would like to thank the organizers of that conference and the RC 09 session for the chance to participate. I would also like to acknowledge the support of the New Zealand Foundation for Research, Science, and Technology, whose generous Bright Future Scholarship supports me during the PhD process. I also take this opportunity to thank the people in Samoa and New Zealand whose assistance during my fieldwork, and contribution in the form of interviews for, and extensive discussion of, my research made this article possible. Among these people, I wish to acknowledge my endlessly supportive supervisors and my department, my long-suffering boyfriend, and, most important, my extremely generous fa'afafine friends.

1 'Samoa' refers to Independent Samoa, formerly known as Western Samoa. Migration to New Zealand is largely from Independent Samoa due to historical, political and cultural links. Because of its close ties to the United States, American Samoa has had a significantly different experience of westernization and pattern of migration, and thus is not considered within the parameters of my research project.

2 See Schoeffel (1979) for an extensive discussion of masculine and feminine labour.

3 This might also explain why many of the stories of fa'afafine husbands were related to me by older women, who may have been more likely to observe such individuals in their domestic environments.

4 See Dolgoy (2000) for a comprehensive analysis of the historical shift in fa'afafine self-presentation.

5 There is a distinct absence in this article of considering the existence of gay-identified Samoans in Samoa, and the impact of globalized discourses of homosexuality on 'traditional' identities within Samoa (Altman, 1996). This can be explained in part because there is no particularly salient population of gay Samoans in Samoa (Dolgoy, 2000: 167), and in part because the focus of my research on fa'afafine did not lead me to explore in depth the issue of gay identities while in Samoa.

Bibliography

Altman, Dennis (1996) 'Rupture or Continuity: The Internationalization of Gay Identities', *Social Text* 14(3): 77–94.

Altman, Dennis (2001) *Global Sex*. Chicago: University of Chicago Press.

Appadurai, Arjun (1991) 'Global Ethnoscapes: Notes and Queries for a Transnational Anthropology', in Richard G. Fox (ed.) *Recapturing Anthropology: Working in the Present*, pp. 191–210. Santa Fe, NM: School of American Research Press.

Besnier, Niko (1993) 'Polynesian Gender Liminality', in Gilbert Herdt (ed.) *Third Sex, Third Gender*, pp. 285–328. New York: Zone.

Bourdieu, Pierre (1977) *Outline of a Theory of Practice*, trans. Richard Nice. Cambridge: Cambridge University Press.

Croall, Heather (n.d.) 'Fa'afafines in Paradise', Reangle Films; reangle.va.com.au (consulted 27 April 2000).

Dolgoy, Reevan (2000) 'The Search for Recognition and Social Movement Emergence: Towards an Understanding of the Transformation of the Fa'afafine of Samoa', PhD thesis, University of Alberta, Canada.

Drucker, Peter (1996) ' "In the Tropics There is No Sin": Sexuality and Gay-Lesbian Movements in the Third World', *New Left Review* 218: 75–101.

Durutalo, Simione (1992) 'Anthropology and Authoritarianism in the Pacific Islands', in Lenora Foerstel and Angela Gilliam (eds) *Confronting the Margaret Mead Legacy: Scholarship, Empire and the South Pacific*, pp. 206–32. Philadelphia, PA: Temple University Press.

Foucault, Michel (1981) *The History of Sexuality. Vol. 1: An Introduction*, trans. Robert Hurley. London: Penguin.

Galuvao, Mufaulu (1987) 'Land and Migration and Western Samoa', *In Search of a Home*, pp. 110–17. Suva: University of the South Pacific.

Holmes, Lowell D. (1987) *Quest for the Real Samoa: The Mead/Freeman Controversy and Beyond*. South Hadley, MA: Bergin and Garvey.

James, Kerry E. (1994) 'Effeminate Males and Change in the Construction of Gender in Tonga', *Pacific Studies* 17(2): 39–69.

Jolly, Margaret (1997) 'From Venus Point to Bali Ha'i: Eroticism and Exoticism in Representations of the Pacific', in Lenore Manderson and Margaret Jolly (eds) *Sites of Desire, Economies of Pleasure: Sexualities in Asia and the Pacific*, pp. 99–122. Chicago: University of Chicago Press.

Keene, Dennis T.P. (1978) 'Houses without Walls: Samoan Social Control', PhD dissertation, University of Hawai'i.

McIntosh, Tracey (1999) *Words and Worlds of Difference: Homosexualities in the Pacific*, Working Paper 3/99, Sociology and Social Policy Working Paper Series, Department of Sociology. Fiji: University of the South Pacific.

MacPherson, Cluny (1997) 'The Polynesian Diaspora: New Communities and New Questions', in Ken'ighi Sudo and Shuji Yoshida (eds) *Contemporary Migration in Oceania: Diaspora and Network*, pp. 77–100. Osaka: National Museum of Ethnology.

Mageo, Jeanette-Marie (1992) 'Male Transvestism and Cultural Change in Samoa', *American Ethnologist* 19: 443–59.

Mageo, Jeanette-Marie (1996) 'Samoa, on the Wilde Side: Male Transvestism, Oscar Wilde, and Liminality in Making Gender', *Ethos* 24(4): 588–627.

Mageo, Jeanette-Marie (1998) *Theorizing Self in Samoa: Emotions, Genders and Sexualities*. Ann Arbor: University of Michigan Press.

Marcus, George (1992) 'Past, Present and Emergent Identities: Requirements for Ethnographies of Late Twentieth Century Modernity Worldwide', in Scott Lash and Jonathan Friedman (eds) *Modernity and Identity*, pp. 309–30. Oxford: Basil Blackwell.

Mead, Margaret (1943) *Coming of Age in Samoa: A Study of Adolescence and Sex in Primitive Societies*. London: Penguin. (Orig. pub. 1928.)

Miles, Paul (2001) 'He's So Fa'afafine', *Gay Times* 277 (October): 126–8.

O'Meara, Tim (1993) 'The Cult of Custom Meets the Search from Money in Western Samoa', in Victoria S. Lockwood, Thomas G. Harding and Ben J. Wallace (eds) *Contemporary Pacific Societies: Studies in Development and Change*, pp. 135–55. Englewood Cliffs, NJ: Prentice Hall.

Ortner, Sherry B. (1981) 'Gender and Sexuality in Hierarchical Societies: The Case of

Polynesia and Some Comparative Implications', in Sherry B. Ortner and Harriet Whitehead (eds) *Sexual Meanings: The Cultural Construction of Gender and Sexuality*, pp. 359–409. Cambridge: Cambridge University Press.

Percy, Mary Ann (2002) 'Having a Fa'afafine Time in Samoa', *Sunday Star Times* 3 February: C15.

Peteru, Andrew Reuben (1997) 'The Sexuality and STD/HIV Risk-Related Sexual Behaviors of Single, Unskilled, Young Adult, Samoan Males: A Qualitative Study', MA thesis, Mahidol University.

Poasa, Kris (1992) 'The Samoan Fa'afafine: One Case Study and Discussion of Transsexualism', *Journal of Psychology and Human Sexuality* 5(3): 39–51.

Radio Australia (n.d.) 'Charting the Pacific'; available at: www.abc.net.au/ra/pacific/default.html (consulted 2 March 2002).

St Christian, Douglass Paul Michael (1994) 'Body/Work: Aspects of Embodiment and Culture in Samoa', PhD thesis, School of Graduate Studies, McMaster University.

Schoeffel, Penelope (1979) 'Daughters of Sina: A Study of Gender, Status and Power in Western Samoa', PhD dissertation, Australian National University, Canberra.

Shankman, Paul (1993) 'The Samoan Exodus', in Victoria S. Lockwood, Thomas G. Harding and Ben J. Wallace (eds) *Contemporary Pacific Societies: Studies in Development and Change*, pp. 156–70. Englewood Cliffs, NJ: Prentice Hall.

Shore, Bradd (1981) 'Sexuality and Gender in Samoa: Conceptions and Missed Conceptions', in Sherry B. Ortner and Harriet Whitehead (eds) *Sexual Meanings: The Cultural Construction of Gender and Sexuality*, pp. 192–215. Cambridge: Cambridge University Press.

Shore, Bradd (1982) *Sala'ilua: A Samoan Mystery.* New York: Columbia University Press.

Sua'ali'i, Tamasailau M. (2001) 'Samoans and Gender: Some Reflections on Male, Female and Fa'afafine Gender Identities', in Cluny Macpherson, Paul Spoonley and Melani Anae (eds) *Tangata o te moana nui: The Evolving Identities of Pacific Peoples in Aotearoa/New Zealand*, pp. 160–80. Palmerston North: Dunmore Press.

Talbot, Dorinda and Swaney, Deanna (1998) *Lonely Planet: Samoa.* Hawthorn: Lonely Planet Publications.

Taouma, Lisa (1998) 'Re-Picturing Paradise: Myths of the Dusky Maiden', MFA thesis, University of Auckland.

Whitehead, Harriet (1981) 'The Bow and the Burden Strap: A New Look at Institutionalized Homosexuality in Native North America', in Sherry B. Ortner and Harriet Whitehead (eds) *Sexual Meanings: The Cultural Construction of Gender and Sexuality*, pp. 80–115. Cambridge: Cambridge University Press.

13

Autochthonous Australian Syncretism

George Morgan

Seventy percent of Aboriginal Australians live in cities and large towns and experience many of the benefits and drawbacks of modern globalized life. Yet most still consider Aboriginality as being defined through pre-colonial tradition. All ethnic identities are subject to being defined and redefined through public representations. Colonial/settler ideology in Australia has cast autochthonous people in a range of roles – the noble savage, the vicious and demoralized fringe dweller, the child-like subject of state and mission- ary paternalism. Such representations endure even where the social con- ditions on which they are built have dissolved. In this article, I argue that contemporary Aboriginality has yet to obtain robust public expression. In their engagement with broader society, many Aboriginal urban dwellers fall back on primordial symbols of their collective selves. In seeking to under- stand why this is so, I look at academic debates around contemporary ethnic identity formation. Many of those who have studied the diasporic movement of people from the South to large metropolitan centres, argue that such movements have produced conditions whereby ethnic identities are no longer fixed to traditions. They argue, migrants are culturally eclectic 'bricoleurs', whose identities are fashioned from a range of contemporary cultural forms – traditional and modern, colonial and postcolonial. We assess these arguments in relation to Aboriginal people who are cultural travellers even though they remain within the borders of one nation.

The Politics of Defining Aboriginality

Non-autochthonous writer David Hollinsworth has considered the criteria conventionally used to define Aboriginality (Hollinsworth, 1992). He identified three general approaches. The first defines Aboriginality accord- ing to 'measure of blood'. In the past, colonial authorities used blood criteria to classify and divide Aboriginal communities. Hollinsworth argued that it is inappropriate to use such criteria any longer. Those deemed 'part-Aboriginal' were separated from their full-blood kin on the assumption that they were more able to be assimilated. Fair-skinned children were deemed to be of lesser Aboriginal blood and were more vulnerable to being taken away from their parents. In Australia today, there is no requirement for claimants to establish that a particular proportion of their forebears were autochthonous in order to gain official recognition of their Aboriginality.

The second common approach sees understanding of traditional culture as the basis of Aboriginal identity. Hollinsworth argues that this argument fails to acknowledge how colonialism has broken the lines of cultural transmission. It is an approach that excludes many of those who wish to identify but have little understanding of autochthonous traditions. This ignorance is not their fault. The state and church missionaries taught Aboriginal people to be ashamed of their culture and many elders were reluctant to share traditional knowledge with young people during and after the assimilation era. The cultural persistence approach defines Aboriginal culture as a vestige. It implies that those who are drawn into the social mainstream thereby undergo a depletion of their autochthonous identity (Chase, 1981). Hollinsworth observes that cultural definitions are often framed in essentialist and reductionist terms in a way that leaves little room for understanding contemporary cultural processes and forms.

Hollinsworth favours defining Aboriginality around resistance to colonial power. This incorporates the possibility of cultural change as well as continuity; it sees Aboriginal identity as formed by contemporary processes, as a relational process and as one which is prospective rather than simply retrospective. This approach avoids essentialist and fixed classifications of identity. It validates the development of a pan-Aboriginal politics instead of leading towards a fragmented localized politics, such as is implied by definitions based on traditional cultural identity. It also permits non-autochthonous people more scope for participation in anti-colonial politics by avoiding defining racial politics around fixed, segregated and incommensurable communities.

Hollinsworth situates his ideas in the context of broader debates about black identity which have been developed in US and British cultural theory. For example, he argues that those who define Aboriginality as cultural descent are guilty of what Paul Gilroy calls 'cultural insiderism' (Gilroy, 1987). Gilroy argues that such insiderism works to exclude those who construct their subaltern identities in contemporary terms. Hollinsworth refers also to Avtah Brah who argues – following Spivak – that defining ethnicity in essentialist terms may be strategically useful when demands are being made on the state (Brah, 1992). But such a process is problematic if it leads to an exclusive assertion of difference.

Hollinsworth incurred the wrath of black writers who sought to defend the strategy of cultural essentialism (Nyoongah, 1992). Dodson argued that it was the prerogative of Aboriginal people to move between different expressions of their own identities ('at times ancient, at times subversive, at times oppositional, at times secret, at times essentialist, at times shifting') (Dodson, 1994: 12). These comments square with Spivak's concept of strategic essentialism, which describes a pragmatic politics of subalternity, articulated in opposition to a disorganizing colonialism (Spivak, 1988).

Postcolonialism and Ethnic Identity

The debates around contemporary autochthonous identity and culture parallel those that refer to the experiences of diasporic people from colonized nations of the South, particularly those who have migrated to the West. Much of this debate has taken place around the concept of postcolonialism, originally a term used by neo-Marxist writers to describe the political, economic and historical dimensions of decolonization but in recent times referring to cultural processes, too (Ahmad, 1995). Slemon observes that postcolonialism denotes 'a category of literary activity which sprang from a new and welcome political energy going on within what used to be called Commonwealth literary studies' (Slemon, 1995: 45). Stuart Hall criticizes postcolonial theorists for failing to incorporate political economy into their analysis, but accepts that postcolonialism represents a conceptually interesting moment for exploring the 'new relations and dispositions of power which are emerging in the new conjuncture' (Hall, 1996: 250). Rattansi defines postcolonial studies as:

> ... the investigation of the mutually constitutive role played by colonizer and colonized, centre and periphery, the metropolitan and the 'native', in forming, in part, the identities of both the dominant power and the subalterns involved in the imperial and colonial projects of the West. (Rattansi, 1997: 481)

Colonial and subaltern cultures intertwine: colonized people absorb some elements of the language, practices and symbolic structures of the dominant culture. Conversely, as Bhabha argues, the presence of native people simultaneously undermines colonialism, holding up the mirror to the colonizer, shattering the comfortable illusions of tradition, the pretension of cultural superiority drawing attention to the fractured underside of colonial life (Bhabha, 1985). For postcolonialists, there is no cultural or physical boundary between the autochthonous and the colonial, no interior and exterior. As Hall points out, transcultural movement and mixing 'has made ethnic absolutism an increasingly untenable cultural strategy' (Hall, 1996: 250).

In another article, Hall claims that the culture and identity of black migrants to Britain, particularly from the Indian subcontinent and the West Indies, are a complex contemporary mixture and not some vestige of tradition (Hall, 1992). He argues that racism 'attempts to fix and naturalize the difference between belongingness and otherness' and advocates a black politics based on recognizing the hybrid nature of black culture. For Hall, 'gone is the innocent notion of the essential black subject' (Hall, 1992: 254).

Other commentators have criticized the assertion that colonized peoples willingly embrace the possibilities offered by global and metropolitan culture. Friedman, for example, believes middle-class Indian intellectuals have inappropriately generalized their own hybrid cultural identities to poor migrants (Friedman, 1994). He claims that the great majority of those who live on social margins have neither the possibility nor the desire to be culturally eclectic, to engage in a playful and self-reflexive process of identity formation. They are much more inclined to hold onto tradition than the postcolonialists would suppose. This observation is supported by Brennan who states that:

> Lost in much of the writing on colonialism and post colonialism is the mood of languorous attachment to native cultures . . . If hybridity can be said to characterize them, then it is a hybridity reclaimed and reinvented as indigenous, defiantly posed against an increasingly insistent metropolitan norm. (Brennan, 1997: 310)

Although Brennan was writing about immigrants in the United States, his observations could equally apply to Aboriginal people living in Australia's towns and cities. They are economically and socially marginal, too. While educated, prosperous middle-class members of ethnic minorities may feel free to explore cultural possibilities, to articulate innovative versions of their collective identities based on combining contemporary and traditional forms, the majority of Aboriginal people are not in such a situation.

Autochthonous Migration to the Cities

When Europeans invaded Australia, they established settlements, towns and cities where previously there had been none. They looked upon Aboriginal people as savages, aimlessly wandering in a harsh landscape. They viewed cities as centres of refinement and culture, which were not appropriate places for those used to living in 'a state of nature'.

When Aboriginal people moved to urban areas in large numbers after the Second World War, they experienced a double sense of alienation. First, their Aboriginality was denied because they lived amongst Europeans. This was the case both for those who lived in fringe settlements and those who arrived later on in order to live in inner-city ghettos or white suburban areas. Second, many felt out of place because they were not living on their own land but on the land of other autochthonous people. They had lost their point of anchorage and had experienced a cultural dislocation far more profound than had those who had emigrated or who had been transported from Europe.

This was the case for Hilary, Millicent, Keith and Tilda, who all moved to Sydney as children during the era in which Aboriginal people were expected to embrace moral respectability, conventional gender roles, wage labour and nuclear family life. Very few were willing or able to assimilate into the Australian way of life as the state expected of them.

Millicent

Millicent[1] was born in Cowra in western New South Wales in 1943. When she was three, her family moved to Sydney because her father refused to live on a government reserve. The family became part of a nascent Aboriginal community in the poor inner suburbs of Sydney that grew rapidly from the 1950s. Her parents thought they would enjoy a better life in the city and were keen on improving their children's life-chances through education – most Aboriginal children experienced racist exclusion in rural schools. The family was part of a process of chain migration that took place from the late 1940s. In urban school, Millicent found very little recognition and consideration of her Aboriginality.

> I always felt that I was expected to be the same as everybody else. There was never any conversation between teachers and Aboriginal students regarding the future. So there wasn't that relationship built between Aboriginal students and teachers. But you were always aware, without analysing it yourself, that you weren't really expected to [succeed] because they, being non-aboriginal teachers, didn't expect you to.

She left school at 15 unable to read and to write. As many other Aboriginal women, she married and had children when she was young. Millicent and her husband were offered new public housing on one of the postwar suburban housing estates on the fringe of Sydney at a considerable distance from her parents' home. Here she felt isolated, socially unworthy and alienated from her non-autochthonous neighbours. In both, the inner city and the suburbs, Millicent informs us that most Aboriginal parents struggled to reinforce their own and their children's autochthonous identities. This involved asserting a claim to a territory and a culture of origin and the disavowal of their urban identity:

> All the families who lived in Redfern did not belong there, they were migrants to Sydney. It's like if I have my kids in Crown St Hospital Surry Hills, they don't belong there. They're Waradjuri people they belong where I came from.

According to her, they travelled back to their home country, often for extended periods:

> In a lot of times, the need overwhelmed the logic. The need to restrengthen their Aboriginality, their spirituality in order to live here [in the city] and remain an Aborigine you have to go back and recharge your battery.

For her, it was as if Aboriginality was something that had to be constantly nurtured and reinforced, something which is tenuous and under threat as a result of living in the city and which can be made solid again by visiting the home country and community. Millicent remained living in the western suburbs of Sydney and became active in urban-based Aboriginal organizations.

Hilary

Hilary was born in Dubbo in western New South Wales in 1955, one of 11 children. The family moved to Sydney when her father could no longer find work as a sheep shearer. They moved between poor makeshift houses on small farms just beyond the outer suburbs. Hilary's mother applied for public housing when her youngest child was a baby, in 1969, and was offered a place on a new estate. Hilary remembers the feeling of confinement when they first moved to the new house. In the fenced, subdivided landscape of the suburbs, her movements were restricted as never before:

We were trapped there. Because all the other places we lived at, we had free rein. We could just wander off, we could go to the river at any time.

She felt the shame of poverty very keenly in these vulnerable teenage years:

All I can remember is that all of the neighbours around us, had all the trappings. You know they all had lovely new curtains, new lino or new carpet ... I felt ashamed about inviting friends back home, because we had bare floorboards, and sheets at the windows.

Her father died when she was 16 and Hilary's family fell on hard times and were forced to accept charity. This was a particularly difficult experience for the teenage girl:

We used to get bags of clothes dropped off, too. That's what I hated ... The fact that we had to pick our clothes out from all these second-hand stuff. I used to drool over all those magazines, that had flash clothes in it, and knowing that I could never buy them. I think that affected my self-esteem, too. Because I had friends around with all the latest gear.

After the death of her father, Hilary was forced to leave school on economic and family support grounds:

This happens a lot in [Aboriginal] families. If you're the eldest at home or you're going to school, you're expected to stay home and help out with the younger ones, and that's what happened with me.

At this time, Hilary's older siblings had left home. She helped her mother during the day and worked as a babysitter for local families at night, handing over her earnings to her mother. As an adult, Hilary took up further studies up to postgraduate level. She is currently involved in urban Aboriginal community politics. She continues to live in public housing in the western suburbs of Sydney.

Keith and Tilda

Keith was born in the early 1950s in Griffith, in the west of New South Wales and moved to Sydney as a young child when his mother, Tilda, separated from his father. Like Hilary and Millicent, she encountered pressures to assimilate that were experienced by Aboriginal people in this time. However, Tilda dealt with those pressures in a very different way. She strenuously resisted settling on a government reserve alongside other Aboriginal people even though her husband, like others, enjoyed the sense of community associated with living in such a setting. Tilda yearned for social improvement and did not wish 'to get caught up with the wrong crowd'. Keith recalled:

Mum tells a classic story ... about how they had a place with hessian walls and dirt floors. He [Dad] said 'you've got a house what more do you want?' And she wants something with floorboards, she wanted something with a roof where she could stay in with her kids ... The other big thing with her, has been all through our lives, is education ... They are the two things which have driven Mum.

Tilda announced that she intended to take the children and to leave for the city in order to 'set up a life properly'. She suggested to her husband going with them but told him if he refused she would cut her ties to him. He did refuse and Tilda burned her bridges. She had internalized the assimilationist idea that Aboriginal culture and community were incompatible with a comfortable modern urban lifestyle. She didn't want an aspect of her old way of life to intrude upon their future. Keith saw his father very occasionally after this decision. In 1965, they were given a tenancy in a new suburban house:

> To Mum at this stage, it was the culmination of everything we wanted . . . It must have been difficult for Mum . . . There has been a very conscious decision by her to walk away from some aspect of her cultural background, and that is to see the [reserve] as dirty and untidy . . . I do know that she had a very strong cultural severance at that time.

Keith was keenly aware that his mother was (and still is) insecure about her Aboriginality. She internalized the negative evaluation of this time:

> You know where you go out and you don't go down the street [looking] untidy because we are not going to be seen with those kind of black people who just go down the streets of Redfern [in the inner city].

Many autochthonous women of Tilda's generation were haunted by these spectres, desperate to be seen as respectable and worthy. Keith suggested obliquely that she was unable to identify publicly as an Aboriginal person:

> . . . it's only been the last couple of years that she can stand up, and even then still finds it difficult . . . People of that generation still find it difficult to stand up and make statements.

Keith was relatively successful at school. He passed his final exams but did not meet the standard required for university entry. He recalls being unsure of the purpose of becoming involved in academic competition with other children. At this time, he was taken under the wing of the Aboriginal Education Council (AEC) and a non-autochthonous teacher who took particular interest in encouraging autochthonous children into higher education. Keith was persuaded to undertake the final year of school again with the offer of a scholarship. The AEC encouraged Keith to move to a new school, one where his prospects would be likely to improve and to board with a white family. Before Aboriginal politics began to be guided by the ethic of self-determination, there were many philanthropically inclined people who sought to assist Aboriginal children.

However, charity can often leave scars and even though Keith won a university place, his mother was deeply disturbed by the process. She had struggled for social mobility, willingly sacrificed her ties to the community and, in spite of all of these efforts, she was deemed to be unable to provide a home environment conducive to her children:

> Mum carries some pretty emotional scars over that time . . . The actual process of going to another school and doing well was not the problem. It was that the home environment was perceived to be the problem.

In 1971, Keith began his university course but struggled from the outset. In those days, there were very few support structures for Aboriginal students and he had very little idea of the purpose of his course. The next year, he left and did not return seriously to university studies until he enrolled in a law degree in the late 1990s. Like Hilary and Millicent, Keith has been an energetic participant in the affairs of Aboriginal community organizations.

Urban Life and Pan-Aboriginal Radicalism

In the 1960s and 1970s, a radical spirit grew among Aboriginal people, in particular among young people living in the cities. The Black Power movement emerged at this time and laid the foundation for subsequent forms of national political representation. Jones and Hill-Burnett define this process as a moment of ethnogenesis, at which pan-Aboriginal politics and culture emerged which began to unite the many hundreds of autochthonous groups that predated colonization (Jones and Hill-Burnett, 1992).

The leaders of this movement, far from promoting an enduring and long-standing culture and community into contemporary political form, were engaged in a process of symbolic construction and reinvention. This process involved, on one side, recruiting specific localized/regional 'traditional' cultural forms (like dot painting, peculiar to the people of central Australia), holding them up as being a symbol of Aboriginal people as a whole. On the other side, it involved developing a radical political rhetoric on behalf of all autochthonous people. While Aboriginal people who moved to cities developed new forms of social and cultural life, their unifying motifs were based on tradition. This movement encouraged people such as Millicent, Hilary and Keith who grew to adulthood in this period, to break the ideological shackles that had been imposed on their parents' generation during the assimilation period. The radical autochthonous movement provided them with a vantage point from which to reflect critically on their earlier life.

The pan-Aboriginal movement has produced a plethora of publicly funded Aboriginal organizations led by autochthonous people. They speak a political language depicting Aboriginality as occupying a separate social space and as being guided by a culture and a value system distinct from that operating in wider society ('our ways' and 'whitefella ways'). They view the process of participating in the white system as a necessary 'evil' but one at odds with the cooperative practices which were characteristic of traditional autochthonous social life. 'Traditional' symbols serve to legitimate the binary divisions that are at the heart of contemporary Aboriginal community action in order to overcome the threat of collapse into a homogenized and atomized politics of citizenship.

It is important to understand the subjective purchase of pan-Aboriginality for contemporary autochthonous urban dwellers. If, as Jones and Hill-Burnett argue, Aboriginal leaders are defining 'a new social category' in both political and cultural terms, of inventing a tradition, does this mean that contemporary Aboriginality is a mere fabrication? Dodson argues strongly against the notion of invention:

> When we talk about an Aboriginality based on the past of our peoples, we are not talking about fabricating an identity based on a past we have rediscovered or dug up . . . The past cannot be limiting because we are always transforming it . . . We do not need to re-find the past because our subjectivities, our being in the world are inseparable from the past. Aboriginalities of today are re-generations and transformations of the spirit of the past, not literal duplications of it. (Dodson, 1994: 10)

It is the 'we' of this passage which is most called into question by Jones and Hill-Burnett's ideas. They correctly suggest that the Aboriginal population is culturally complex and variegated, that they are not amenable to such rhetorical closures. Autochthonous people occupy a range of life-worlds from the remotest desert settlements to inner urban communities; from those conversant in traditional language and ceremony to those who lost those links generations ago. Dodson is correct in arguing that contemporary Aboriginal lived culture involves the regeneration and transformation of inherited cultural repertoires. However, many of those who live in cities and towns embrace and articulate strategically essentialist representations of Aboriginality.

Raymond Williams considers the question of cultural continuity in general terms. In exploring the operation of hegemony, he identifies the interplay of dominant, emergent and residual cultural forms. For Williams, culture is never static but always in the process of being made and remade. Subaltern groups neither simply abandon their inherited forms when social relations change, nor uncritically accept dominant cultural constructions. Rather they forge their collective identities at the junction of the dominant, the residual and the emergent. Culture is a process of negotiation between the old and the new. Williams is thus keen on distinguishing residual culture from archaic cultures:

> By residual I mean something different from the 'archaic' though in practice these are often very hard to distinguish . . . I would call the 'archaic' that which is wholly recognized as an element of the past, to be observed, to be examined, or even on occasion to be consciously revived, in a deliberately specializing way. What I mean by the 'residual' is very different. The residual, by definition, has been effectively formed in the past, but is still active in the cultural process, not only and often not at all as an element of the past, but only as an effective element of the present. (Williams, 1977: 121)

Jones and Hill-Burnett claim that the process of ethnogenesis involves the revival of what are for most – although not all – of those who make up the pan-Aboriginal imagined community, archaic autochthonous forms.

However, these forms do not make up the total sum of urban autochthonous cultural identity. There are indeed residual and emergent forms that are authentically autochthonous even if they do not have the stamp of primordiality. In common with the majority of global citizens, Aboriginal people produce emergent cultures from the material available through international/global cultural flows. Since the 1960s, for example, young people have appropriated the symbolism of black American protest and youth cultures. Thirty years ago, many of the Land Rights protestors sported the afro hairstyles, headbands and appropriated the slogans of the US Black Power movement. Today, many young autochthonous people embrace the styles of rap and hip-hop, and identify with the ghetto kids of New York and Los Angeles. Many young men have been inspired by the politics of Malcolm X and Louis Farrakahn. They are not simply cultural mimics. They adopt motifs that receive local significance. They acquire a subcultural meaning that is very different from the original setting.

I have already suggested that contemporary urban Aboriginal politics is based on the idea of a separate autochthonous community united around what are ostensibly grounded traditions which are mainly produced through a process of contemporary reinvention in order to serve an existential need. For Aboriginal people living currently in cities and towns, ancient symbols provide a point of anchorage against the pressures to assimilate, a counter-weight to bland modernity. While they practise forms of residual culture, its symbols are less visible (and less celebrated) than the unifying symbols of 'tradition'. Fanon observed that those who live under the yoke of colonialism frequently internalize the negative evaluations which colonial ideology throws up (Fanon, 1967). According to this understanding, the popular assumption that Aboriginal people living around European population centres are fringe dwellers, demoralized and bereft of their culture, will generally lead these people to support a political culture based on recovering aspects of the past rather than identifying the residual collective forms of the present.

The implication of this argument is that the frameworks offered by Hollinsworth for judging Aboriginality are inappropriate. Hollinsworth contends that autochthonous Australian identity should not be defined around cultural tradition or essence but rather should be based on a notion of resistance. This idea fails, however, to acknowledge that many of the resistant public expressions of contemporary Aboriginality are constructed precisely in traditional and essentialist terms. His second criterion for assessing Aboriginality collapses into the third.

The Broader Context of Essentialism

In order to understand why the essential–primitive distinction dominates public representations of Aboriginality, it is necessary to look beyond the internal dynamics of Aboriginal cultural production and to grasp general political and social processes that contribute to construct and perpetuate this image of Aboriginality.

Several commentators have noted that an enduring attachment to the idea of the 'noble savage' is central to Australian national identity.

Hamilton argues that Australian nationalism has long been based on a yearning for a deeper attachment to the land than non-autochthonous Australians have been able to achieve. She claims that Australians have drawn on Aboriginal culture and spiritual attachment to landscape without acknowledging this debt. This fact has allowed Australians to 'claim both a mythological and spiritual continuity of identity that is otherwise lacking' (Hamilton, 1990: 18).

The strategic essentialism that is often advanced by Aboriginal people is complemented (or perhaps encouraged) by a growing contemporary interest in autochthonous tradition. This emphasis is underlined by middle-class citizens of a liberal/progressive bent for whom the colonial past is a source of shame, and by groups who identify with cultural counter-move-ments. The current New Age interest in autochthonous culture is an expres-sion of this quest for cultural purity and authenticity, for a counterweight to the shallow and ephemeral relations of modernity. Autochthonous tradition combines an ecological ethic with spirituality. It is untainted by modern life. This authentic culture is found in ancient places, not in cities. Tacey explores this trend towards a romanticism of Aboriginal culture (Tacey, 1995). He considers this movement as reflecting a popular disillusion with western rationality and modernity, and a yearning for inner spiritual fulfilment forged through a connection with nature and the land. According to him, Australians are engaged in a search for something that transcends the super-ficial and instrumental relations of our times and, as a consequence, they place Aboriginal Australia on a pedestal:

> The values of the past [have been] reversed: not we superior and they merely shadowy figures on the floor of hell, but we spiritually barren and they spiritually rich and well endowed. (Tacey, 1995: 129)

Tacey's work deals with the play of culture and ideas but not with political dimensions of autochthonous essentialism. The concept of hegemony is useful here. Like postcolonialism, hegemony deals with the process of cultural negotiation but it requires that culture is explored by taking account of political and economic relations. Gramsci considered how nation-states secure the consent of the governed, and safeguard the interests of dominant groups, through means other than coercion (Gramsci, 1971). In his opinion, this process involves the creation of a national-popular ideology in order to defuse social conflict. In societies characterized by social inequality, the project of garnering social order is inherently complex and fragile. A hegemonic project involves the incorporation of elements of lived culture and political demands of subaltern groups into the national-popular whole without compromising the primary interests of dominant groups. When a conflict occurs between dominant and oppressed social groups, the pre-existing 'hegemonic discourse is abandoned as scorched earth [and] a different discourse forged in a process of disobedience and combat ... is enunciated' (Parry, 1995: 43). By contrast, postcolonialism encourages us to see the link between culture and power as happening without any conjunctural point of anchorage and with no sense that this relation is institutionalized.[2]

In recent times, the state has come to accept, and even to promote, autochthonous traditionalism as a hegemonic response to an Aboriginal movement that has won considerable sympathy and support for its causes within the Australian urban middle class. In the Mabo and Wik decisions, the Australian High Court – moved in a left-liberal direction by a series of progressive appointments in the 1980s – recognized the existence of native title and posed a challenge to mining and pastoral interests. The political and legislative response was to circumscribe these rights and to restrict the groups who can make successful land claims. Claimants must demonstrate descent from the traditional owners of the land under claim, a continuing attachment to that land and a familiarity with 'traditional' culture. The Act is predicated on a notion of culture as ossified around 'tradition', something fixed both prior to and after colonization (MacDonald, 1998). There is little scope for those who have moved to cities and towns to argue a case for native title on the basis of residual culture in the sense Williams uses the term. Native title law in Australia operates to exclude the majority of Aborigines in south-eastern Australia.

Similar criteria for assessing contemporary autochthonous cultural identity applied in litigation surrounding a celebrated American native title claim that was examined by anthropologist James Clifford (Clifford, 1988). A group of people claiming to be Mashpee Indians, original owners of land that was subject to development proposals, sought legal recognition for their claims to ownership. The case hinged on whether they could establish their autochthonous bona fides: bloodlines and cultural continuity. Most of the claimants were integrated into the lives of local towns and had apparently accepted the trappings of modern life. The counsel for the developers tried to show that the claimants had lost their connection with their original culture and were simply fabricating 'tradition' for the purpose of controlling land. The Mashpee for their part brought forward evidence of their ongoing practice of culture. Clifford accepted that some of the witnesses were involved in reinventing tradition but criticized the terms under which the case was constructed. He attacked the notion that cultural authenticity was solely based on continuity and argued that culture is a living, dynamic system, rather than a vestige:

> How rooted or settled should one expect 'tribal' Native Americans to be – aboriginally in specific contact periods, and now in highly mobile 20th-century America? Common notions of culture persistently bias the answer towards rooting rather than travel.
>
> Moreover the culture idea, tied as it is to assumptions about natural growth and life, does not tolerate radical breaks in historical continuity. Cultures, we often hear, 'die'. But how many cultures pronounced dead or dying by anthropologists and other authorities have, like Curtis' 'vanishing race' or Africa's diverse Christians, found new ways to be different? Metaphors of continuity and 'survival' do not account for complex historical processes of appropriation, compromise, subversion, masking, invention and revival ... The history of the

Mashpee is not one of unbroken tribal institutions or cultural traditions. It is a long, relational struggle to maintain and recreate identities. (Clifford, 1988: 338–9)

The claims of the Mashpee were unsuccessful. The court ruled that they had no native title rights. Clifford's observations are equally applicable to autochthonous Australians. The production of identity is rather complex and cannot be reduced to a notion of the endurance of the 'traditional' into the present. It involves the articulation of archaic forms, collectively reinvented in the process of ethnogenesis, with residual forms, deeply rooted in the past but much changed from their traditional shape, and contemporary cultural materials that circulate widely in the public sphere. Many of those who do not participate in 'traditional' practices, are generally popularly and officially viewed as culturally bereft, even if their residual culture is strong.

A Recovered Aboriginality

The same limited criteria used to define who is a legitimate claimant to native title have been used by conservative forces to challenge the Aboriginality credentials of many of those living in south-eastern Australia. In the mid-1990s, the right-wing One Nation Party emerged in Australia and placed racial issues on the public agenda. Party representatives were able to obtain seats in state legislatures, as the comments of leader Pauline Hanson struck a popular chord, particularly with voters in depressed rural areas. Aboriginal people living in urban centres in south-eastern Australia were a central focus of Hanson's attacks. She accused them of being counterfeit, of identifying solely for the purposes of obtaining special government assistance. She stated that:

In 1971, there were just under 116,000 Aboriginals. In the 1991 census, there were approximately 260,000. We had an increase of 129 per cent – everybody is out there, wanting to claim to be an Aboriginal and jumping on the gravy train. (*Sydney Morning Herald*, 8 August 1998: 1)

Hanson gives expression to what may well be a popular view of Aboriginality: autochthonous people are drawn into white society, a fact that diminishes their Aboriginality. Only those who live in concentrated communities in remote areas with a preponderance of Aboriginal forebears can, in Hanson's view, legitimately claim to be Aboriginal. Currently, in Australia, the process of certifying Aboriginality is left in the hands of Aboriginal organizations like Lands Councils. Although the Howard coalition government has not yet sought to undermine this self-managed system, this may well form part of a future conservative agenda.

Hanson questioned the authenticity and the motives of those who have recently identified as Aboriginal. She is not alone. Aboriginal people occasionally express similar sentiments about those seeking to be received back into the fold after a period of passing. Occasionally, these misgivings surface in public. They undermine the appearance of autochthonous unity and the general tolerance of difference that, in general, has characterized Aboriginal community politics.

Such issues were discussed in debates around the publication of Sally Morgan's autobiography, *My Place* (Morgan, 1987). During the mid 20th century some Aboriginal people, including Tilda, whose life we explored earlier, sought to pass as non-autochthonous if they were able to sever communal ties in pursuit of social advancement. Some passers and their children have sought to re-establish bonds that were in the past renounced – thus to reidentify. Ross observes that of the total increase in autochthonous population in Australia between 1991 and 1996 – from 265,371 to 352,970 or a 33 percent growth – 'only about 40 per cent can be attributed to natural increase' (Ross, 1996: 12). Undoubtedly, some of those who have recently identified are genuinely remorseful about past decisions that they (or their parents) took to sever ties, and see the process of reconnection as enriching. Others may be encouraged by the greater public sympathy and, as Hanson suggests, increased public support provided by the state for autochthonous people. There is little doubt that in recent times autochthonous culture has been held in greater public esteem than in the past and that this has led people to 'rediscover' their Aboriginal roots. Pan-Aboriginality has also made it possible for those who previously passed to assert their autochthonous credentials without having to live on or close to their ancestral lands.

My Place describes how Sally Morgan became aware that she was Aboriginal in spite of the efforts of her mother and grandmother to conceal this fact. They had passed during the assimilation era claiming Indian ethnic origin. Morgan describes the sense of shame and secrecy that characterized her domestic life, describing her grandmother's reluctance to allow her to bring school friends home – as if the cover would be blown if this occurred. This is characteristic of the insecurities about appearance and domestic life which were (and are) expressed by those Aboriginal people who had experienced the intrusive social engineering surveillance of the assimilation era. *My Place* describes the author's coming to terms with her autochthonous past almost in terms of a spiritual quest.

The response to this book from academics was not uniformly favourable. Attwood, a non-autochthonous historian, questioned the metaphysical way in which Sally Morgan defined her sense of Aboriginality but stopped short of denying her claims to an Aboriginal identity (Attwood, 1992). He argued in favour of a definition that is based on historical rather than supra-historical, essentialist terms. Aboriginal writer Jackie Huggins backed up Attwood's views and in doing so launched an uncompromising attack on those who had lived 'under-cover' in white society (Huggins, 1992). She endorsed Attwood's suggestion that those who came from families that had suffered the brutalities and humiliations of colonialism without ever denying their Aboriginality are, and should form, the vanguard of the movement: 'Aboriginality cannot be acquired overnight. It takes years of hard work, sensitivity and effort to "come back in" . . . The debt has to be repaid in various ways' (Huggins, 1992: 461). Huggins suggests that Morgan has not done that work and is hostile to the sanitized version of Aboriginality presented in this book for white, middle-class consumption.

The strategic problems that the Aboriginal movement faces when confronting any racist reaction are of two types. First, internal autochthonous politics is characterized by frequent divisions. Some of these relate to whether a person should be accepted as authentically Aboriginal. In circumstances of intense political scrutiny, these divisions are inevitably exploited. Second, many Aboriginal people in cities accept, and even support, public representations of autochthonous collectivity which are only based on petrified tradition. They appear to undermine their own claims to identity. The majority of autochthonous Australians are currently better served by promoting an awareness of the residual culture than by holding exclusively to 'tradition'. I concur with McKee, who has argued that contemporary suburban images of Aboriginality should be developed in the mainstream electronic media (McKee, 1997).

Conclusion

In this article, I have explored the attraction of autochthonous tradition both for Aboriginal people themselves and for the broader public. Traditionalism and essentialism are double-edged swords. On the one hand, they allow autochthonous city dwellers to define a distinctive space for their culture and politics in order to claim legitimacy based on being part of an ancient culture. On the other hand, they have the effect of obscuring the reworked, contemporary residual forms of autochthonous culture and social life.

Traditional representations of Aboriginality are not solely generated from within the Aboriginal community. As Langton argues, media and non-autochthonous people working within the media play a key role in shaping the public definition of Aboriginality (Langton, 1993). Dodson observes in relation to these public representations: 'It's as if we've been ushered onto a stage to play in a drama where the parts have already been written.' However, he goes on to say:

> We have never totally lost ourselves within the other's reality . . . We have never fallen into the hypnosis of believing that those representations were our essence. Alongside the colonial discourses we have always had our own Aboriginal discourses in which we have continued to create our own representations and to recreate identities which escaped the policing of authorized versions. (Dodson, 1994: 9–10)

Much more ethnographic exploration of urban Aboriginality as subculture is necessary: its manners, ways of speaking and relating, forms of enjoyment, practices of mutual support as well as processes of appropriation of global commodities and symbols, and given autochthonous meaning have to be studied. Most autochthonous cultural production takes place at alternative sites – at sporting, carnivals, music and dance performances, in pubs and clubs. Much of these events cannot be characterized in the same romantic terms as are cultural forms based on a restaged 'tradition'.

The autochthonous identity of most Aboriginal people living in cities is not something which is invented or contrived: it is a residual and living set of relationships, something quite different from that which is presented in essentialist public representations. Aboriginal culture has a contemporary form that is far from being a facsimile of ancient tradition. As the social circumstances in which Aborigines find themselves change, as they are forced to adapt to the pressures which are placed on them, the everyday significance of many inherited forms recedes – connections to land, ancient rituals, forms of spirituality – and new articulations emerge. These phenomena do not represent a breach with the past or a point of disjunction. They continue to be forms that serve to constitute Aboriginal solidarity and they are no less autochthonous culture than are Corroborees and body painting.

Notes

1 All names in this article are fictitious.

2 Like many of those who define themselves as postmodernists, postcolonial writers generally disaggregate the state into a series of disparate sites. They argue that state power is ambiguous. It is not, as is suggested in the Marxist literature, unified around the project of defending the interests of capital or other dominant forces. They claim that their approach opens up a space to explore, for example, pedagogy in state education without being trapped into binary and reductionist formulations. This may well be an appropriate counterweight to economism but not every conception of state power needs to operate economistically. It is also possible to accept that the state is not monolithic, that it contains sites that pull in opposite directions (for instance when the Wik decision was handed down by the High Court to the chagrin of mining and pastoral interests, and the surprise of the Howard government). Moreover, it is possible to hold that at moments of political crisis a sustained net tendency towards protection of dominant interests exists. Gramsci's use of hegemony allows us to see ways in which the micro-sites of cultural engagement are framed by political and social contexts of which state power is a key element.

Bibliography

Ahmad, A. (1995) 'The Politics of Literary Postcoloniality', *Race and Class* 36(3): 1–20.

Attwood, B. (1992) 'Portrait of an Aboriginal as an Artist: Sally Morgan and the Construction of Aboriginality', *Australian Historical Studies* 25(9): 309–18.

Bhabha, H. (1985) 'Signs Taken for Wonders: Questions of Ambivalence and Authority Under a Tree Outside Delhi', *Critical Inquiry* 12(1): 144–65.

Brah, A. (1992) 'Difference, Diversity and Differentiation', in J. Donald and A. Rattansi (eds) *'Race', Culture and Difference*, pp. 126–45. London: Sage.

Brennan, T. (1997) *At Home in the World: Cosmopolitanism Now*. Cambridge, MA: Harvard University Press.

Chase, A. (1981) 'Empty Vessels and Loud Noises; Views about Aboriginality Today', *Social Alternatives* 2(1): 23–7.

Clifford, J. (1988) 'Identity in Mashpee', in J. Clifford (ed.) *Predicament of Culture. Twentieth Century Ethnography, Literature and Art*, pp. 277–346. Cambridge, MA: Harvard University Press.

Dodson, M. (1994) 'The Wentworth Lecture: The End in the Beginning: Re(de)finding Aboriginality', *Australian Aboriginal Studies* (1): 2–13.

Fanon, F. (1967) *The Wretched of the Earth*. New York: Random House.

Friedman, J. (1994) *Cultural Identity and Global Process*. London: Sage.

Gilroy, P. (1987) 'Problems in Anti-Racist Strategy', Runnymede Lecture, London, 23 July.

Gramsci, A. (1971) *Selections from Prison Notebooks*. London: Lawrence and Wishart.

Hall, S. (1992) 'New Ethnicities', in J. Donald and A. Rattansi (eds) *'Race', Culture and Difference*, pp. 252–9. London: Sage.

Hall, S. (1996) 'When Was "The Post-Colonial"? Thinking at the Limit', in I. Chambers and L. Curti (eds) *The Post-Colonial Question*, pp. 242–60. London: Routledge.

Hamilton, A. (1990) 'Fear and Desire – Aborigines, Asians and the National Imaginary', *Australian Cultural History* 9: 14–35.

Hollinsworth, D. (1992) 'Discourses on Aboriginality and the Politics of Identity in Urban Australia', *Oceania* 63(2): 137–55.

Huggins, J. (1992) 'Always Was Always Will Be', *Australian Historical Studies* 25(100): 459–64.

Jones, D. and Hill-Burnett, J. (1992) 'The Political Context of Ethnogenesis: An Australian Example', in M. Howard (ed.) *Aboriginal Power in Australian Society*, pp. 214–46. St Lucia: University of Queensland Press.

Langton, M. (1993) *'Well I Heard it on the Radio and I Saw it on the Television'. An Essay for the Australian Film Commission on the Politics and Aesthetics of Film Making by and about Aboriginal People and Things*. Sydney: Australian Film Commission.

MacDonald, G. (1998) 'Contextualising Cultural Continuities in New South Wales', in G. Morgan (ed.) *Urban Life, Urban Culture – Aboriginal Indigenous Experiences*, pp. 1–25. Conference Proceedings: University of Western Sydney.

McKee, A. (1997) ' "The Aboriginal Version of Ken Done . . ." Banal Aboriginal Identities in Australia', *Cultural Studies* 11(2): 191–206.

Morgan, S. (1987) *My Place*. Fremantle: Fremantle Arts Centre Press.

Nyoongah, M. (1992) 'Comments on Hollinsworth', *Oceania* 63(2): 156–8.

Parry, B. (1995) 'Problems in Current Theories of Colonial Discourse', in B. Ashcroft, G. Griffiths and H. Tiffin (eds) *The Post-Colonial Studies Reader*, pp. 36–44. London: Routledge.

Rattansi, A. (1997) 'Post-Colonialism and its Discontents', *Economy and Society* 26(4): 480–500.

Ross, K. (1996) *Population Issues, Indigenous Australians*, Occasional Papers, no. 99. Canberra: Australian Bureau of Statistics.

Slemon, S. (1995) 'The Scramble for Post Colonialism', in B. Ashcroft, G. Griffiths and H. Tiffin (eds) *The Post-Colonial Studies Reader*, pp. 45–52. London: Routledge.

Spivak, G. (1988) 'Subaltern Studies: Deconstructing Historiography', in R. Guha and G. Spivak (eds) *Selected Subaltern Studies*, pp. 330–63. Oxford: Oxford University Press.

Tacey, D. (1995) *Edge of the Sacred – Transformation in Australia*. Melbourne: HarperCollins.

Williams, R. (1977) *Marxism and Literature*. Oxford: Oxford University Press.

Index